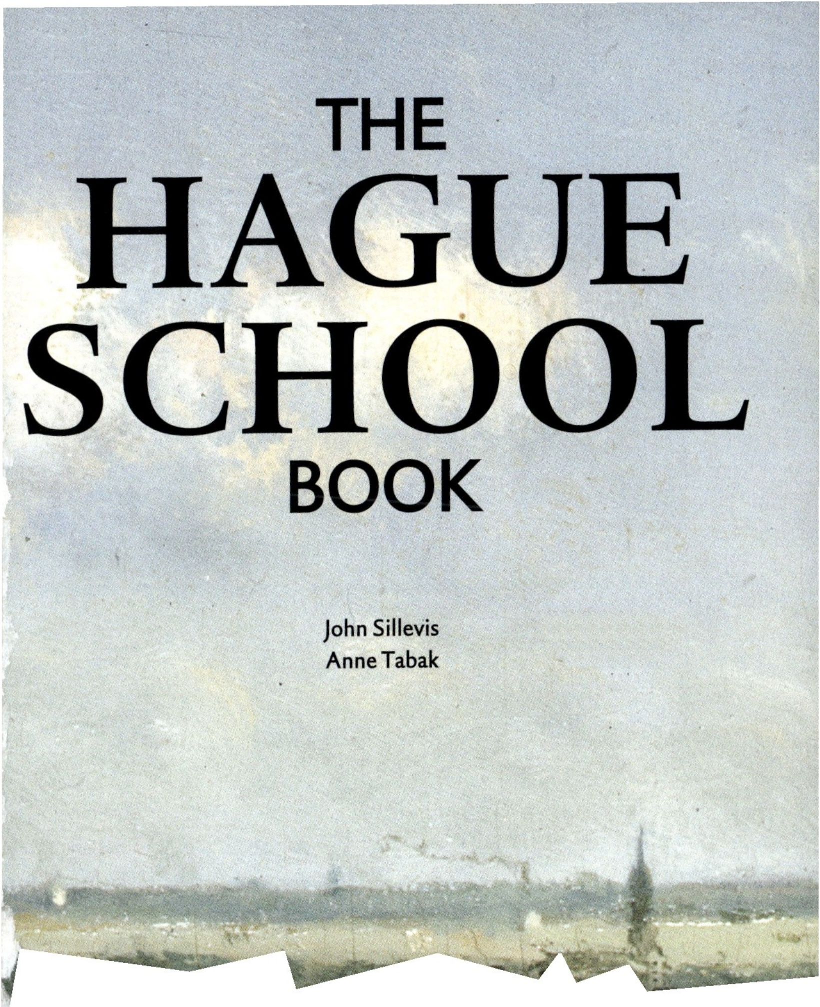

THE HAGUE SCHOOL BOOK

John Sillevis
Anne Tabak

TABLE OF CONTENTS

BIOGRAPHIES

Anne Tabak

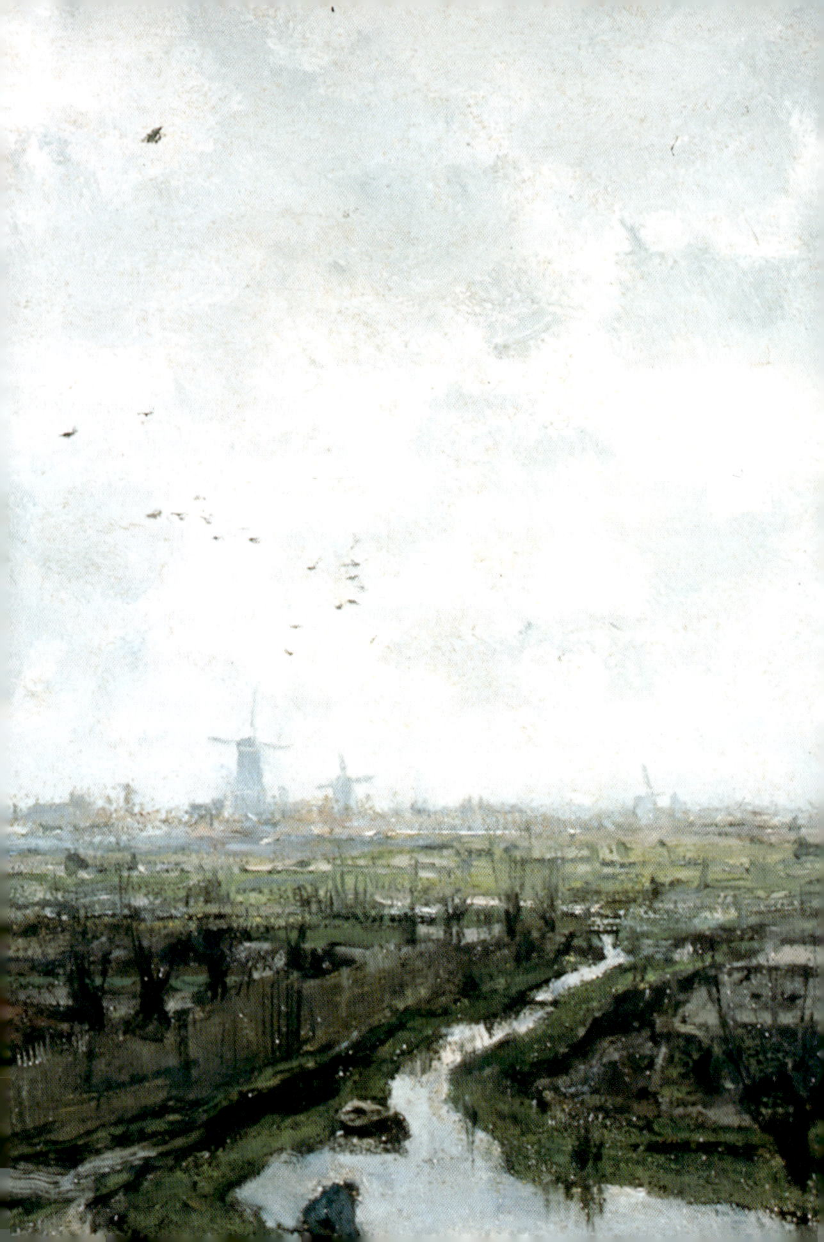

FOREWORD

The Hague Gemeentemuseum's primary importance lies in its three great collections from the 19th and 20th centuries: its Hague School, Escher and Mondrian collections. Besides the masterpieces by Picasso, Schiele, Monet, Toorop and others on display in the museum, each of these three collections now has its own wing. In 2001, the permanent Mondrian and Hague School exhibitions were established in the Berlage Building, and in 2002 the Escher exhibition was created in the Museum Het Paleis. The three exhibitions in turn led to the creation, in collaboration with Waanders Publishers, of a new series of publications intended for a broad public. The present book, eye-catching through both its completeness and content, is the first in the series. In combination with the exhibition itself, it will help give the Gemeentemuseum the high status it deserves. Already renowned as the Netherlands' most beautiful museum, it is now setting the tone with its contents, as well.

Wim van Krimpen
director Gemeentemuseum Den Haag

Jacob Maris, *Allotments near The Hague,* ca. 1878 (detail)

p. 6:
Willem Maris, *Cows by a pool* (detail)

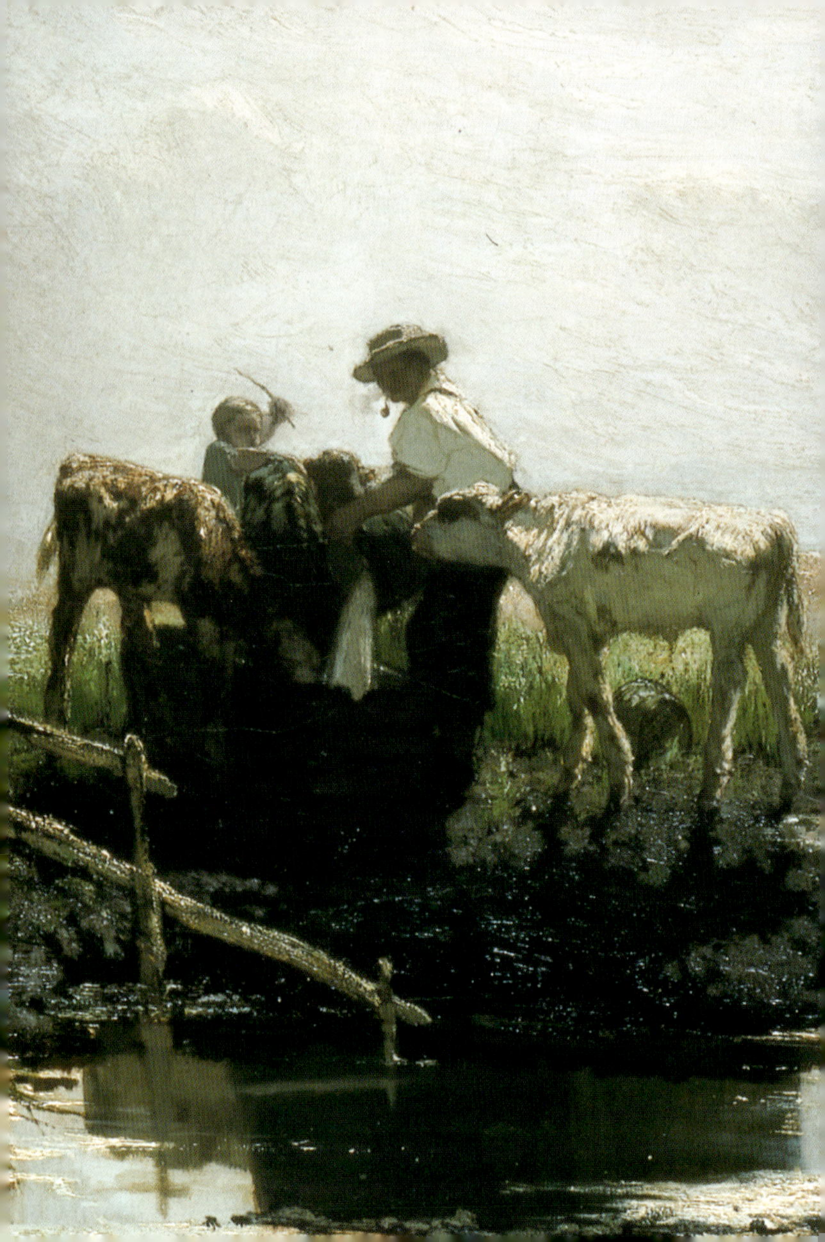

INTRODUCTION

When he was starting out as an art dealer, the famous young Daniel Wildenstein was advised by his father: 'Cows don't sell,' and Wildenstein would go on to specialise in the gallant works of the French Regency period, with their lustrous silks and perfumed boudoirs. With his fascination for the commonplace, the sober-minded Dutch art lover had, however, traditionally felt more for such subjects as the much-revered cow, for so long the mainstay of the Dutch economy, and the only object which broke up the monotony of the endless flat expanse of polder grass. Similarly, while his contemporaries, the French impressionists, found nothing quite as beautiful as the sunlight's reflection in a pond strewn with water lilies or the façade of a cathedral, for Willem Maris, like Aelbert Cuyp or Paulus Potter before him, the sheen of a cow's hide was enough to set his brush adance.

For a period of thirty years, from ca. 1870 to 1900, the two generations of artists comprising what is now called the Hague School set the artistic tone in the Netherlands. Their themes were as unelevated as they were classic: landscapes, livestock, interiors. With ever-greater subtlety and intimacy, they depicted the Dutch polder landscape, derived poetry from a view of a kitchen or stall and brought to life the joys and sorrows of life in fishing villages such as Katwijk or Scheveningen. Although contemporaries of the colour-mad impressionists, with whom they shared the ideal of painting from nature, they remained true to the grey tonality of the Dutch countryside. And while the impressionists were devoted painters of the Paris night life of their time, the Hague School eschewed all expressions of worldliness. They avoided Scheveningen's seaside visitors as subjects, preferring to portray the fishing community.

Cows do not have an easy time today, and the same applies to fishermen. But thanks to the Hague masters' subtle re-creations of 'grey sentiment,' we will always be able to enter the misty atmosphere of pastures forever gone and penetrate the dimly lit fisher's cabins which then faced threats far greater than today's fishing quotas. When the Hague School was in its prime, the industrial revolution was already an established fact, Europe's urbanisation had begun and idyllic unspoiled nature had long been consigned to the past. Israëls, the Marises, Mauve and Weissenbruch painted their Scheveningen canvases with their backs to the *Kurhaus*, well-aware of the transience and preciousness of what they were recording, and today, more than a century on, we are still aware of our deep indebtedness to them.

While, initially, some exponents of the Hague School had found it difficult to live from their painting alone, as the end of the 19th century approached, the group was able to benefit from growing public acclaim. Eventually, their work became popular with prominent collectors in England, Scotland and the United States, including the famed magnate, Henry Clay Frick, in whose New York museum a masterpiece by Jacob Maris still dares compete with Velazquez. After the First World War, however, the School became definitively overshadowed by French impressionism, and their names disappeared from the art history handbooks.

A reappraisal of the Hague School came, slowly but surely, in the second half of the 20th century, initially, as is so often the case, via the art market. For the first time in years, The Hague's

Gemeentemuseum decided, in 1965, to mount a retrospective devoted to the masters of the Hague School, with W. Jos de Gruijter, whose two-volume work (1968/69) would long remain the standard work on the School, in charge of the exhibition. It was not until 1983 that another large exhibition was organised, this time not only held in The Hague, but in Paris' Grand Palais and London's Royal Academy, as well.

As one of the organisers of that exhibition, together with John Sillevis and Charles Dumas, I still recall how little art-historical research had been done on the Hague School since De Gruijter, so that there were precious few new facts available to us. Another problem stemmed from the fact that De Gruijter himself had hardly made an attempt at attaining a synthesis. To be sure, he had provided his readers with well-written portraits of individual artists. However, he had made no effort to give a picture of the achievements of the group as a whole, something underlined by the fact that the book's introduction was not written by him, but by Victorine Hefting, former director of the Gemeentemuseum.

In 1983, our aim was to study the role of the Hague School as an innovative movement. While up to then, these painters had, quite one-sidedly, been valued primarily for their landscapes, their fascination for the life of the fishing community was now given greater emphasis. We distinguished between an incipient phase, a period of flowering and a long period of decline, and examined the School's relationship with the two greatest figures in painting around 1900, Vincent van Gogh and Piet Mondrian. In addition, authors were requested to write articles on the history of the collecting of works by the School, the role played by the art trade and the School's following in the Netherlands and abroad.

Through our choice of the title, 'Dutch masters of the 19th century,' we were unambiguously declaring the Hague painters to be the heirs of the great Netherlandish painters of the 17th century.

In our view, it was a disservice to these artists to regard them, as was then customary, as the Dutch equivalent of the impressionists. Their origin in the Dutch romanticism of Schelfhout and Koekkoek, their confrontation with the artistic inheritance of the Dutch 17th century and their receptivity for the Barbizon School's innovative impulses in landscape painting gave their art a new élan and an unmistakably unique character. At the end of the 19th century, art critics outside the Netherlands took note of this, referring to 'the New Dutch School.'

In my view, the 1983 exhibition also helped counteract a certain static quality in the reception of these painters. It seems to have led to greater attention being paid to development in their work, even in the period when Toorop and Breitner had come onto the scene. It may also have inspired the organisers of the 1990 exhibition 'The Painters of '80' to present the late works of Maris, Gabriël, Weissenbruch and Israëls in dialogue with the avant-garde of the Amsterdam impressionists and symbolists.

Following the exhibitions in Paris and London, the Gemeentemuseum continued to work toward widening awareness of the Hague School. In the 80s and 90s, it continued its rehabilitation offensive with exhibitions in Munich, Mannheim, Madrid and Vienna. These efforts may not have resulted in universal fame for the School; as a result of them, however, the period in which mention of these artists was confined to footnotes to treatments of Van Gogh and Mondrian was definitively over. Moreover, works from the Hague School are now included with increasing frequency in international publications, and the acquisition by Washington's National Gallery of a large landscape by Jacob Maris can be viewed as a sign of things to come.

In the Netherlands, the last twenty years have witnessed an increase in the importance attached to art-historical research. Much has now been written concerning the social aspects of the lives of 19th century artists, e.g., artists' societies and the art market. The School's substantial influence on European and American artists has, as well, undergone further investigation. A number of doctoral dissertations have shed light on the important role played by Brussels as a meeting point between the Dutch and French art worlds, and some exponents of the Hague School have been the subjects of new monographies. Numerous small and mid-sized Dutch museums have also made their contribution. The museums of Gouda, Dordrecht and Oss mounted exhibitions devoted to Tholen, Gabriël and Weissenbruch and the Groninger Museum put its spotlight on Jozef Israëls, while Amsterdam's Jewish Historical Museum held a parallel exhibition on the Jewish aspects of his œuvre.

A turning point in appreciation for the works of the School was also reflected in a change in the fortunes of The Hague's Museum Mesdag. Interest in this museum of modern art, once the leader in its field, had diminished to such an extent that its future existence had become threatened, its beautiful Hague and Barbizon collections notwithstanding. However, in 1996, after already having been closed for a few years, the museum rose, as it were, from its ashes. Not only was the museum returned to its former glory through large-scale restoration work, but the adjacent house in which Mesdag had lived was acquired as well and incorporated into the museum.

Thanks to purchases, generous gifts and, especially, bequests, the Dutch museums are well-supplied, – if not saturated – with the works of the Hague School. As a result, there was hardly a time in the last 25 years that the Dutch museums were involved with large-scale acquisition of works by the group. In the 1960s, only the Gemeentemuseum was actively involved with the purchase of their works, acquiring a small view of Haarlem by Weissenbruch, a view of Monmartre by Matthijs Maris and the magnificent 'Allotments' of his brother Jacob. From that time on, museum's acquisitions became increasingly seldom, and the purse-strings were only loosened when a truly extraordinary work presented itself. Expanding its collection of works by artists within the context of Vincent van Gogh, the relatively young Van Gogh Museum in Amsterdam acquired a dozen oil paintings and watercolours by artists of the Hague School, including Matthijs Maris' masterpiece, 'Woman with the goats' and Jozef Israëls' exquisite watercolour, 'Sewing class at Katwijk.' The museum received as a gift from the well-known Mesdag collector and expert, Johan Poort, the re-discovered 'Les Brisants de la Mer du Nord,' with which Mesdag established his international career at the Paris Salon of 1870.

The Dutch national collection was also augmented by two extraordinary and important works from the Hague School: a stormy landscape by Roelofs dating from 1850, purchased to mark the departure of Simon Levie as director of the Rijksmuseum, and a 'View of Rouen,' a canvas from the romantic early period of Johannes Bosboom that had hung in the Gemeentemuseum on extended loan.

As inspiring as temporary exhibitions may be, it is the permanent exhibitions in museums that fix one's attention on a work of art and give the public the opportunity to deepen their love for it. Thanks to the permanent exhibitions devoted to the Hague School in the Rijksmuseum, Museum Mesdag and the Gemeentemuseum, its place is now firmly anchored in the Netherlands' public collection of art treasures. Each of these museums has its own area of concentration and approach. In the Rijksmuseum, the School is presented as the 19th century renaissance of Dutch 17th century landscape and genre art. In Museum Mesdag, the spontaneous sketch in oils and the group's dialogue with their French colleagues in the Barbizon School receive special prominence. The Gemeentemuseum offers, of the three, certainly the most balanced overview. Here, one can follow the Hague masters' development: their first tentative steps; how they freed themselves from their breeding ground in the Biedermeier-like Dutch romantic movement; at the end of the century, their confrontation with the urban impressionism of the generation of Breitner and Isaac Israëls. In addition, the presentation demonstrates how the works of the Hague School led the way to the fascinating art of Mondrian.

A particularly attractive facet of the Hague School is formed by its watercolours. In this difficult medium, some of the group's members demonstrated an ability to obtain atmospheric effects of an incredible refinement. Unfortunately, though, due to concerns about the detrimental effects of excessive light, this very portion of their œuvre can only be put on view from time to time. The time is long gone, when watercolours were on permanent display in the Drucker Extension of the Rijksmuseum and the rooms of Museum Mesdag. However, thanks to the technique of printing, such a publication as the present one can provide some degree of consolation in this regard.

As rich as it is compact, this book on the Hague School in the collections of the Gemeentemuseum offers an attractive overview of the works of the group. As one could expect from the Gemeentemuseum of The Hague, its collection is unquestionably of high importance, rich and many-facetted. Granted: in Amsterdam one can see Bilders and Mauve at their best, and as regards Israëls, Jacob Maris and Roelofs, the honours are equally distributed among the Dutch museums. However, the Gemeentemuseum is unequalled in its choice collection of Matthijs Maris and, above all, its unique series of works by J.H. Weissenbruch. Nowhere else is the lyrical, transparent art of this painter – in the light of history perhaps the greatest of all the Hague masters – represented as impressively.

Ronald de Leeuw
director Rijksmuseum Amsterdam

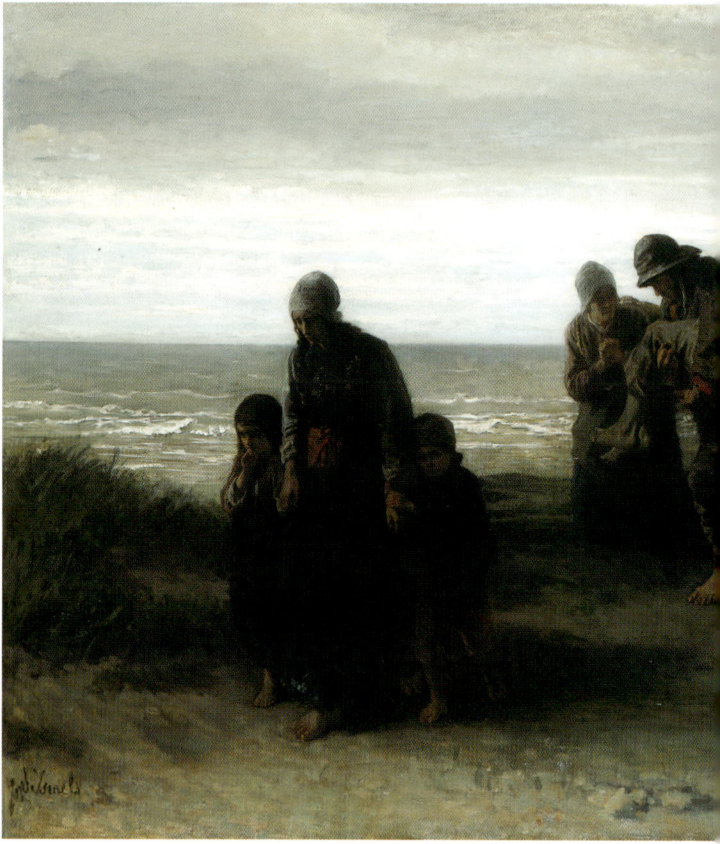

Jozef Israëls, *The drowned fisherman,* 1861 (National Gallery, London)

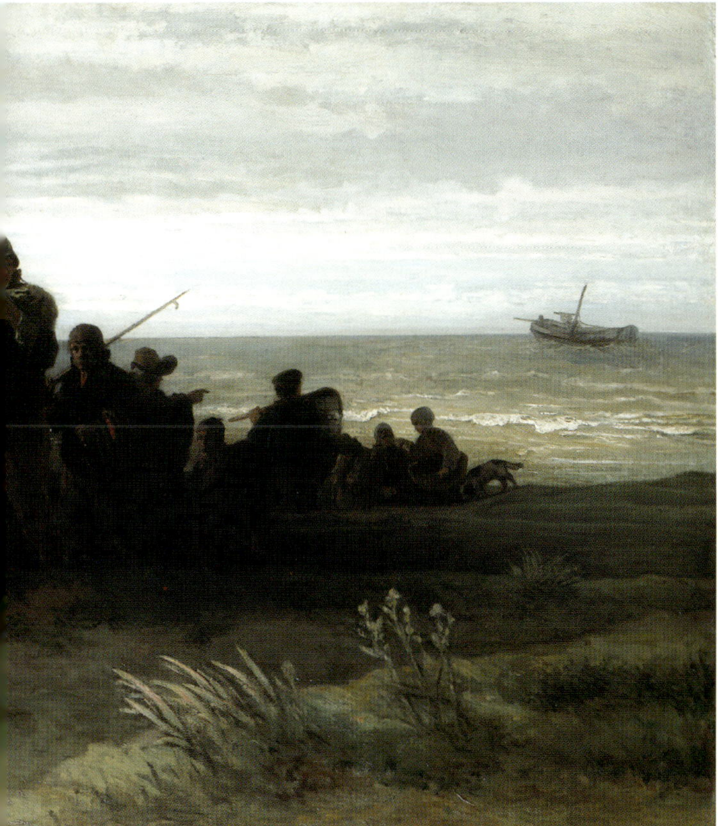

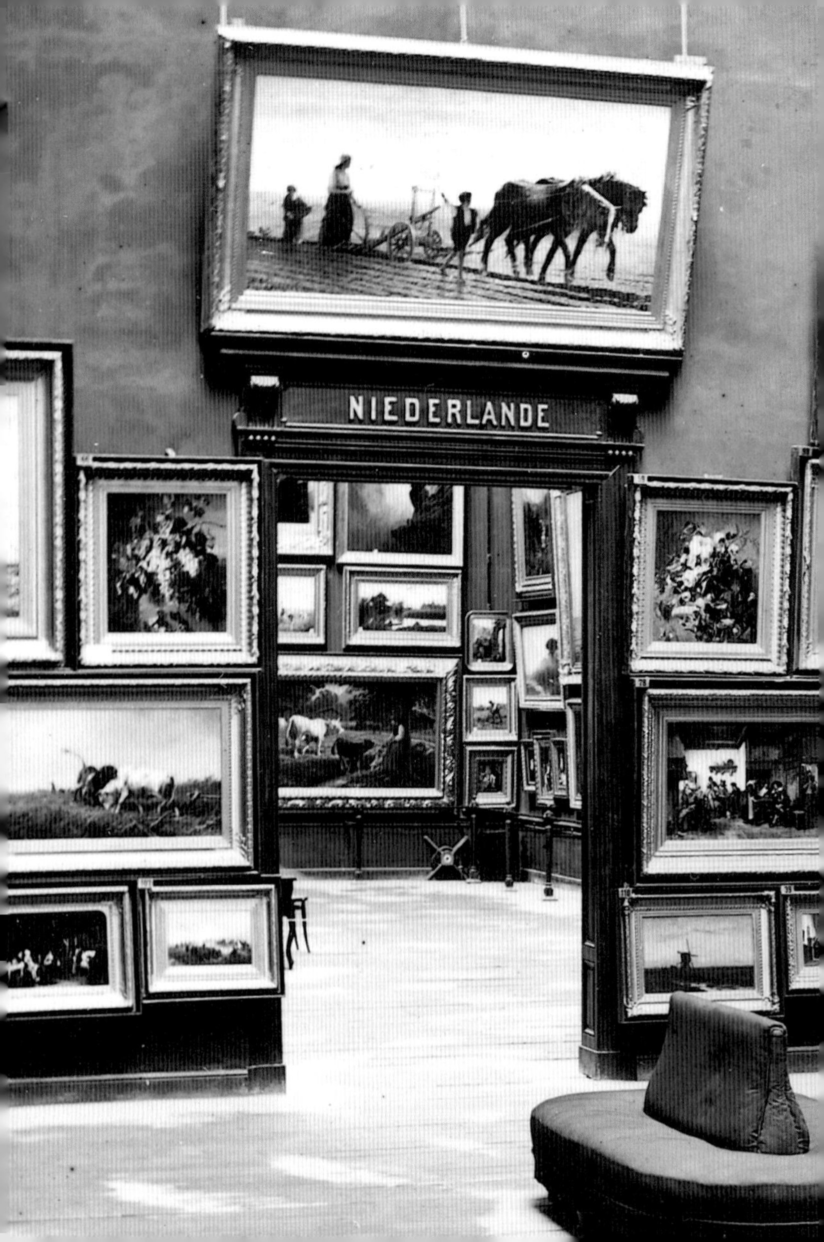
NIEDERLANDE

INTERNATIONAL FAME

John Sillevis

The 19th century was the century of great international exhibitions. The first world exhibition, the Great Exhibition held in 1851 in London's Crystal Palace, functioned primarily as a showcase for the products of commerce and industry. The second, which took place in Paris in 1855, included, for the first time, a section devoted to the work of contemporary artists. The world exhibitions presented the newest inventions and developments in the field of technology, and also offered the visitor impressions of distant lands and peoples.

Progress was the dominant underlying concept of these exhibitions, but nationalism, at its acme at that time, also played a role in the submissions of the participant countries. Art – especially in France – was an important component of national prestige, and the artists selected were regarded by both public and press as representative of the artistic situation in their respective countries.

Jozef Israëls was one of the artists taking part in the International Exhibition of 1862 in London. Following the example of Paris, at this exhibition, too, considerable space was made available for contemporary visual art. Israëls' contribution, 'The drowned fisherman,' became an immediate success with the public. It was even referred to as 'the most touching picture of the whole exhibition' and was reproduced and discussed in detail in *The London Illustrated Times.* The painting fell within the new movement known as realism, introduced by Courbet during the Paris World Exhibition of 1855. Although invited by the French authorities to take part in the exhibition, Courbet had chosen to display his work outside the exhibition in his own separate pavilion, sensationally named the 'Pavillion du Réalisme.' Courbet had already attracted much attention with his monumental painting depicting a village funeral in Ornans: neither the public nor art critics had been accustomed to seeing the lives and deaths of simple peasants represented in a format normally reserved for the heroic acts of elevated figures drawn from history, the Bible or mythology. In that sense, Israëls' painting was equally unusual, as it did not show the shipwreck itself – a theme popular with painters of the romantic period – but, rather, the sorrow following the disaster: the fisherman's widow with her two children, who had lost their breadwinner, and the fishermen who had to carry their mate to the grave. The painting was purchased in London and subsequently entered the famous collection of Alexander Young. It is now part of the collection of London's National Gallery.

The success of his realistic theme was for Jozef Israëls a clear signal that he could readily create a sensation abroad with a subject drawn from contemporary Dutch life. It was, however, as yet too early to speak of a *Hague School.* It was not until the world exhibition held in Vienna in 1873 that a connection could be pointed to between the work of Jozef Israëls and a number of his Dutch contemporaries. In the midst of more than 6,000 works of art from all over the world, the Dutch submission – consisting of 167 works – made, in the words of art critic Friedrich Pecht, 'a harmonious and salutary' impression.[1] In Vienna, Israëls again succeeded in attracting attention with a funeral scene, this time in a peasant interior. The body of the deceased peasant is brought outside, while his despairing widow remains behind with her small children. French art critic René Ménard wrote in the influential

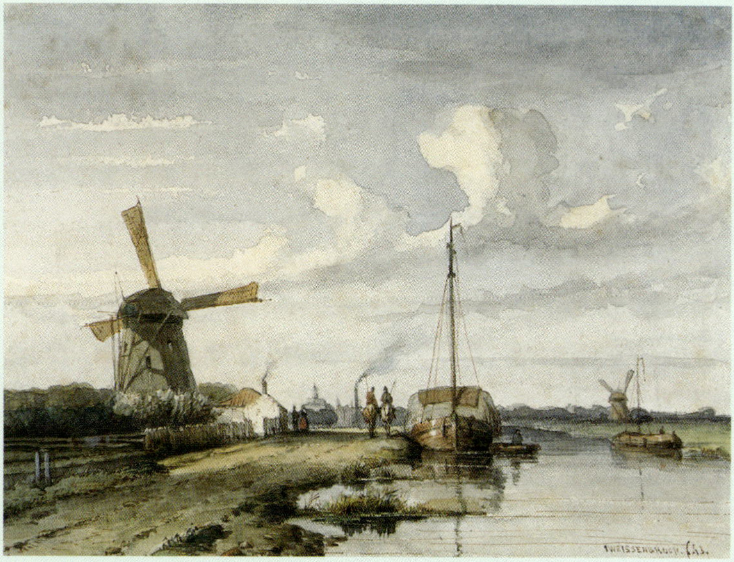

Jan Weissenbruch, View of the Trekvliet near The Hague, 1843 (watercolour)

p. 16:
The Dutch section at the Vienna World Exhibition of 1873

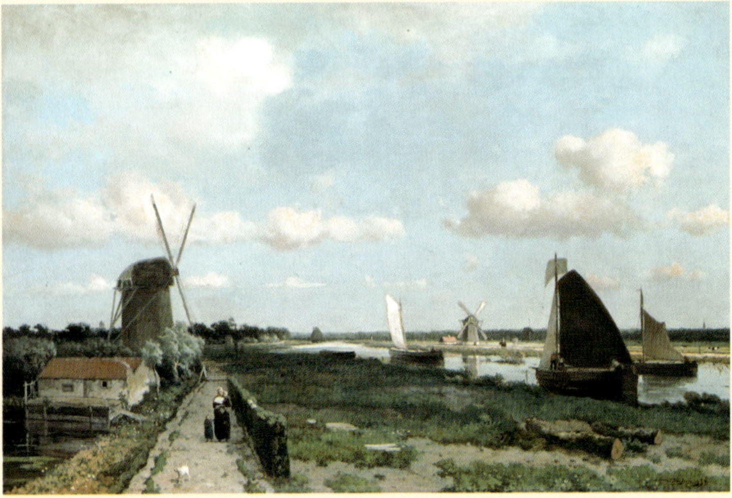

J.H. Weissenbruch, View of the Trekvliet near The Hague, 1870

pp. 22-23:
detail of p. 20

Gazette des Beaux-Arts of the work, which was exhibited in Vienna under the title 'Durch Finsternis zum Licht' (through the darkness to the light): 'I believe that the "Funeral" shall come to be considered one of his best works.'[2] Willem Roelofs exhibited two works, 'On the river Gein,' and 'Pasture landscape with cows' (now in the collection of Amsterdam's Stedelijk Museum), Anton Mauve presented his 'Draught horses on the banks of the Rhine' and J.H. Weissenbruch was represented by his 'View of the Trekvliet near The Hague,' at that time part of The Hague's municipal collections. Bosboom, as well, was among the contributing artists. With great clarity, critic Ménard observed of the Dutch section: 'Landscape art is on the eve of a new development. Slowly but surely, and without much ado, the Dutch painters have returned to their roots.' He praised their feeling for realism, use of *couleur locale* and no-nonsense approach.[3] He spoke of 'a small group of painters [who were] taking root on the Dutch coast.'

Critic L.E. Duranty, as well, referred to a group of twelve to fifteen closely associated artists, this in his discussion of the Dutch contribution to the Paris World Exhibition of 1878. In his view, only now could the Netherlands again rightfully consider themselves a nation of painters, following, as he put it, a malaise during the romantic period.[4]

With so much being said on the matter internationally, it was not long before Dutch art critics were also voicing their opinions. In 1875, writer J. van Santen Kolff published a long article in the magazine *De Banier*, in which he coined the term 'Hague School' and characterised the group as 'a new, ultra-radical movement in painting.'[5] He referred to Mesdag, Jacob Maris, Jozef Neuhuys and Anton Mauve, as well as Louis Apol, Jan Vrolijk, Théophile de Bock, Fred du Chattel, E.J. Boks and F.P. Ter Meulen as 'trail-blazing masters' and Sadée, Jozef Israëls and Artz as custodians of the art of 'painting in grey.' In his view, the group's aims could

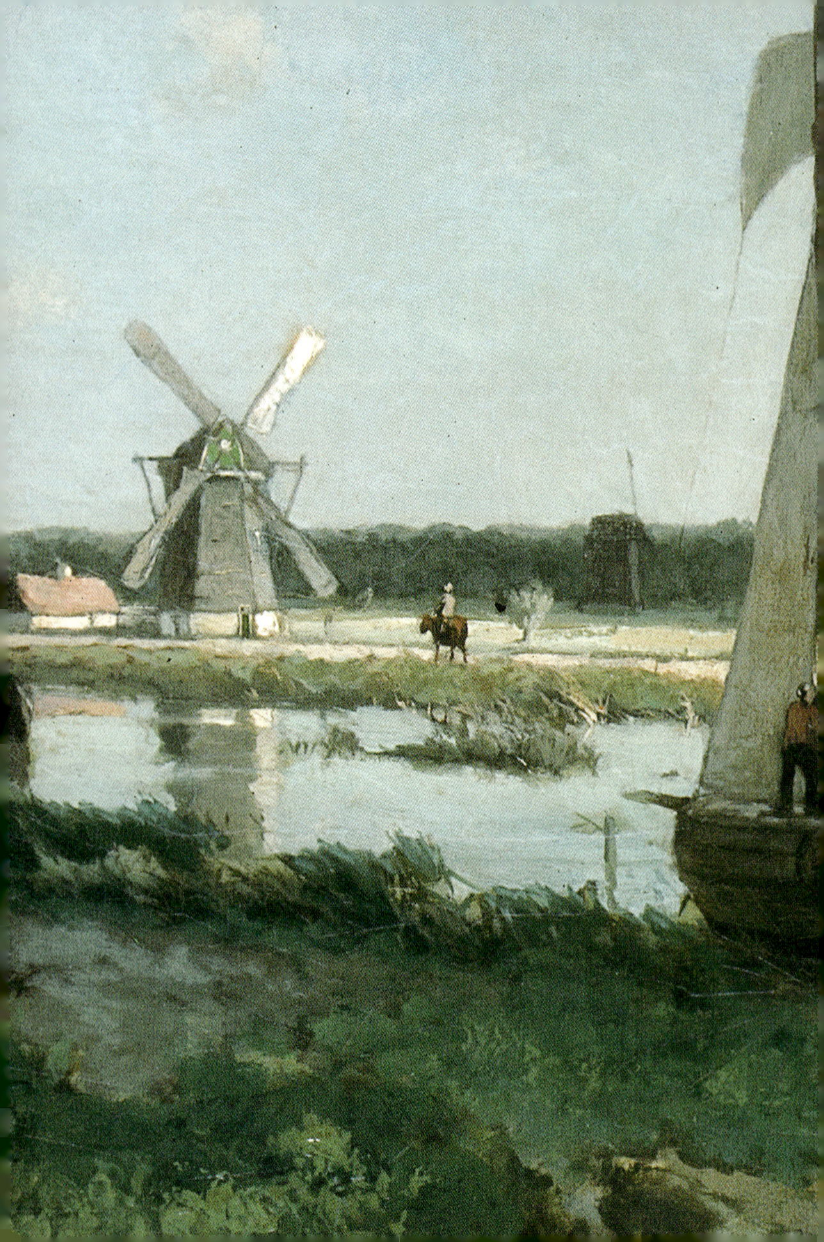

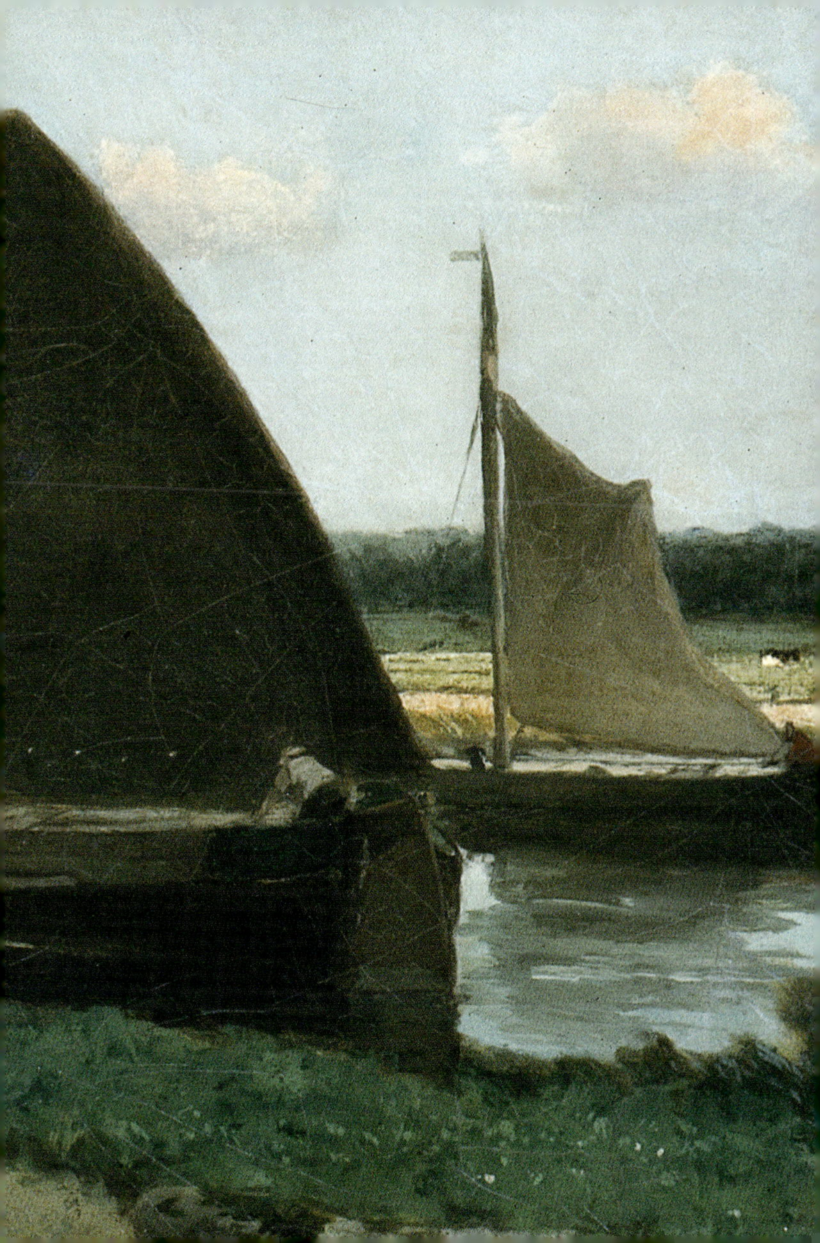

be epitomised by its representation of *atmosphere* and preference for *tone* above *colour*. He considered Mesdag the clearest exponent of the new realism, as well as a pioneer and example for the modern landscape and seascape painters of his time. While such a positive reception of the art we today refer to as 'the Hague School' was consistent with current trends in international art criticism, it continued to be an exception in the art criticism appearing in the Dutch press. The older members of the Dutch painters' society, Pulchri Studio, reacted to the new school with repugnance, finding these young artists 'mud painters,' and director J.P. Koelman of the Haagse Teekenacademie (Hague Academy of Art) classified a submission of theirs as 'realistic filth.' True to tradition, Koelman had provided the Exhibition of Living Masters, of which the painters of the Hague School formed part, with exhibition space, as facilities large enough to accommodate the exposition's many works were nowhere else to be found in The Hague. The Gemeentemuseum had already been established, but its modern collection had, for the most part, yet to be acquired, and the historic collections were housed in the Sebastiaansdoelen. Only at the end of the century would Pulchri Studio be given its own exhibition rooms, first on the Prinsengracht and later on the Lange Voorhout.

Besides such international events as the world exhibitions already mentioned, artists' societies also played a very important role in spreading the fame of the Hague School during the 19th century. An example is the *Montreal Society of Artists*, founded in 1847, the year in which Pulchri Studio was also founded in The Hague; from 1860, this organisation, whose name had been changed to *Art Association of Montreal*, began organising its 'loan exhibitions,' featuring works supplied by local collectors, art dealers and artists, whereby the emphasis was on old masters and the Barbizon and Hague Schools. As early as 1879, a work by

Matthijs Maris could be viewed at the 9th exhibition of the Art Association, and at the 1888 exhibition, of the 136 catalogue items, 22 were works of the Hague School. Mauve and Tholen were especially popular, as was J.H. Weissenbruch. Following the death of Jacob Maris in 1899, a 'Special Loan Exhibition' was organised, devoted to the three Maris brothers: Jacob, Matthijs and Willem. The exhibition included 48 paintings, all from private Montreal collections.[6] One of the participating collectors, E.B. Greenshields, even wrote a book entitled 'Landscape Painting and Modern Dutch Artists.' The book, published in Toronto and New York in 1906, was to exert considerable influence on both Canadian and U.S. collectors.

At the time, it was viewed as a very natural thing to combine the Hague and Barbizon Schools, a notable example being Charles Taft, half-brother of U.S. president William Howard Taft, who filled one wall of his music room with the Hague School and the opposite wall with the Barbizon School.[7]

Many art dealers established additional locations, in order to meet the great demand for works of the Hague School, e.g., the French Gallery, which had branches in London, Edinburgh and Montreal. Another company which flourished at the time was the Amsterdam firm, E.J. Wisselingh & Co., which, from 1898, organised sale exhibitions in Montreal. In the U.S., Boston, Washington, D.C. and New York were the most important places for purchasing works of the Hague School. The Toledo Museum of Art (Ohio) was able to draw on the private collection of Edward Drummond Libbey, which contained works by Anton Mauve, J.H. Weissenbruch, Jozef Israëls and the Maris brothers. From art dealer Knoedler, New York collector Frank Frick purchased several works from the Hague School which ultimately found their way into the famed Frick Collection. Later, the museum would sell off a number of the works, but one masterpiece by Jacob Maris, a

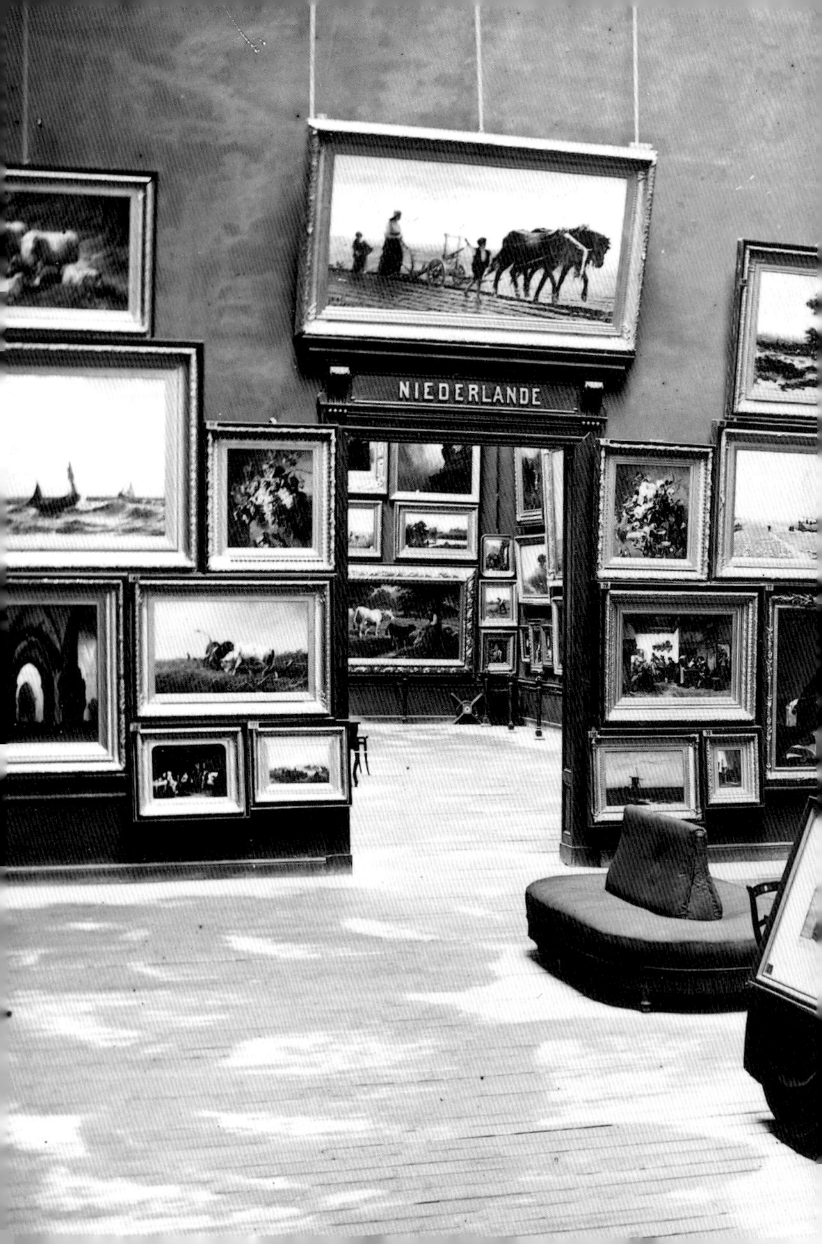
NIEDERLANDE

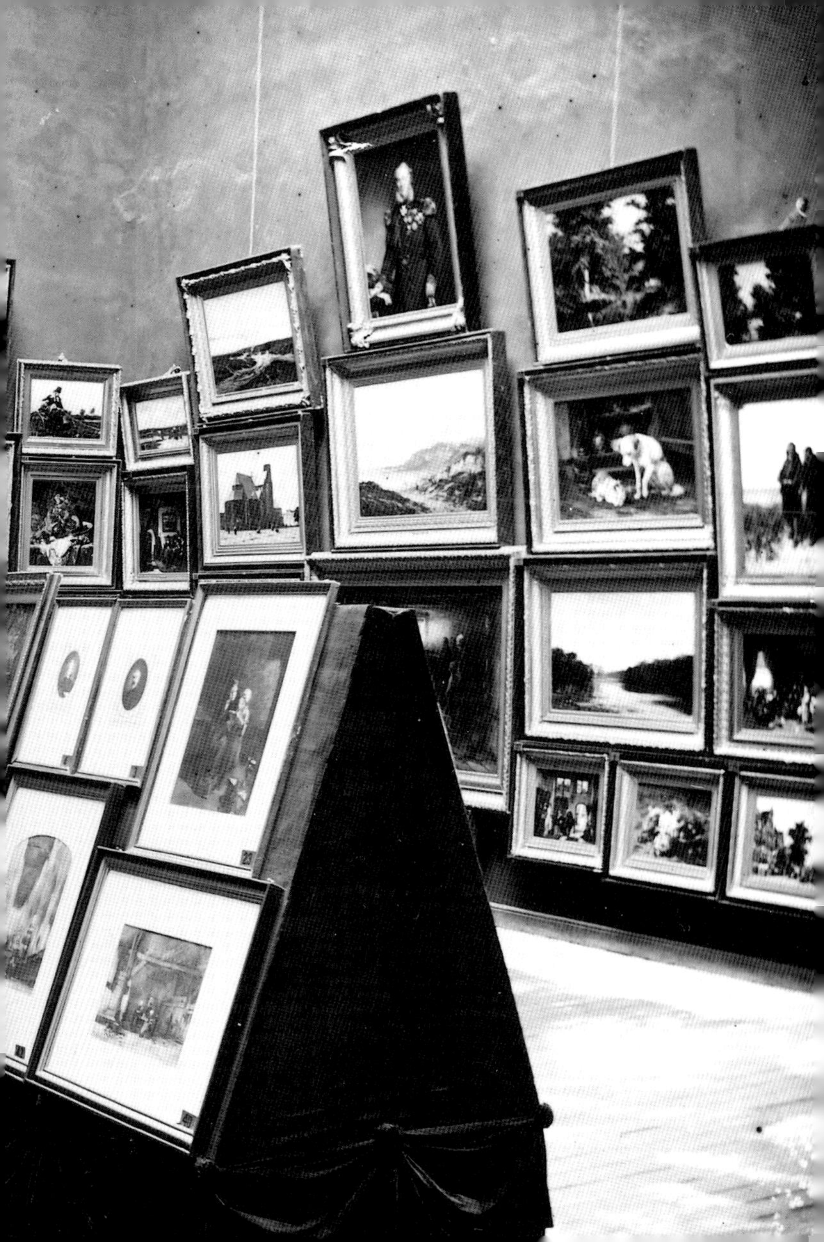

view of a small bridge near Rijswijk, continues to hang in its permanent collection.[8]

In Europe, Munich was, from 1879, the site of exhibitions of works of the Hague School. Works by Jacob Maris, Anton Mauve, Mesdag, Gabriël, Willem Roelofs and Willem Maris were exhibited at the second International Art Exhibition held in the city's Glaspalast. Work by Jozef Israëls was, however, conspicuously absent,[9] and at the third International Art Exhibition in 1883, a number of important members of the group were not represented. Painter J.J.L. de Haas was enlisted by the group to function as a supervisory director and ensure a balanced selection of artists. Through de Haas' efforts, important works of the Hague School were purchased with regularity by the Bavarian Collection of Paintings from 1888. Many German art critics reacted enthusiastically, with Richard Muther regarding the confrontation with the Hague School a revitalisation cure for German art. However, not everyone was as enthusiastic. The conservative Friedrich Pecht, who had already written on the Dutch submission in Vienna, described the stormy clouds in the Mesdag's skies as 'riesige Knödel' (gigantic dumplings) flying through the air, and subjected Israëls and Bisschop, as well, to ridicule.[10]

In Budapest, Counts Esterházy and Palffy bought important works by Jozef Israëls ('Sewing class at Katwijk'), Gabriël, Mesdag and Tholen which eventually became part of the collection of the Hungarian National Museum.

Never before had art been so accessible to a large public, and not only in the Netherlands, but all over the world. For such artists as the members of the Hague School it must have been a new experience to know that their work was being exhibited, purchased, judged and awarded prizes from London to Paris, Milan to Montreal and Vienna to Washington. Anton Mauve rapidly became overstrained from the constant demand in England

and America for 'sheep coming' and 'sheep going' – whereby there was a clear difference in price between the two subjects –, and Blommers had the unusual experience of learning that his paintings were being sold before even having been painted. Fame and success seemed in endless supply – a heyday which began only ten years after a 'Hague School' had first been referred to and one which lasted until the outbreak of the First World War.[11]

pp. 26-27:
The Dutch section at the World Exhibition in Vienna, 1873

pp. 30-31:
Wall of the music room of Charles Taft with works by Mauve, the Maris brothers and Jozef Israëls

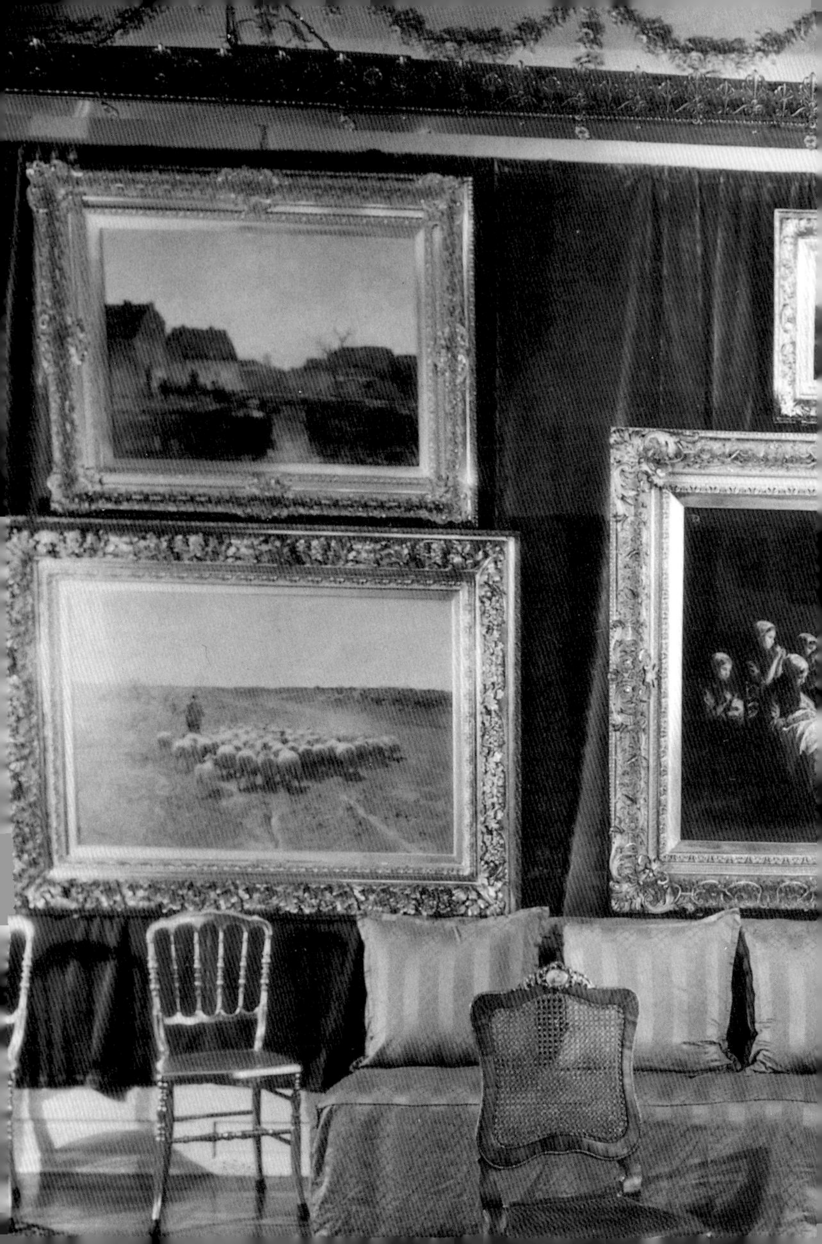

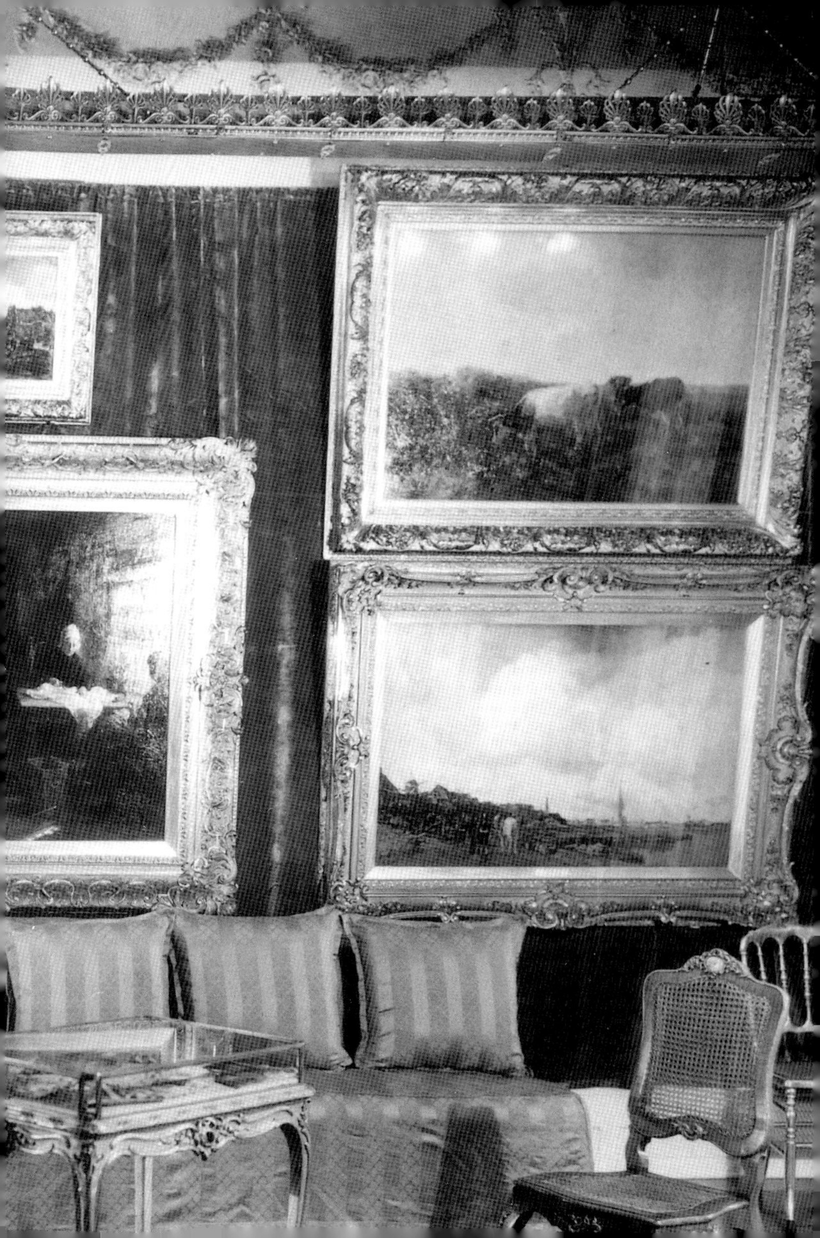

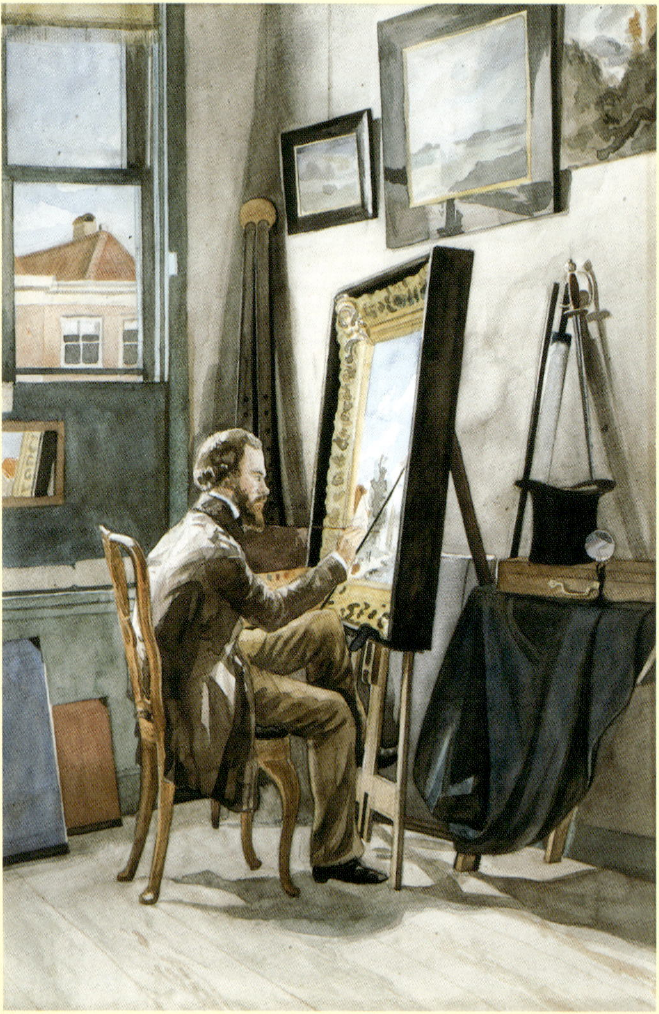

LESSONS FROM NATURE

John Sillevis

While its ostensible starting point was realism, the Hague School's roots go back unmistakably to the romantic movement. Dutch romanticism was, certainly in visual arts, not a period of infectious enthusiasm or irrepressible inspiration. The artistic traditions which had made Holland great were paid artificial lip service, with the emphasis on the landscape and genre scene. These Dutch painters were not cut out for the great drama of the historical piece: in their hands, the representation of great heroics drawn from history, mythology or the Bible frequently became awkward, banal or even unintentionally humorous. The romanticism which flourished in Germany, England and France called for the great gesture, emotional upheaval and theatrics. The Dutch romantics avoided all-too-strong emotions and preferred expressing themselves with small-scale, precisely measured works. An approaching storm or the threat of snow are the height of drama for a landscape by Andreas Schelfhout. His ice landscapes were filled with skaters, sleds and refreshment stalls, but did not show people falling through the ice, let alone a romantic pursuit of a hero who tries to save his skin by jumping from ice floe to ice floe. Dutch romantic painting was perfectly suited to the proper, bourgeois lives led by the Stastok family from Hildebrand's 'Camera Obscura' (a collection of humoristic reflections and short stories dating from 1839); in the Dutch home, the clock always kept good time, and outside,

p. 32:
Jan Weissenbruch,
Self-portrait in the studio, n.d.
(watercolour)

Johannes Bosboom,
Quai de Paris in Rouen, n.d.
(watercolour)

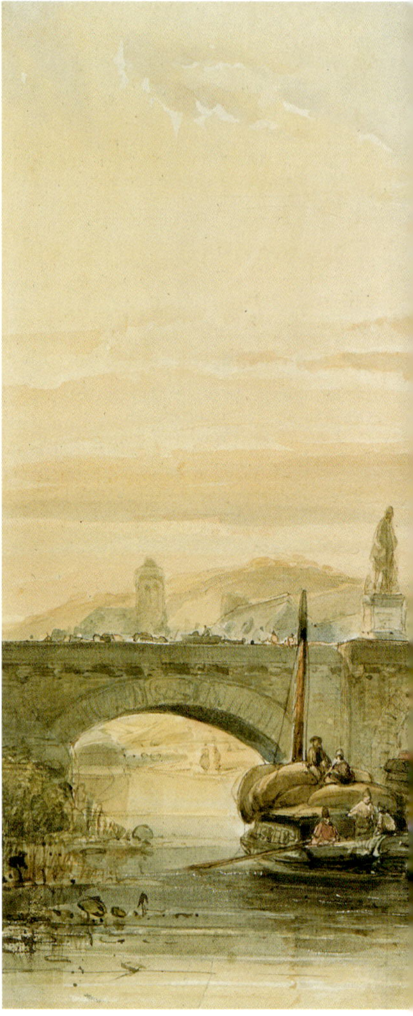

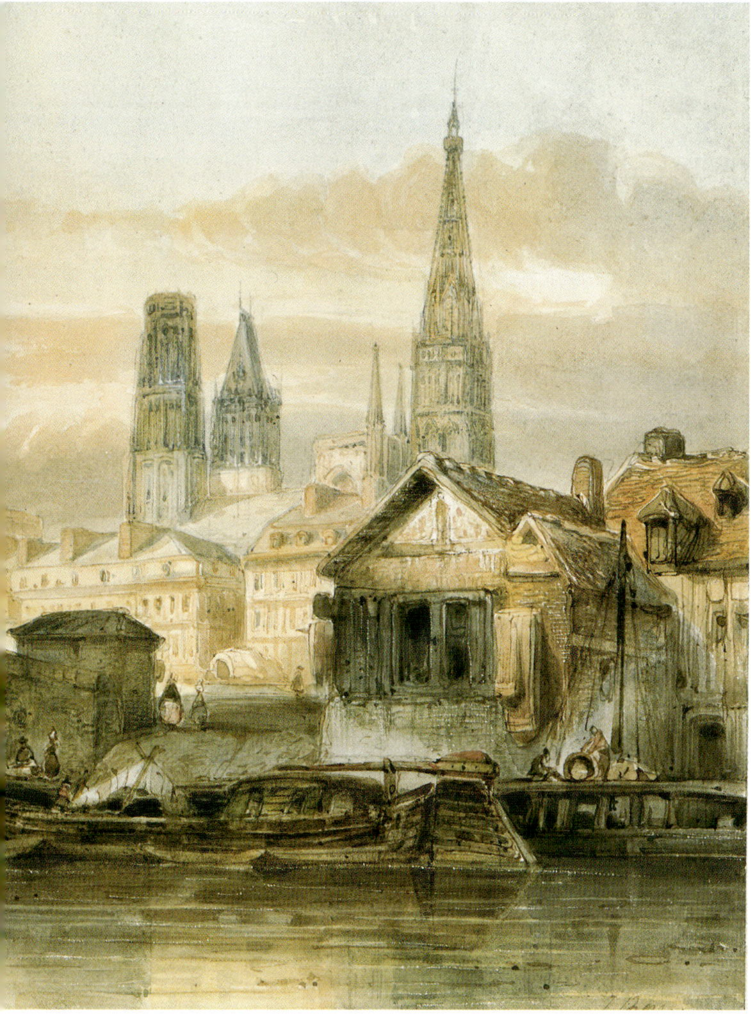

the stage-coach went by every day with predictable punctuality. Breaking through this regular rhythm required much nerve and fantasy, and artists who tried to free themselves from this rigidly defined scheme could expect strong opposition from the press. For example, Wijnand Nuyen's desolate shipwrecks, these dramatic depictions of the Normandy coast with their strong colours and sharp contrasts of light and shadow, were characterised as the work of a 'young and very promising artist who, with each work comes nearer to a false, romantic taste.'[12] Romanticism was regarded as an import, the product of an un-Dutch mentality. Nuyen had gone on study trips to France and Germany; he was familiar with the paintings and lithographs of Eugène Isabey and his penchant for the rough coastal landscape of Normandy and Brittany. Nuyen was familiar with the new fishermen's genre then experiencing a heyday in the so-called Düsseldorf School, in which Scandinavian painters played an essential role. He painted fishermen in traditional dress and sloops on the beach of Scheveningen accompanied by ship's rigging and the paltry homes of the fishing villages. He studied the prints of Bonington, Samuel Prout, Harding and Cooke and collected illustrated editions of the Waverly Novels of Sir Walter Scott and of the works of Byron. Nuyen's paintings and drawings revealed a preference for gothic architecture – a preference he shared with his friend Johannes Bosboom. Following Nuyen's example, Bosboom journeyed to Normandy in 1838, in the company of Cornelis Kruseman. A year later, Bosboom painted a monumental view of the mediaeval centre of Rouen. The work presents a view of the cathedral from the banks of the Seine near the Quai de Paris in a style highly reminiscent of Nuyen, who died unexpectedly in the same year, aged 26. Gothic churches, especially their interiors, would ultimately become the dominant theme of Bosboom's œuvre. However, Bosboom was also highly skilled, in both oils and watercolours, when it came to landscapes, for which he typically chose unusual subjects, such as lime excavations and beach scenes with seaside visitors.

The young Hendrik Jan ('Hein') Weissenbruch also made 'watercolour drawings from nature,' as he himself called them. Weissenbruch diffidently showed his work to the famous Schelfhout, who, to his surprise, reacted enthusiastically, and even invited the young artist to work in his studio. Bosboom was, however, opposed to such a step, saying: 'You shouldn't do it, Weiss, you need to learn to stand on your own two feet.'[13] Schelfhout was not an advocate of painting from nature: in his view, it was a good way to waste paint. At the time, the Hague art world was characterised by a closely knit network of various familial connections. Andreas Schelfhout was first cousins with the painter, Bart van Hove, who taught at the Haagse Teekenacademie (Hague Academy of Art). One of Schelfhout's daughters married Wijnand Nuyen; Bart van Hove's sister married the best friend of Wijnand Nuyen, painter Antonie Waldorp.[14] In the time of the Hague School, too, family connections played an important role. Hein Weissenbruch was a cousin of romantic painter Jan Weissenbruch, the Maris brothers, Jacob, Matthijs and Willem, formed a prominent triumvirate and Anton Mauve was married to a niece of Vincent van Gogh. The initial friendships among the painters of the Hague School were formed in Oosterbeek, where, immediately preceding the middle of the 19th century, many artists could be found making their first explorations in painting from nature.[15]

One of the 'discoverers' of Oosterbeek was Johannes Warnardus Bilders, who, after 1840, spent the summer months painting outdoors, accompanied by his wife and children, and often in the company of such young artists as Gabriël, Anton Mauve, Willem Roelofs and the Maris brothers. A favourite spot was Wolfheze, known for the Odin's oaks which stood there. Another meeting place was the estate 'De Hemelsche Berg', owned

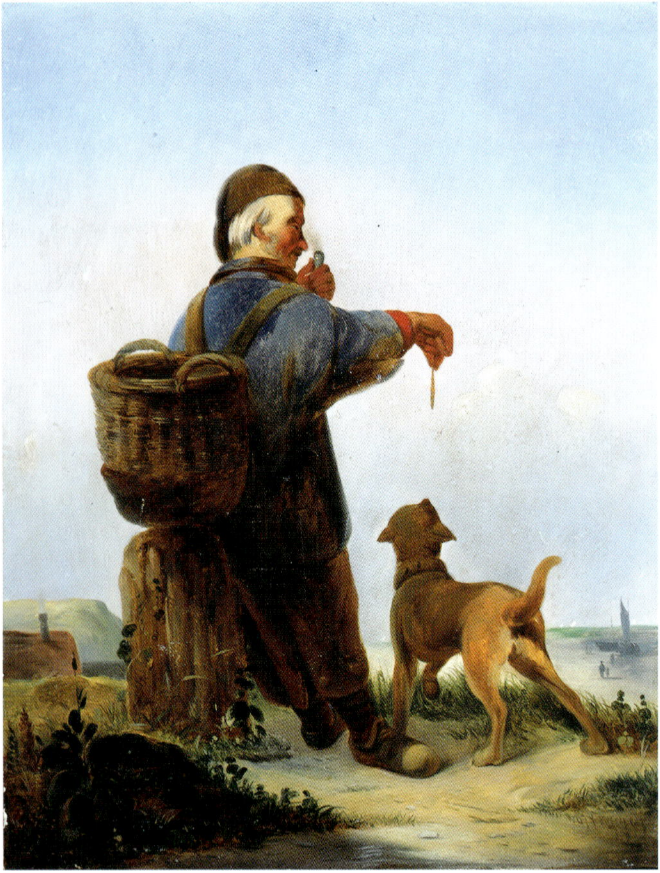

Wijnand Nuyen, *Scheveningen man,* n.d. (private collection)

Andreas Schelfhout, *Scheveningen woman,* n.d. (watercolour)

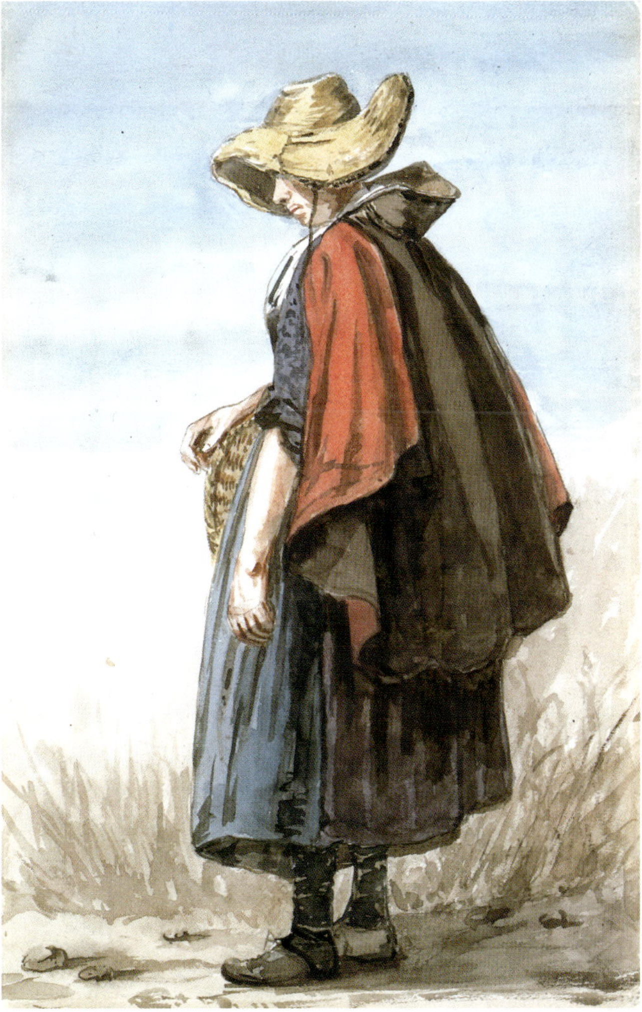

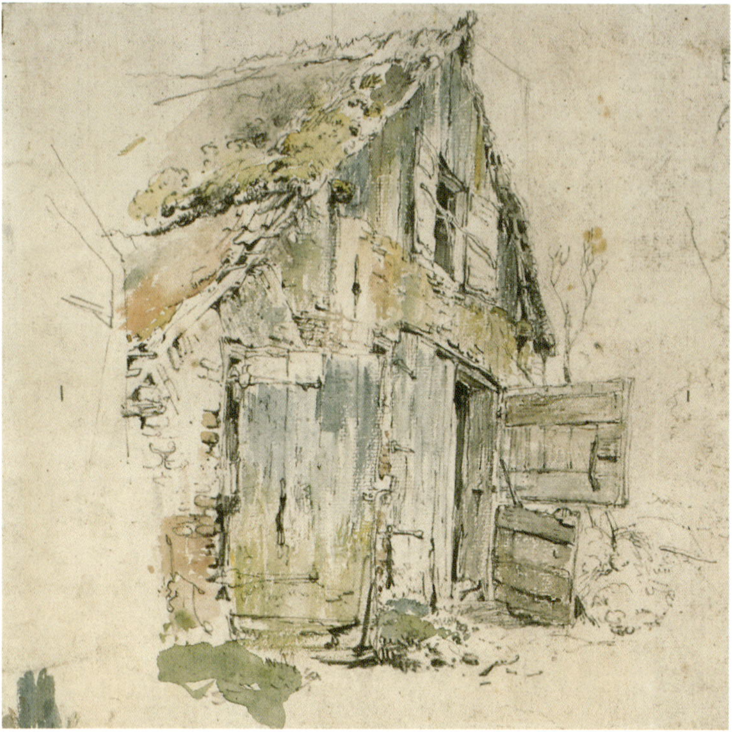

Willem Roelofs, *Old shed,* n.d. (watercolour)

by writer and art patron Johannes Kneppelhout, who, in his student years, had made a name for himself as a writer about student life under the pseudonym Klikspaan. In later life, he came to consider it his mission in life to offer professional training to promising young artists, even writing a book entitled 'L'éducation par l'amitié' (education by friendship). Among those he helped were the young violinist, Jan de Graan, and J.W. Bilders' son, Gerard. Although imbued with the best of intentions, Kneppelhout's efforts also had a tyrannical side. Gerard Bilders, who had received training from the Hague painter, Simon van den Berg, would have preferred completing his training in Paris, but was sent by Kneppelhout to Switzerland to study with the extremely mediocre landscape painter, Charles Humbert. Part of the instruction he had received had consisted in drawing from classical plaster models at the Hague Academy of Art and copying Potter's 'Bull' in the Mauritshuis. However, the young Bilders' interests went in a completely different direction: in 1860 he visited, together with his father, the Exposition générale des Beaux-Arts in Brussels. J.W. Bilders had frequently exhibited works of his here – views of woods near Nijmegen and Wolfheze –, but what Gerard interested were the paintings of the Barbizon School on view there, including studies from nature by Diaz de la Peña, Jules Dupré, Millet, Corot, Courbet and Troyon. In these works, he saw before him what he himself aspired to: a tone in which all colours came together, a 'coloured grey.' Gerard Bilders wrote: 'Maintaining the feeling of grey in even the brightest green is extraordinarily difficult...'[16]

Bilders' landscapes of the Betuwe district and the edge of the Veluwe district nevertheless remained colourful, and sometimes exhibited the warm glow of the setting sun on a summer evening. Bilders, who was unsure of his own abilities, received little moral support from his father, or even his patron, Kneppelhout, who would have actually preferred a literary career for him. The young artist contracted tuberculosis and, despite a great will to live, died, aged 27, in 1865.

Art critics were not inclined to encourage the new interest in 'coloured grey.' Bilders had been informed that his work was too grey, one critic advised that Matthijs Maris should take off his 'grey eyeglasses,' and another wrote of Anton Mauve that his eyes were covered with a mourning veil.[17] Sombreness was, however, not the effect these young artists intended. Anton Mauve repeatedly wrote Willem Maris, enthusiastically inviting him to come wandering with him in the environs of Oosterbeek and paint outdoors. ('Divinely beautiful, that Wolfhezer country with its brooks and pines.') From the age of eleven, Willem Maris had been taken hiking through grazing land by his older brothers, Jacob and Matthijs, to draw and paint. In the summer, they painted outdoors, and in the winter they worked in sheds and stalls. The instruction Mauve had received from horse painter Wouterus Verschuur came in handy when he painted outdoors. Mauve and Gabriël also worked in close conjunction, and even collaborated on a large wood landscape, with Gabriël painting the trees, and Mauve the goats and cows. Sadée, Kaemmerer, Blommers and Nakken could also regularly be found painting in Oosterbeek, where the new notions on painting from nature could be put to the test. The friendships which started here later provided the basis for the strong internal cohesion among the members of the Hague School.

The similarity to the Barbizon School in this regard, is striking.[18] Barbizon, too, was characterised by a 'va-et-vient'; only a few artists, e.g. Millet and Rousseau, lived there on a permanent basis, with the local auberge of father Ganne serving as a place to meet and hold discussions. The products of their work in the open air could be viewed at the great art exhibitions, such as the yearly Paris Salons, where the contribution from landscape painters

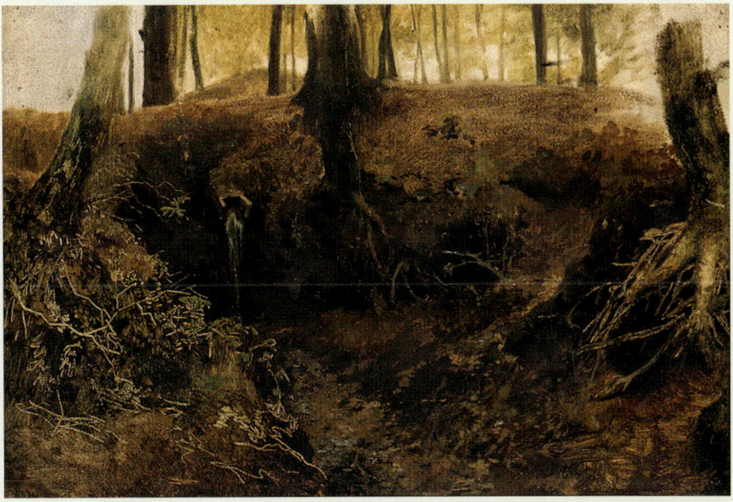

Matthijs Maris, 'The origin' (wood landscape near Oosterbeek), ca. 1860

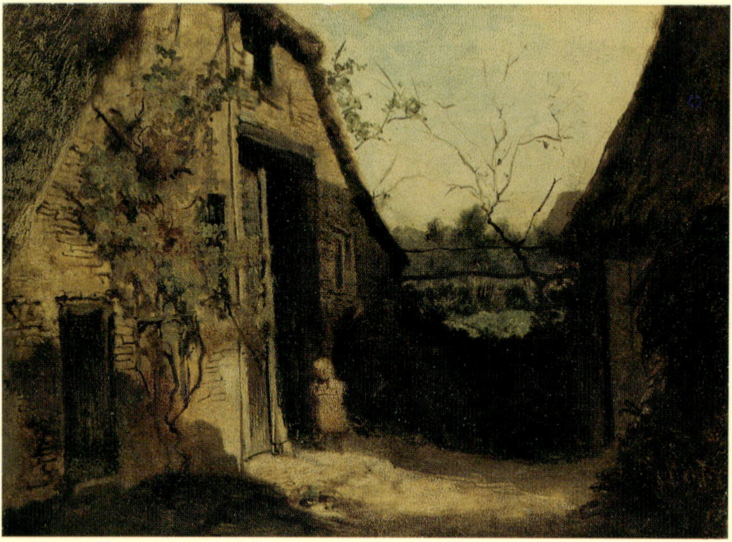

Matthijs Maris, *Landscape with peasants' sheds,* ca. 1860

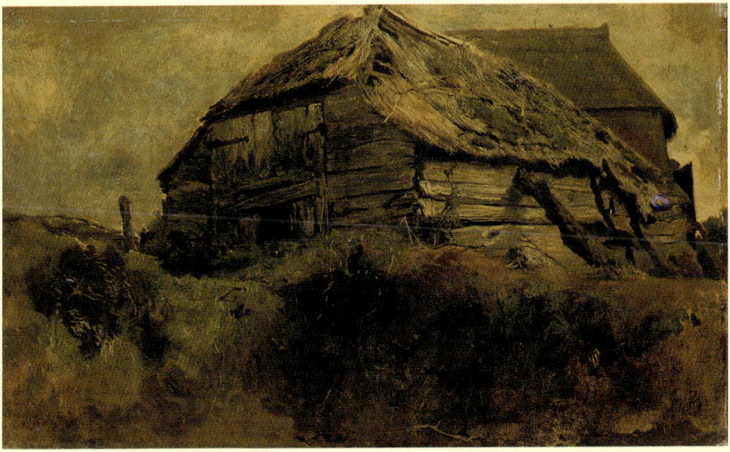

Matthijs Maris, *Sheep barn near Wolfheze,* ca. 1860

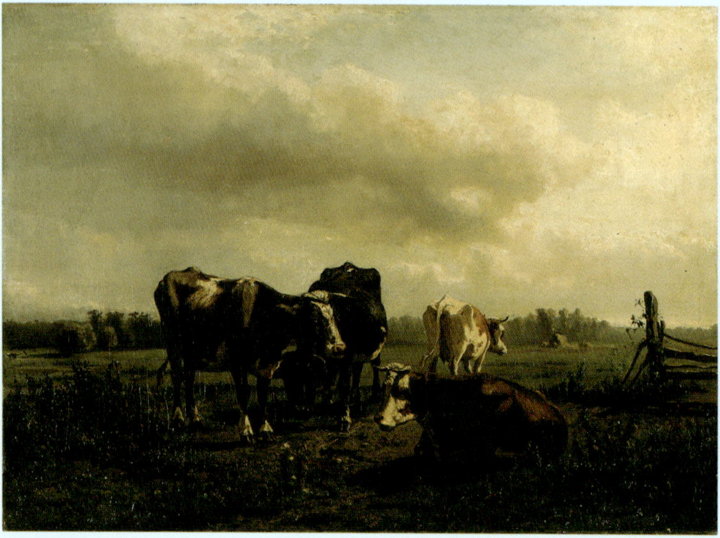

Gerard Bilders, *Cows in polder landscape,* ca. 1857-1860

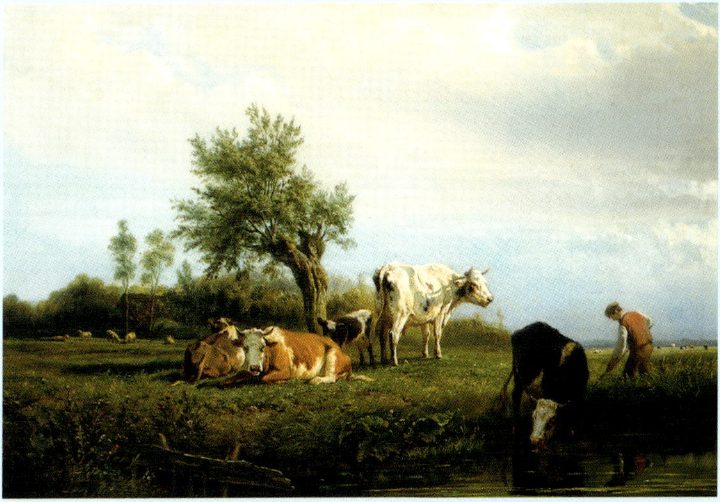

Anton Mauve, *Cows in Oosterbeek,* n.d.,
Caldic Collection, Rotterdam

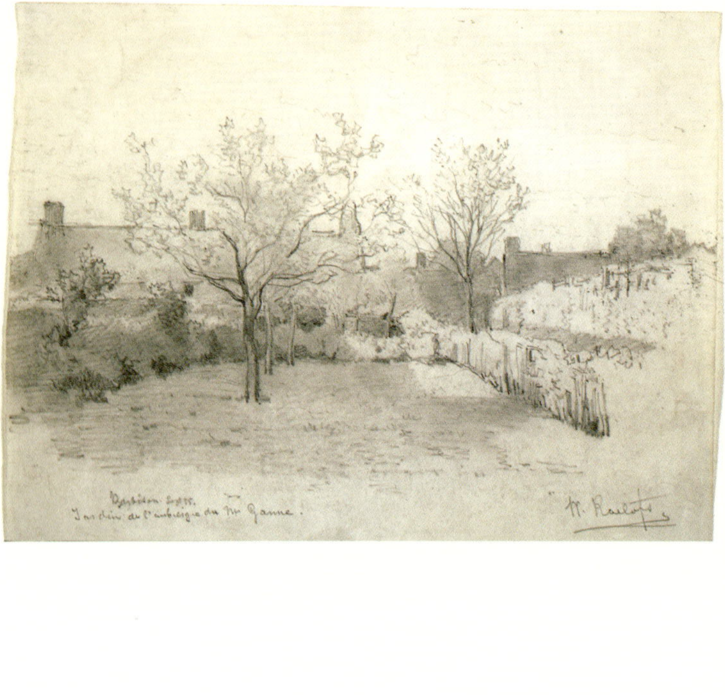

Willem Roelofs, *The garden of Ganne's auberge in Barbizon,* sketch, 1855

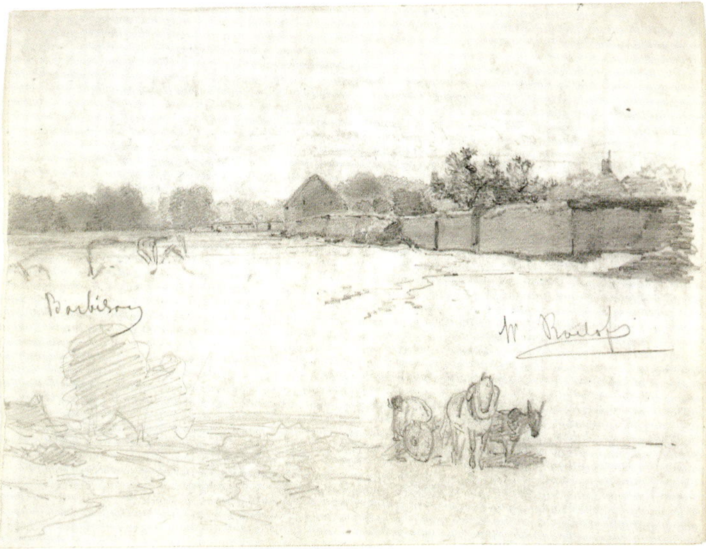

Willem Roelofs, *Country road with cart,* leaf from a sketchbook, n.d.

increased with each year. Willem Roelofs, Jacob Maris and Jozef Israëls even travelled to Barbizon in order to experience at first hand its inspirational powers. Jacob Maris painted in the Forrest of Fontainebleau on the outskirts of Barbizon, Jozef Israëls took traditional peasants' clothing with him when he left the district and Willem Roelofs sketched the garden of the auberge of father Ganne. Barbizon became synonymous with receiving direct inspiration from nature – painting spontaneously, and as much as possible, in the open air, and the quick registration of changing effects of light and shadow. This very method of painting was rapidly met with incomprehension and disapproval in conservative art criticism circles, where it was asserted that the method's exponents were impatient, hasty and sloppy, and where the new vision immanent in their works often went unnoticed.

Jacob Maris, *Painter at work,* 1860

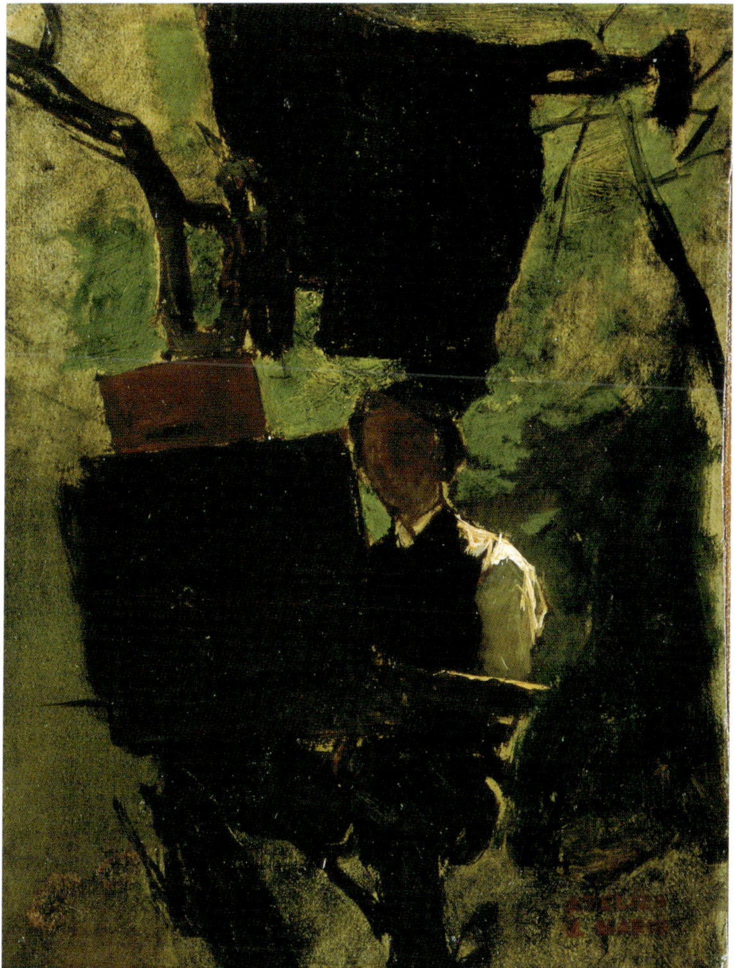

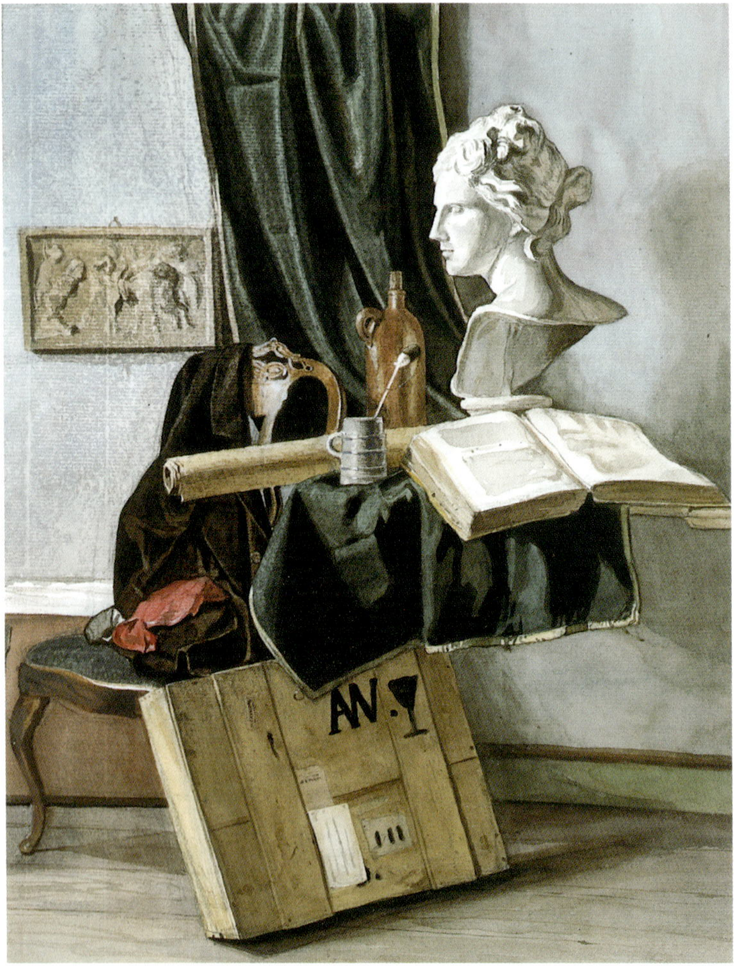

J.H. Weissenbruch, *Still life in the studio,* n.d. (watercolour)

THE RULES OF ART

John Sillevis

Gerard Bilders' letters to his meddling patron Johannes Kneppelhout, give us a clear picture of the artistic development of a prospective painter. He enrolled in the Haagse Teekenacademie (Hague Academy of Art) to draw and paint plaster casts of Greek and Roman sculptures, such as the 'Achilles Gladiator' and 'Apollo Belvedere.' In the Mauritshuis he copied portions of Potter's 'Bull,' first the sheep and lamb, and then the bull's head. His teacher, Simon van den Berg, recommended him for admission to Pulchri Studio as a working member, as this would give him the opportunity to draw from clothed models. Although he once obtained a sheep's head from the butcher's to use it as a model, as he himself said: working from models bored him to death. In the Trippenhuis, the precursor of the Rijksmuseum in Amsterdam, he admired Ruysdael and Cuyp, but most of all, Rembrandt. 'I not only find Rembrandt's works beautiful,' he wrote, 'but if this were still the time of gods and goddesses, I would worship him.' In the 'Night watch,' he saw 'a world aglow, filled with light and unparalleled power.' This he compared to his own paintings: '[...] poor cows, dairy farms and sheep compositions. And I doubt if I will ever amount to anything.'[19]

Bilders was present at a talk given by the well-known art collector, C.J. Fodor, at Arti et Amicitiae, a society affiliated with the artists' community in Amsterdam. Upon viewing Fodor's

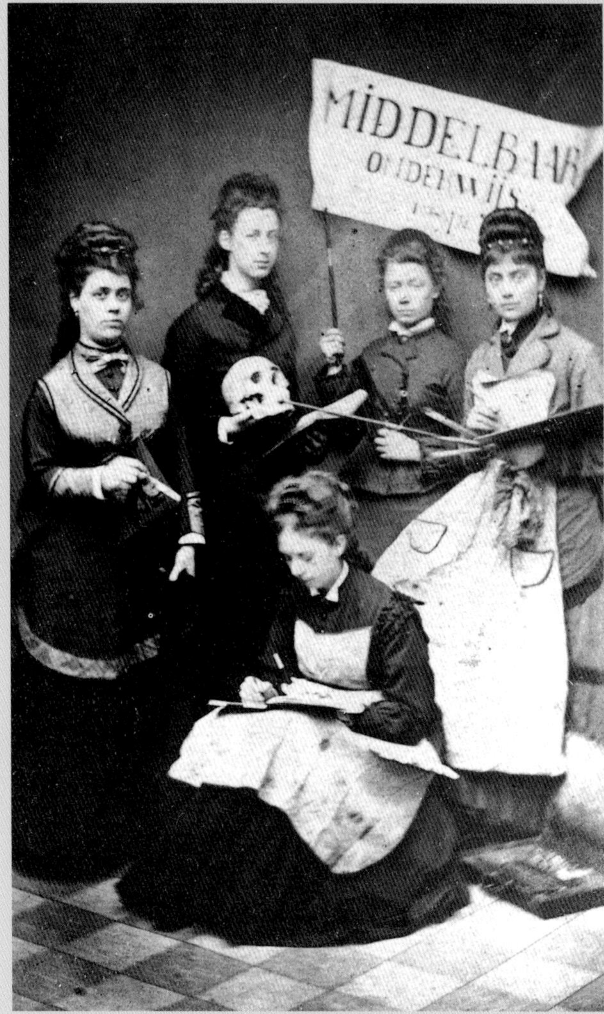
MIDDELBAAR
ONDERWIJS

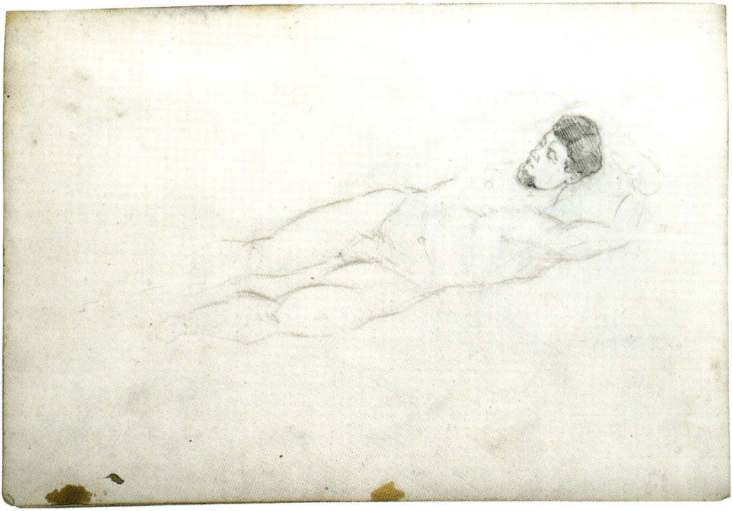

Suze Robertson, *Male nude,* n.d.

The first female students at the Hague Academy of Art, with Suze Robertson as flag-bearer

p. 56:
Matthijs Maris, *Head of an Arab,* study, ca. 1855-1858

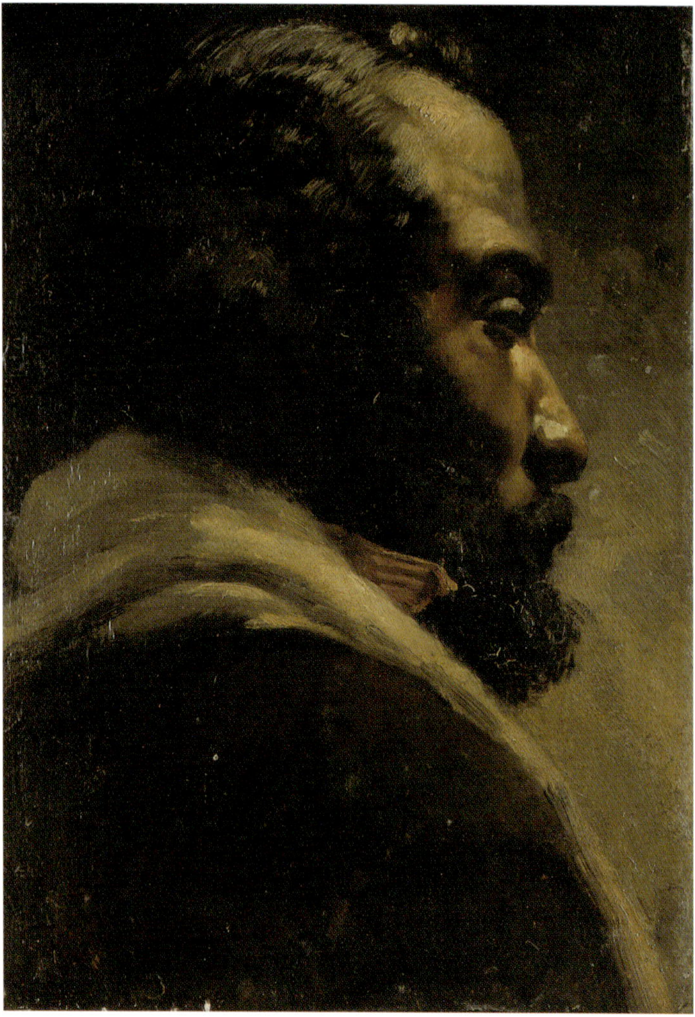

collection of French drawings, presented by him at the same occasion, Bilders found them in no way superior to the work of Rochussen, Bosboom or Schelfhout. A sign that Bilders was already regarded as an accomplished artist was his admission, in March of 1860, as a member of the Royal Academy of Visual Art, this despite the great insecurity about his own work which would remain with him until his death. Kneppelhout was, however, not impressed with the coveted designation, finding it sufficient to remark that the membership had been conferred upon him only because he would then have to pay the membership contribution. According to him it was 'nothing more than an assault on your purse.'[20]

Although Kneppelhout found his protégé a far-from-exemplary student, the training Gerard Bilders received was exemplary for art instruction in the Netherlands at that time. Instruction at the Academy of Art consisted primarily of lessons in sketching from plaster casts and bronzes after classical Greek and Roman models; this was followed by drawing from models, clothed in historical or folk costumes, or from nudes, the latter being exclusively male, as posing by female nudes was considered improper. It should be pointed out in this connection that until the end of the 19th century, women were not admitted to the class in drawing from nudes. One of the first female students admitted to the Hague Academy, Suze Robertson, protested against this rule because she (rightly) believed that without this class her training would not be complete, but her demand was interpreted as a provocation. The masters of the 17th century were regarded, just as the sculptors of classical times, as perfect models who would enable students to improve their skills.

The most important part of the training consisted in imitation. When drawing from a model, an extremely realistic reproduction of the model's individual features was far less important than

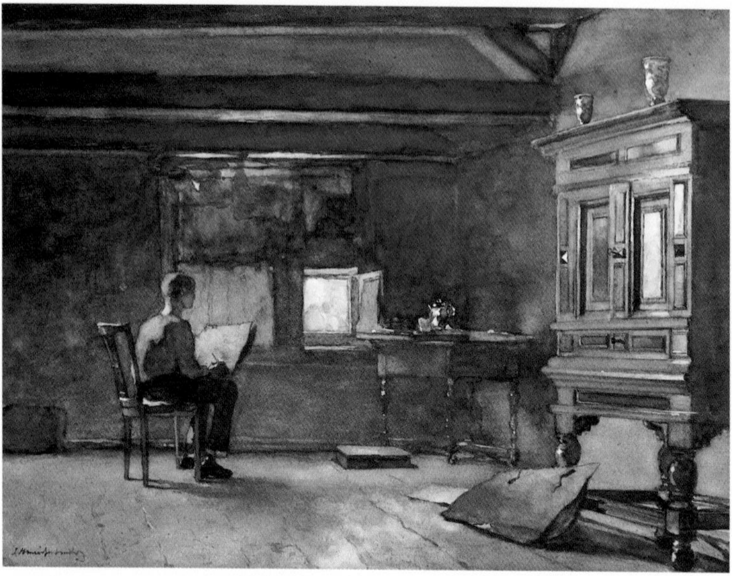

J.H. Weissenbruch, *The artist's studio,* n.d. (watercolour)

J.H. Weissenbruch, *In the studio,* n.d. (watercolour)

J.H. Weissenbruch, *View from the studio,* n.d. (watercolour)

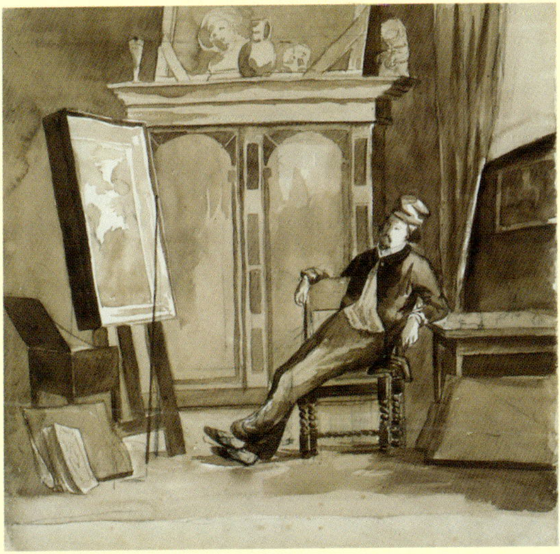

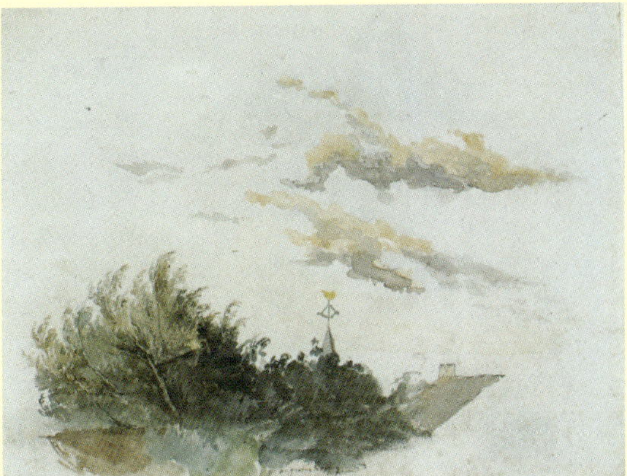

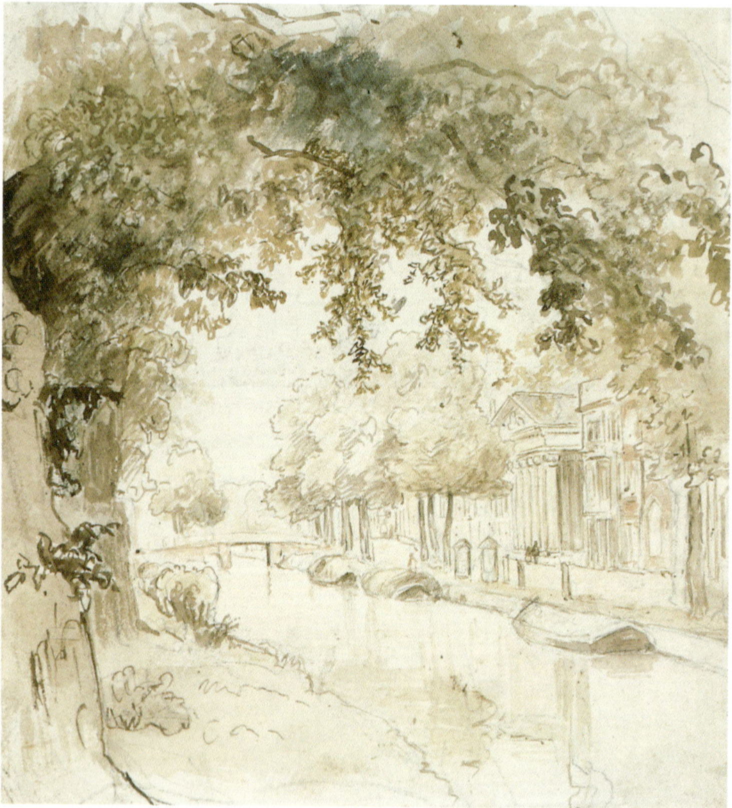

Charles Rochussen, *The Hague Academy on the Koninginnegracht,* n.d. (watercolour)

showing that one applied the masters' perfect proportions with technical mastery, even if the model in and of him/herself did not completely fulfil classical ideals of beauty. A graceful youth could serve as Adonis, a muscular labourer as Hercules, an old man with a paunch as Silenus; and in France a 'beau vieillard' or 'beau nègre' was always in demand. Whether black or old: beauty was always the first requirement.

At the end of each year, the drawings were judged and some were awarded with a prize. The highest honour one could receive at the conclusion of one's studies was the Prix de Rome, which meant a government grant for a period of study in Italy, intended to let the most talented student be inspired directly by the art of ancient Rome and the Italian Renaissance. The chosen student was, however, required continually to submit examples of his work, and if these were found to be below standard, the grant was ended.

While Dutch art – particularly that of the 17th century – was highly esteemed abroad, the level of art instruction in the first half of the 19th century left much to be desired. It is possible that the transformation of the academies' status from that of artists' societies to that of state-run institutions played a role. The period starting with French domination of Holland under King Louis Bonaparte turned art into a matter of state, after the French model. The Hague Academy of Art was given an imposing building in the style of a Greek temple, with columns and a pediment and a collection of plaster and bronze models for the students. Nevertheless, they were, by the time they received their diplomas, not yet well-equipped with the qualifications then expected of a trained artist, and some were advised to take additional training in Antwerp, where the level of training was much higher, or in Brussels, where the students did not even have to pay for their tuition. Antwerp was considered progressive; in Brussels the influence of neo-classicism was still strong. The highly-rated art academy of Düsseldorf

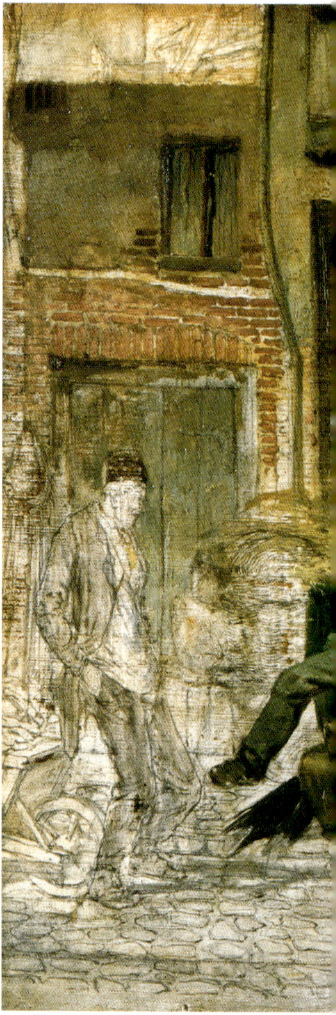

Matthijs Maris,
Market in Antwerp, n.d.

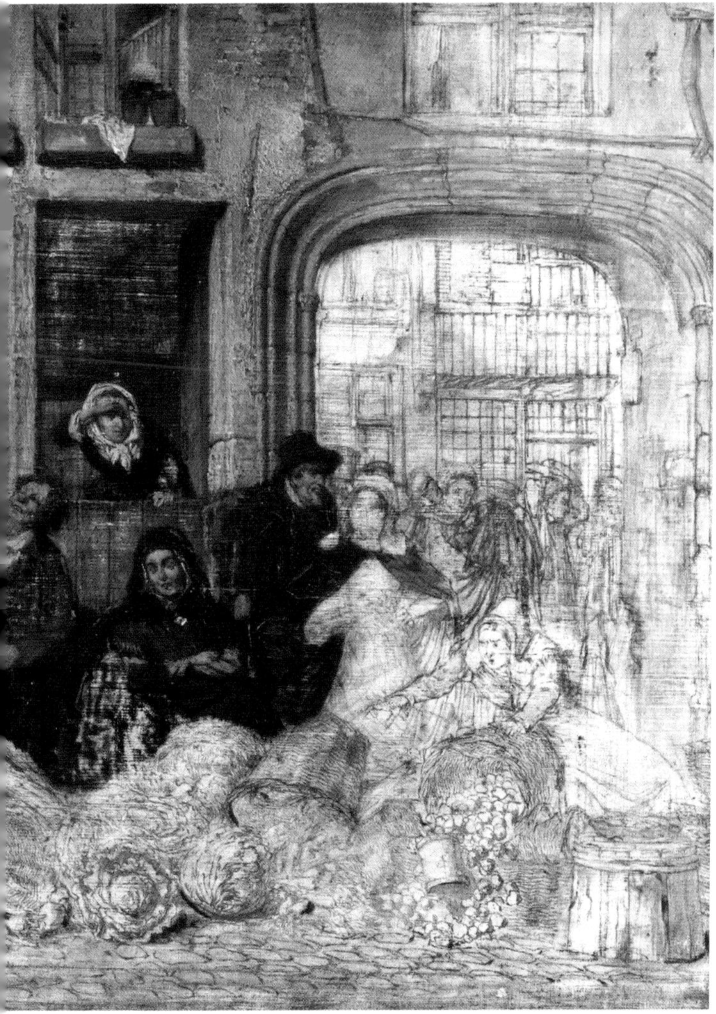

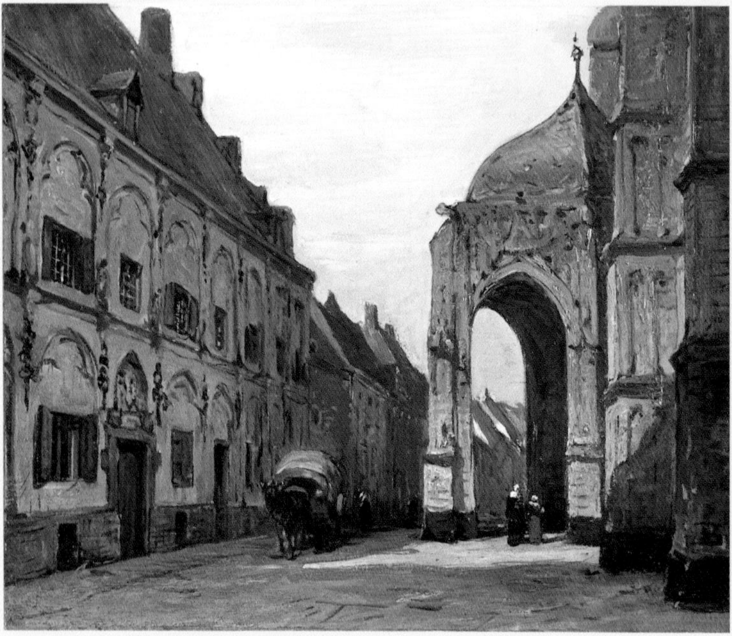

Johannes Bosboom, *View of the Church of St. Steven in Nijmegen,* ca. 1850

attracted a large number of foreign students, especially from Scandinavia. Here, the instruction programme was enriched by a so-called 'Meisterklasse,' in which the most promising students benefited from additional supervision by artists affiliated with the academy.

In the 19th century, Paris retained its central position in the art world, including in the area of training. In addition to the authoritative École des Beaux-Arts, there were numerous studios where, during certain periods, artists would take students, who could thus perfect their skills under the supervision of the master – a kind of 'Meisterklasse' in privatised form.

Jozef Israëls studied for a time under the French painter, François-Édouard Picot, who had a studio with some seventy *élèves* under his supervision, and took evening classes under Horace Vernet and Paul Delaroche at the École des Beaux-Arts. Jacob and Matthijs Maris completed their studies at the Academy of Art in Antwerp, studying under, among others, Nicaise de Keyser, who had collaborated with the Hague romantic, Wijnand Nuyen. Albert Neuhuys, too, stayed in Antwerp for four years, possibly on the advice of his older brother, Jan Antoon, who had also been trained there. Roelofs lived in Brussels and taught H.W. Mesdag there; Gabriël also lived for many years in the Belgian capital, where he taught W.B. Tholen. Vincent van Gogh followed the pattern set by the Hague School: after a period of instruction under Anton Mauve, he continued his training in Antwerp, and subsequently in Brussels, albeit without concluding his studies there.

It is not documented that the painters of the Hague School, with the exception of Philip Sadée, ever enrolled at the Düsseldorf Academy. We do, however, know for certain that Bosboom and Jozef Israëls travelled to Düsseldorf in order to keep abreast of the newest artistic developments. For their part, painters of the so-called Düsseldorf School participated in the Living Masters

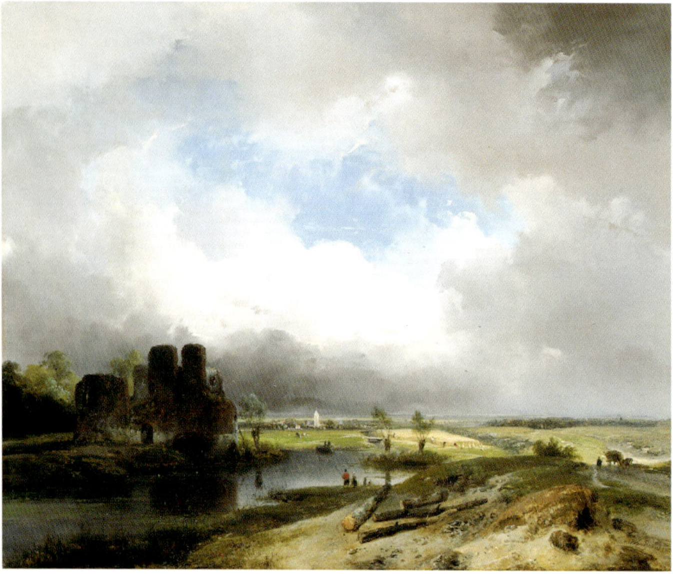

Andreas Schelfhout, *Landscape with ruins,* 1834

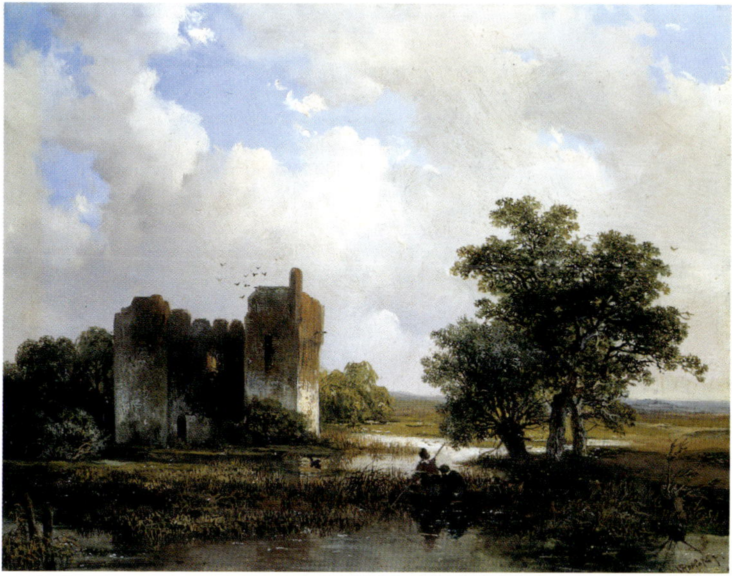

Willem Roelofs, *Landscape with ruins,* ca. 1845

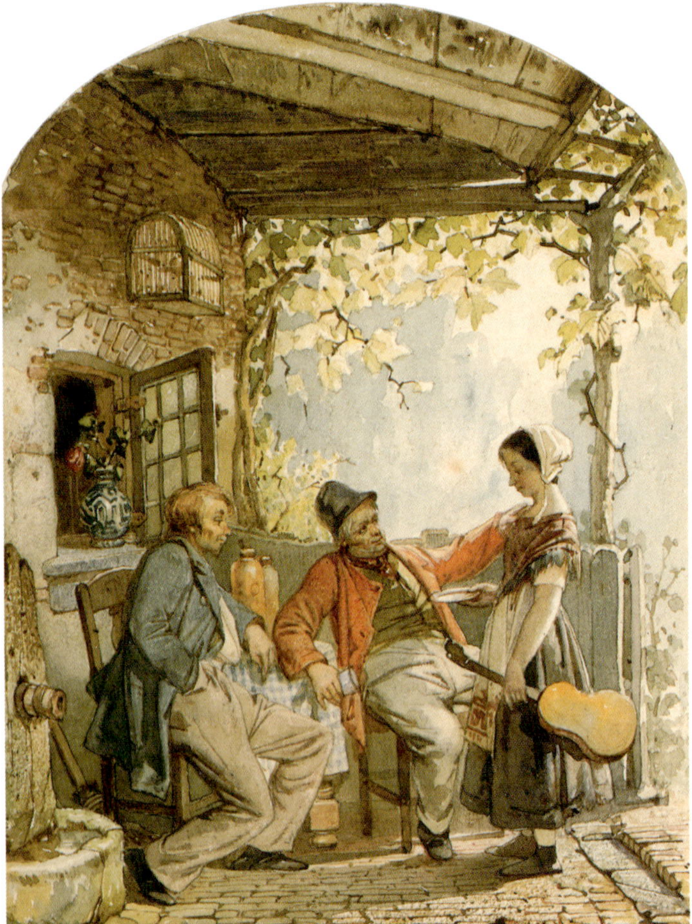

Jacob Maris, *Tavern scene* (summer cottage with men and female street musician), 1859

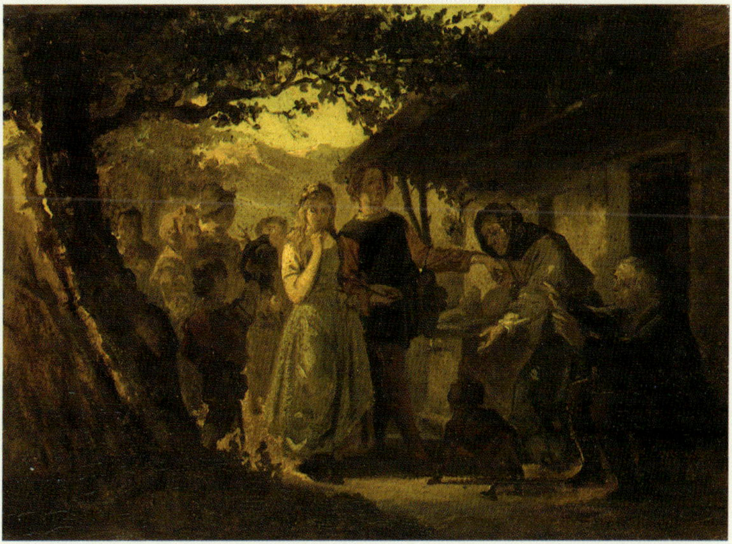

Jacob Maris, *The wedding procession,* ca. 1862

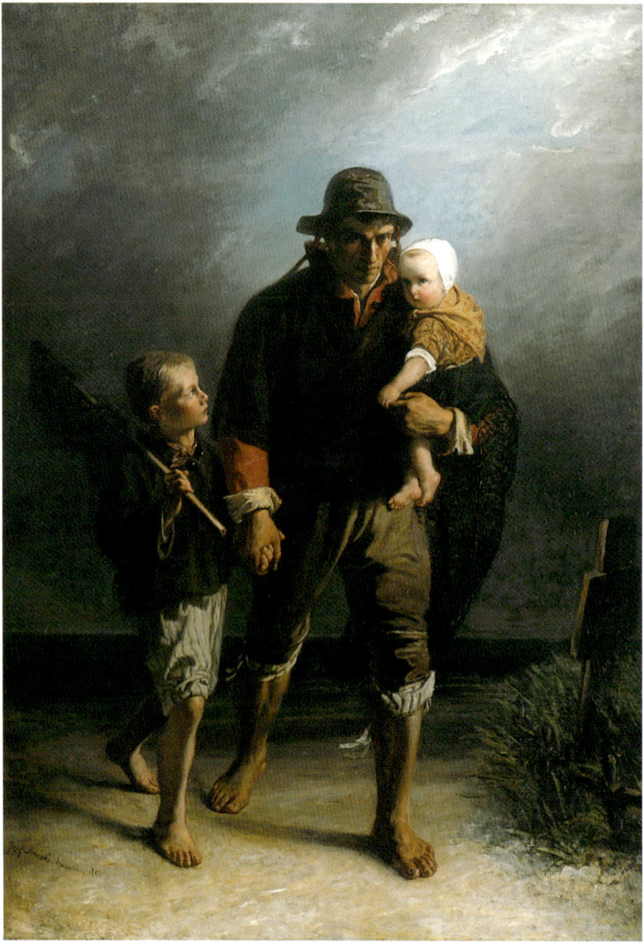

Jozef Israëls, *By mother's grave*, 1856,
collection of the Stedelijk Museum, Amsterdam

exhibitions in the Netherlands. Rudolf Jordan, who, already in the 1830s, had devoted himself to the fishermen's genre, played an important role in this regard. He had started painting scenes drawn from the lives of the fishermen on the German island of Helgoland, but subsequently found inspiration in Scheveningen and on the Dutch island of Marken as well. The fishermen's genre rapidly became a Düsseldorf speciality: such artists as Adolph Tidemand, Ferdinand Fagerlin and Eduard Hildebrandt were emulated by Blommers, Sadée and the young Jozef Israëls. Such paintings as 'By mother's grave' by Jozef Israëls and 'Welcome home' by Sadée, were directly inspired by the Düsseldorf school.[21]

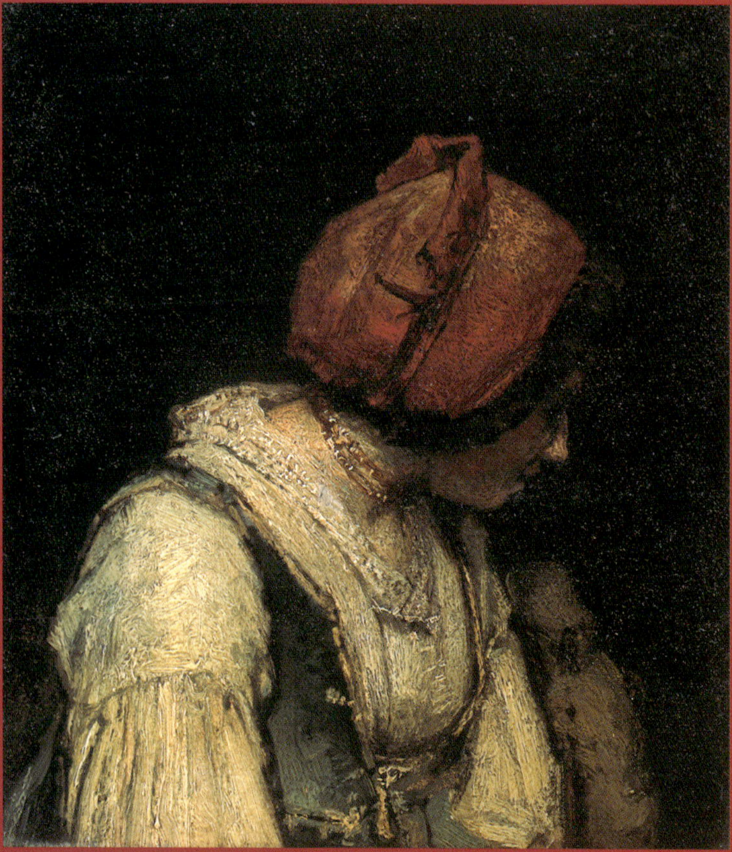

Matthijs Maris, *Spinner,* ca. 1870-1874

THE ROLE OF THE ART TRADE

John Sillevis

Around 1850, there were relatively few art dealers to speak of in The Hague. The most interesting art shop was Maison Vincent van Gogh, run by an uncle of the painter, with the family nickname 'Uncle Cent.' From 1842, the shop, which originally also sold artists' supplies, was located on Spuistraat. Uncle Cent had good contacts with the Paris art dealers, in particular with the dealer, Goupil, who supplied him with works by French artists.[22] Uncle Cent also dealt in works by Dutch – and particularly Hague – artists, who, if they sold well, could count on financial support from Van Gogh. In 1861, Uncle Cent entered into a partnership with Goupil and soon moved his shop to No. 14 on *de Plaats*, a more fashionable address. Here, not only modern paintings were offered for sale, but engravings and photos of internationally known works of art, as well – the latter being a novelty at that time. Uncle Cent envisaged possibilities for the sale of works by young Dutch artists in Paris, and with his support, Jacob and Matthijs Maris set off for the French capital, to paint there. One condition was that they had to limit themselves to genres which sold well, such as that of portraying young girls in traditional Italian folk costumes. Kaemmerer, too, was a protégé of Van Gogh's; he developed into a painter of genre tableaux in a slick Empire style with a somewhat frivolous tendency. After a time, Jacob Maris began to regard it as a burden always having to dance to the tune of the art market and art collectors. Matthijs Maris, as well, was left with a life-long aversion to painting 'potboilers,' as he called them. When Jacob Maris made it clear to his Paris dealer that he preferred to paint landscapes, a conflict resulted. This in turn became one of the reasons for his definitive return to The Hague. His desire to paint landscapes turned out not to be a problem for his business relations in The Hague: at the start of the 1870s, the landscapes of Jacob Maris found their way back into the sales books of Goupil's Hague branch, beside Matthijs Maris, Bosboom, Artz and Mesdag. Depictions of the life of the fishing community by Jozef Israëls, Sadée and Blommers also turned out to be very popular. Anton Mauve, too, was closely connected to the art house of Goupil, not only as an artist, but also because he had married a niece of Vincent van Gogh's. Uncle Cent moved to Paris, continuing his activities as an art dealer there. He left his Hague business in the hands of his acting manager, H.G. Tersteeg, who, later on in the 1870s would become the boss of the young Vincent van Gogh, who as a 16-year-old came to work for his uncle as a shop assistant. The resulting contact with members of the Hague School, as well as the opportunity he had here to familiarise himself with artistic developments in Paris, Brussels, London and Vienna through the shop's engravings and photographic reproductions, enabled him to familiarise himself with the art of his time – even before he himself began to paint. But this was not all: Uncle Cent also made it possible for Vincent to work in the Paris and London branches of the house of Goupil, with Vincent's brother, Theo, becoming manager of the branch on the Boulevard Montmartre.

Around 1865, The Hague had only five art dealers to its name; thirty years later, their number had grown to thirteen.[23] Until 1917, Goupil (later under the name Boussod, Valadon & Cie.) was The Hague's leading dealer, with such firms as Maison Artz and the house of Couvée also playing important roles. The leading

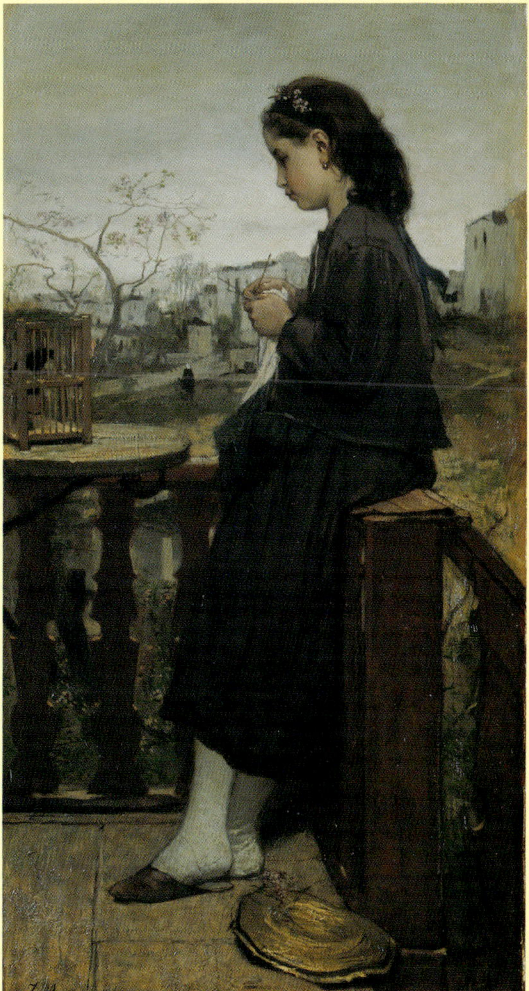

Jacob Maris, *Girl knitting on a balcony, Montmartre,* 1869

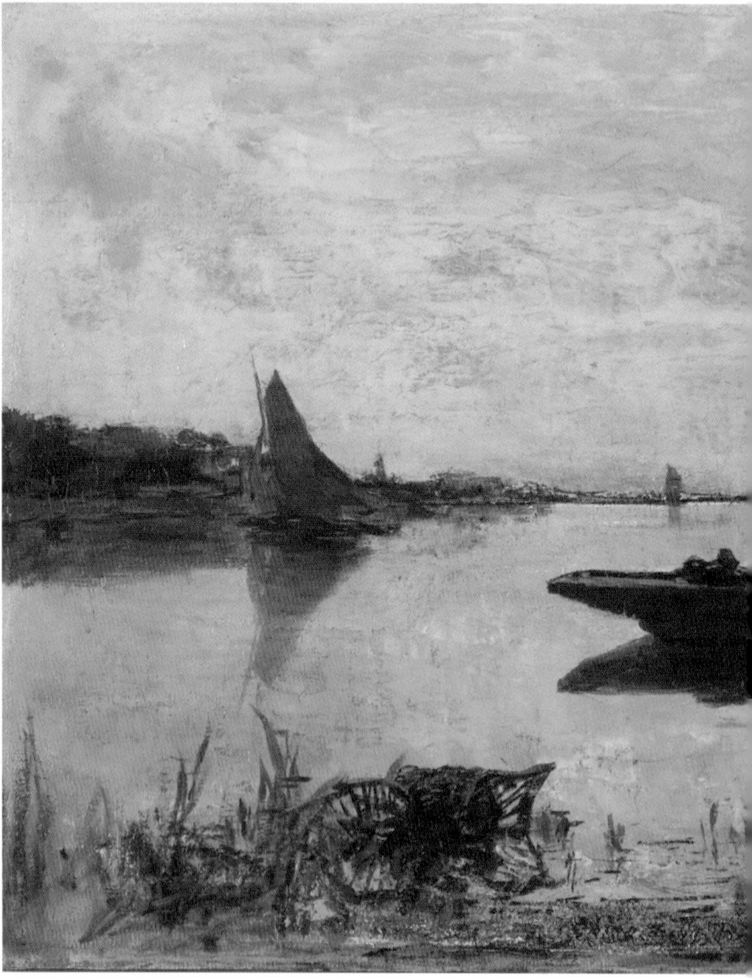

Jacob Maris, *Ferryboat,* 1870

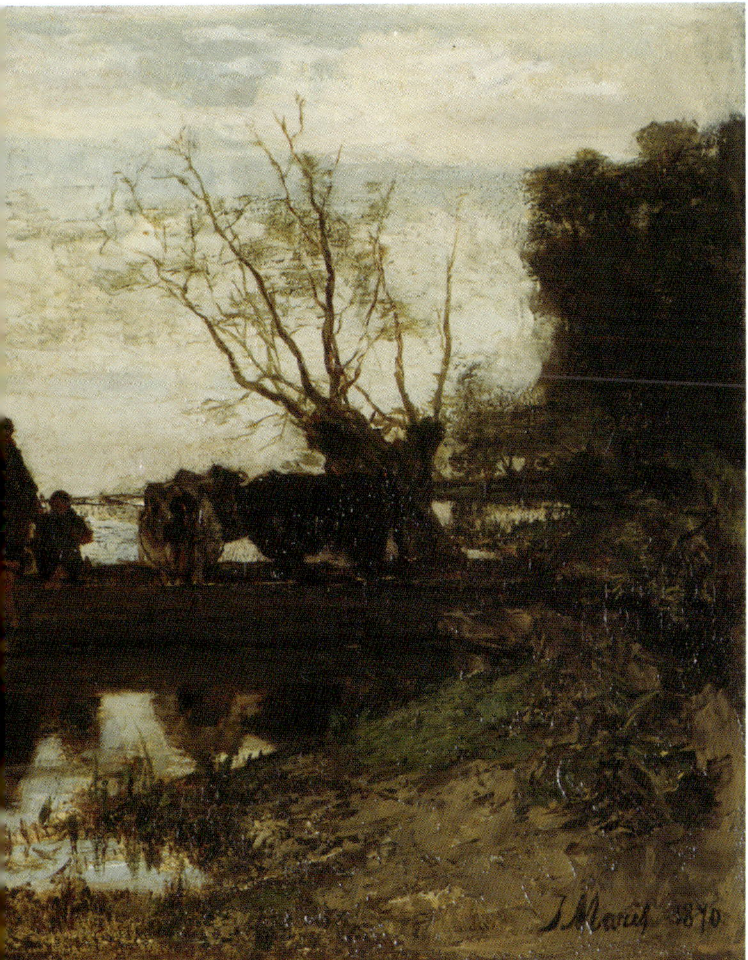

Amsterdam dealers were Van Wisselingh and Fr. Buffa en Zonen. Michael Knoedler, a Goupil employee, started his own business in New York City, where a lively market for Dutch landscapes and city views was developing. The London dealer Wallis discovered Jacob Maris' qualities as a landscape painter at the Paris Salon, just when Maris had broken with Goupil. Wallis ensured good sales for Maris' work in his 'French Gallery.' Goupil however continued to play a role in the London market, under the name, 'Goupil Gallery in New Bond Street.' The manager of the branch was David Croal Thomson, who made it his business to familiarise the English art public with the Hague School, with an emphasis on Jacob and Matthijs Maris. Thomson also wrote a book entitled 'The Barbizon School of Painters' (1890), which paved the way for the fame of the Barbizon School in England and the United States.[24]

The Holland Fine Art Gallery of C.M. van Gogh and W.J. van Hoytema, and the Dutch Gallery, the London branch of the Amsterdam house of Van Wisselingh, specialised in the sale of Dutch art; in Scotland, Alex Reid and Daniel Cottier were influential in this market segment. It was indirectly because of the latter that Matthijs Maris would learn at first hand how important support from the art trade could be in an artist's life. Cottier brought Van Wisselingh to London. In 1877, Matthijs Maris also came to London, at Cottier's invitation, and wound up lodging with him for ten years. Until his death, he was supported and cared for by Van Wisselingh, this despite the fact that, in his last years, he hardly painted at all.[25] Aside from the above-mentioned dealers, the works of the Hague School were also sold In France by the gallery of Arnold and Tripp, at 8, rue St. Georges. The firm was run by Arnold Eversteyn, originally of The Hague, and his partner, Richard Howard Tripp. Portions of the correspondence between Jozef Israëls, H.W. Mesdag and Anton Mauve and this firm are preserved at the Fondation Custodia in Paris.[26] Arnold and Tripp

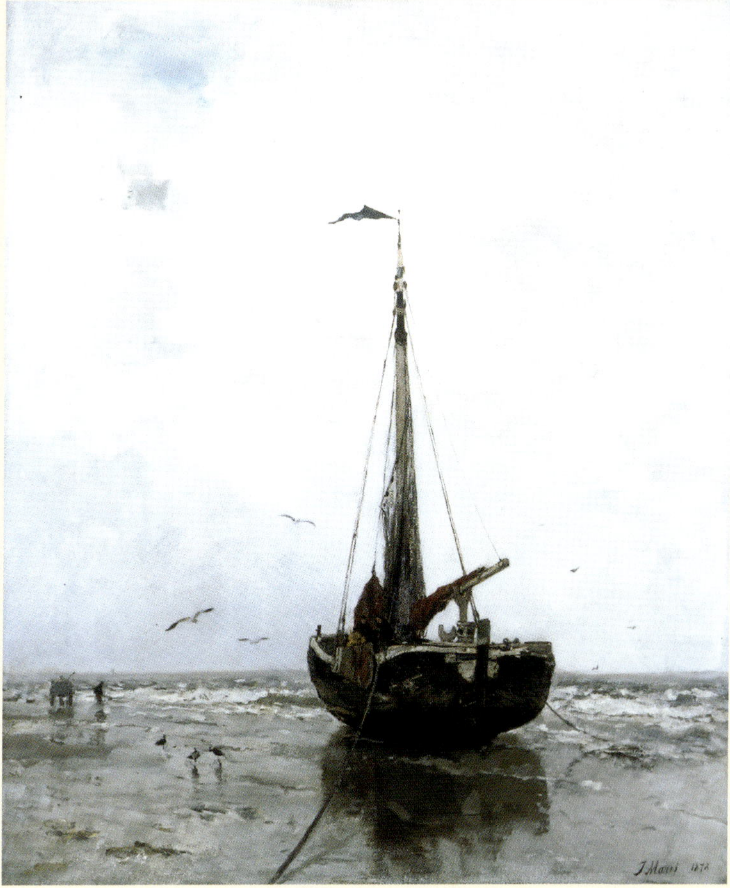

Jacob Maris, *Fishing boat,* 1878

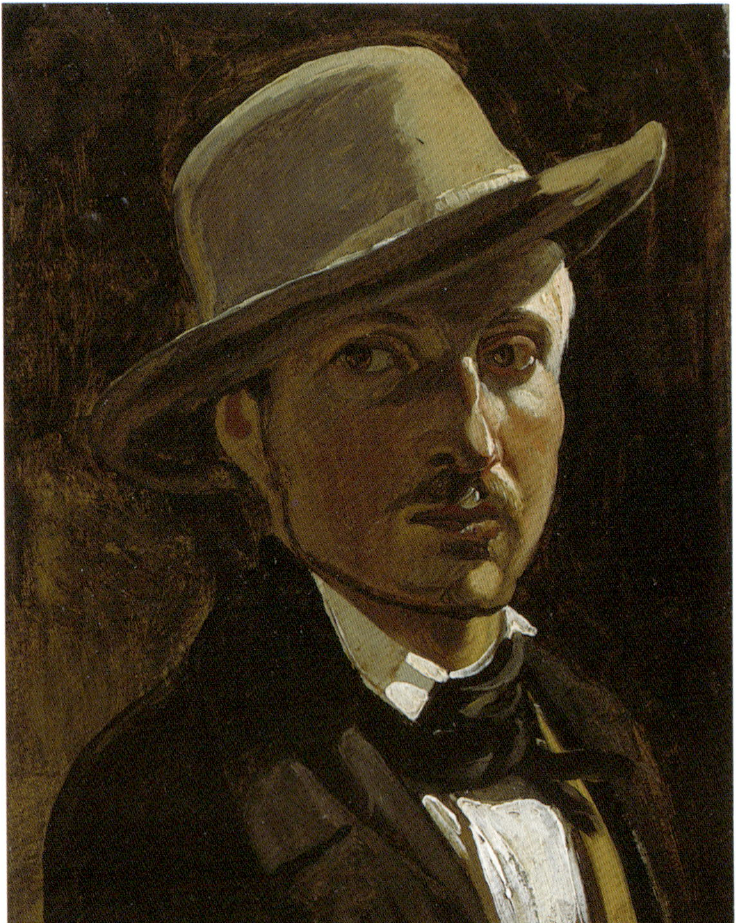

Matthijs Maris, *Portrait of a man (Self-portrait?)*, ca. 1857-1859

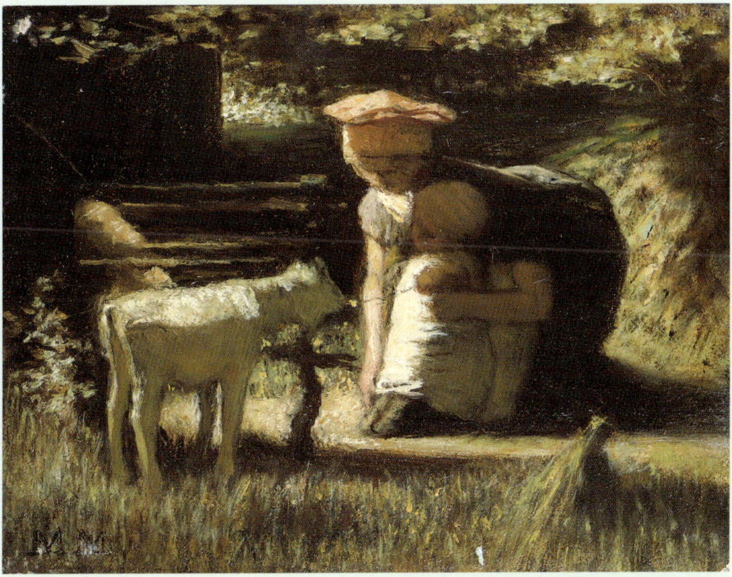

Matthijs Maris, *The introduction (The little goat)*, ca. 1865-1866

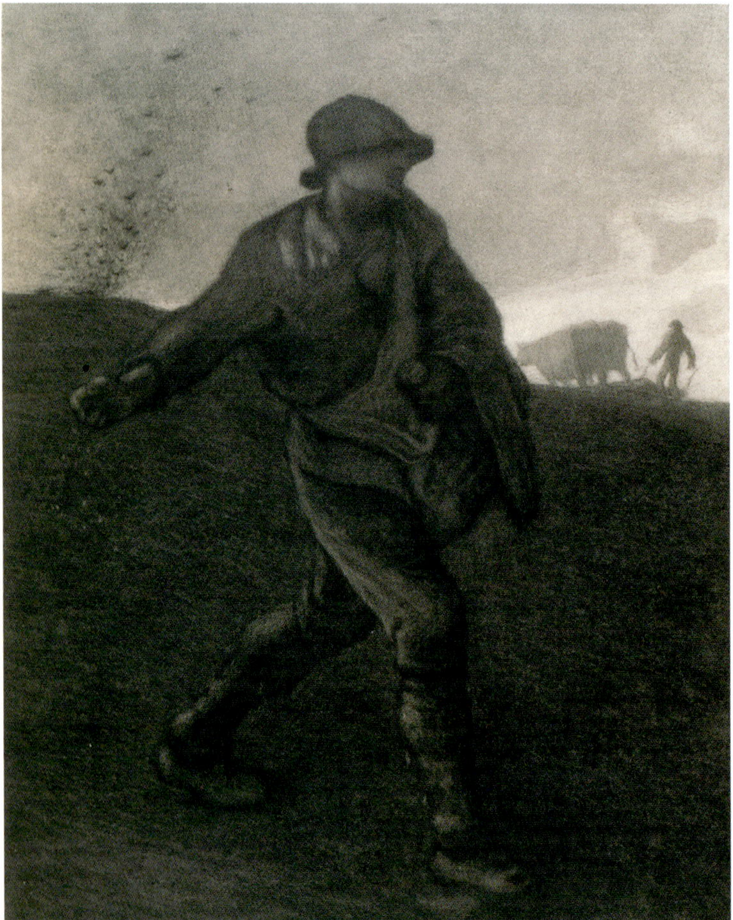

Matthijs Maris, *The sower* (after Millet), n.d.

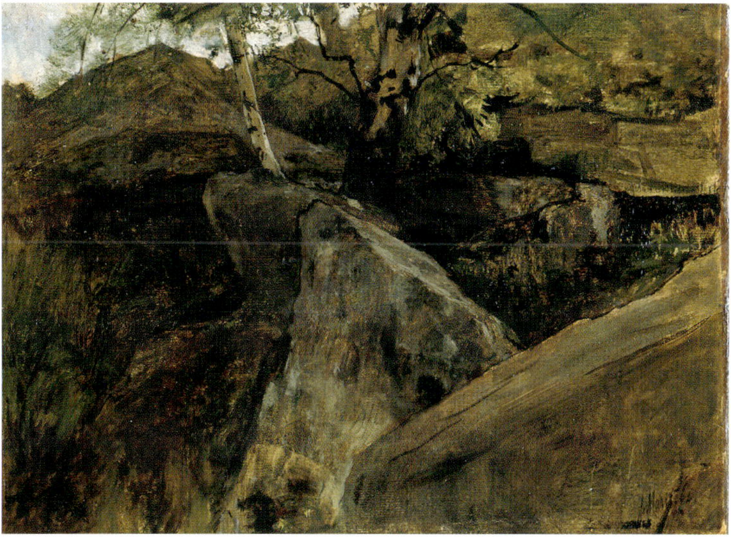

Jacob Maris, *Rocky landscape near Barbizon,* n.d.

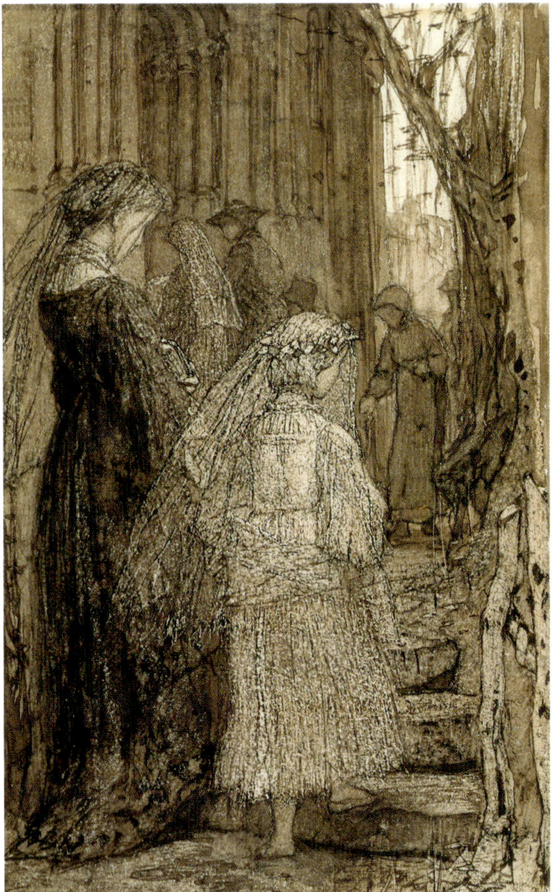

Matthijs Maris, *Christening procession,* ca. 1862-1864

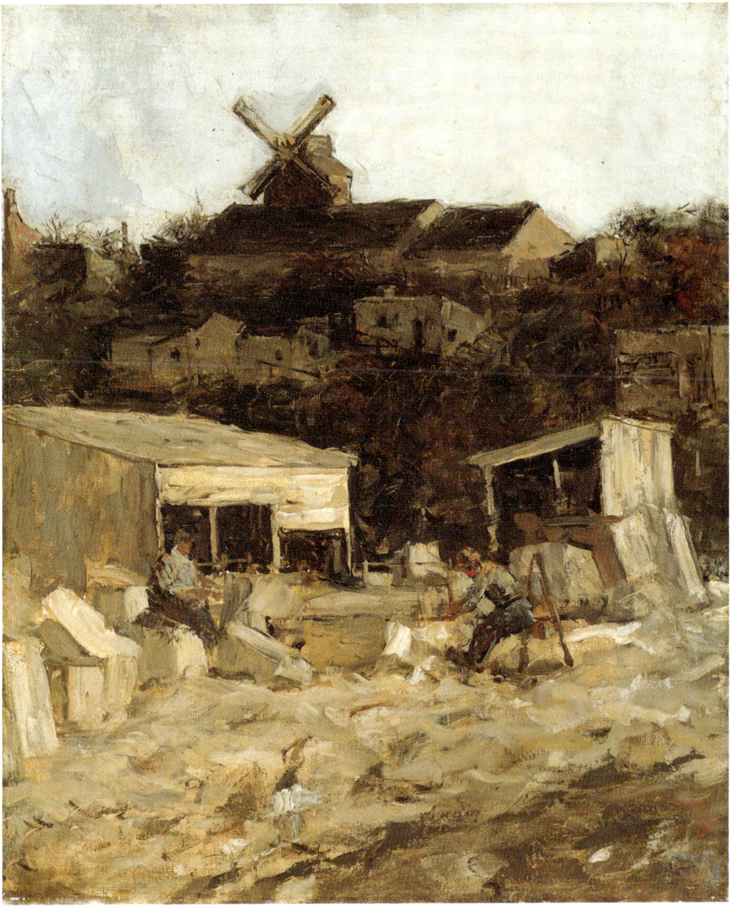

Matthijs Maris, *Stone quarry near Montmartre,* ca. 1870-1873

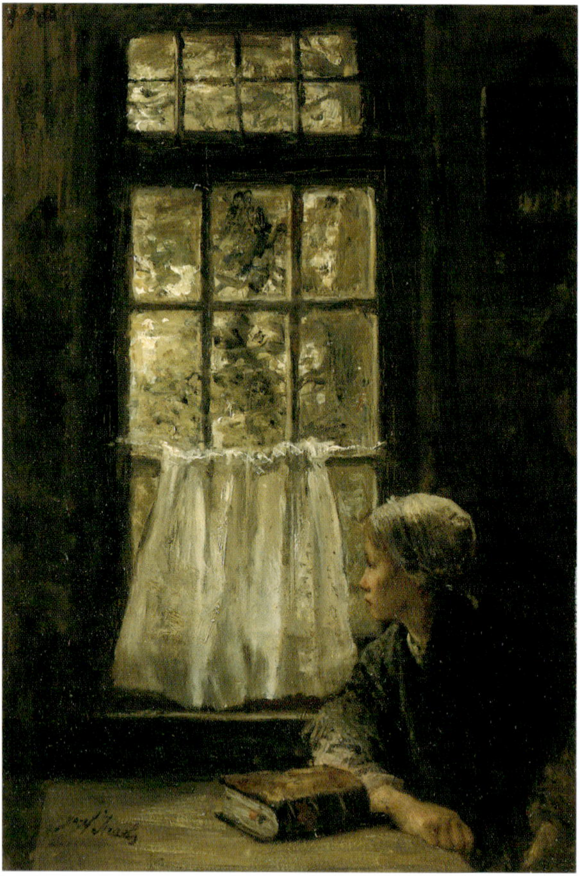

Jozef Israëls, *Sunday morning,* ca. 1880

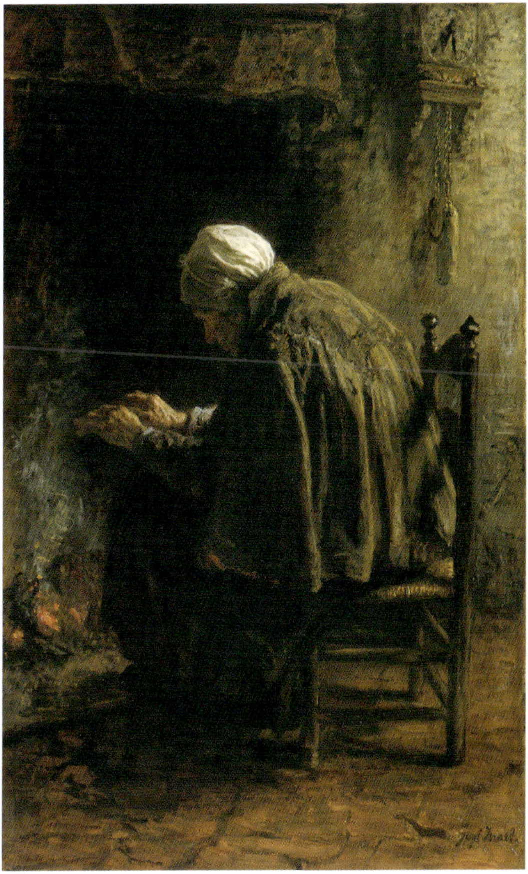

Jozef Israëls, *Growing old,* ca. 1878-1883

p. 88:
detail of p. 87

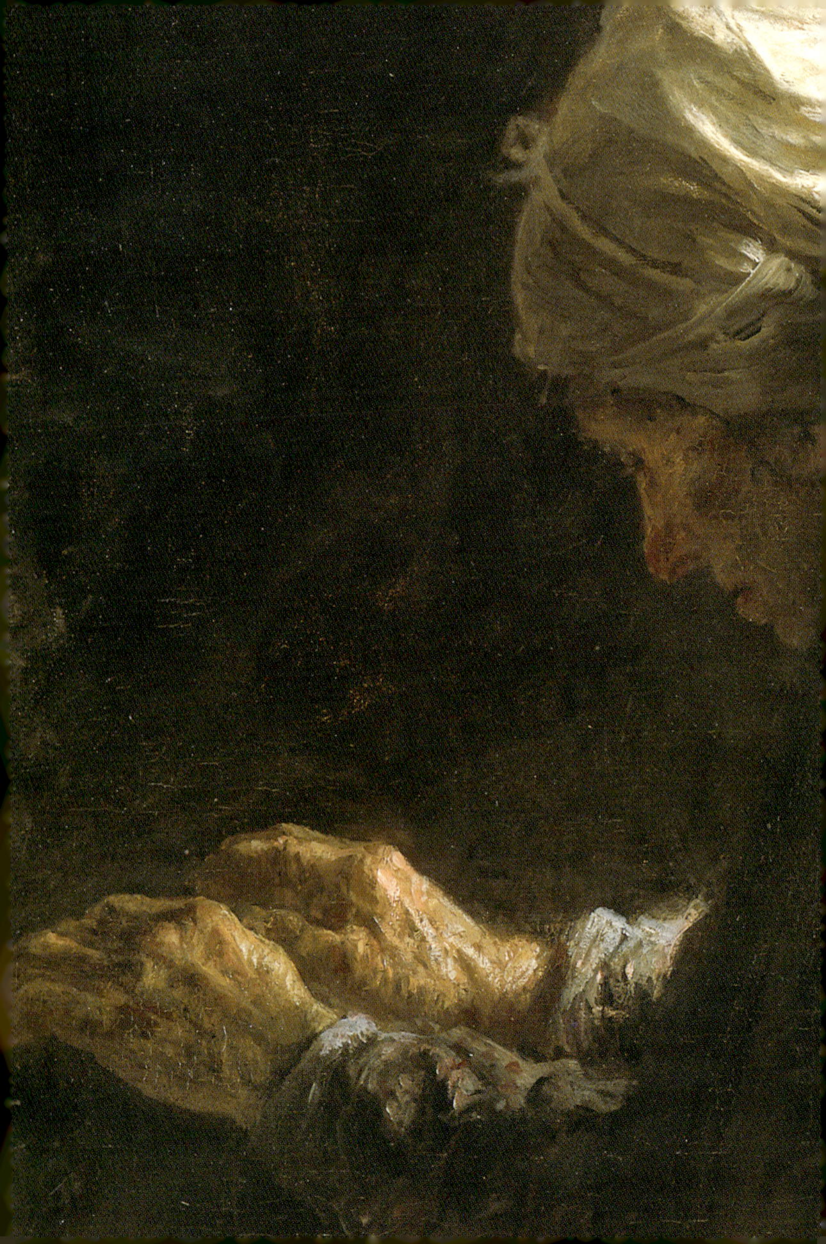

not only dealt in paintings and watercolours by Israëls, but also had etchings prepared by Israëls in Holland printed in Paris by the firm of A. Salmon. Although Arnold and Tripp's correspondence with Israëls has not been preserved, it appears that they did not hesitate at times to make comments critical of the works he sent them. Sometimes they found his oil paintings too coarse, or his watercolours 'unfinished.' Israëls would in turn protest politely, or offered to withdraw his work and sell it elsewhere. Jozef Israëls was a great exponent of the notion that a watercolour could be just as complete a work of art as a painting in oils, even though it was not painted on canvas, but on paper; he declared in a letter: 'You will see that these are no sketch-watercolours, but true 'pictures in watercolour,'' adding: 'I am setting the price at 5,000 francs for all three.'[27] In fact, Arnold and Tripp wound up paying only *f* 3,600 for the watercolours. Jozef Israëls was now a very well-paid artist. His painting 'By fields and roads' (now in the collection of the Rijksmuseum)[28] was offered for sale in 1892 for the, at that time, extremely large sum of 12,000 guilders. The fact that Israëls prepared his own prints made him an exception among the members of the Hague School; most of the painters had their canvases reproduced in etched form by such graphic artists as Philippe Zilcken and Storm van 's-Gravenzande. It remained for the second generation of the Hague School, e.g., W.B. Tholen and Willem de Zwart, to discover the etching as a full-fledged medium. As technical possibilities increased, photo-reproduction gradually took the place of the print.

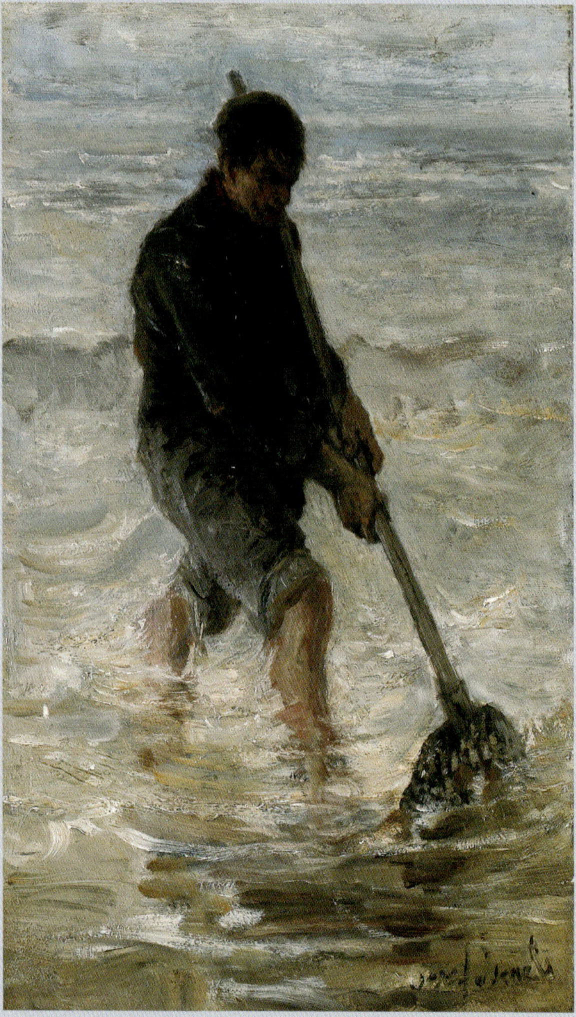

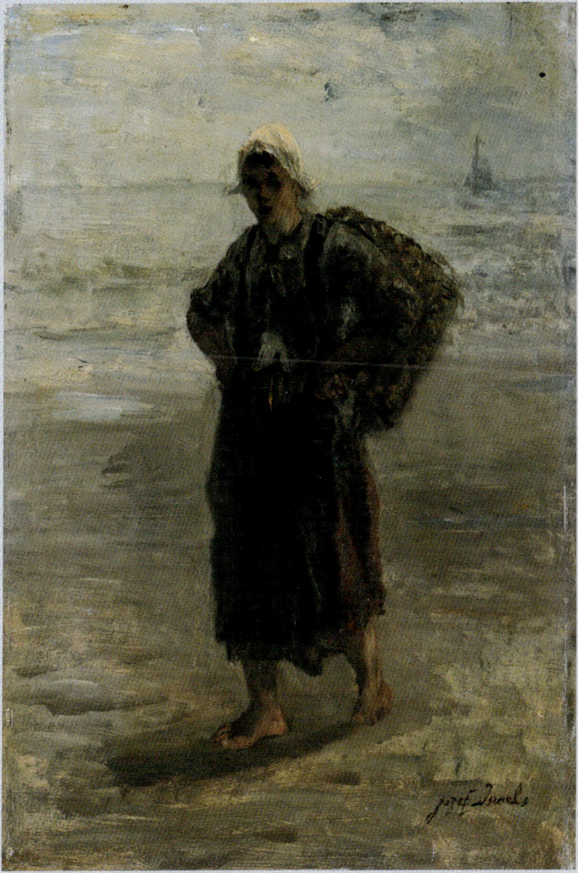

Jozef Israëls, *Prawn fisherman,* ca. 1900

Jozef Israëls, *Fisherman's wife,* ca. 1890

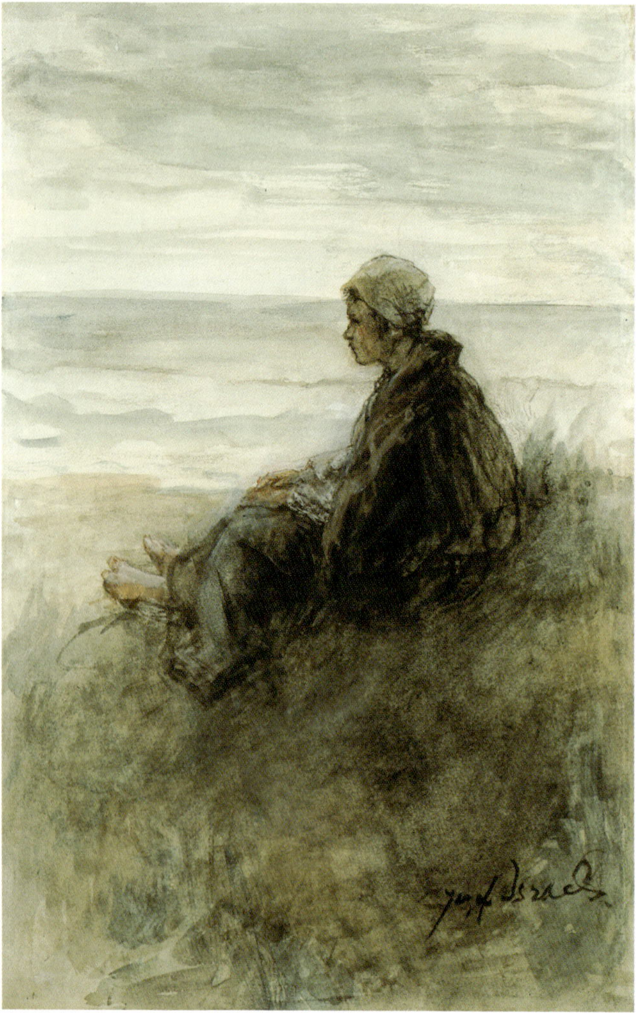

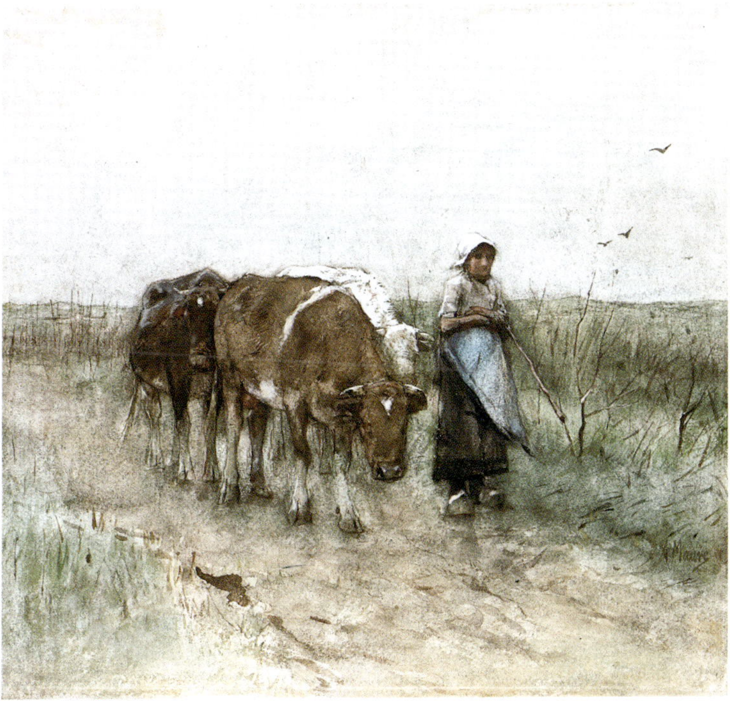

Jozef Israëls, *Girl on a dune,* n.d. (watercolour)

Anton Mauve, *Cowherd (Homeward),* n.d. (watercolour)

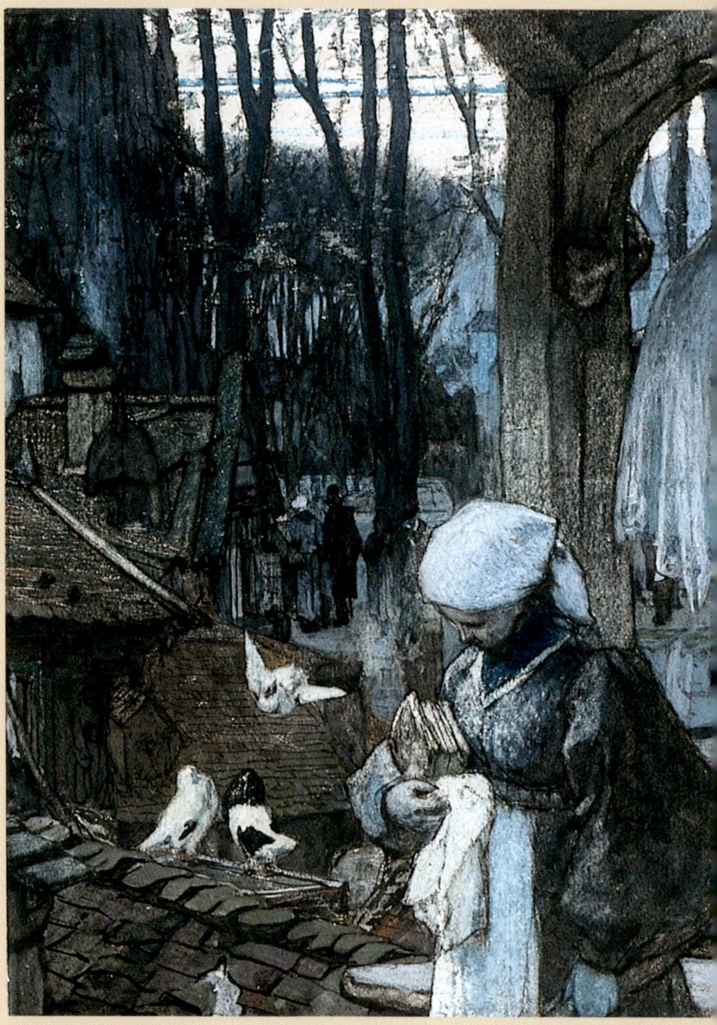

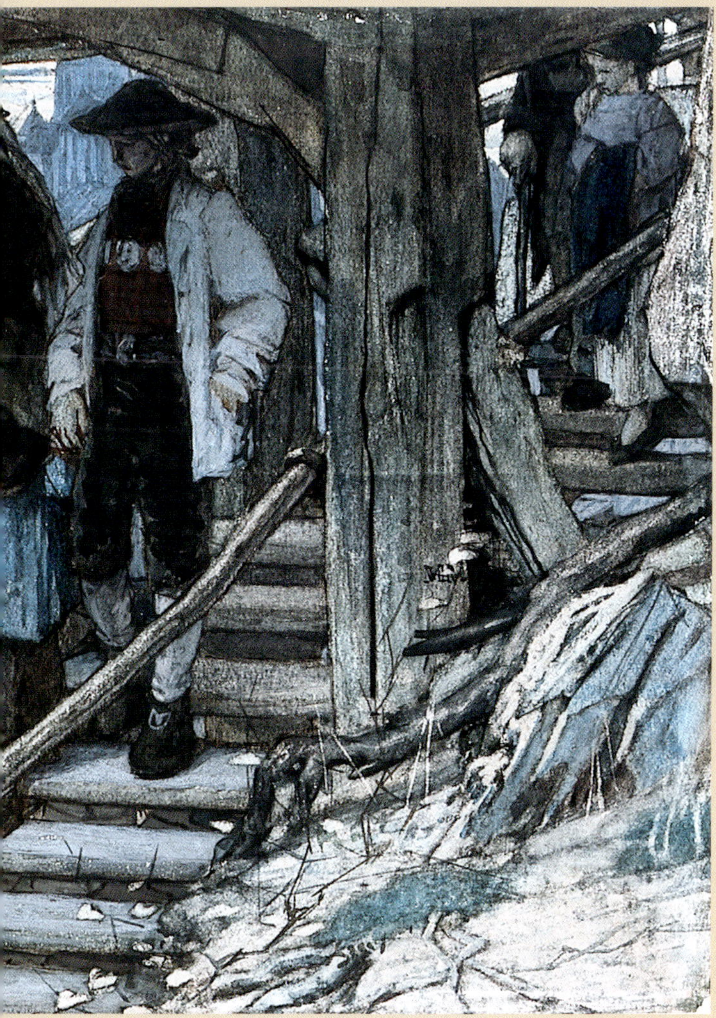

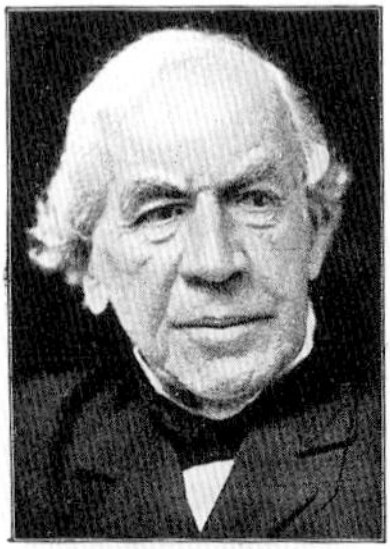

J. Staats Forbes.

UITNOODIGINGSKAART
voor de opening
aan
HOUDER MET DAMES
Zaterdag 17 Juni,
te 2 uur.

Een belangrijk gedeelte der beroemde verzameling van wijlen J. STAATS FORBES te LONDEN en andere MODERNE SCHILDERIJEN en AQUARELLEN bijeengebracht door A. PREIJER 2 Paleisstraat, 's GRAVENHAGE, wordt tentoongesteld in PULCHRI STUDIO, 's GRAVENHAGE tot 31 Juli 1905.

Invitation to the exhibition of the collection of Staats Forbes in the Preijer gallery, The Hague

pp. 94-95:
Matthijs Maris, *Christening procession in Lausanne,* n.d. (watercolour)

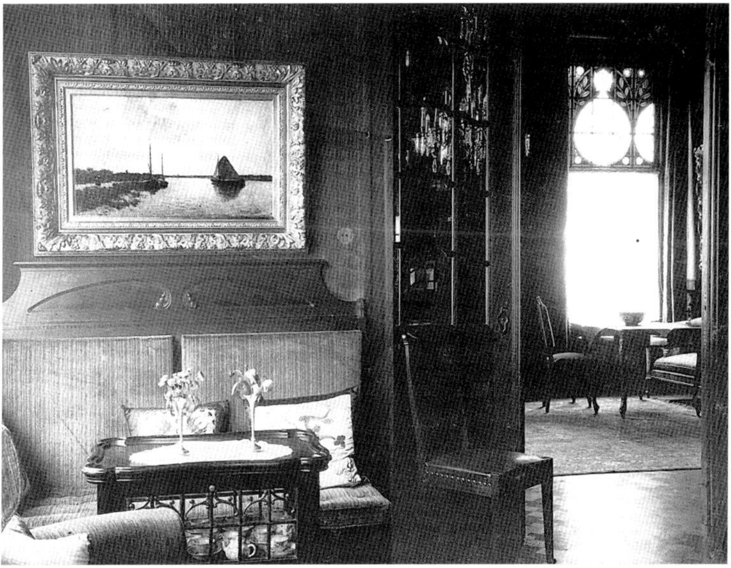

Interior of the home of Amsterdam collector E.H. Crone on the Keizersgracht, 1902

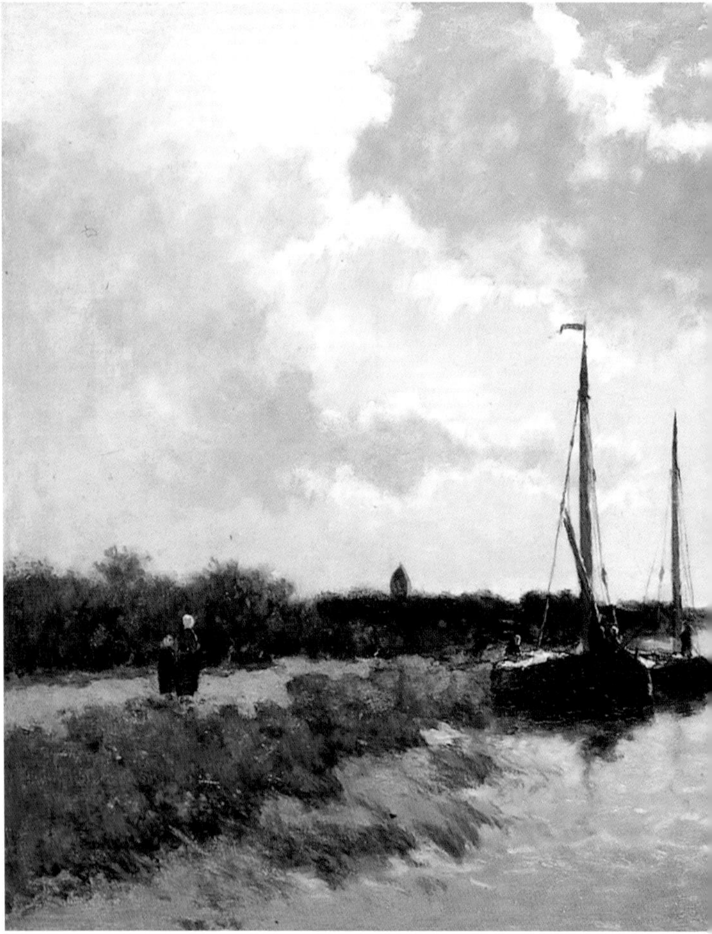

J.H. Weissenbruch, *Ship with tanned sail,* 1875

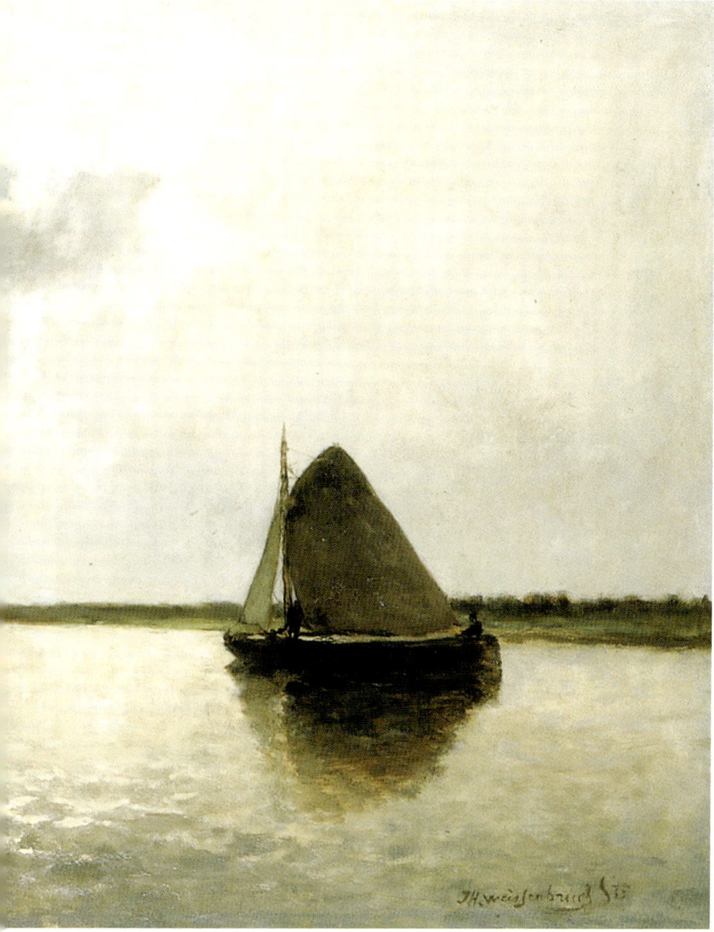

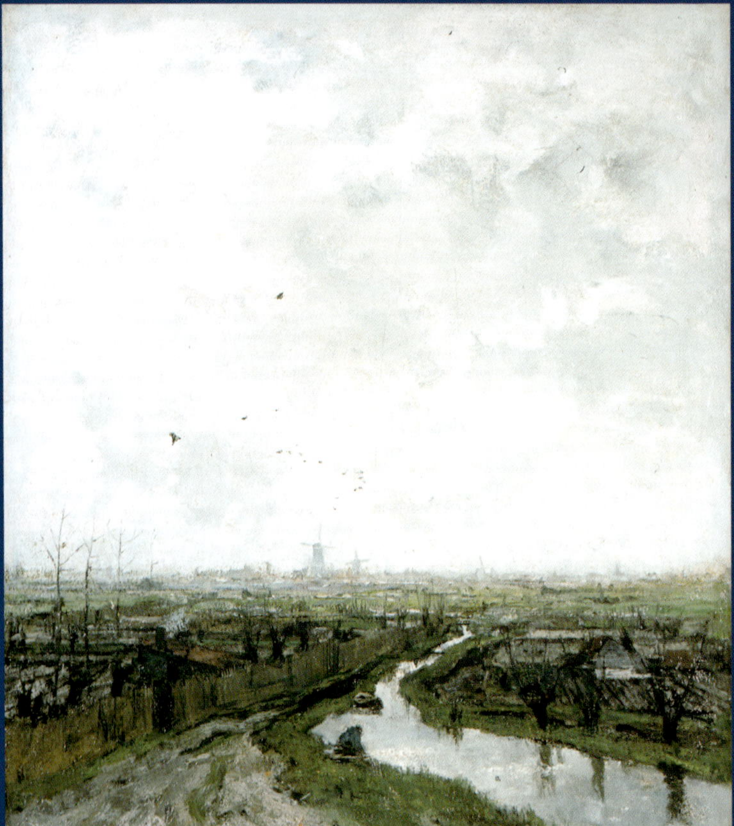

Jacob Maris, *Allotments near the Hague,* ca. 1878

THE SECOND GENERATION

John Sillevis

The last quarter of the 19th century was a period of rapid change, not only in the field of art, but in economic and social terms as well. The industrial revolution which, elsewhere in Europe, had taken place much earlier, had now also reached the Netherlands. Modernity penetrated the timeless tranquillity of the countryside and the static image of the old cities. New residential areas were being built for both labourers and trades people, the railway network was growing and numerous technological innovations found their way into everyday life.

For the first generation of Hague School painters, these changes came as a shock. Mesdag's beloved vantage point on the Seinpost Dune was partially levelled to make way for the café 'Seinpost,' the fishing boats no longer sailed by the beach, but could now lay anchor in the Scheveningen fishing port, and in the silhouette of The Hague, there appeared factory chimney stacks and buildings with cast iron roofs. The quiet spots in walking distance from the studio gradually disappeared; the painters sought alternative spots in the polders near Leidschendam and Voorschoten, or the lakes near Noorden. Brabant and Drente also became popular with the painters, as did the heaths around Laren. The younger generation did not choose to flee the new order, but rather, regarded it as a source of new inspiration: construction projects, industrial sites, stations, harbours, shops, display windows, urban traffic and the

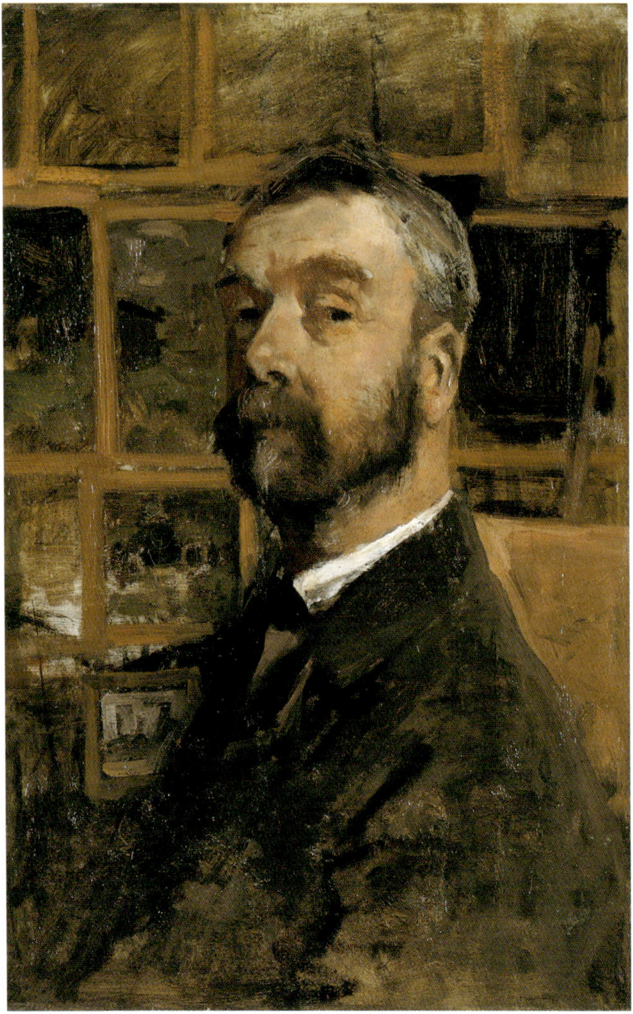

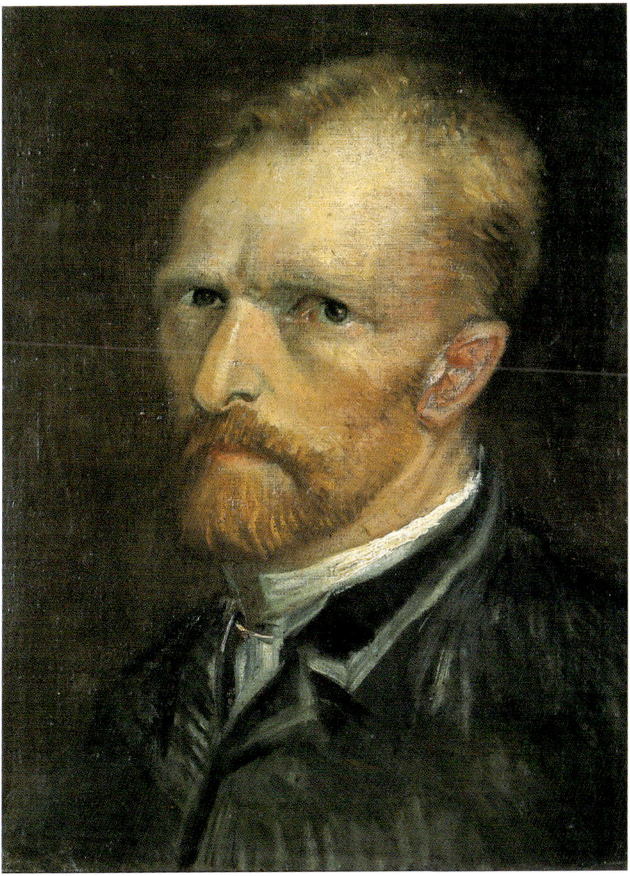

p.102:
Anton Mauve, *Self-portrait,* ca. 1884-1888

Vincent van Gogh, *Self-portrait,* 1886

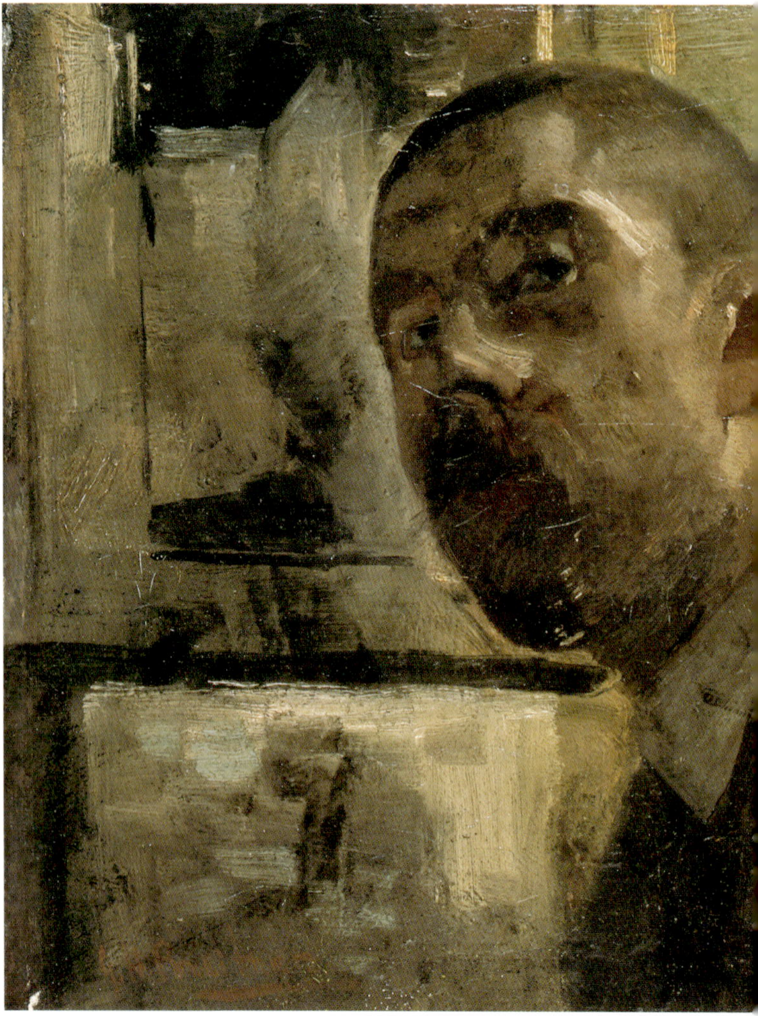

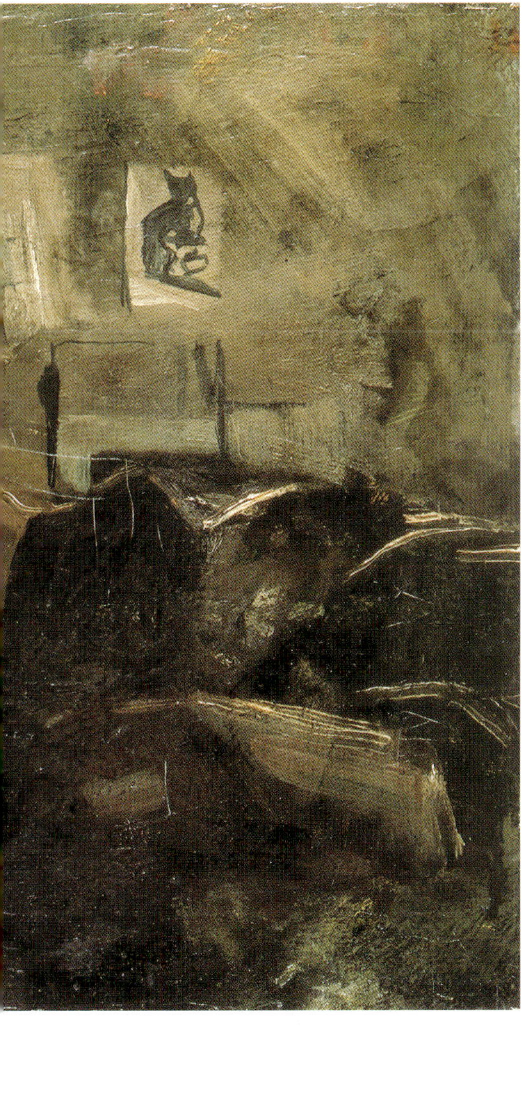

G.H. Breitner,
Self-portrait, 1885

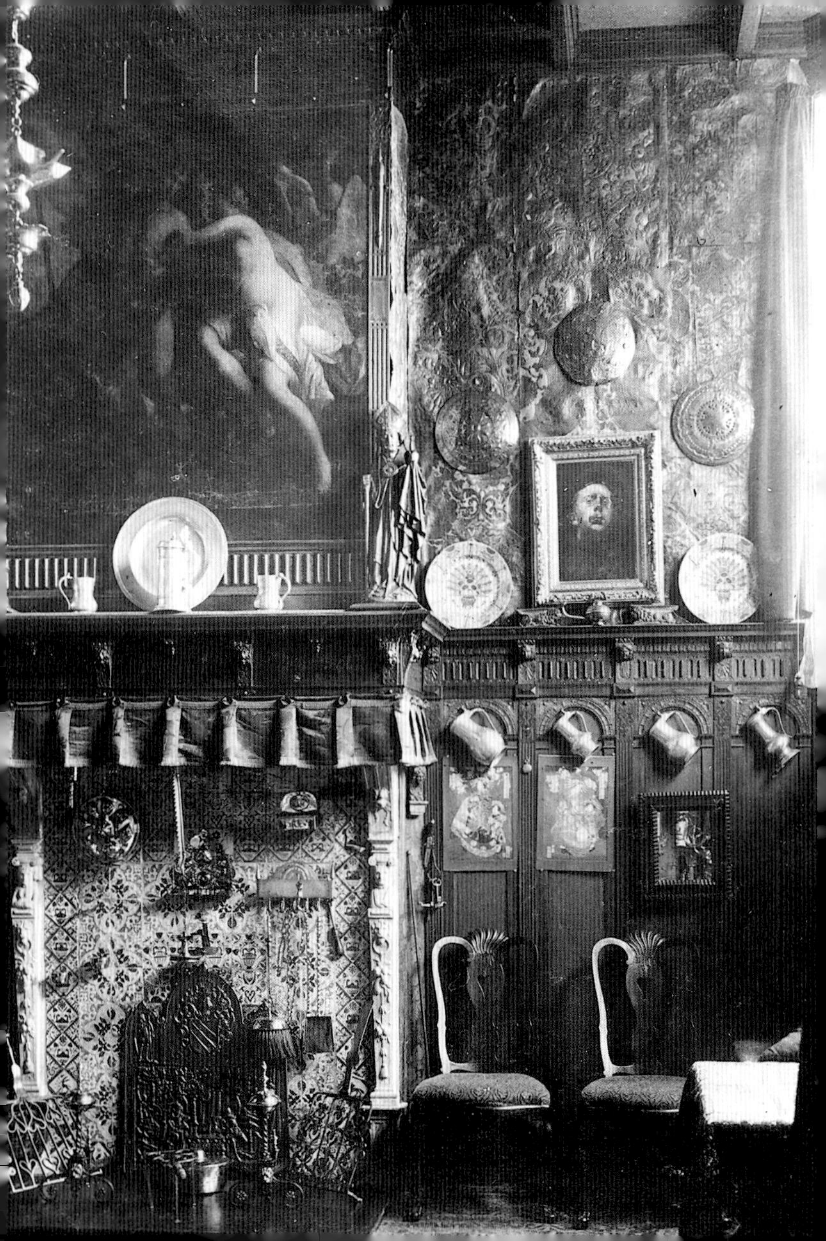

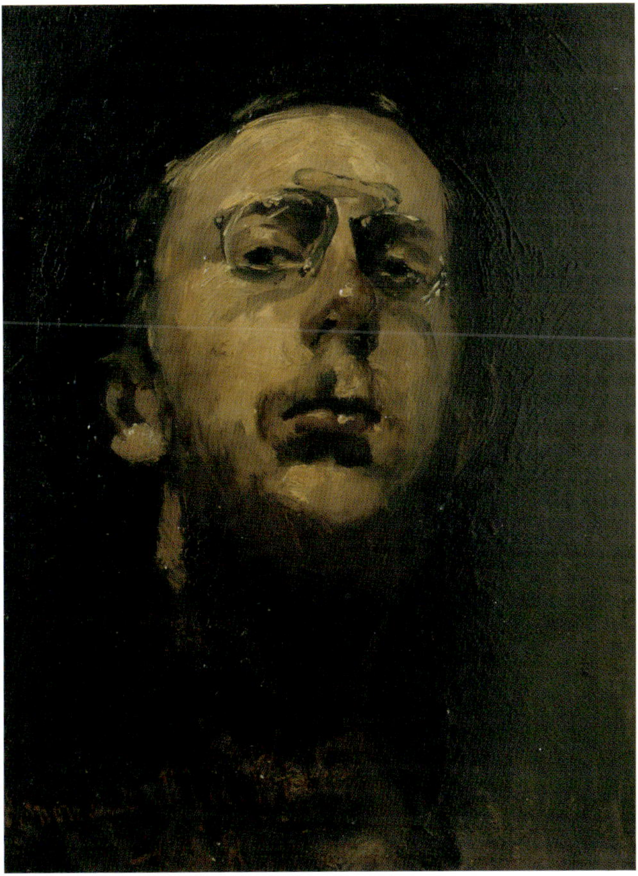

Interior of H.J. van der Weele's home

G.H. Breitner, *Self-portrait with pince-nez,* 1882

pleasures of the big city, such as the circus, the *café-chantant* and the fair. 'Modernity is all there is – there is nothing else,' declared Isaac Israëls, whose aspiration it was to be 'le peintre du peuple' in the tradition of Breitner and the De Goncourt brothers.[29]

In the same period, Vincent van Gogh wrote his brother: 'You see, Theo, my boy, I cannot produce Types of Beauty, my ideal shall be Heads of the People,'[30] alluding here to the English illustrated magazine, The Graphic. Because of their exemplary function for him, Van Gogh preserved these illustrations with great care. Vincent declared that, if he could, he would simply take 'men, women or children' right off the street and use them as models to paint from in his studio. Only then would he be able to produce figures from the people, for the people.[31]

For a time, it seemed as though Breitner and Van Gogh were pursuing the same objective, searching together for motifs to draw and paint from in the slums of The Hague, with their soup kitchens and muddy streets. In the waiting room of the railway station, they chose their models from the waiting travellers, but Van Gogh annoyed everyone, including Breitner, by scratching exaggeratedly hard with his pencil across the paper. Van Gogh also criticised Breitner, comparing his watercolours to mouldy wallpaper.[32] Following Van Gogh's death, Breitner wrote to painter Herman van der Weele, a common friend, that he regarded Van Gogh's paintings as 'art for Eskimos,' coarse and rude.[33]

Van Gogh actually felt more appreciation and affinity for Van der Weele. They shared an interest in English magazine illustrations, e.g., those of Herkomer in The Graphic. In Van der Weele's studio, Van Gogh admired his friend's studies of excavators, horses and sand-filled wheelbarrows. Together, they went to the sand excavations and construction sites where The Hague's new districts were to be built, such as the Statenkwartier, where Van der Weele would also eventually live. He enjoyed his conversations with Van

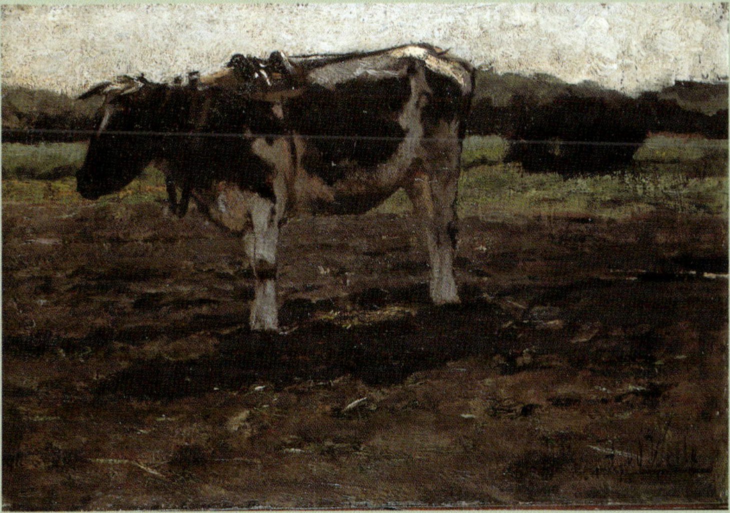

H.J. van der Weele, *Cow in a pasture,* n.d.,
L. van Sinderen collection, The Hague

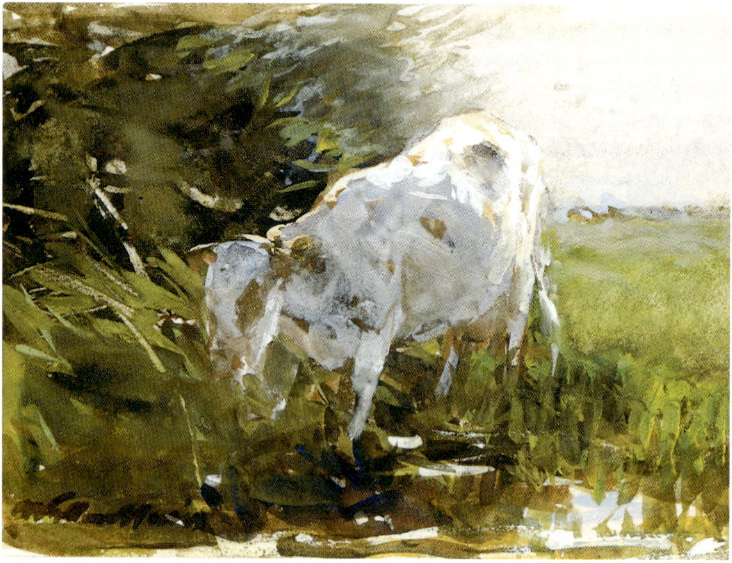

Willem Maris, *Cow by a pond,* 1896 (watercolour)

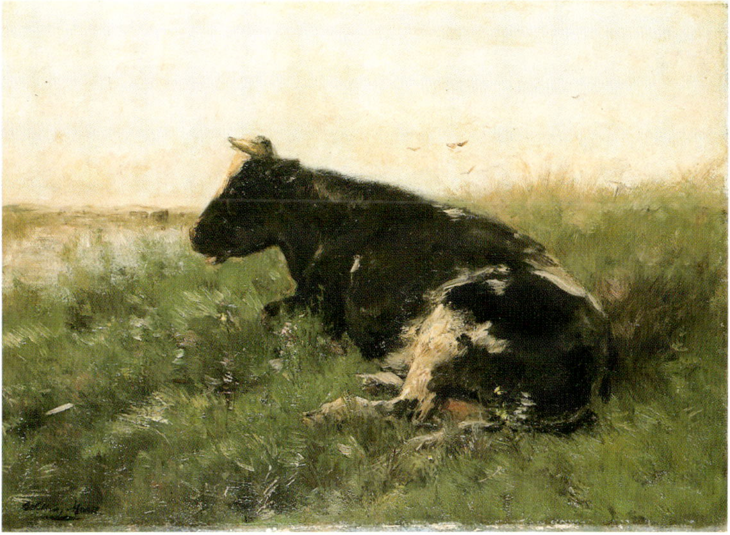

Willem Maris, *Reclining cow,* ca. 1893

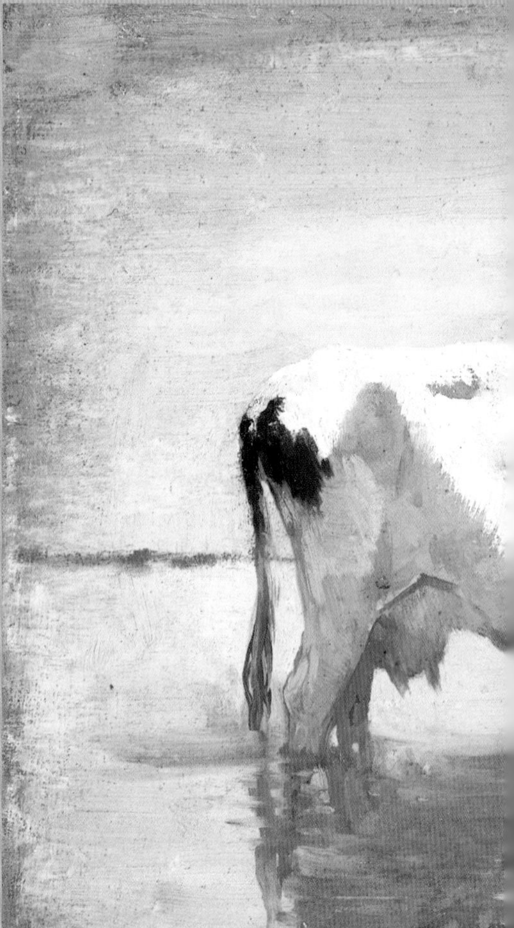

Anton Mauve,
White cow, ca. 1884

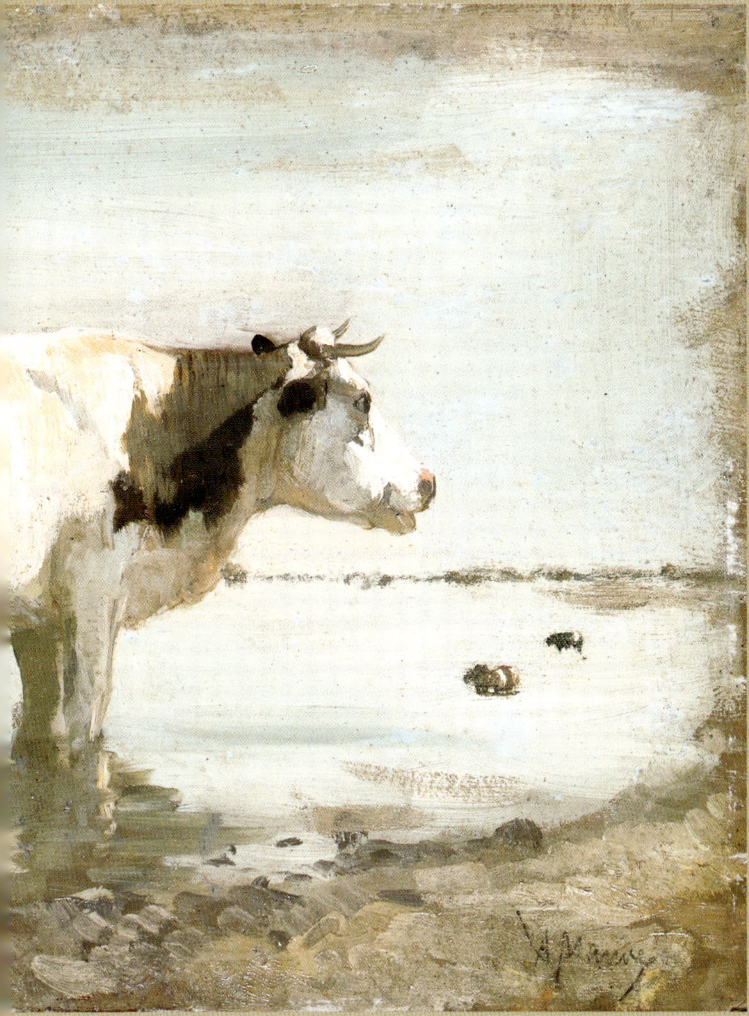

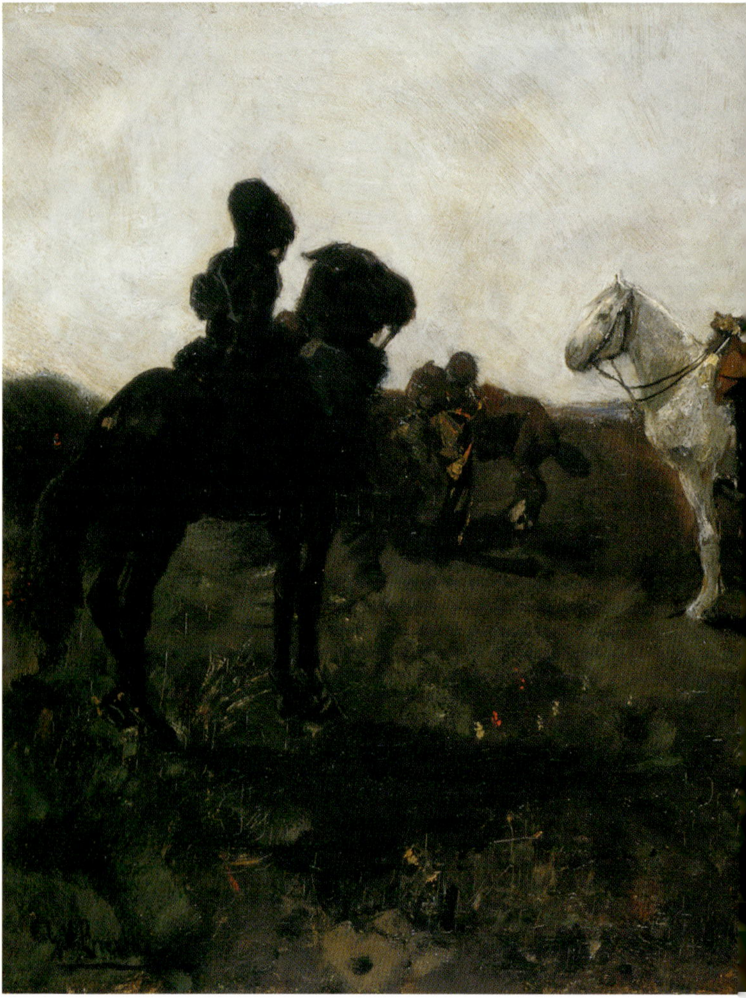

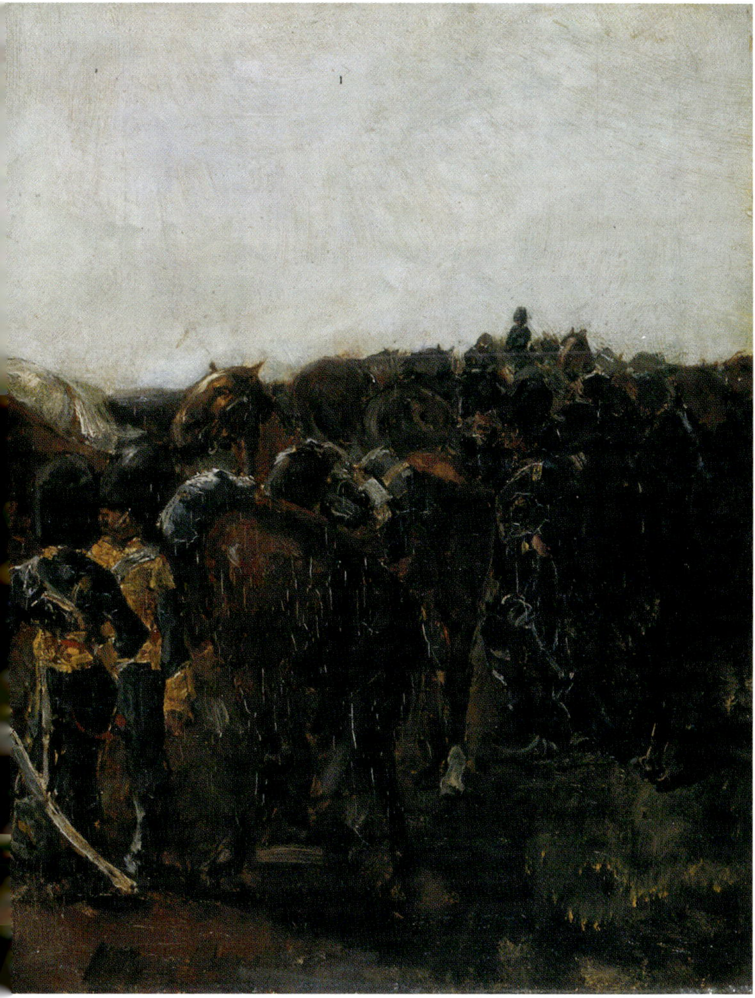

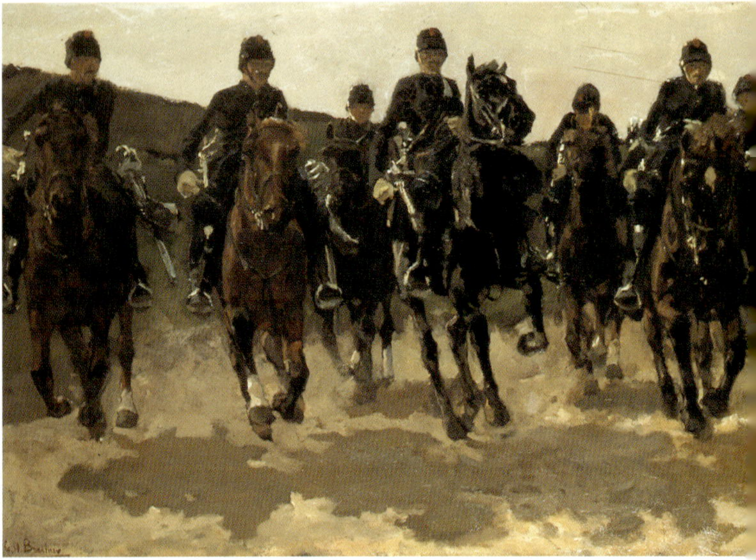

pp. 114-115:
G.H. Breitner, *Soldiers in the dunes,* ca. 1880-1881

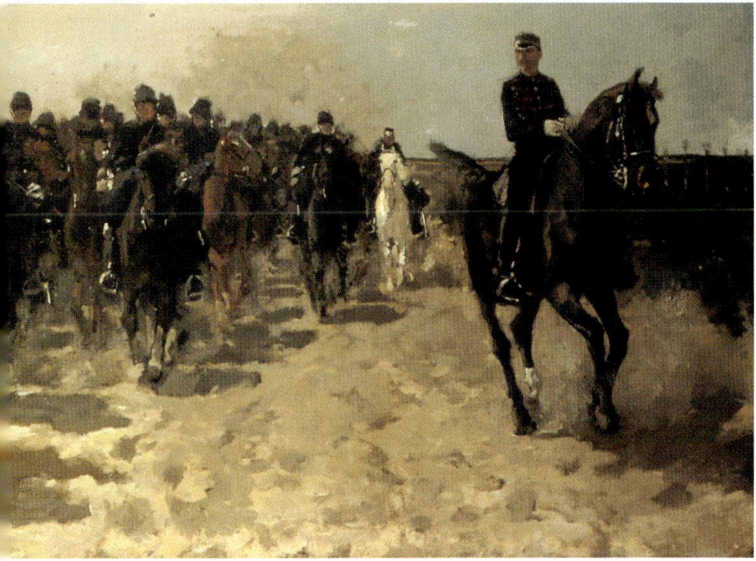

G.H. Breitner, *Cavalry,* 1883-1888

der Weele about the painter's profession, and wrote his brother: 'And, above all, when kindred spirits work and search together, they are able to give each other much strength and stimulation.'[34] Van der Weele, now a relatively forgotten name from the ranks of the Hague School, was a skilled landscape painter who created fine backlighting effects, which he used with much success in his studies of animals.

Van Gogh continued to model himself after the painters of the Hague School. In 1883 he wrote: 'Now, for me, I, too, am searching for the path that is best for me, the path of, shall we say, Israëls, Mauve, Maris – I do not know how far I have advanced along this path – much less how far I shall continue on it. But I have done my best in this, and shall keep doing my best.'[35]

Breitner, in contrast, had more admiration for the work of Willem de Zwart, together with whom he had studied at the Hague Academy of Art. Willem de Zwart was Jacob Maris' only pupil. In Maris' studio, Willem de Zwart made still life studies with, as motifs, old books and sheet music in the foreground and a self-portrait of Matthijs Maris in the background. Willem de Zwart drew and painted in the direct vicinity of where he lived, e.g., in the dunes near the Kanaalweg in Scheveningen, or by the arterial road to the Loosduinen, near the Beeklaan. Willem de Zwart travelled together with Breitner to Drente to sketch, in turn using his sketches as a source of ideas for the tiles he painted for the Hague delftware works, 'Rozenburg.' In 1885 he became a member of the painters' society, Pulchri Studio.[36] In 1894 De Zwart left The Hague, and went to live in Soest, subsequently moving to Hilversum and, then, Laren.

Willem Bastiaan Tholen was trained at the Rijksacademie in Amsterdam, but in 1879 journeyed to Brussels to study under Gabriëls. Together with Gabriëls, he painted studies in oils from nature in the vicinity of Kampen and Giethoorn. His friendships

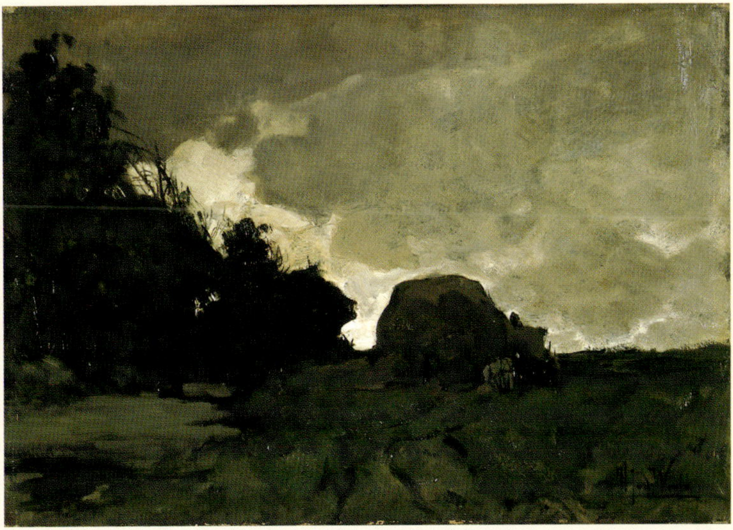

H.J. van der Weele, *Landscape under stormy skies (Approaching storm)*, n.d.

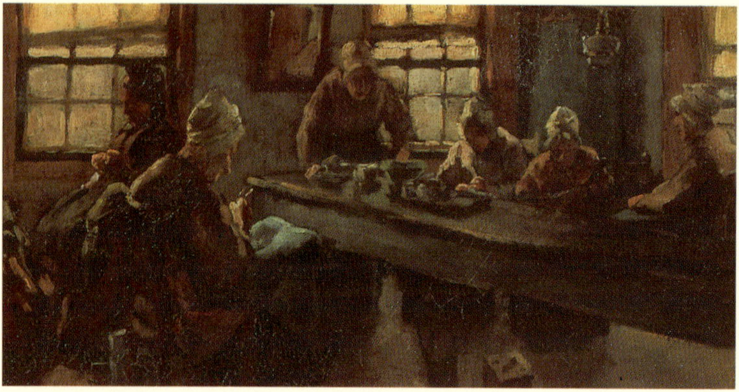

Anthon van Rappard, *The home for elderly women on West Terschelling,* 1883

with Willem Witsen and Anthon van Rappard, who in turn was friends with Vincent van Gogh, dated from his academy days. It was not until 1887 that Tholen settled in The Hague. Like Willem de Zwart, Tholen painted the sand excavations in preparation for the construction of the Statenkwartier and the district Duinoord, and in turn used the construction of the new buildings as a source of motifs, something Breitner had also done. From 1900, Tholen had his own boat, a sailing barge named 'The Eudia.' On it, he travelled from his house, the 'Kanaalvilla' near the White Bridge in The Hague, to the Zuiderzee, where he would seek inspiration in Enkhuizen and Volendam, among other places. Tholen's choice of colours remained close to the tonalities of the Hague School.

Suze Robertson studied together with Breitner and De Zwart at the Art Academy of The Hague. In 1884, she established herself as a painter in The Hague, where she quickly gained admittance to the circle of Pulchri Studio. Above all, it was Mesdag who demonstrated great admiration for her exceptional talent and included work of hers in his own collection. Her contemporaries, e.g., Breitner and Witsen, also indicated their admiration for her. Suze Robertson made powerful portraits and other depictions of women at work on the farm. In addition, she painted village views and interiors in expressionistic colours. Her drawings, as well, are impressive, with an intensity comparable to that found in Van Gogh's later works.

The early works of Mondrian reflect her influence. Like Willem de Zwart, Robertson often employed a dark background as her starting point, gradually working toward lighter colours, with the result that many of her paintings make a somewhat sombre impression on the viewer. Suze Robertson's works are characterised by a robust use of colour and strength of vision.

Through the years during which the Hague School experienced its flowering, some of the themes cultivated by the group turned

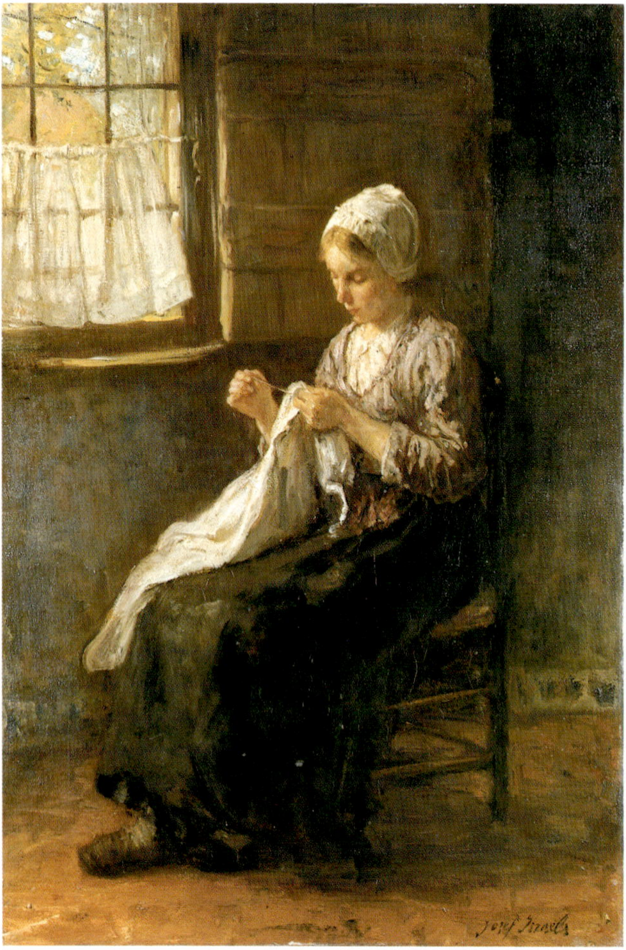

Jozef Israëls, *Woman sewing (for her trousseau)*, ca. 1880

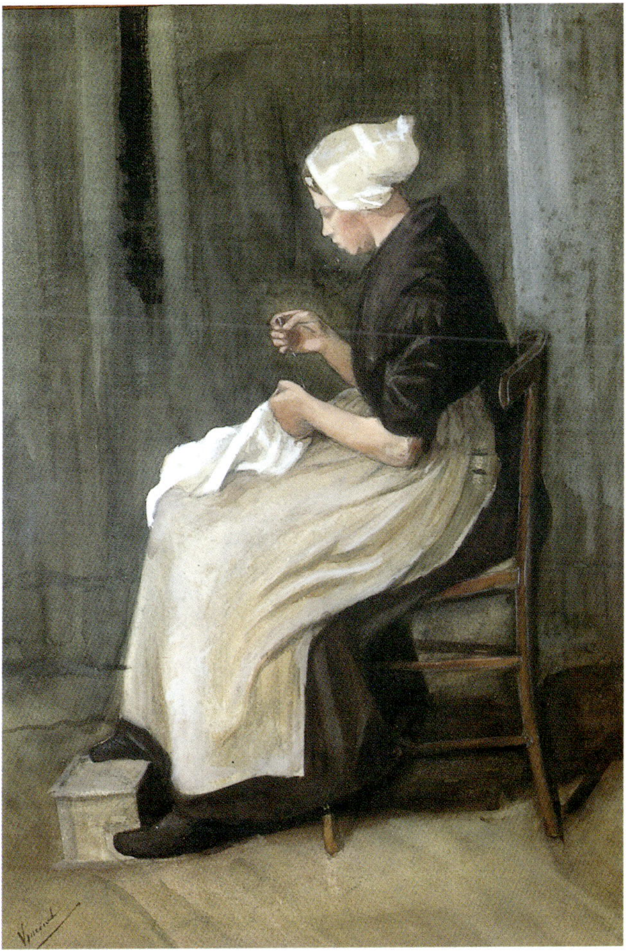

Vincent van Gogh, *Woman in traditional Scheveningen dress, sewing,* n.d. (watercolour) (De Boer collection)

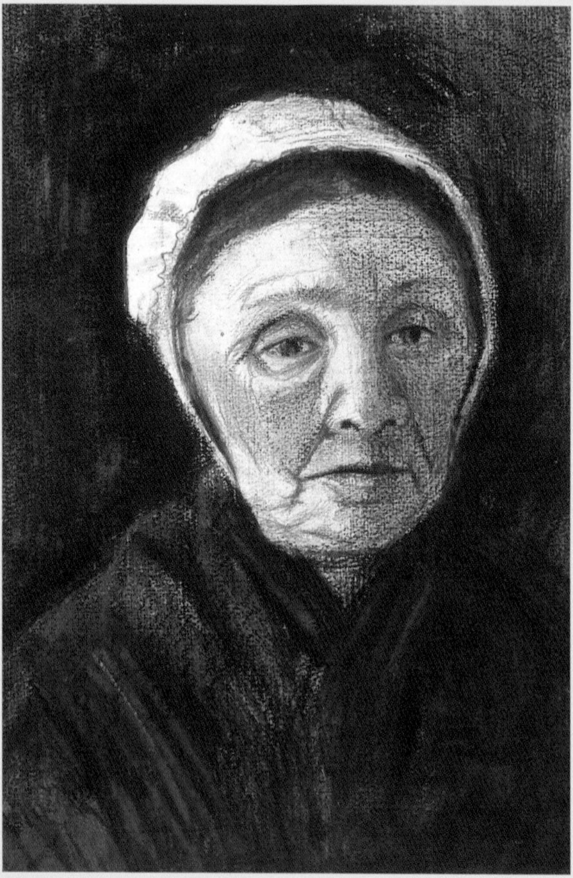

Vincent van Gogh, *Scheveningen woman (Sientje Hoornik's mother)*, ca. 1882-1883 (drawing)

Vincent van Gogh, *Woman pealing potatoes (Sientje Hoornik)*, ca. 1882 (drawing)

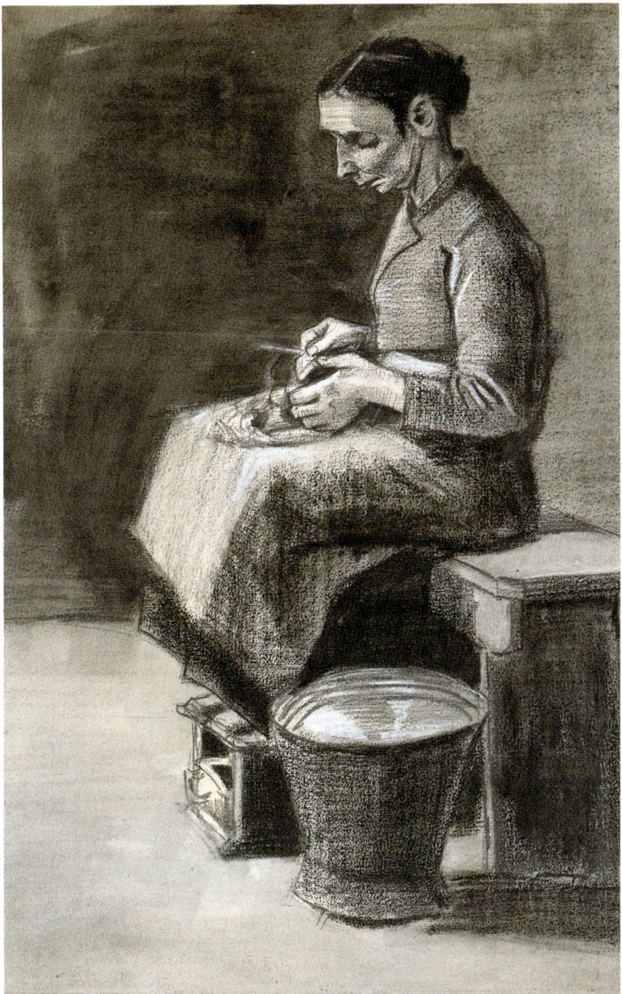

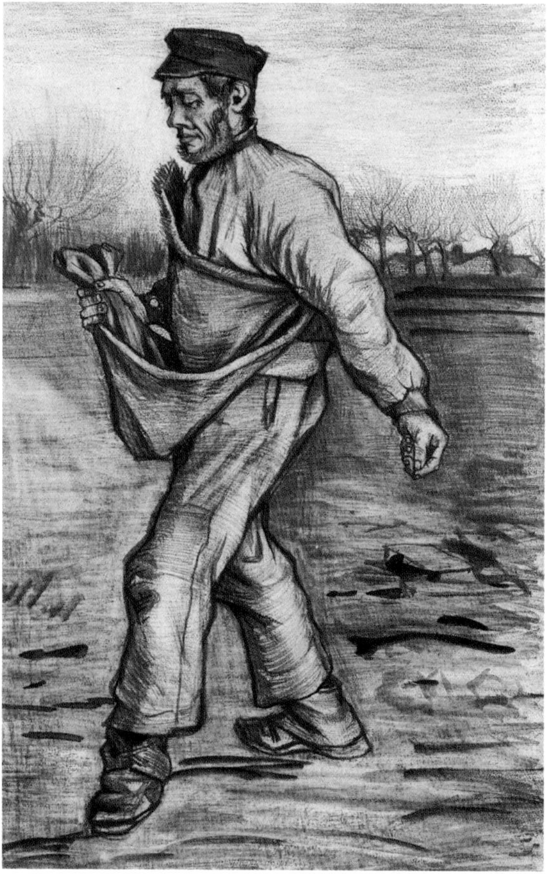

Vincent van Gogh, *Sower,* n.d. (drawing) (De Boer collection)

Vincent van Gogh, *Street sweeper,* n.d. (drawing)

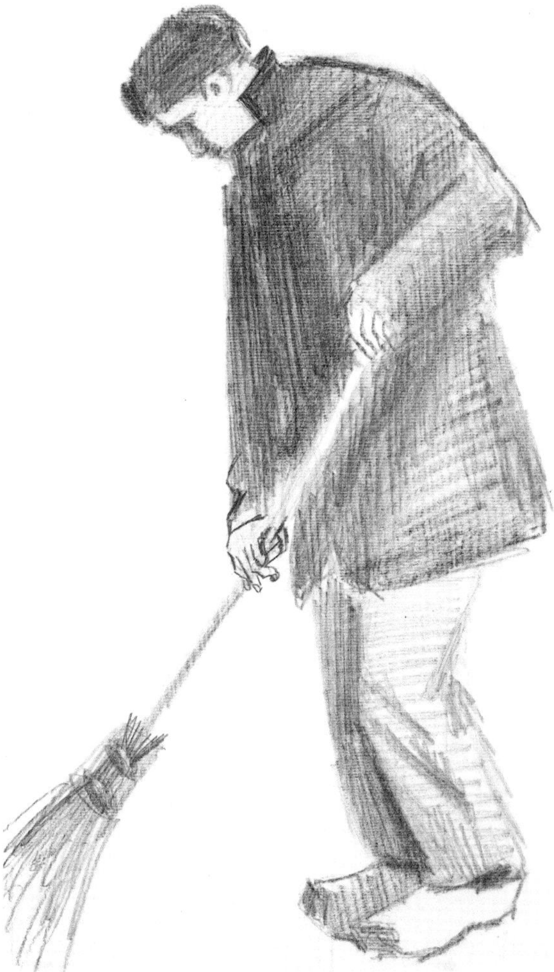

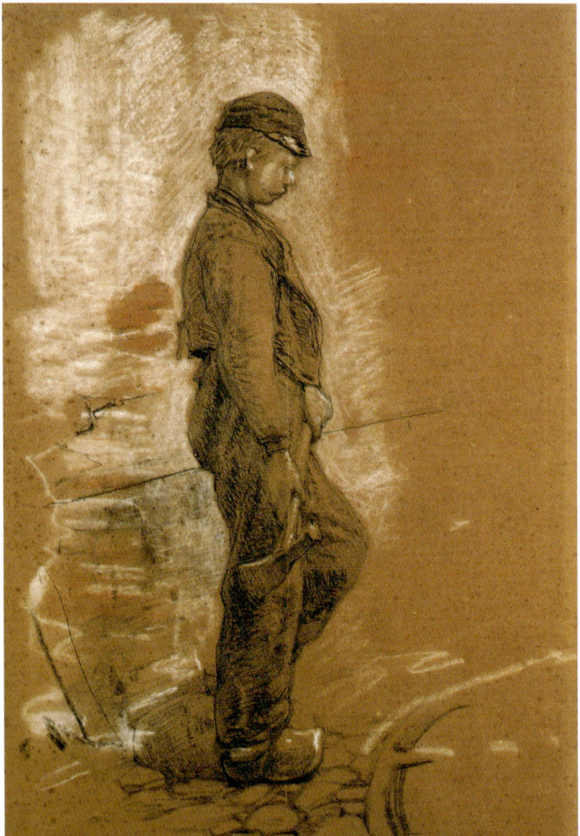

Willem Maris, *Youth with pickaxe,* n.d. (drawing)

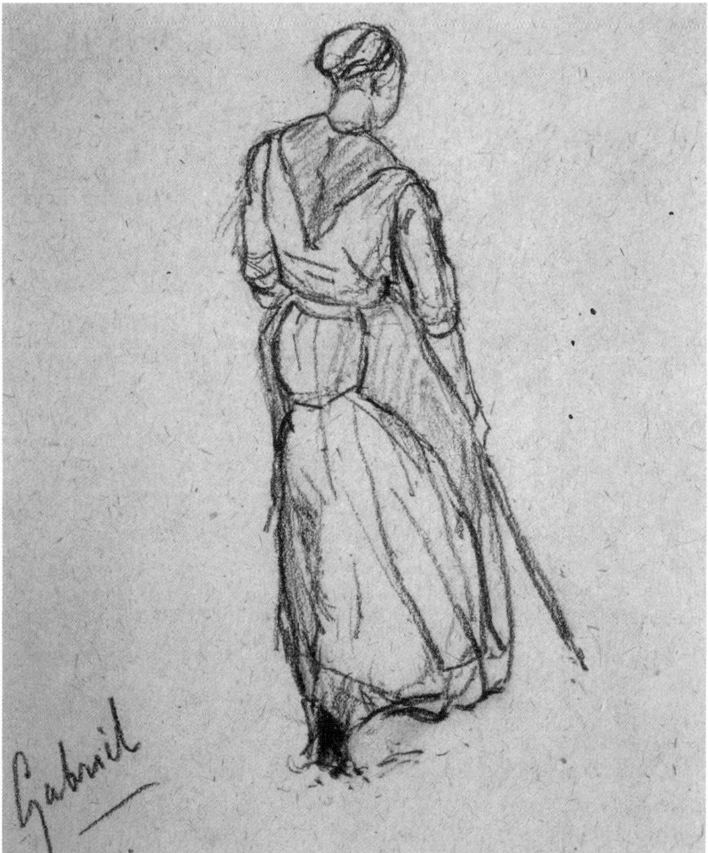

Paul Gabriël, *Woman working the land,* n.d. (drawing)

pp. 130-131:
Anton Mauve, *The corn harvest,* n.d. (watercolour)

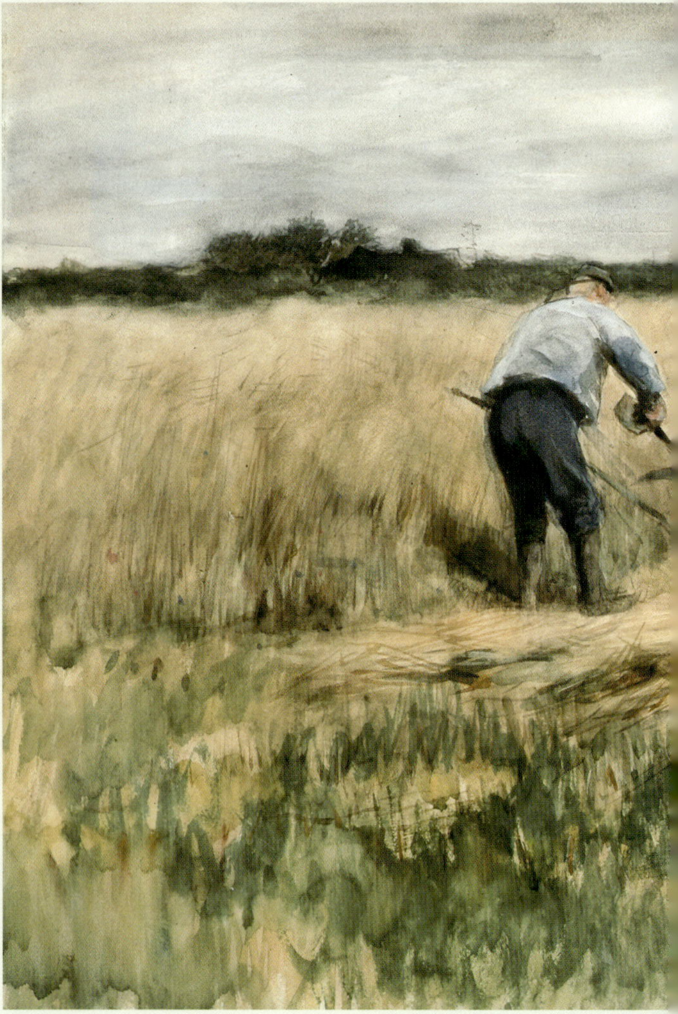

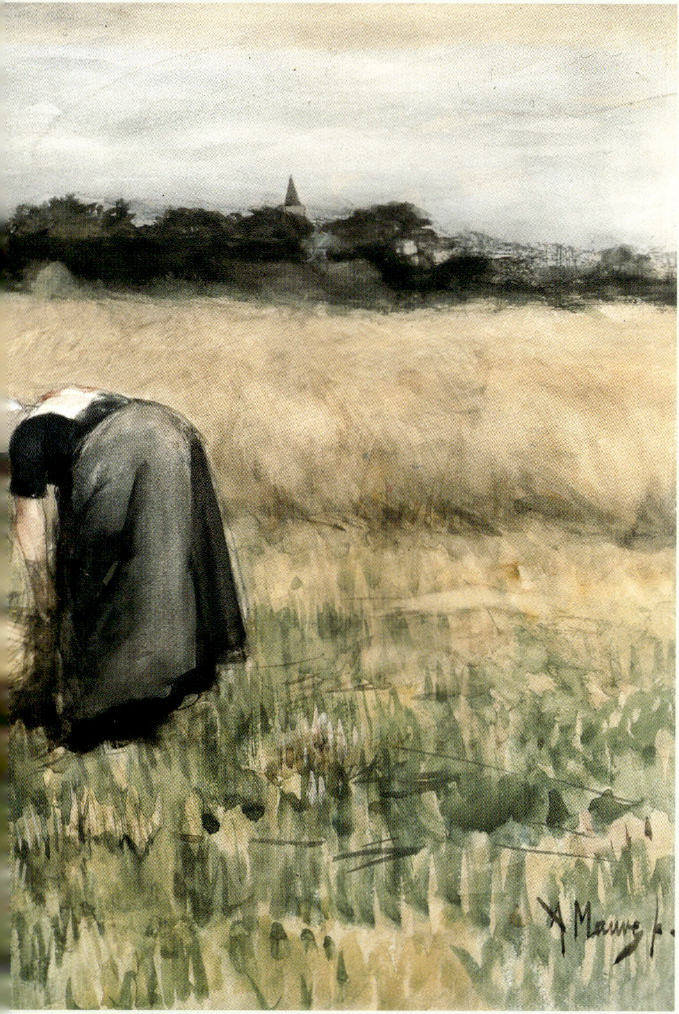
A Mauve f.

out to be particularly successful. After having caused a furore at the start of his career with his interiors and funeral scenes, in the 1870s Jozef Israëls introduced the theme of a peasant family at the table, painting, in 1876, his 'The frugal meal,' now in the collection of the Glasgow Art Gallery. In 1882, Israëls employed the same theme in expanded form: the entire family is assembled around the table, before the open hearth, a work now in the collection of Amsterdam's Van Gogh Museum, under the title, 'A peasant family at the table.' In 1884, the house of Goupil, which had exclusive reproduction rights for Jozef Israëls' works, published a portfolio of photo-reproductions entitled 'Les grands peintres français et étrangers,' which included reproductions of two works by Jozef Israëls: 'The Frugal Meal' (here under the title 'Intérieur hollandais') and a drawing whose composition bore a strong resemblance to that of the 'Peasant family' of 1882. (In 1882, Van Gogh had referred to a submission of Jozef Israëls to the Paris Salon: '[...] with, I think, 5 or 6 figures: a peasant family sitting at the table.'[37])

In 1889, Jozef Israëls produced a new variation on this theme: now, the family was seated around a single bowl filled with potatoes; the interior was illuminated on either side of an open hearth by two windows. The painting has been dated ca. 1884.

Inspired by the series, 'Heads of the people,' mentioned above, Van Gogh had, in his Hague period, gone about sketching an analogous series consisting of typical figures from the Dutch populace. After leaving The Hague, he continued the series during his stay at his parents' home in Nuenen in the province of Brabant, making sketches and studies in oils of peasants, and commenced work on his first important work, 'The potato eaters.' The painting's composition, to which he devoted much time and attention, is very similar to the family groups depicted by Jozef Israëls, with the difference being that Van Gogh opted for a close-up with greater

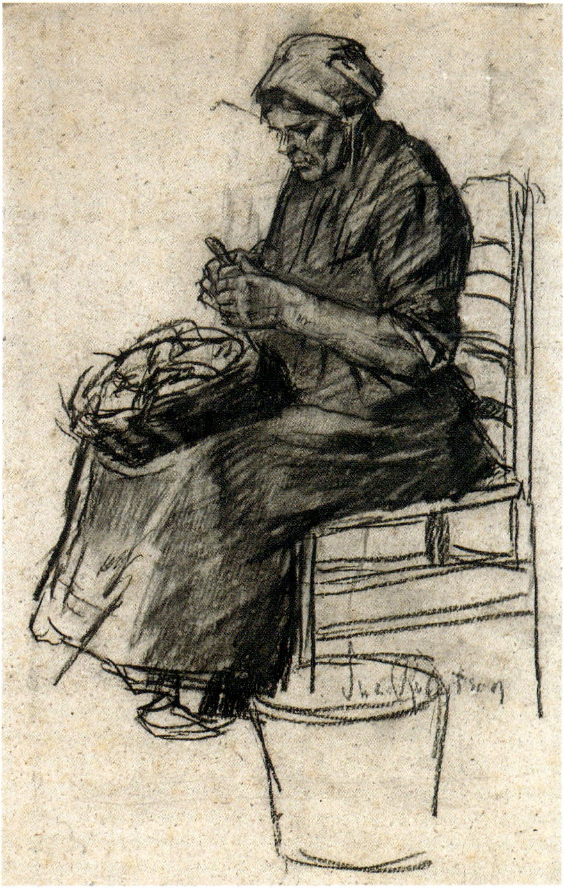

Suze Robertson, *Woman pealing potatoes,* n.d. (drawing)

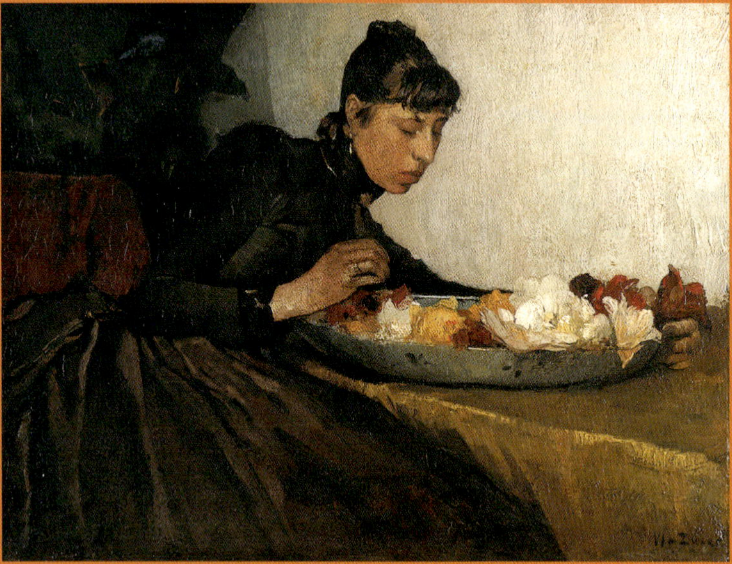

Willem de Zwart, *Arranging flowers,* ca. 1900

Suze Robertson, *Black man,* n.d. (drawing)

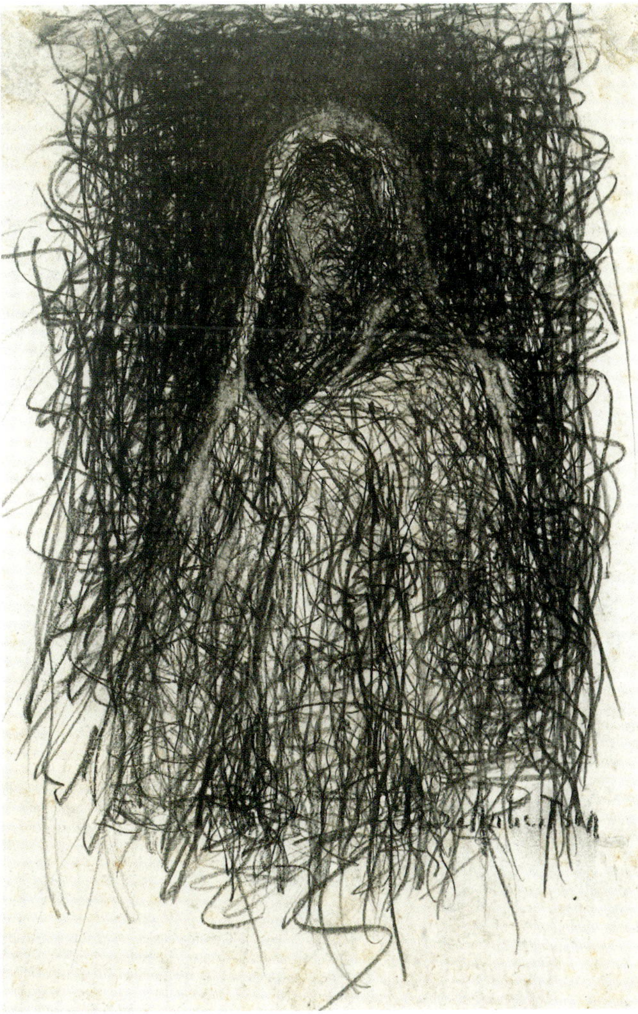

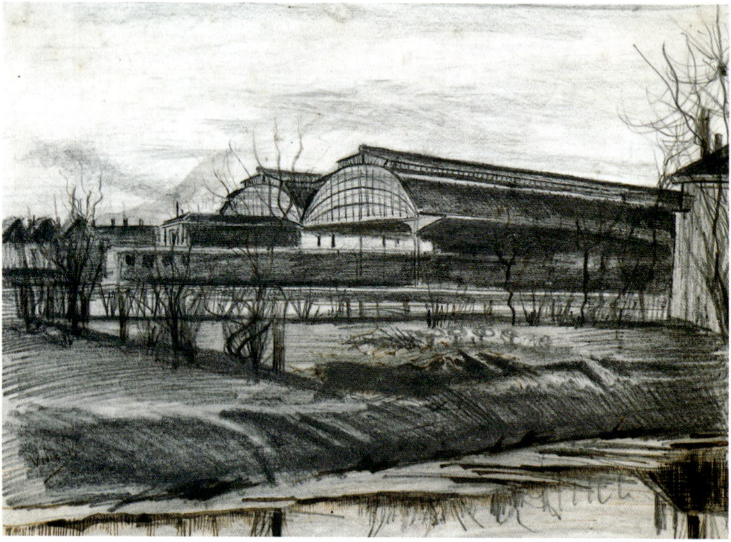

Vincent van Gogh, *Behind Rijnspoor Station (Hollands Spoor)*, 1882 (drawing)

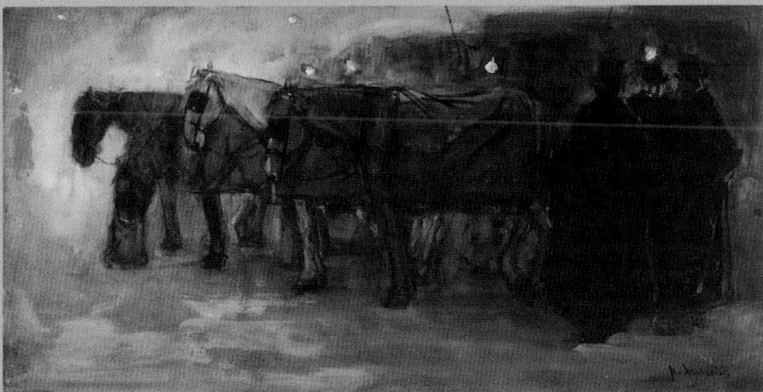

Floris Arntzenius, *Waiting cabs,* n.d. (watercolour)

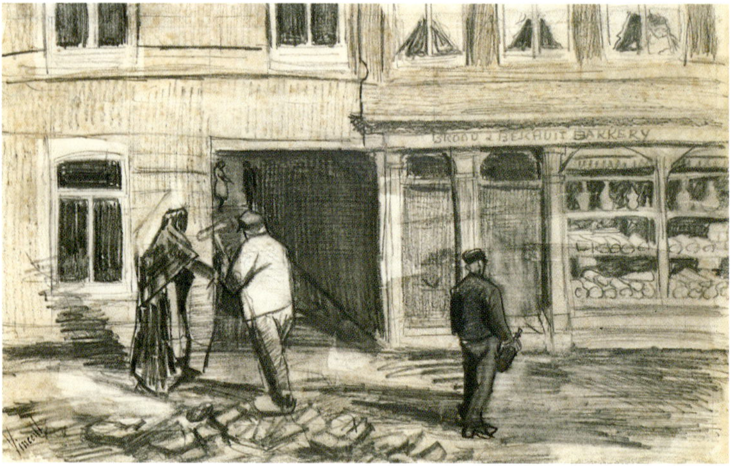

Vincent van Gogh, *Bakery, The Hague,* 1882 (drawing)

Vincent van Gogh, *In the rain (Dans la pluie),* 1882 (watercolour)

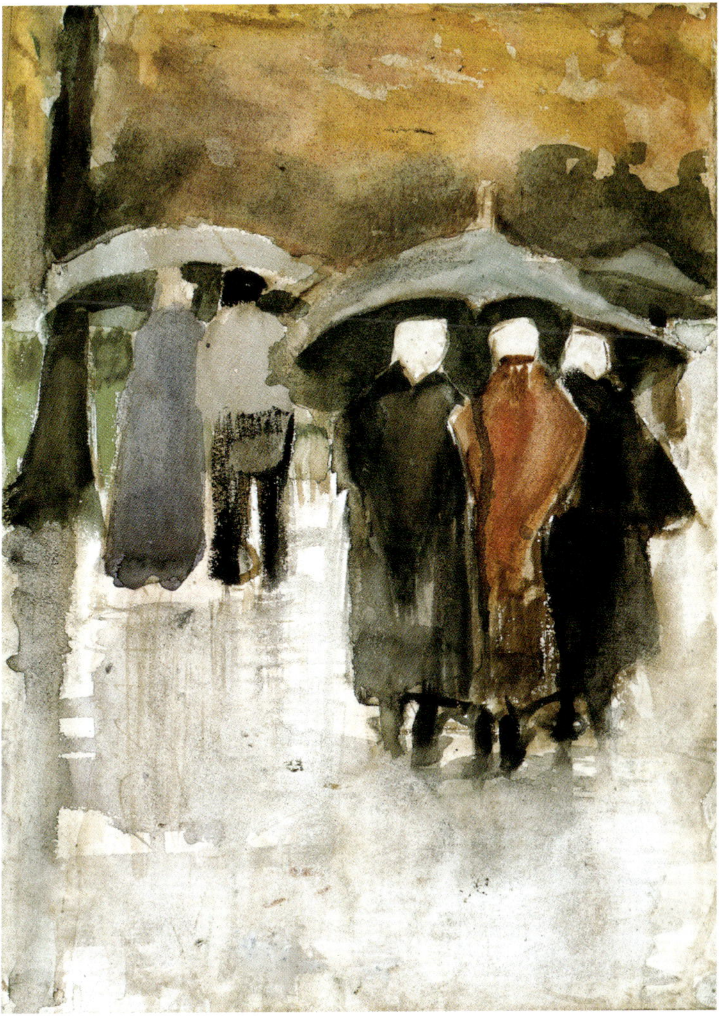

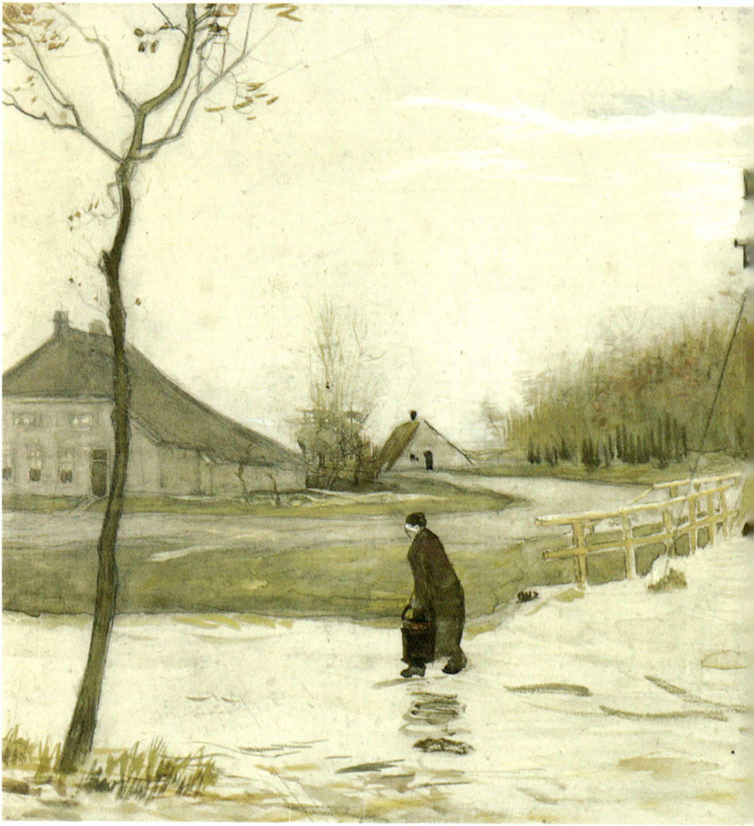

Vincent van Gogh, *The draw bridge in Nieuw Amsterdam,* 1883 (watercolour)

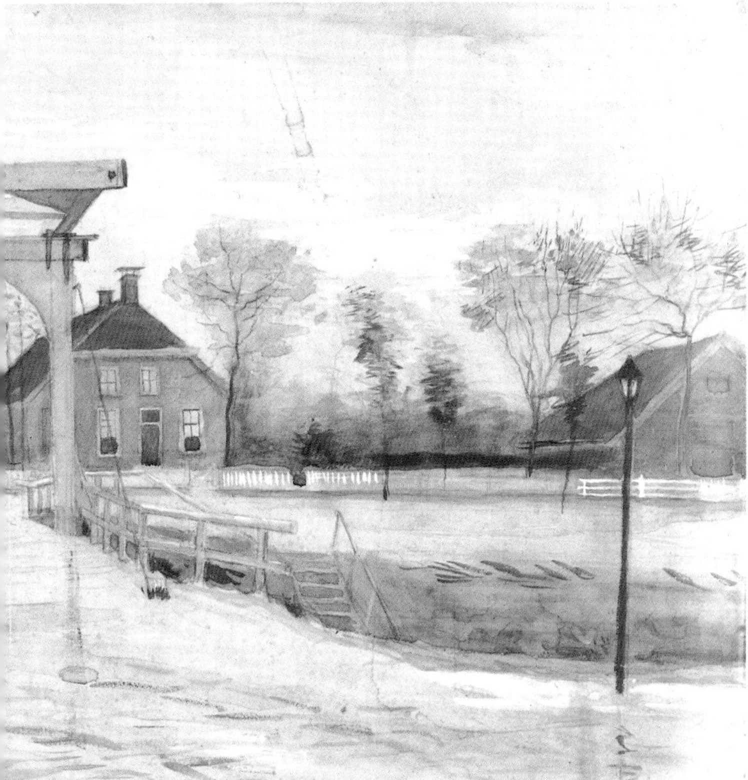

accentuation of the peasants' faces, while eliminating the problem of an anatomically correct representation of the different figures.

In 1902, Jozef Israëls took up this theme once again, possibly after having seen Van Gogh's version. He now also chose the title, 'The potato eaters,' and the composition features the same close-up approach to the four figures around the table. The painting now forms part of the collection of the Hague's Gemeentemuseum.[38] In 1910, the 'Peasant family at the table' dating from 1889 was among the works included in an exhibition in honour of Jozef Israëls at the Venice Biennale, where it was purchased by the renowned Scottish collector, John Reid.

Van Gogh's Hague years were of decisive significance: the many contacts he formed and the many impressions of artists and artistic movements he collected here revealed to him the course he would take. And after his departure from the city, as well, his admiration for the school of painters bearing its name continued. Even in Arles he thought back with gratitude to his lessons under Mauve and the great importance of making studies from nature, as championed by the Hague School.

Detail of p. 145

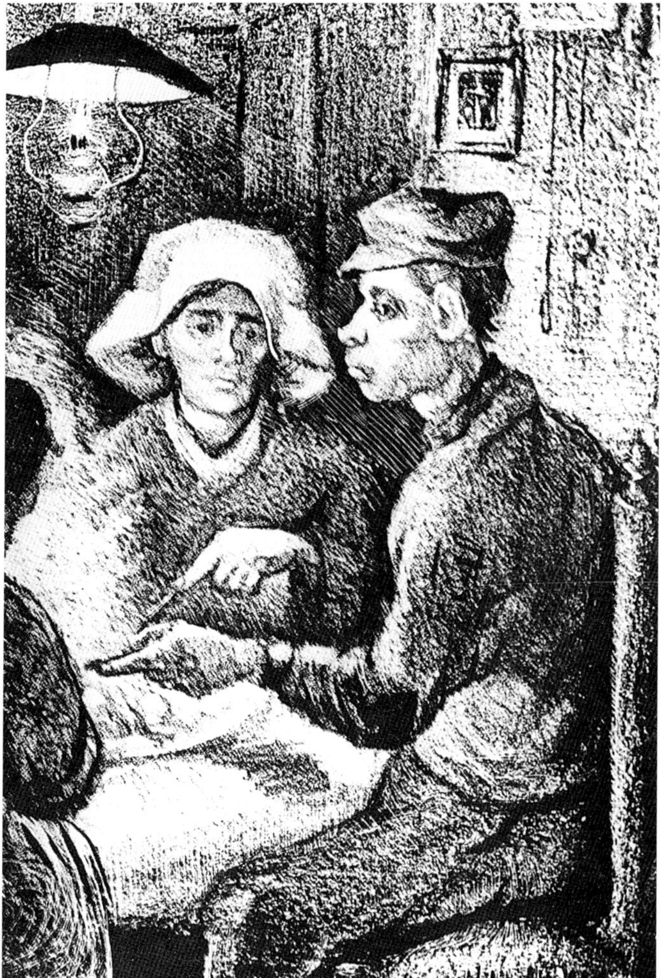

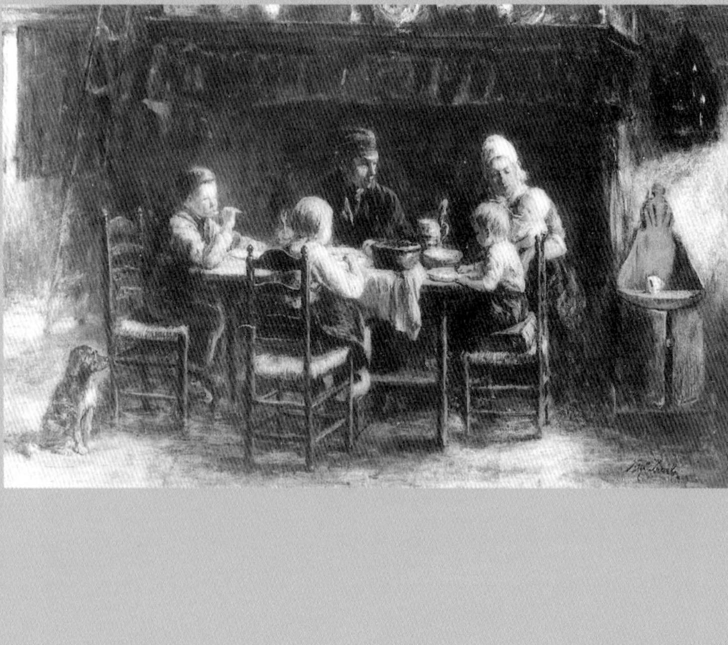

Jozef Israëls, *The frugal meal,* n.d.
(private collection)

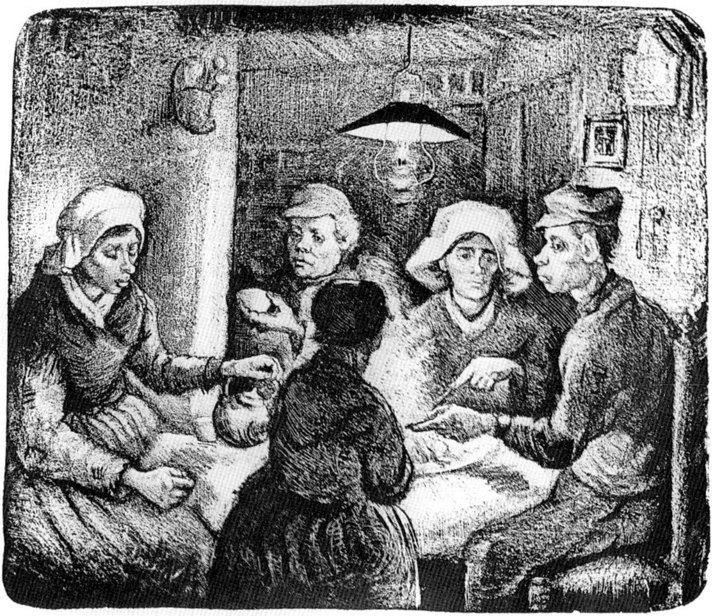

Vincent van Gogh, *The potato eaters,* n.d. (lithograph)

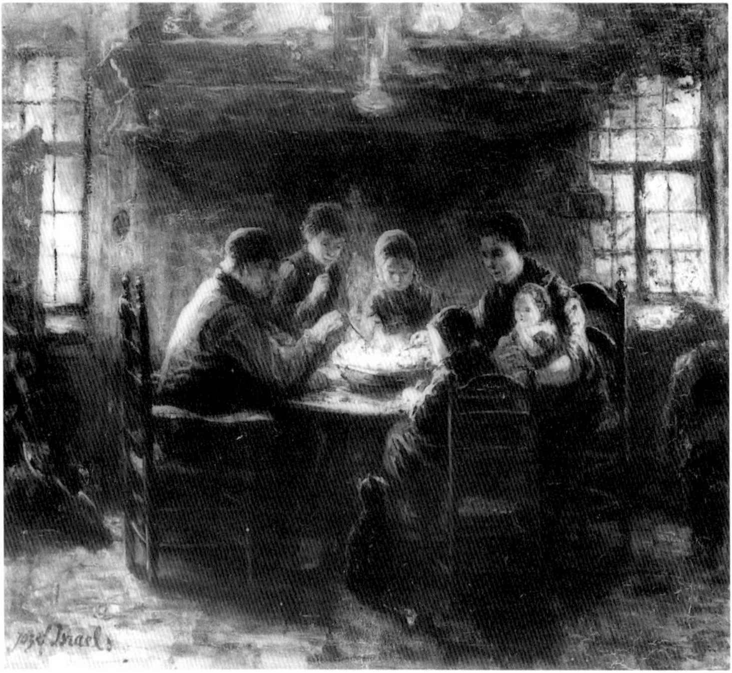

Jozef Israëls, *Potato eaters,* 1907
(private collection)

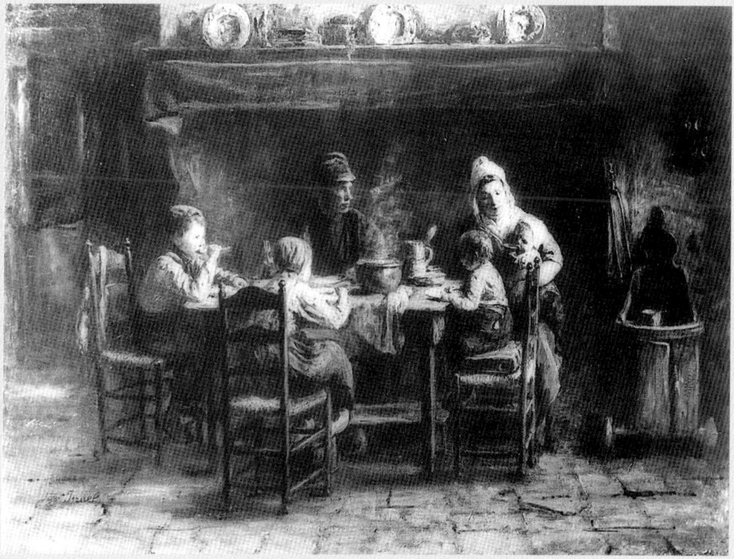

Jozef Israëls, *The frugal meal,* 1876
(private collection)

pp. 148-149:
Jozef Israëls, *At the table,* 1902

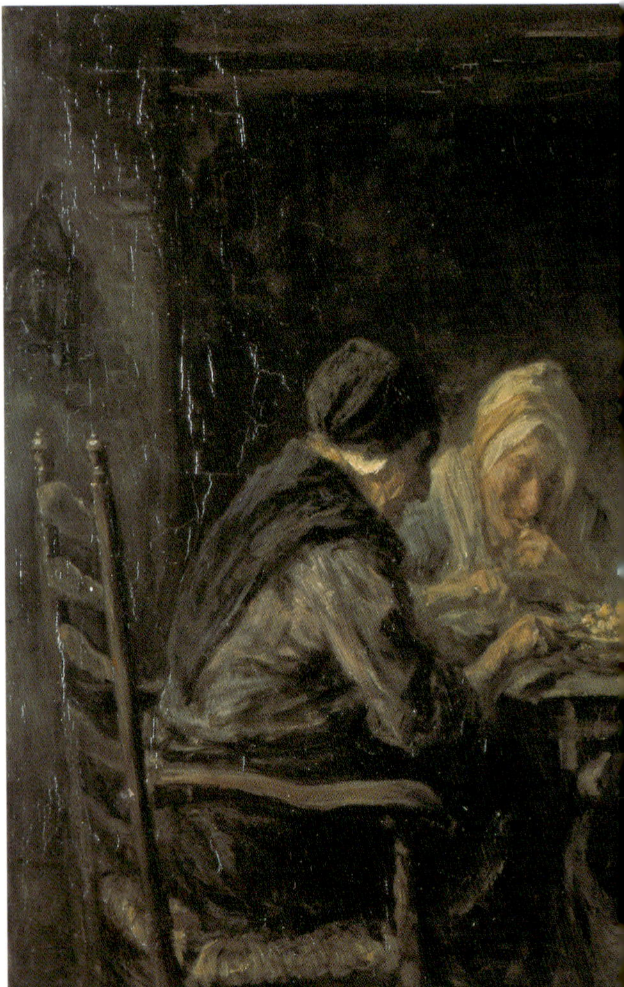

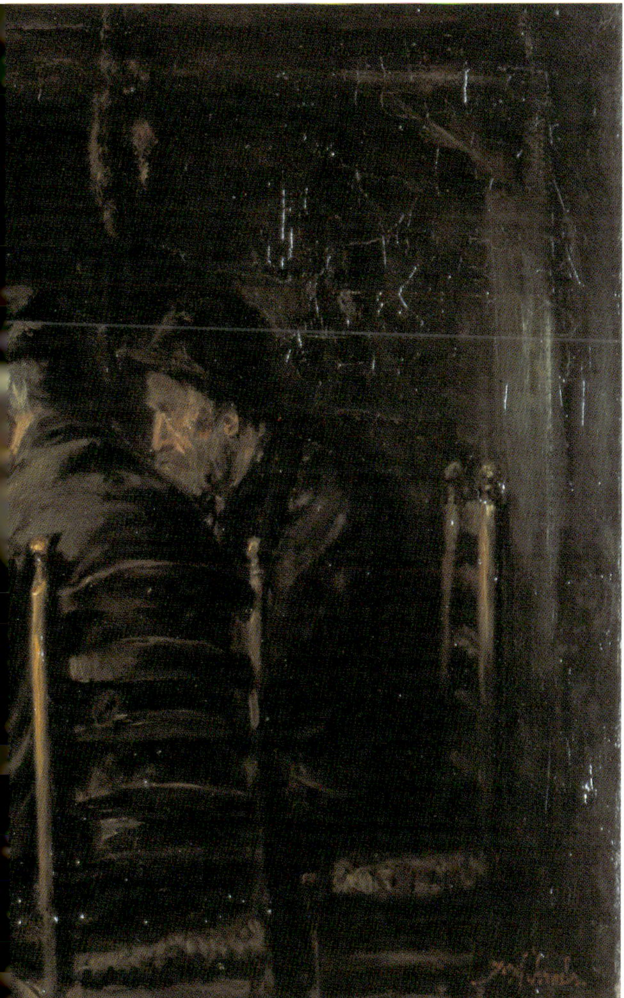

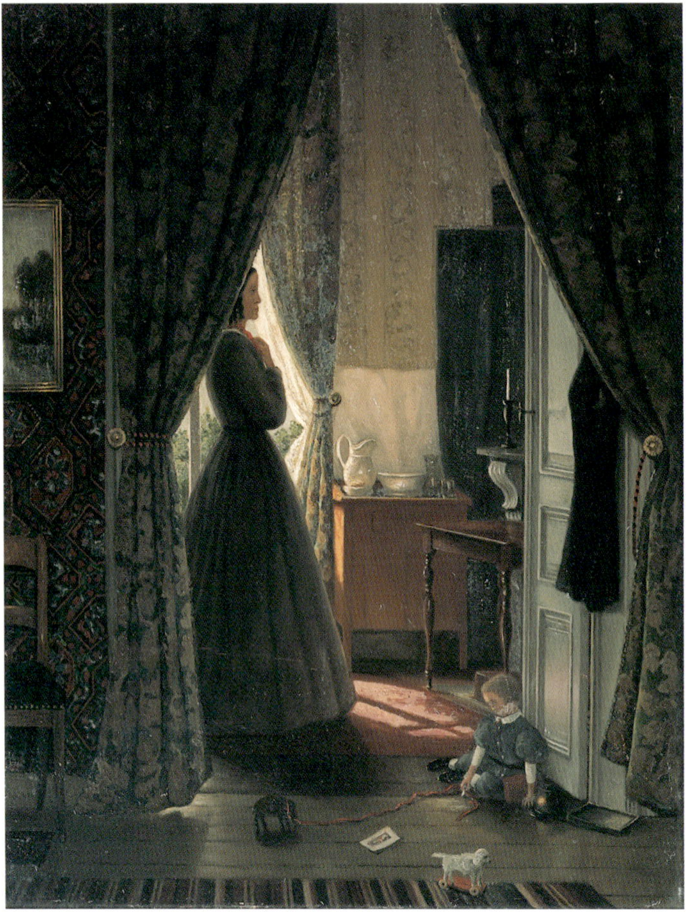

H.W. Mesdag, *Woman in interior (mrs Mesdag and her son Klaas)*, 1868
Panorama Mesdag collection, The Hague

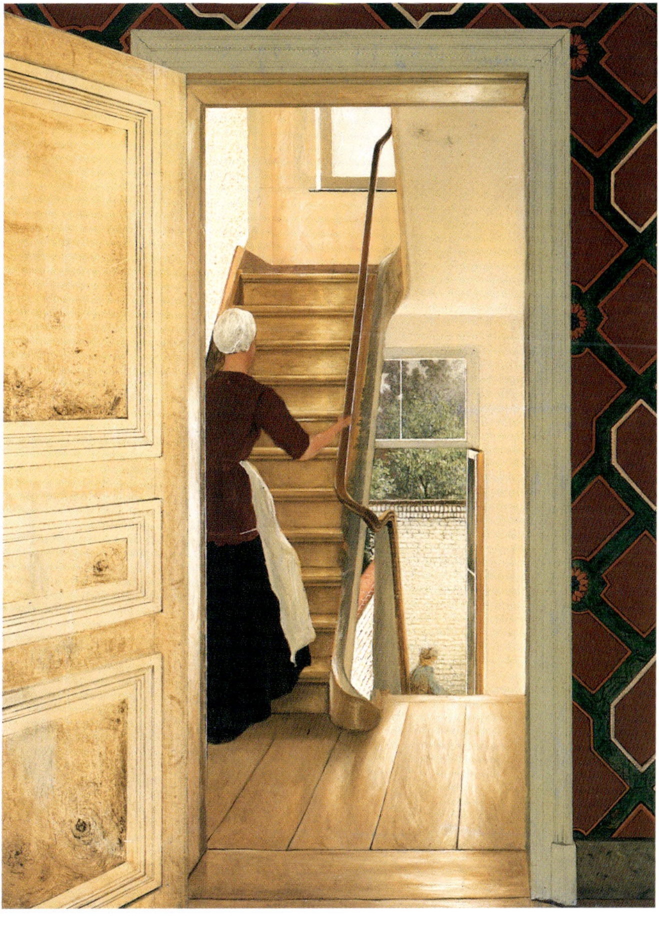

H.W. Mesdag, *Study of a staircase,* 1868
Panorama Mesdag collection, The Hague

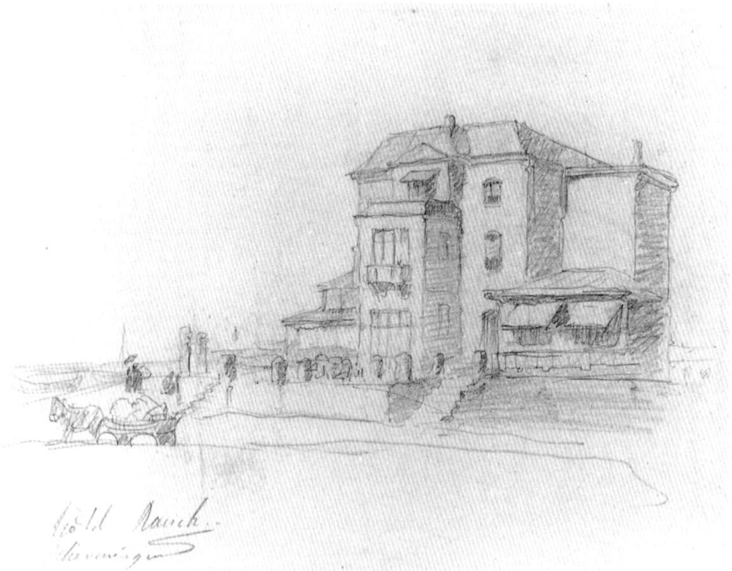

H.W. Mesdag, *Hotel Rauch in Scheveningen,* n.d. (drawing)
J. Poort collection, Wassenaar

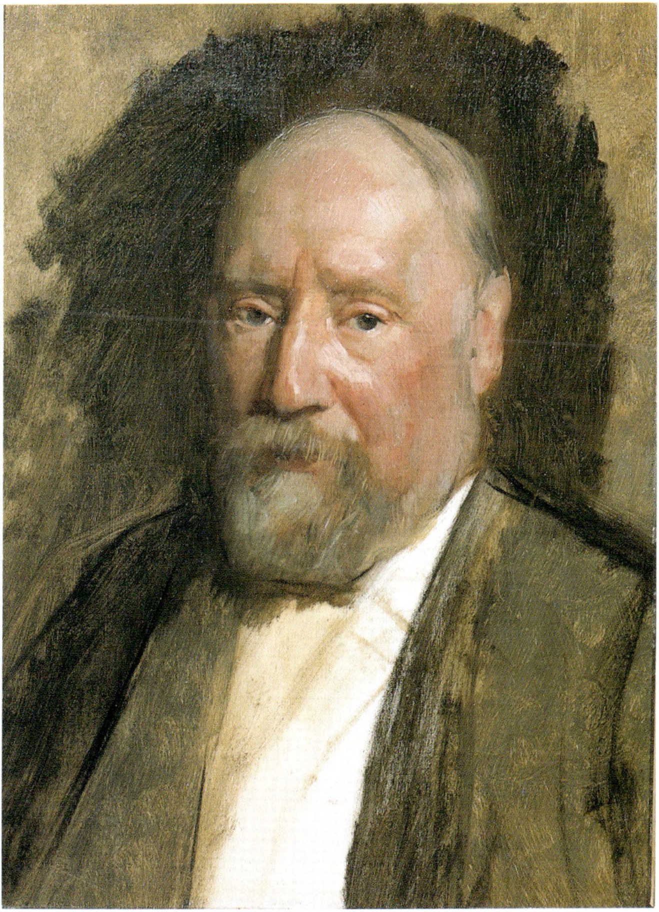

Portrait of H.W. Mesdag, n.d.
Panorama Mesdag collection, The Hague

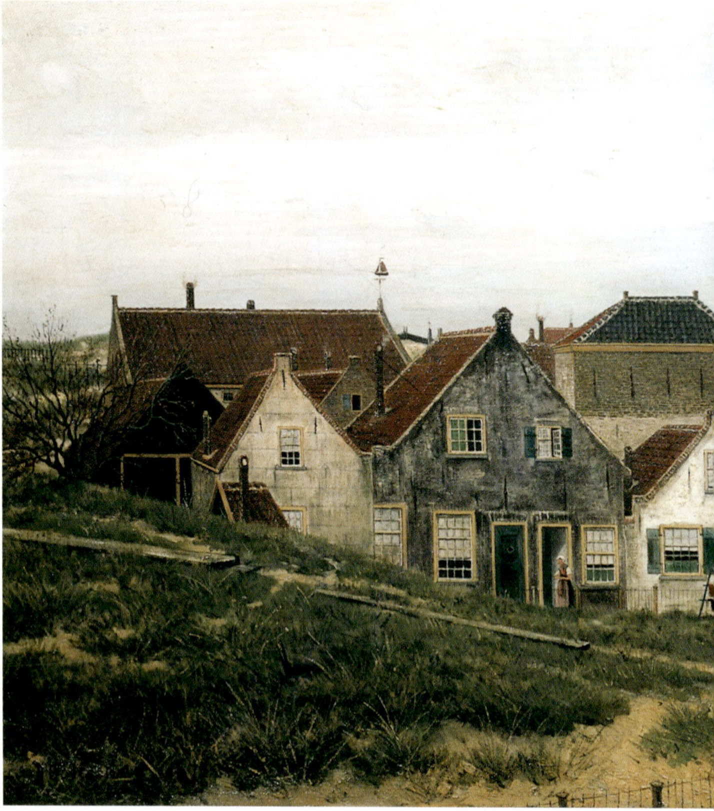

H.W. Mesdag, *View of the village of Scheveningen,* 1873
Panorama Mesdag collection, The Hague

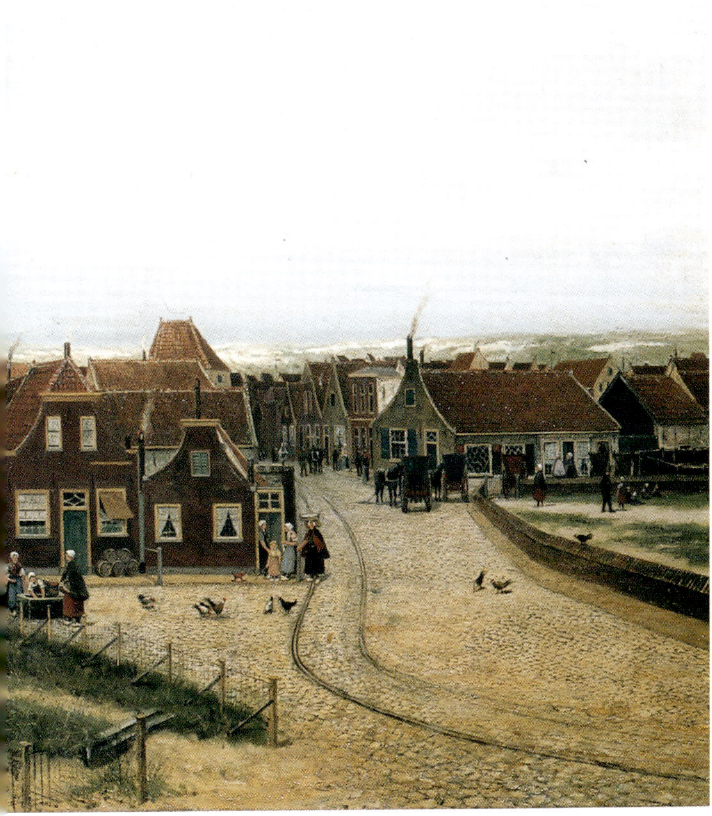

pp. 156-161:
Panorama Mesdag, The Hague, 1882

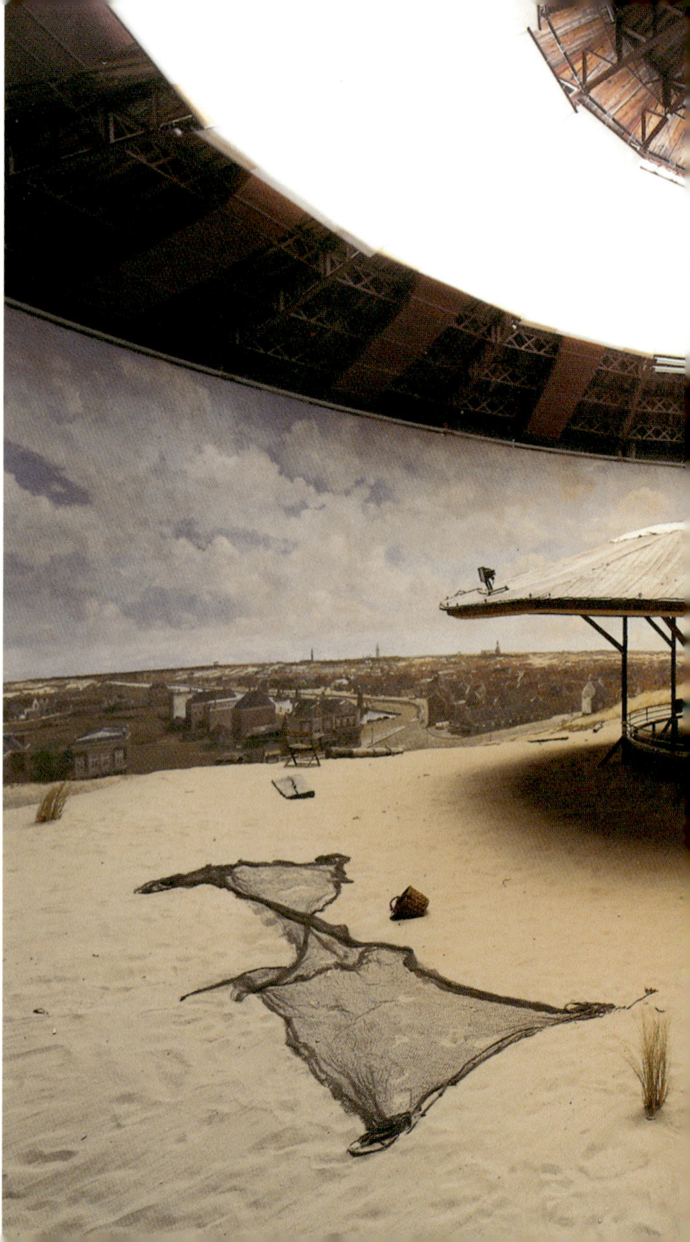

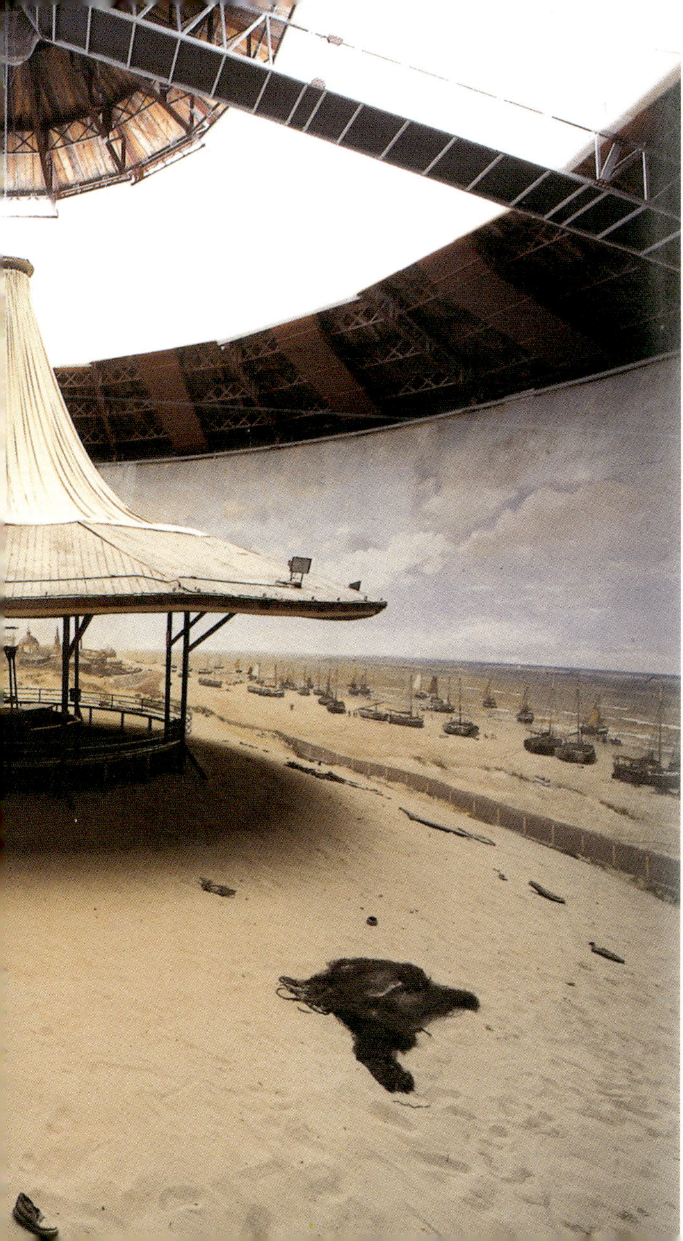

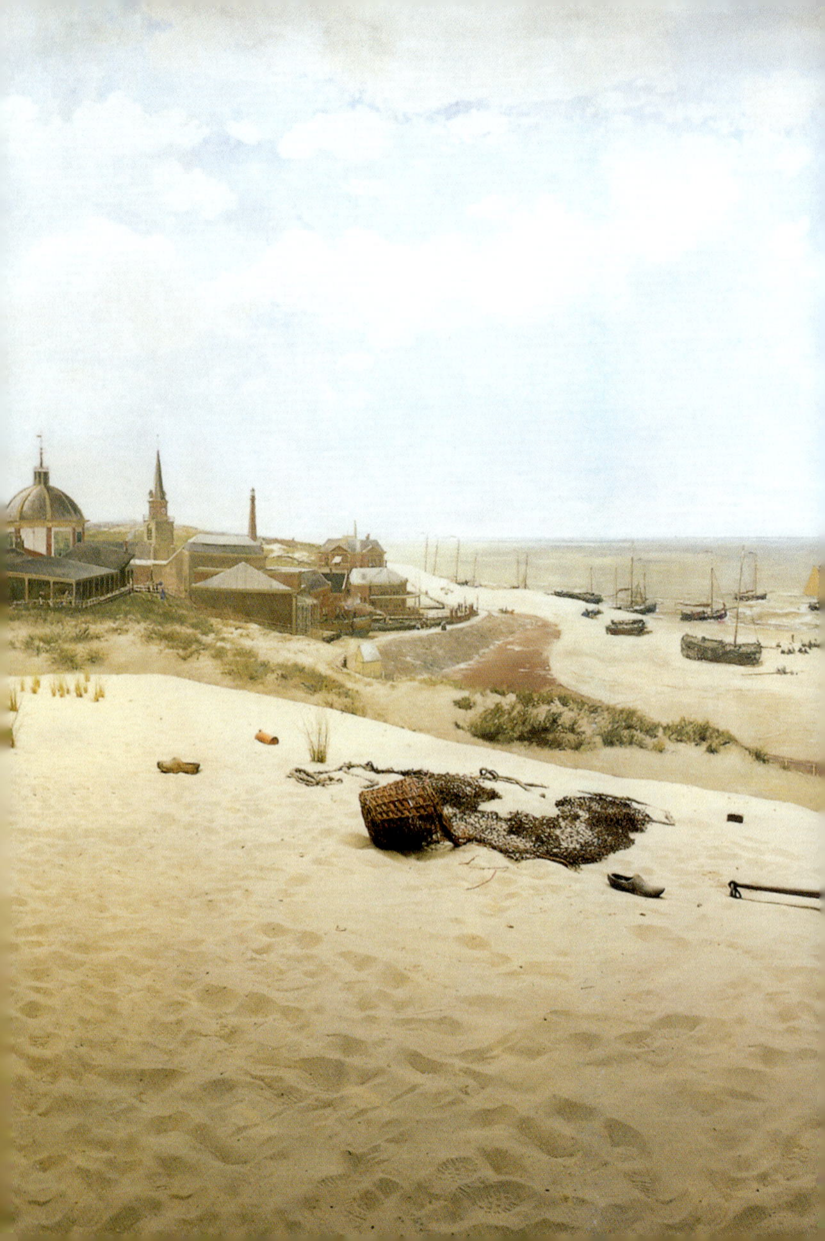

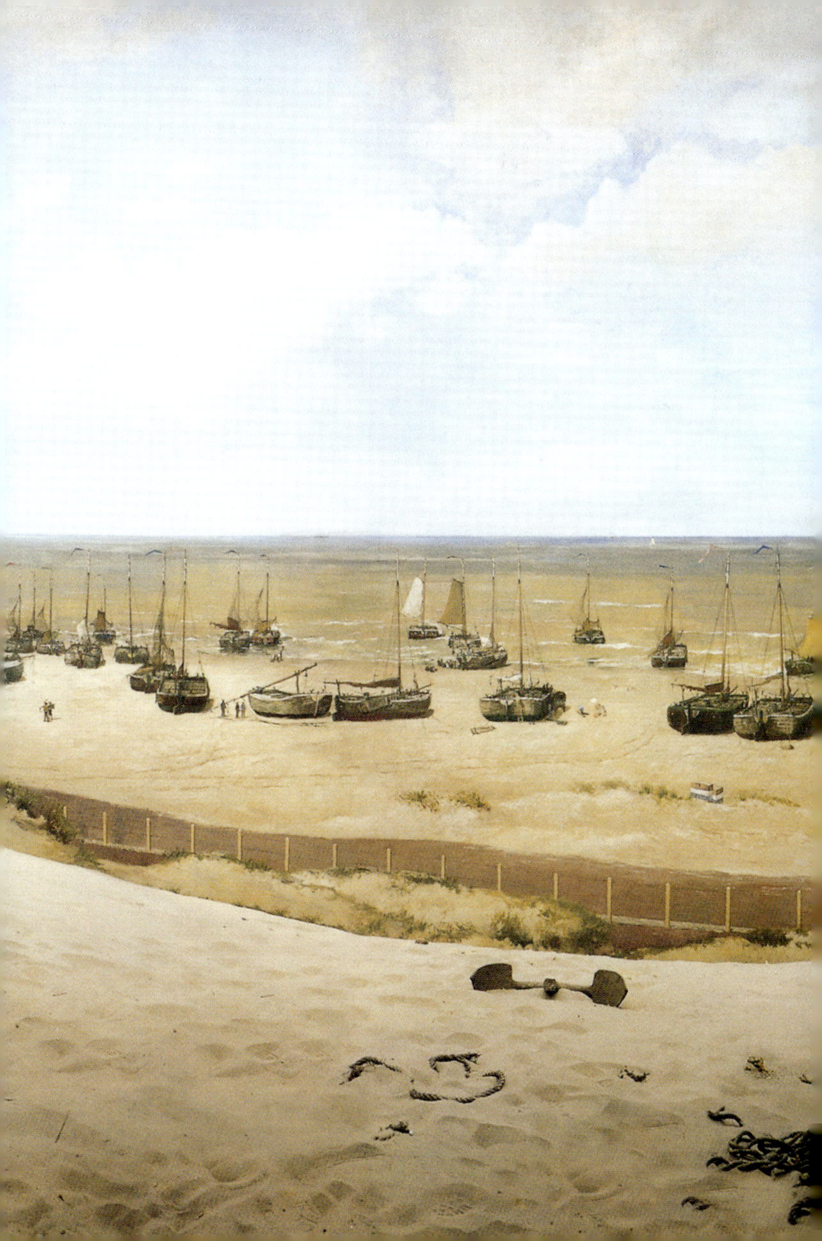

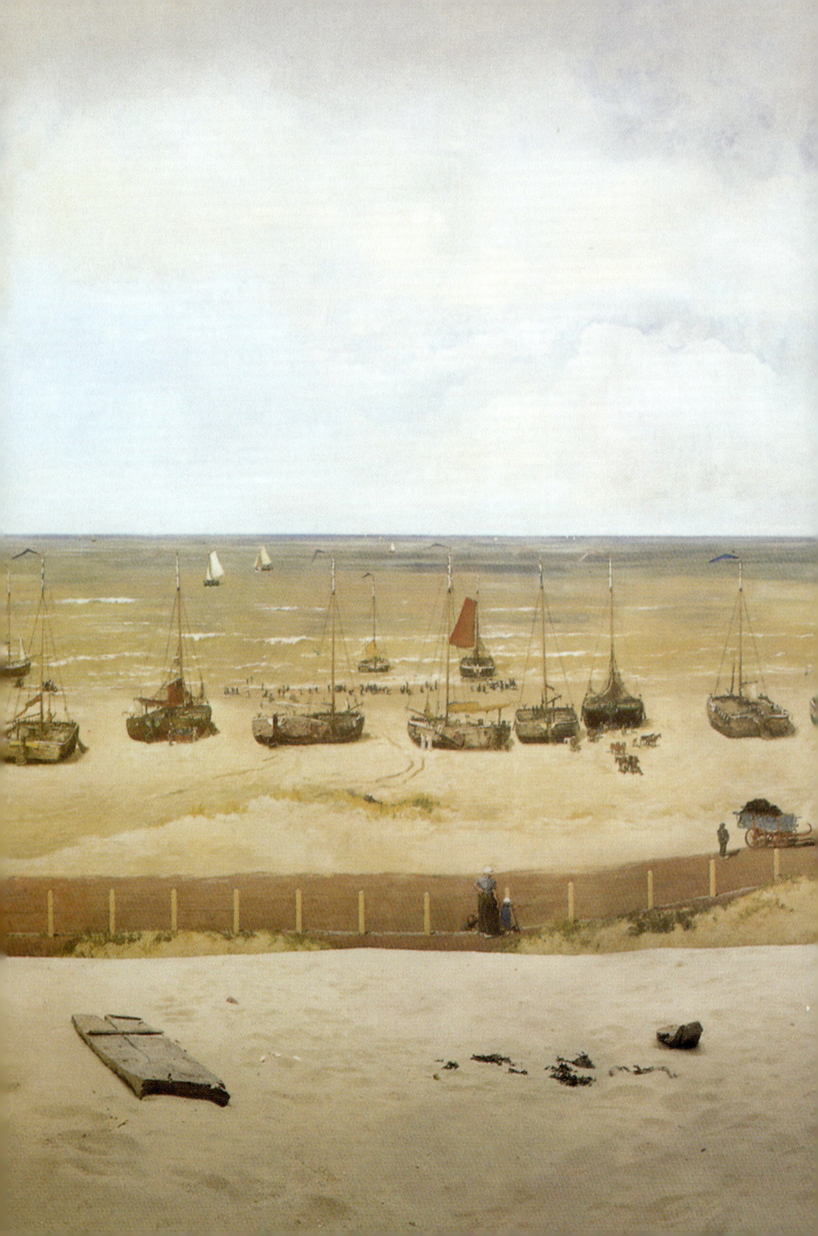

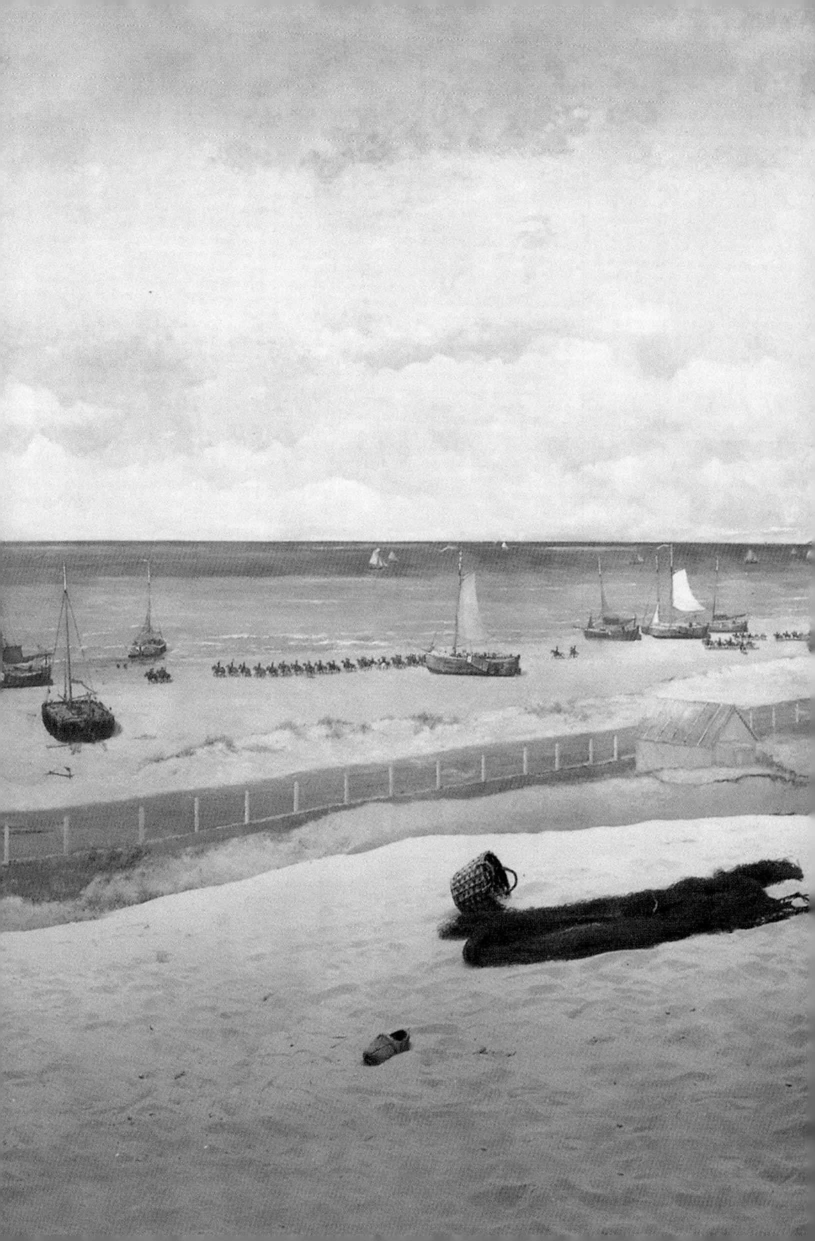

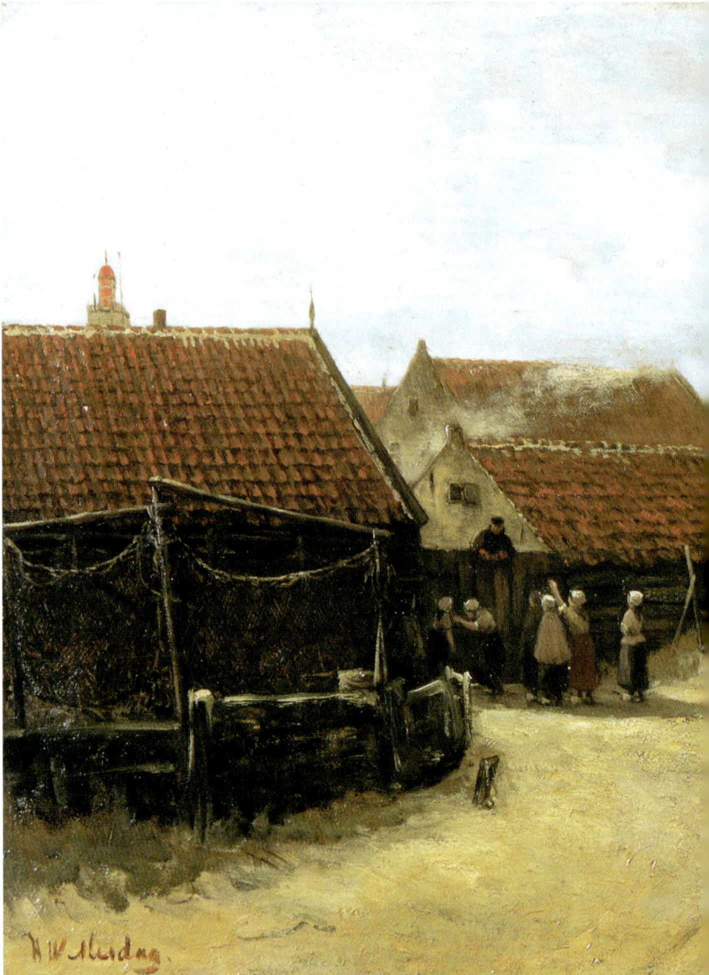

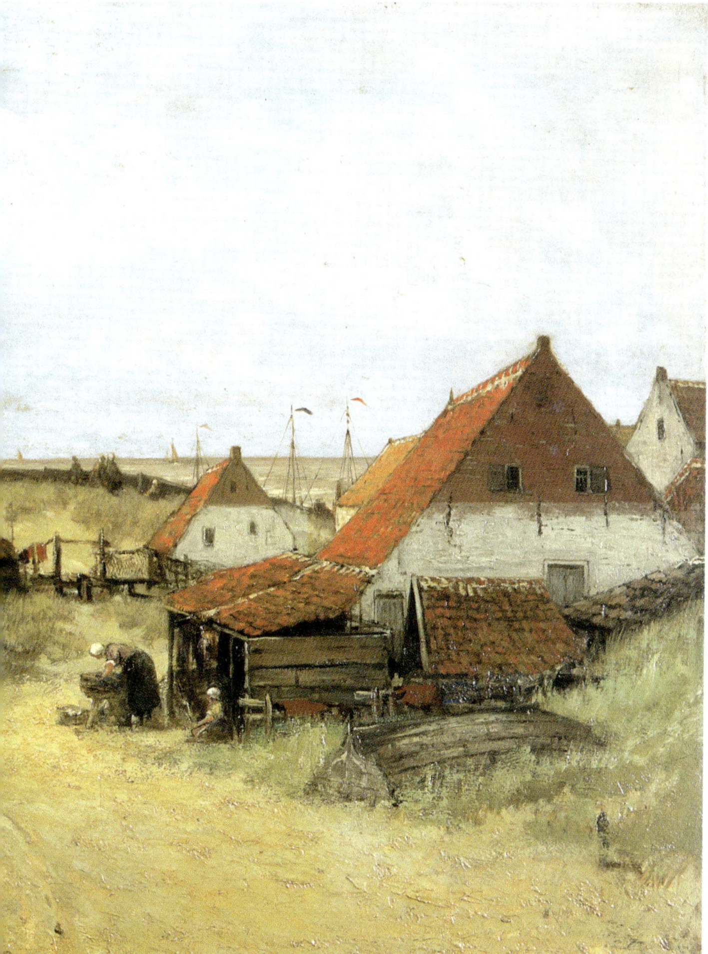

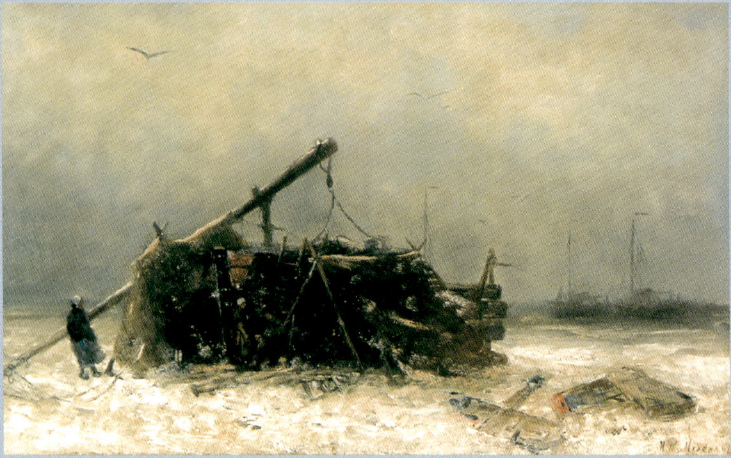

pp. 162-163:

H.W. Mesdag, *Neighbourhood by the lighthouse of Scheveningen,* n.d.
J. Poort collection, Wassenaar

H.W. Mesdag, *Repairs,* n.d.
J. Poort collection, Wassenaar

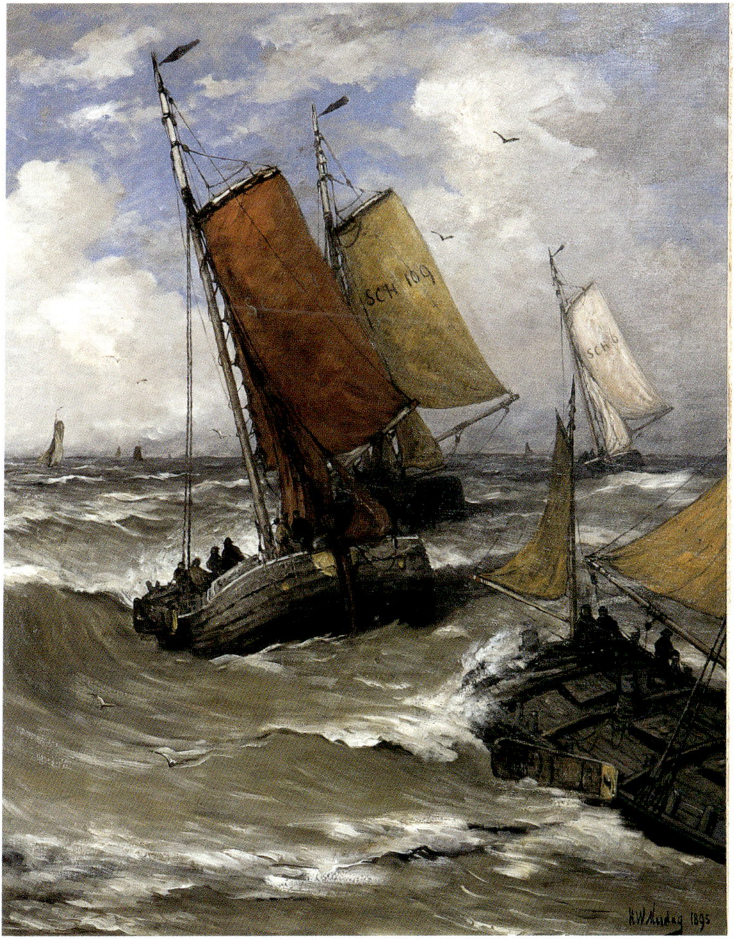

H.W. Mesdag, *Winding the anchor,* 1895
J. Poort collection, Wassenaar

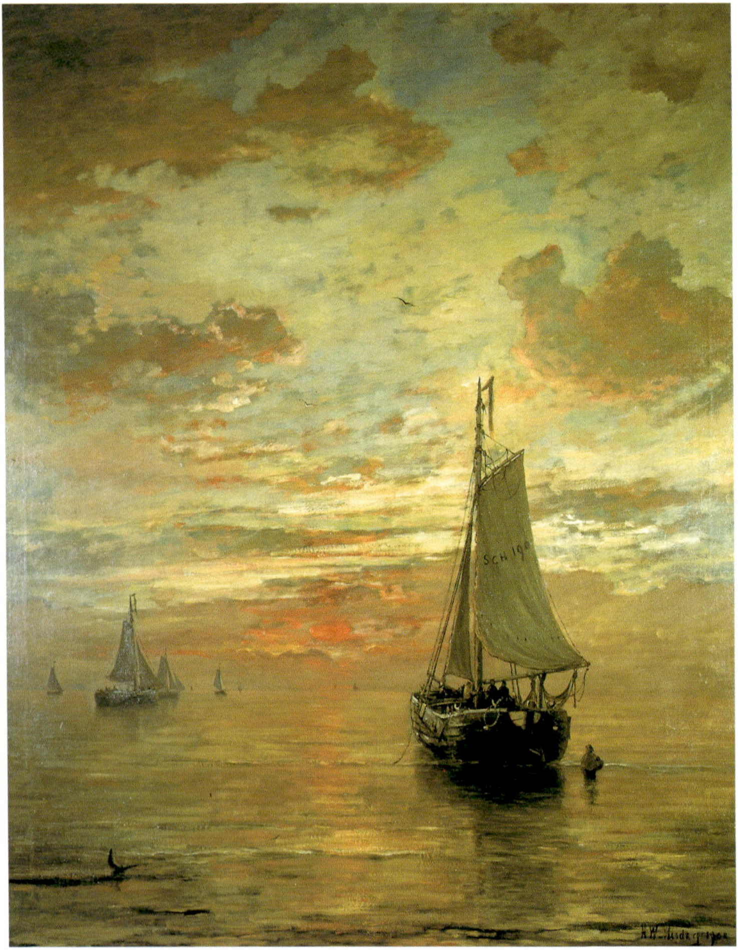

H.W. Mesdag, *Summer evening on the beach,* 1900
J. Poort collection, Wassenaar

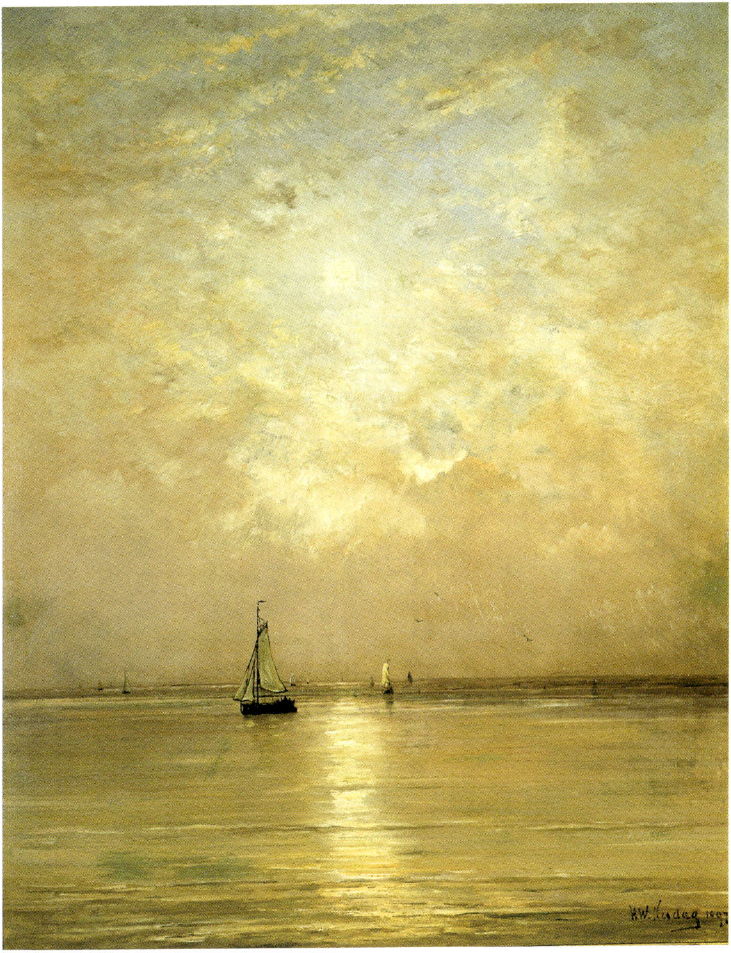

H.W. Mesdag, *Boats in the sunset,* 1897
J. Poort collection, Wassenaar

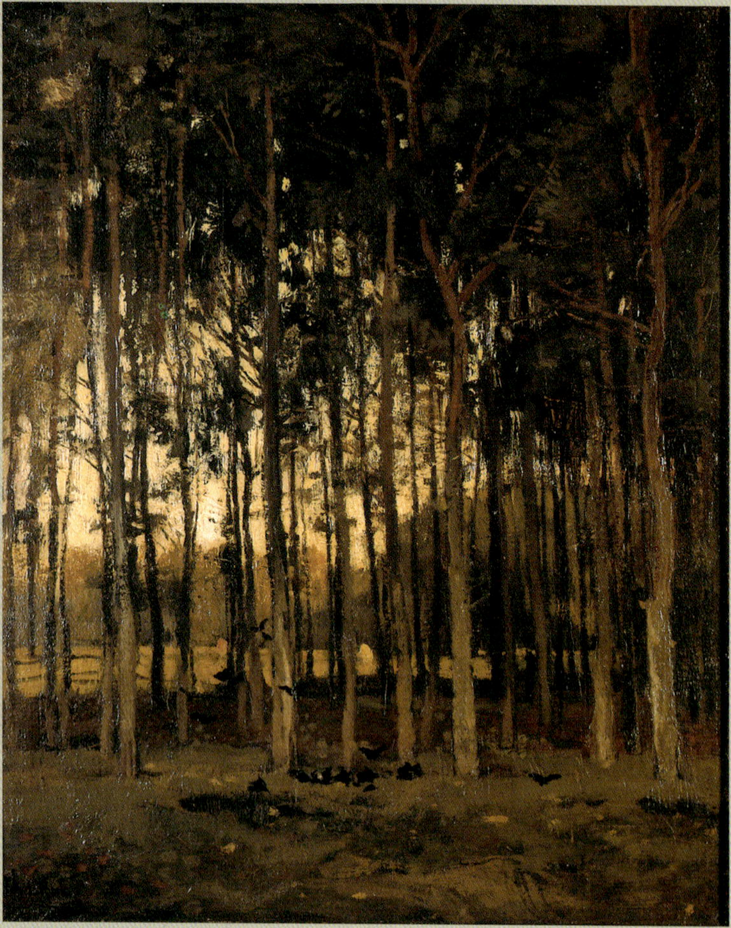

Théophile de Bock, *Wood landscape,* n.d.

AVANT-GARDE AND TRADITION

John Sillevis

The exhibition of works from the estate of Vincent van Gogh in May 1892 was greeted with surprise by The Hague's art-loving public. The exhibition had been organised by the recently founded Haagsche Kunstkring (Hague society of artists) and the works exhibited had been selected by Jan Toorop from the estate of Theo van Gogh, who had died six months after the death of Vincent. Theo's widow, Jo van Gogh-Bongers, had made it her cause to help Vincent's works gain greater recognition – she was also preparing the publication of his letters –, but she was anxious about the kind of reactions Vincent's works might elicit. Even Jan Veth, one of the progressive artists of the time, confessed that he initially had been shocked by 'the unbridled violence of a number of ugly Van Goghs.'[39] Jozef Israëls, who was present at the opening of the exhibition, complimented Jo van Gogh on the beauty of the work exhibited, his view notwithstanding that one could not paint the sun in Vincent's manner.[40]

The Haagsche Kunstkring came into being on 1 May 1891 in the Café Riche in The Hague's *Passage*, with Théophile de Bock, the organisation's first chairman, presiding. Among the founding members of the Kunstkring were Jan Toorop and writer Marcel Emants. Unlike Pulchri Studio, the Kunstkring was not exclusively devoted to painting, and already at its founding, the need was underscored for furthering 'the visual, literary and musical arts as well as the art industry,' and the collaboration between the practitioners of these branches of the arts.[41] In addition to the Van Gogh exhibition, the Kunstkring also organised the city's first Rodin exhibition.[42] Music, theatre, architecture, design, applied art, dance: they were all topics of discussion for the Kunstkring, and the wide range of events it organised made this society synonymous with The Hague's artistic avant-garde. Presided over by Mesdag as its high priest, 'Pulchri' had become the revered bulwark of the Hague School, now a bastion of the establishment. During his long chairmanship, 'Pulchri' had moved to its new exhibition rooms on the Lange Voorhout, where the first memorial exhibitions honouring deceased members of the School would also be held.

The Haagsche Kunstkring, originally an idea of Jan Toorop's, initiated contact with Brussels' Groupe des XX, and the enthusiasm among its members for pointillism, and subsequently symbolism, was great. Seemingly unfazed, the painters of the Hague School continued to work in their tried-and-true style, with little sign of innovation. At most, Jozef Israëls, J.H. Weissenbruch and Jacob Maris were able, in the final phase of their artistic careers, to demonstrate their ability to produce works of high quality and have some effect on the next generation of artists. The Hague School's success formula had, however, also attracted artists of a lower echelon: these repeated endlessly the group's best-selling themes in watered-down form, something which did not contribute positively to the reputation of the School or Pulchri Studio. A number of artists decided, in addition to their membership of 'Pulchri,' to also try their luck with the Kunstkring, and it was because of this link that some of the wind was taken out of the sails of the rivalry between the two societies. Of the members of either society, Jan Toorop entertained the largest number of international contacts in the art world, with ones in London,

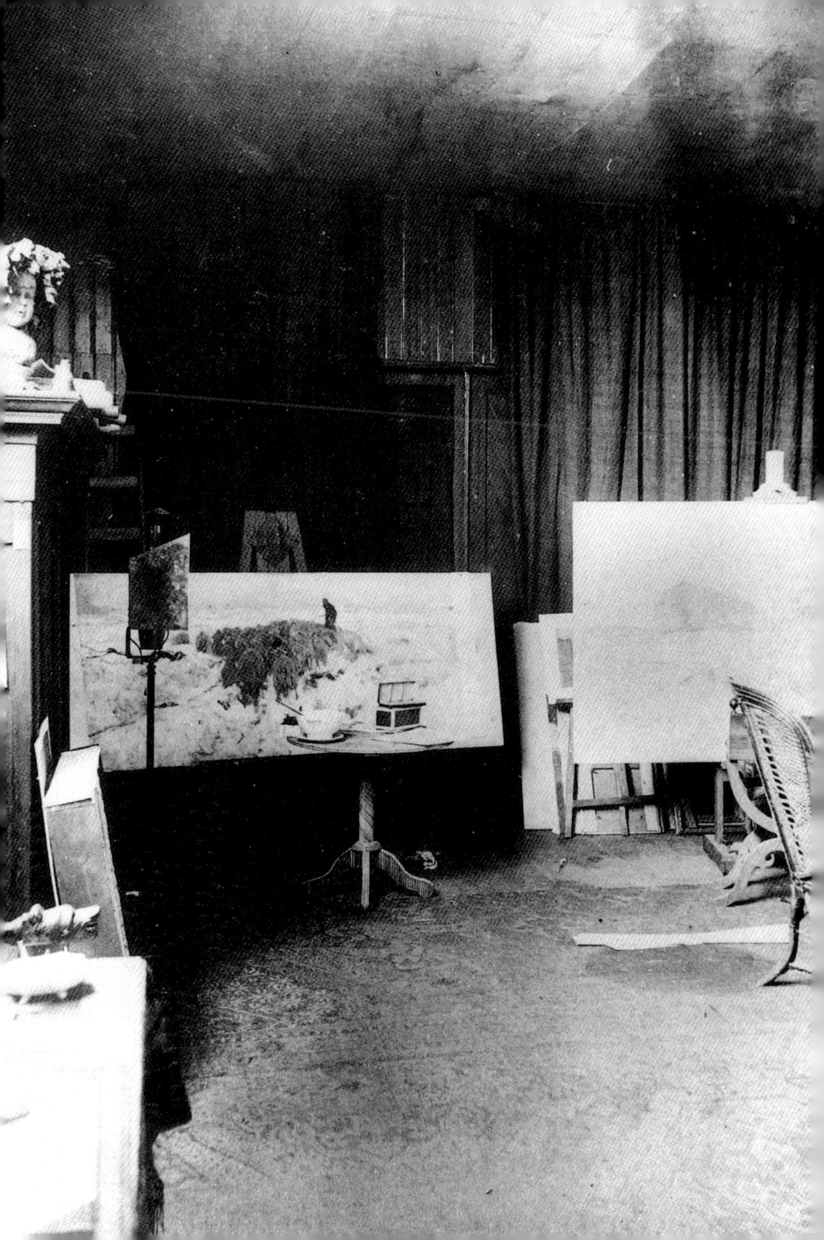

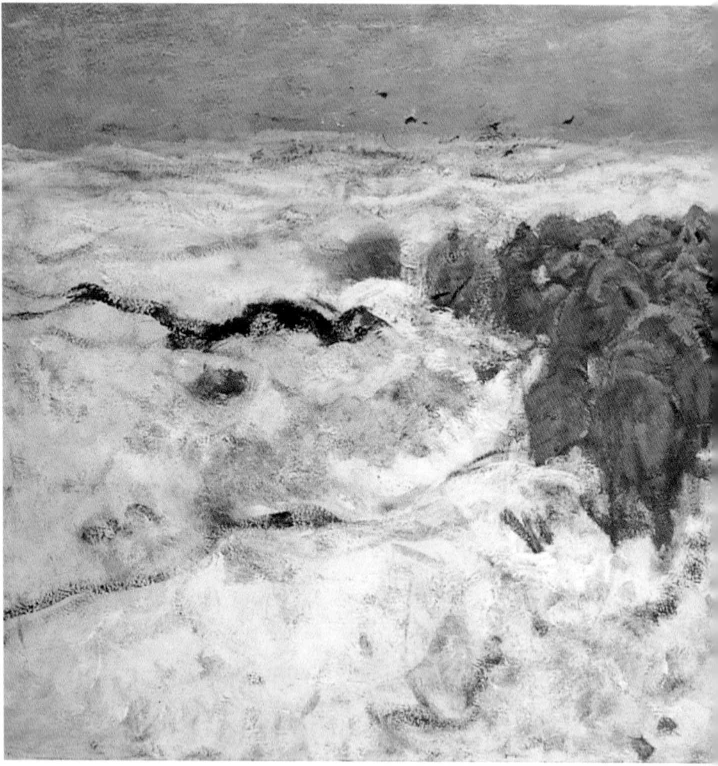

p. 171:

Anton Mauve's studio after his death in 1888, on the easel:
Flock of sheep in the snow, with shepherd

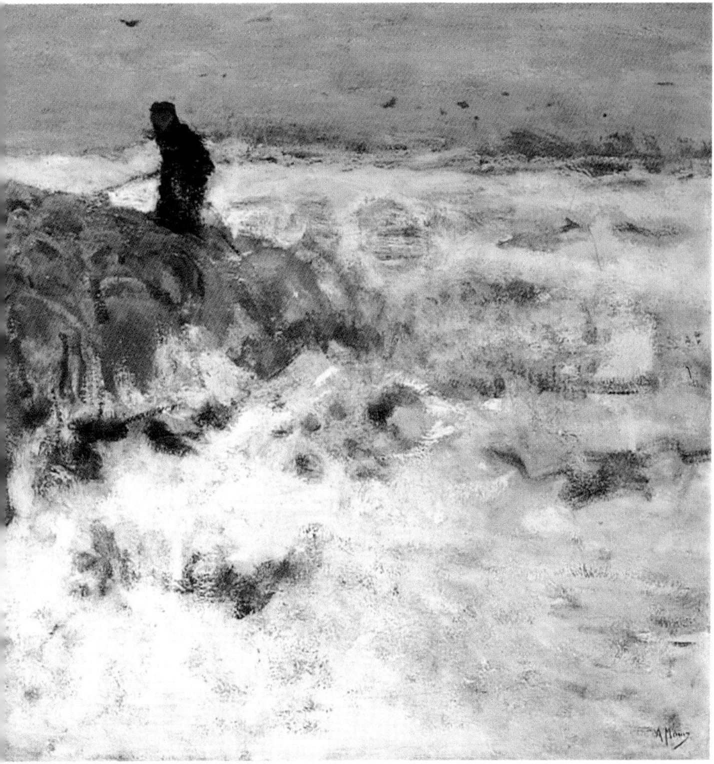

Anton Mauve, *Flock of sheep in the snow, with shepherd,* 1887

pp. 174-175:
Philip L.J.F. Sadée, *The share of the poor,* 1901

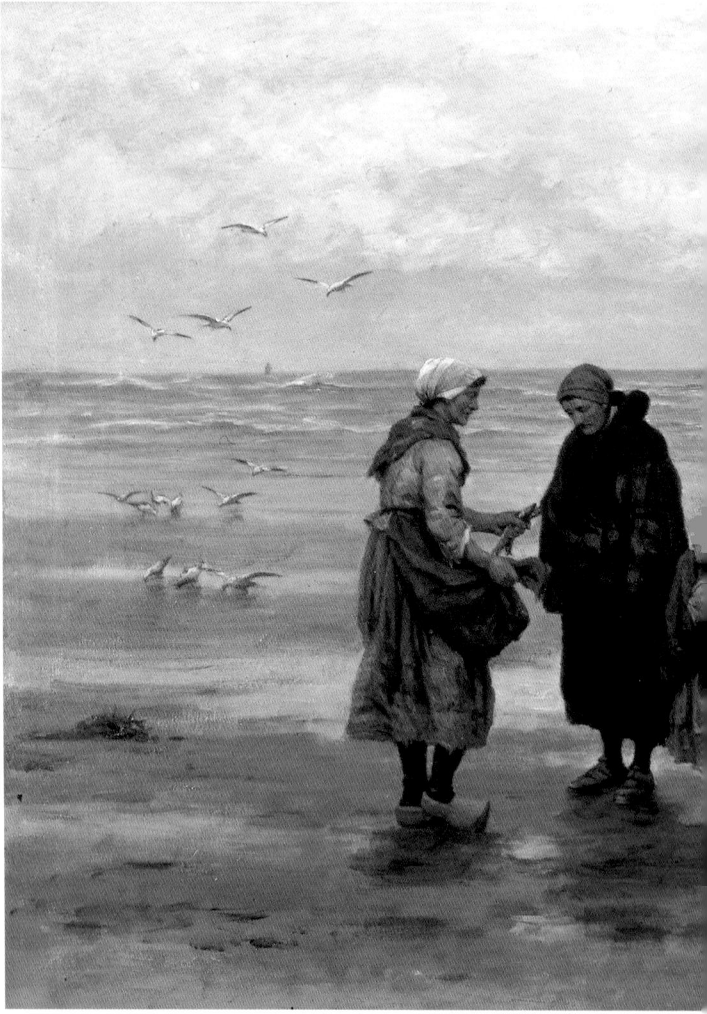

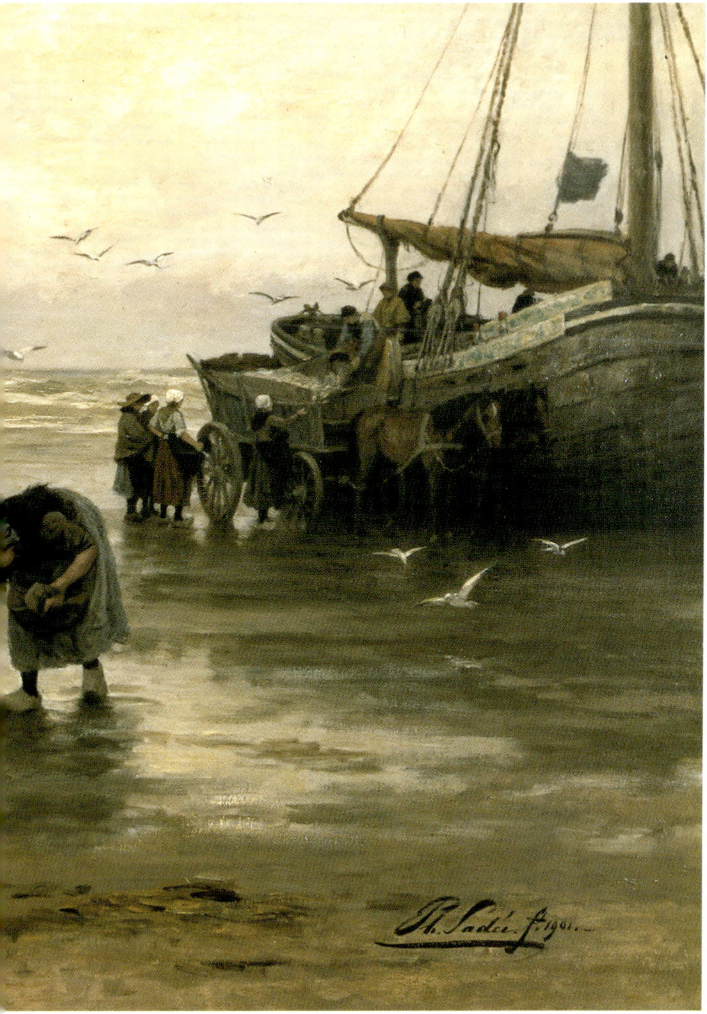
Ph. Sadée f. 1901.

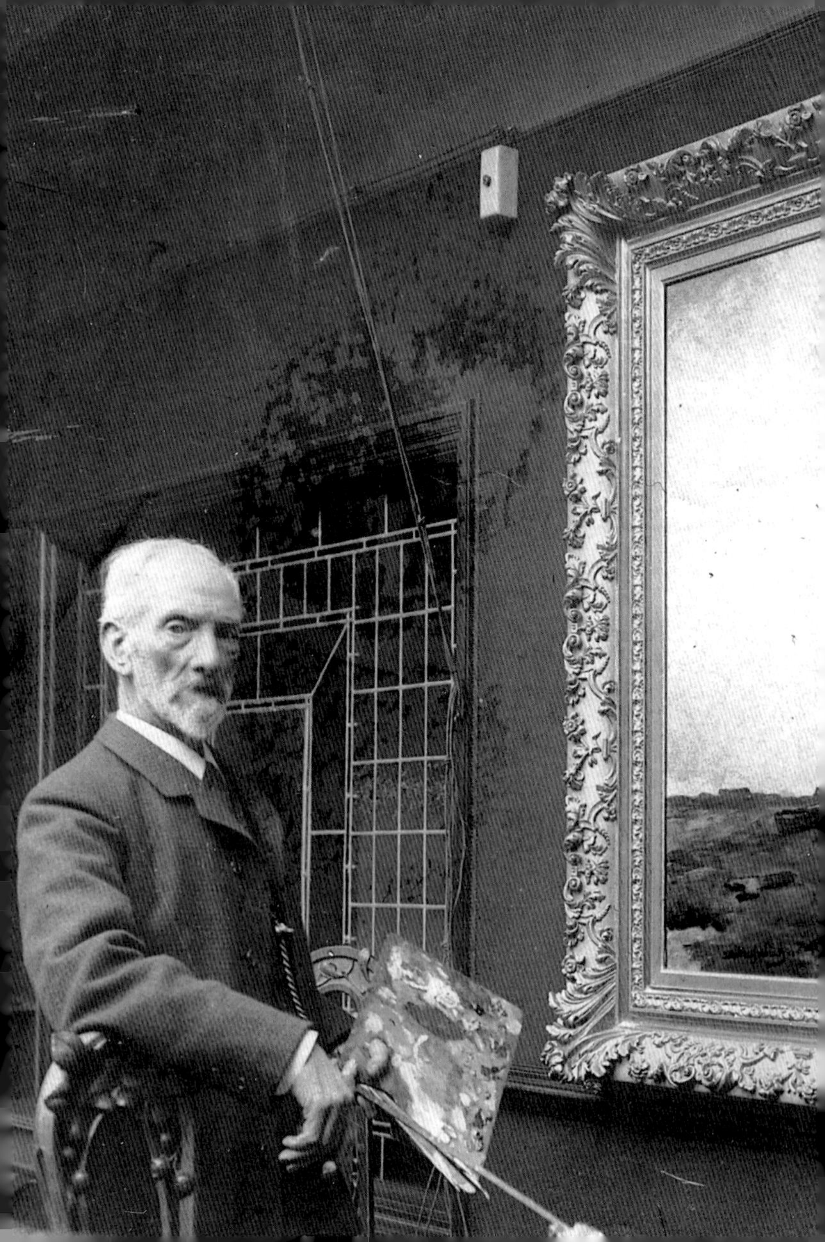

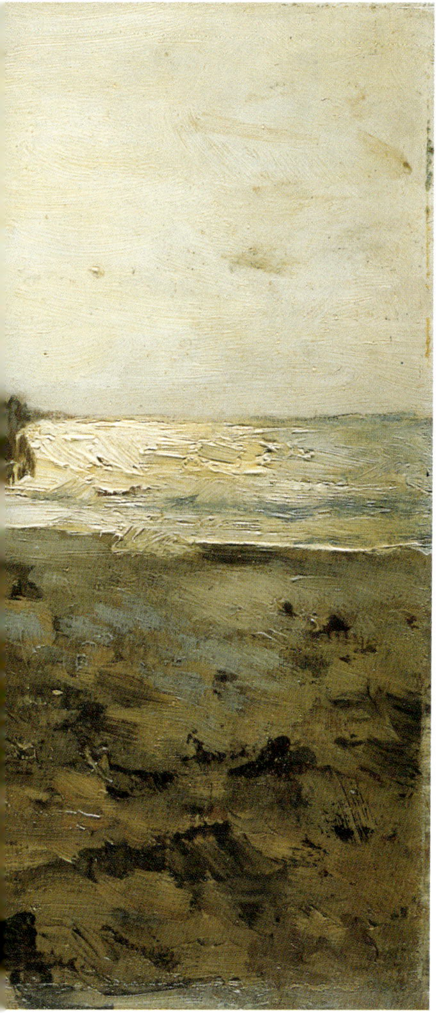

pp. 176-177:
J.H. Weissenbruch in front of his *Storm on the coast of Zeeland,* his submission to the 1900 World Exhibition in Paris

J.H. Weissenbruch,
Shellfish carts, ca. 1890

J.H. Weissenbruch, *Beach,* 1901

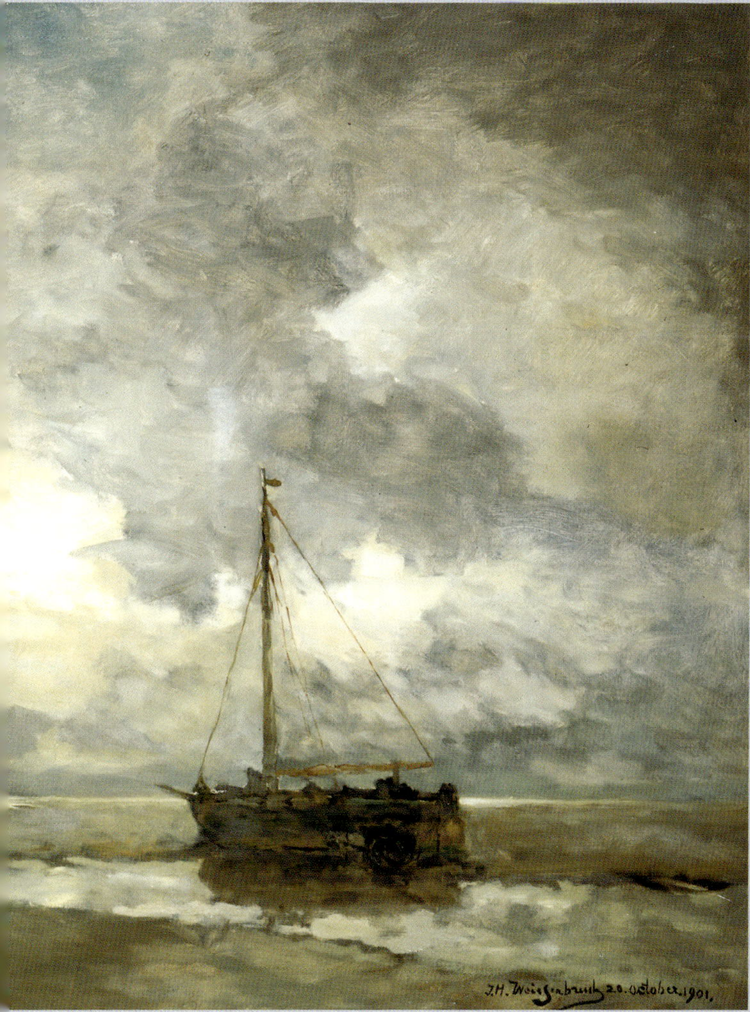
J.H. Weissenbruch 20. October 1901.

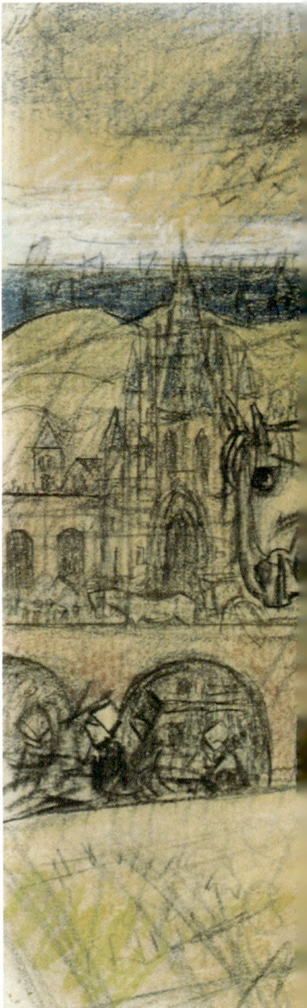

Jan Toorop, *Katwijk aan Zee,* 1890
(drawing)

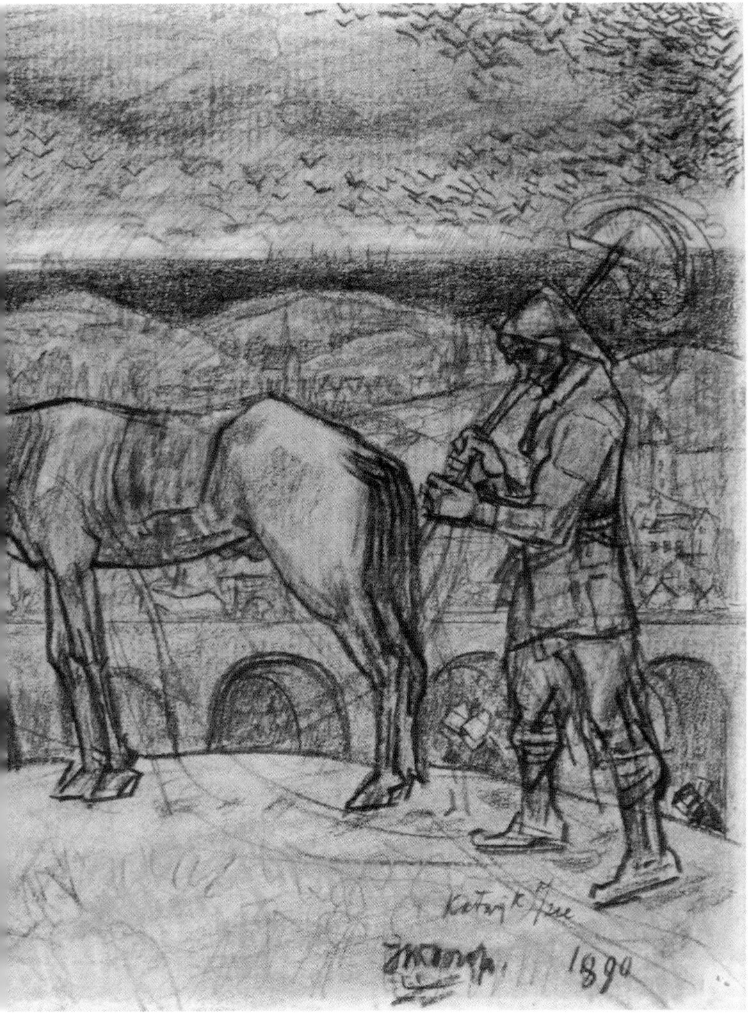

Brussels, Paris and Vienna, and reflected in his own work, modern concepts concerning visual and applied art. The rise of modernism, the art of the 20th century, was unstoppable.

The painters of the Hague School did not end up in obscurity – on the contrary. Jozef Israëls was honoured with a solo exhibition at the Venice Biennale, and following his death, with a memorial exhibition in the new Toledo Museum of Art (Ohio); Mesdag's funeral was a national event, and most of the group's other members became the recipients of numerous honours and awards. Following the Second World War, there was renewed interest in the School, especially spurred on by the publications of, and exhibitions organised by, Pieter Scheen and Jos de Gruyter. Anna Wagner did research on, among others, Matthijs Maris and Isaac Israëls, and in 1983 the Dutch Rijksdienst Beeldende Kunst (national agency for visual art) organised, in cooperation with The Hague's Gemeentemuseum, an exhibition devoted to the Hague School which was seen in Paris, London and The Hague. The international attention given the School increased greatly: exhibitions followed in Mannheim, Munich, Cincinnati, Budapest, Madrid and Vienna, and the stream of expositions and catalogues devoted to individual painters from the group continues without interruption. The Hague School shows no sign of having lost any of its expressive power.

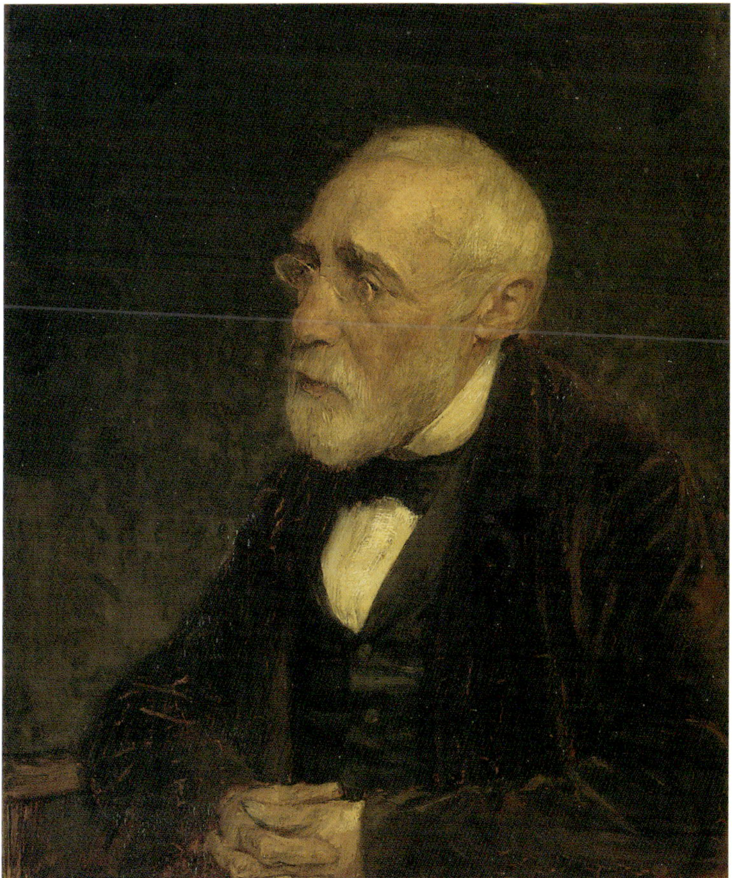

Jan Veth, *Portrait of Jozef Israëls,* n.d.

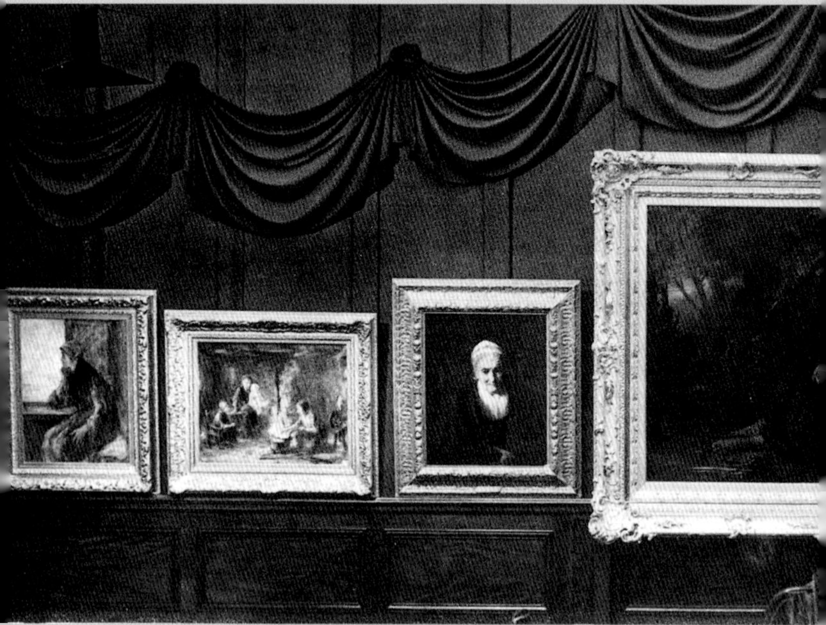

Wall from the exhibition in honour of Jozef Israëls at the Toledo Museum of Art (Ohio), 19

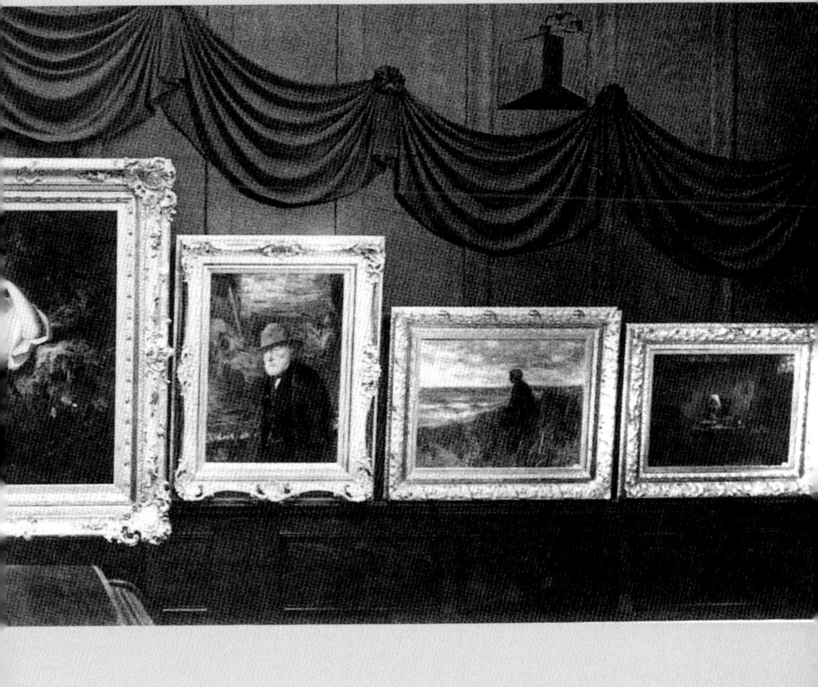

NOTES

1 A. Winkelbauer, 'Kunst für Künstler, Wien und die Haager Schule,' cat. exhib., *Van Gogh und die Haager Schule*, Kunstforum Wien 1996, pp. 319–350.

2 R. Ménard, 'Exposition de Vienne,' *Gazette des Beaux-Arts* VIII (1873), pp. 203-206.

3 Ibid. (note 2), p. 203.

4 Duranty, 'Exposition universelle, Les écoles étrangères de peinture,' *Gazette des Beaux-Arts*, XVIII (1878), pp. 166, 167.

5 J. van Santen Kolff, 'Een blik in de Hollandsche Schilderschool onzer dagen,' part IV, *De Banier, Tijdschrift van 'Het Jonge Holland'* I (1875), pp. 158-187.

6 M.H. Hurdalek, cat. exhib., *The Hague School, collecting in Canada at the Turn of the Century*, Art Gallery of Ontario, Toronto 1983, pp. 14, 15.

7 See: cat. exhib., *Dutch Drawings from the Age of Van Gogh*, Taft Museum, Cincinnati 1992, p. 3.

8 C. Dumas, 'Haagse School verzameld,' in: cat. exhib., *De Haagse School, Hollandse Meesters van de 19de eeuw*, Paris, London, The Hague 1983, pp. 125-136.

9 Th. Vignau-Wilberg, 'München und die Haager Schule,' in cat. exhib., *Die Haager Schule in München, Meisterwerke der holländischen Malerei des 19. Jahrhunderts aus dem Haager Gemeentemuseum und den Bayerischen Staatsgemäldesammlungen*, Munich 1989, pp. 383-412.

10 F. Pecht described the fourth Internationale Kunst-Ausstellung in *Kunst für Alle* III (1887/1888), p. 358 ff. See also: M. Bringmann, Friedrich Pecht (1814-1903), *Maßstäbe der deutschen Kunstkritik zwischen 1850 und 1900*, Berlin 1982. Pecht was clearly a member of the conservative camp.

11 J.J.Th. Sillevis, 'De gevestigde Haagse School (1885–1910), cat. exhib.: *De Haagse School, Hollandse meesters van de 19de eeuw*, Paris, London, The Hague 1983, pp. 89-100.

12 See: 'Gedachten over den tegenwoordigen toestand der Beeldende Kunsten in ons Vaderland, bij het zien der Haagsche tentoonstelling van kunstwerken in 1833,' *Algemene Konst- en Letterbode*, dl. II (1833), pp. 229, quoted in: J.J.Th. Sillevis, 'Wijnand Nuyen,' cat. exhib., *Wijnand Nuyen, 1813-1839, Romantische werken*, Haags Gemeentemuseum, The Hague 1977, pp. 9-30.

13 Cat. exhib., *Schilderijen en aquarellen door J.H. Weissenbruch*, Kunsthandel Buffa & Zn., Amsterdam 1899. Includes an interview with the artist (unpaged).

14 A. Hoogenboom, *De stand des Kunstenaars, De positie van kunstschilders in Nederland in de eerste helft van de negentiende eeuw*, Leiden 1993, p. 103.

15 V. Hefting, *Schilders in Oosterbeek 1840-1870*, Zutphen 1981; J. Wesselink, *Schilders van den Veluwezoom,* Amsterdam 1946.

16 Letter from Gerard Bilders to Jan Kneppelhout, dated: Amsterdam, 10 July 1860. See: J. Kneppelhout (ed.), *A.G. Bilders, brieven en dagboek*, Leiden 1876, p. 153.

17 See: 'Tentoonstelling van schilder- en andere kunstwerken van Levende Meesters in Arti et Amicitiae,' *Algemeen Handelsblad*, 15 October 1863.
See: R. de Leeuw, 'Het hart geopend voor de schoonheden der natuur,' cat. exhib., *De Haagse School, Hollandse Meesters van de 19de eeuw*, Paris, London, The Hague 1983, pp. 51-76.

18 J.J.Th. Sillevis, J.H. Kraan, *De School van Barbizon, Franse Meesters van de 19de eeuw*, Ghent, The Hague, Paris 1985/86.

19 Letter from Gerard Bilders to Johannes Kneppelhout, dated: Amsterdam, 27 November 1859, in: J. Kneppelhout, op.cit. (note 16), pp. 115-117.

20 Letter from Johannes Kneppelhout to Gerard Bilders, dated: Leiden, 21 March 1860; in: J. Kneppelhout, op.cit. (note 16), p. 139.

21 See: J.H. Kraan, 'Erkenning en invloed in het buitenland,' in: cat. exhib., *De Haagse School, de collectie van het Haags Gemeentemuseum*, The Hague 1988, pp. 27-56; see also: J.H. Kraan 'Holland in zwang,' in: cat. exhib., *De Haagse School*, Paris, London, The Hague 1983 pp. 115-124; J.H. Kraan 'Als Holland Mode war, Deutsche Künstler und Holland im 19. Jahrhundert,' *Nachbarn* no. 31, Bonn 1985.

22 D. Dekkers, 'Goupil en de internationale verspreiding van Nederlandse eigentijdse kunst,' *Jong Holland* no. 4, year of publication 11 (1995), pp. 22-36.

23 C. Stolwijk, op.cit., p. 188.

24 J.J.Th. Sillevis, cat. exhib., *De School van Barbizon, Franse meesters van de 19de eeuw*, Ghent, The Hague, Paris 1985/86, p. 49.

25 Ch. Dumas, 'Haagse School verzameld,' in: cat. exhib., *De Haagse School*, Paris, London, The Hague, 1983, pp. 125-136.

26 See: J.J.Th. Sillevis, 'Lettres de Jozef Israëls à Arnold et Tripp, marchands de tableaux,' *Archives de l'art français*, part XXIX (1988), pp. 141-162.

27 Letter from Jozef Israëls to Arnold & Tripp, dated: The Hague, 1 December 1890; in: op.cit., (note 26), p. 159.

28 *Tentoonstelling van kunstwerken van levende meesters te Amsterdam*, 1892 cat. no. 200; now: Rijksmuseum Amsterdam inv. no. A2601.

29 A. Wagner, *Isaac Israëls*, Venlo 1985, p. 22; R. Bergsma, P. Hefting, *George Hendrik Breitner, schilderijen, tekeningen, foto's*, Bussum 1994, pp. 8–29. Breitner made this statement in a letter dated 28 March 1882.

30 H. van Crimpen and M. Berends-Albert (ed.), *De Brieven van Vincent van Gogh*, 4 parts. The Hague 1990, letter 294.

31 Ibid. (note 31), letter 293. See also: J. van Lindert, 'Scènes uit het alledaagse volksleven' in: cat. exhib., *Van Gogh en Den Haag*, The Hague/Zwolle 1990, pp. 118-145.

32 Ibid. (note 31), letter 363.

33 P.H. Hefting, 'Brieven van G.H. Breitner aan H.J. van der Weele,' *Nederlands Kunsthistorisch Jaarboek*, 27 (1976), p. 129.

34 Ibid. (note 31), letter 354.

35 Ibid. (note 31), letter 343.

36 See: R. Bionda, cat. exhib., *Willem de Zwart 1862-1931*, The Hague, Alkmaar, Laren 1984.

37 Ibid., letter 181.

38 See: J.J.Th. Sillevis, cat. exhib., *De Haagse School, de collectie van het Haags Gemeentemuseum*, The Hague 1988, cat. no. 21: Jozef Israëls *De Aardappeleters*, inv. no. 11-1949, pp. 138-141, with illustrations; D. Dekkers, cat. exhib., *Jozef Israëls 1824-1911*, Groningen/Amsterdam 2000, cat. no. 46: Jozef Israëls, *Boerengezin aan tafel*, private collection, pp. 222-224.

39 Jan Veth, in: *De Amsterdammer* 27 March 1892.

40 M. Op de Coul, 'De Van Gogh-tentoonstelling in de Haagsche Kunstkring,' cat. exhib., *Vincent van Gogh en Den Haag*, The Hague 1990, pp. 166-169.

41 E. Fernhout, H. Mühl, J. Verstegen, *De Haagse Bohème op zoek naar Europa, Honderd jaar Haagse Kunstkring*, The Hague 1992, p. 28.

42 J.J.Th. Sillevis, 'Rodin in Nederland,' cat. exhib., *Rodin*, The Hague/Laren 1995.

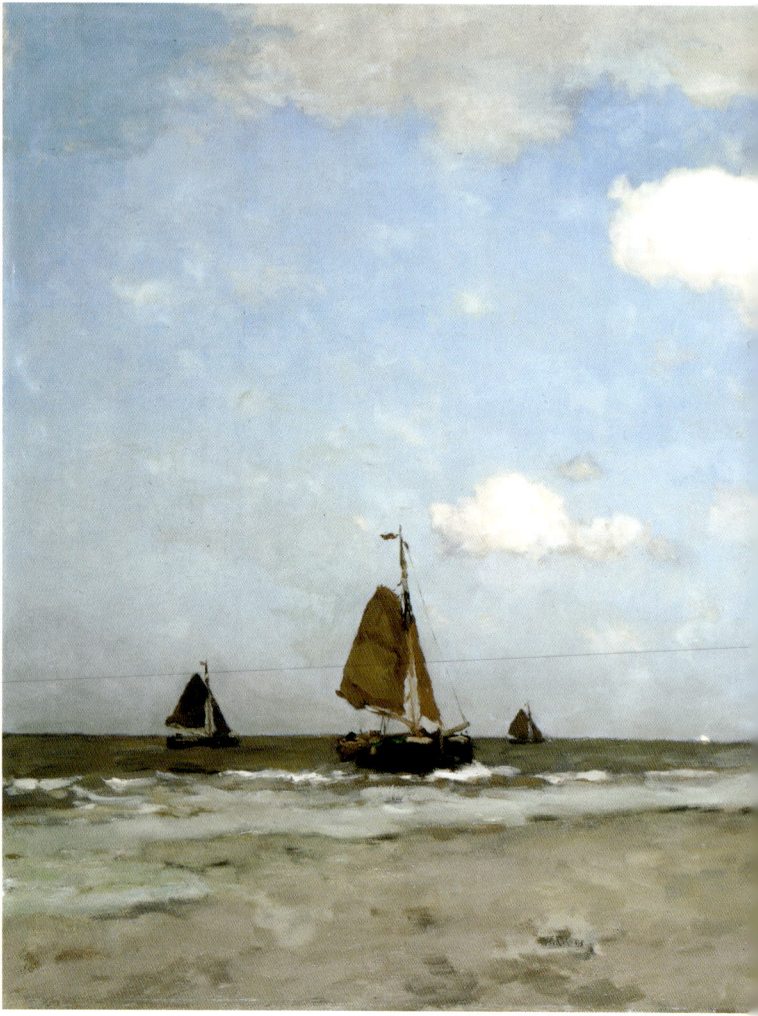

J.H. Weissenbruch,
Beach, 1887

pp. 192–193:
Willem Tholen,
Skating in the Hague Woods, 1891

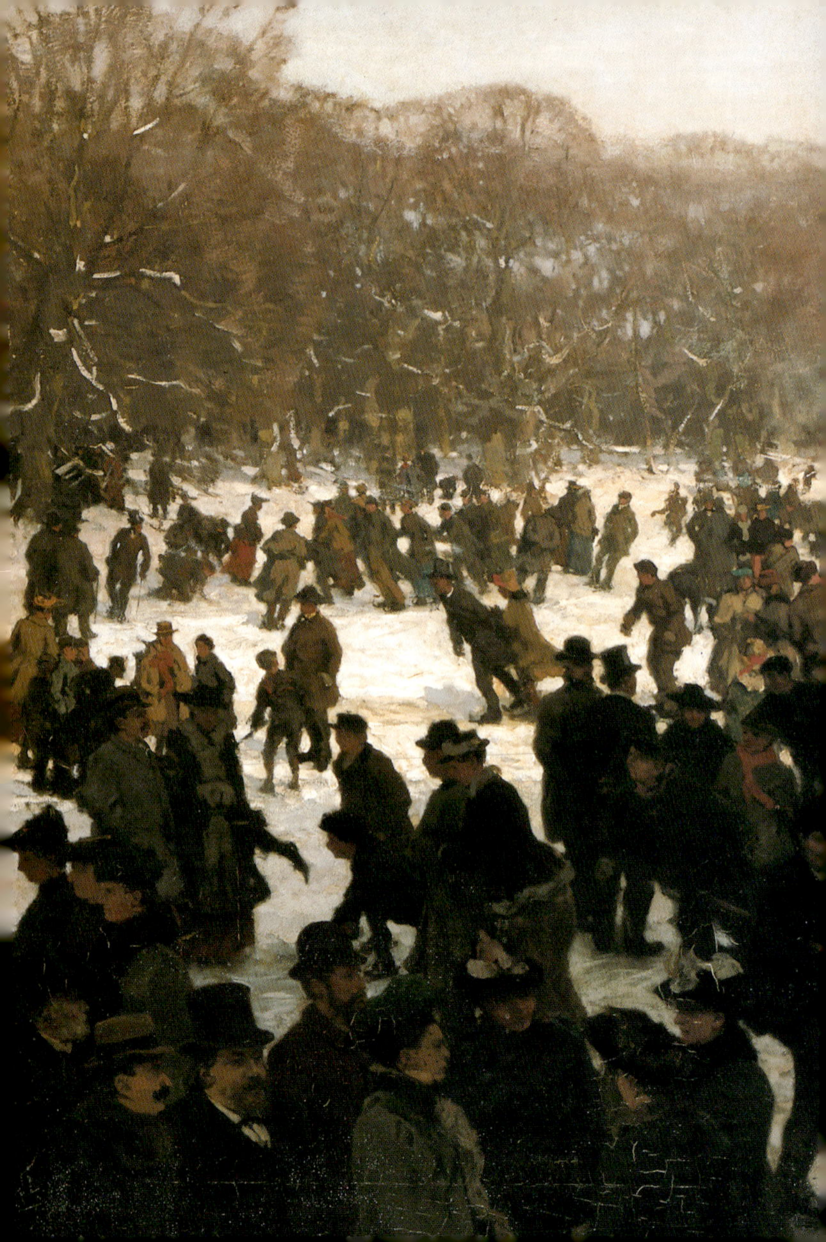

BIOGRAPHIES

Anne Tabak

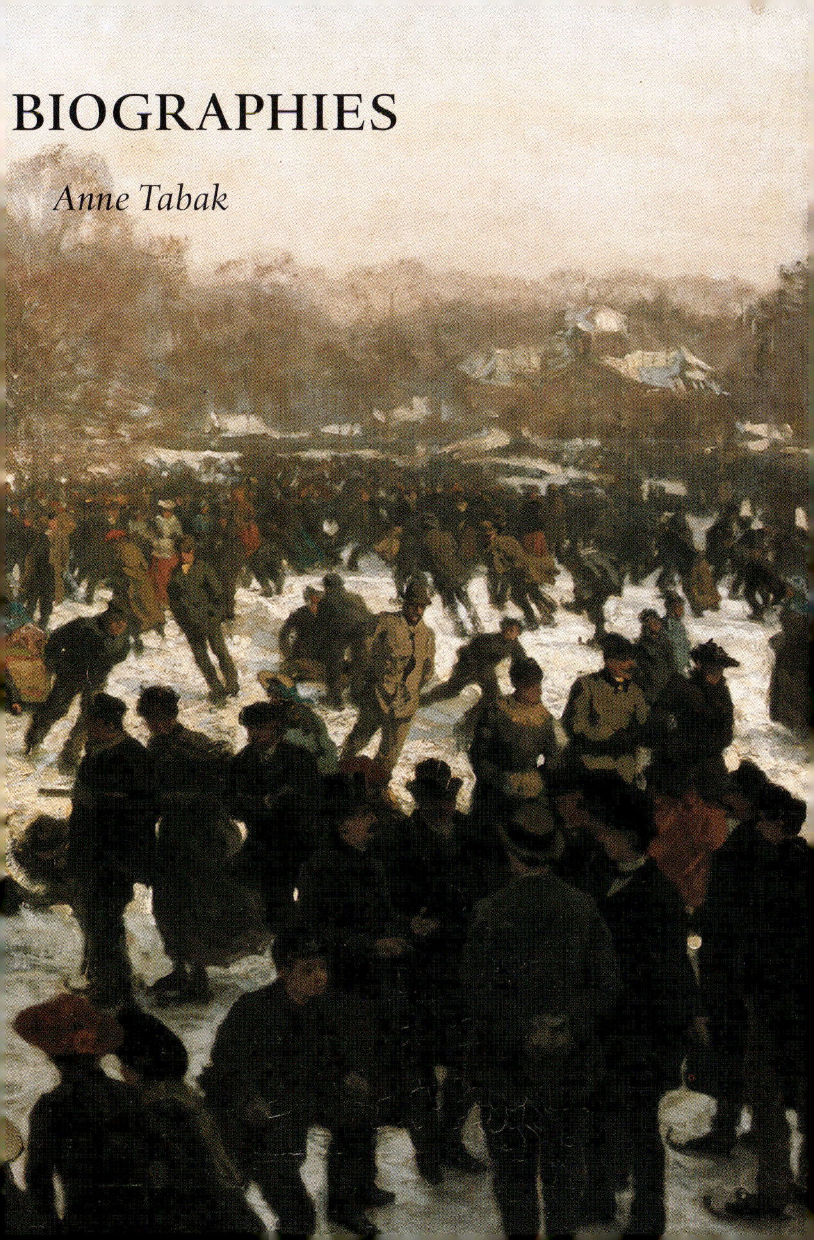

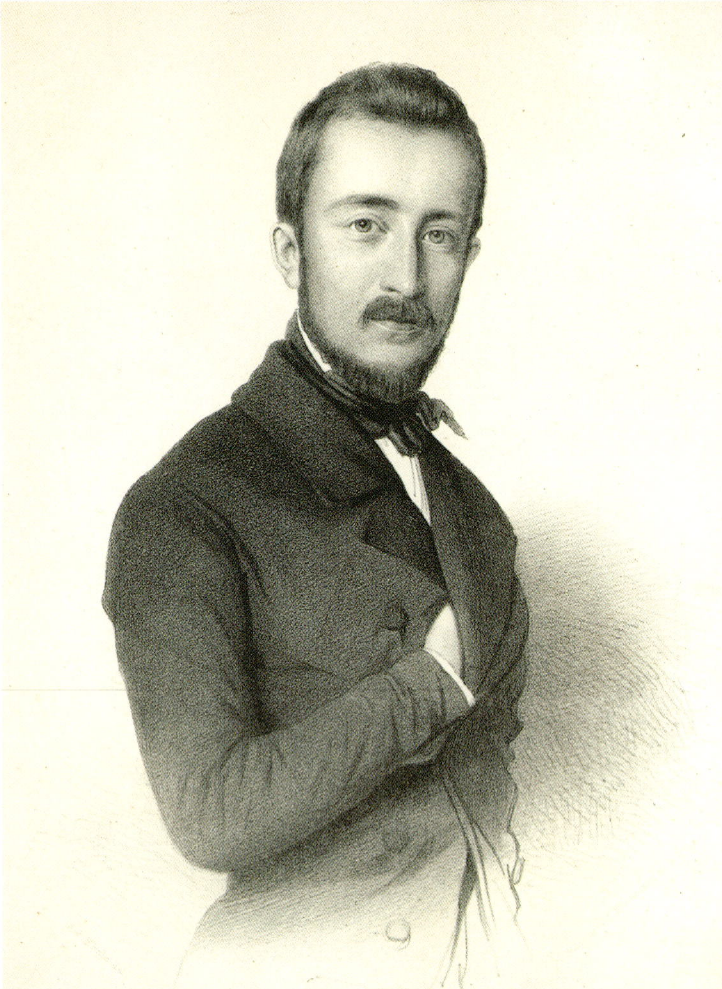

Johannes Bosboom

(1817-1891)

Johannes Bosboom and his twin brother Nicolaas were born on 18 February 1817 in The Hague. Bosboom loved to draw, and when he was twelve this predilection received an extra impulse: the painter Bartholomeus van Hove became a neighbour of the Bosboom family, living on the Dunne Bierkade. Van Hove specialised in idyllic landscapes. When he was fourteen Bosboom exchanged his school bench for his neighbour's studio. Van Hove's son Huib and Sam Verveer were Bosboom's fellow students. Together they worked on the pieces of scenery that Van Hove created for the Royal Theatre in The Hague. In addition, Bosboom took lessons from 1831 to 1835 and again from 1839 to 1840 at the Haagsche Teekenacademie (Hague Academy of Art). Here he made the acquaintance of Antoine Waldorp and Wijnand Nuijen, who was somewhat older.

In 1833, when he was sixteen, Bosboom made his debut, submitting three city views of The Hague to the exhibition of Living Masters in The Hague. Two years later, on the advice of Nuijen, Bosboom, Sam Verveer (and possibly Antoine Waldorp) travelled to Utrecht, Nijmegen, Düsseldorf, Cologne and Coblenz. Bosboom incorporated his experiences from this trip in the watercolour 'View of the Mosel bridge at Coblenz', which was purchased by Andreas Schelfhout himself. Bosboom wrote that although Schelfhout became his confidante and friend from that date, he refused to become one of his students because he feared that Schelfhout would have had an overpowering influence on his development. In 1836 he started working in his own studio in his parents' home.

In 1836, Bosboom's participation in a contest by the 'Felix Meritis' society earned him a gold medal. He was to receive many more honours, both in his own country and abroad. In 1837, Bosboom stayed for a few weeks in Antwerp, and in 1839, he again travelled with Cornelis Kruseman to Paris and Rouen, following in the footsteps of Nuijen. He received a silver medal for 'The Paris quay and the cathedral at Rouen' at an exhibition in The Hague. He also painted a number of church interiors, a relatively traditional genre in which the seventeenth-century painters Pieter Saenredam and Emanuel De Witte served as important examples. Bosboom had a great deal of success with these pieces, and for the rest of his career he would repeatedly return to this theme, which was the one in which he would achieve his greatest fame.

Bosboom did not approach church interiors as religious spaces but rather as pictorial spaces. In this first period he mostly painted the rich interiors of churches in Brabant and Belgium. In his emphasis on spatial architecture, strengthened by the wing-like division of foreground, middle ground and background, the influence of theatrical decor is evident. His predilection for historical costumes and his use of eye-catchers such as chandeliers and banners as staffage are indications of this influence. For his spatial light effects, Bosboom was guided by the romantic approach of Wijnand Nuijen. Following Nuijen's style, Bosboom sought a way to infuse light into the church by means of an invisible light source and thus to bring out the mystical aura of the space. In using this method the linear, perspective rendering of the architecture is gradually relegated to the background.

In the summer of 1846, Anna Louisa Geertruida Toussaint from Alkmaar visited Bosboom in his studio. She was a celebrated writer of historical novels. In September Bosboom travelled to Alkmaar, creating many sketches in the Great or St. Lourens Church there. Toussaint and Bosboom met often, and from that time on became a couple. In 1851, they were married in the Great Church in Alkmaar. Bosboom would often paint the interior of this church.

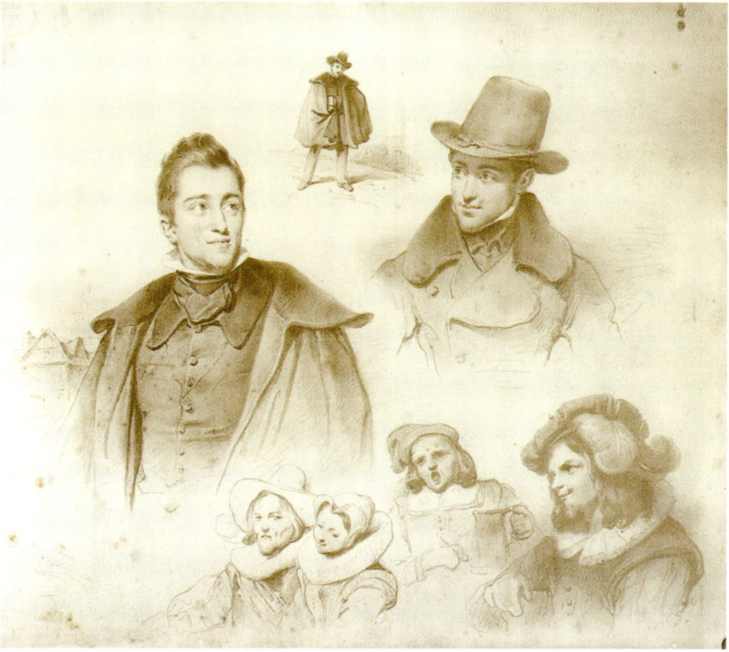

p. 194:
A.J. Ehnle, *Portrait of Johannes Bosboom,* n.d.
Collection of the Gemeentearchief, The Hague.

Cornelis Kruseman, sketch during a stay in France, including two portraits of Johannes Bosboom, 1839
RKD collection

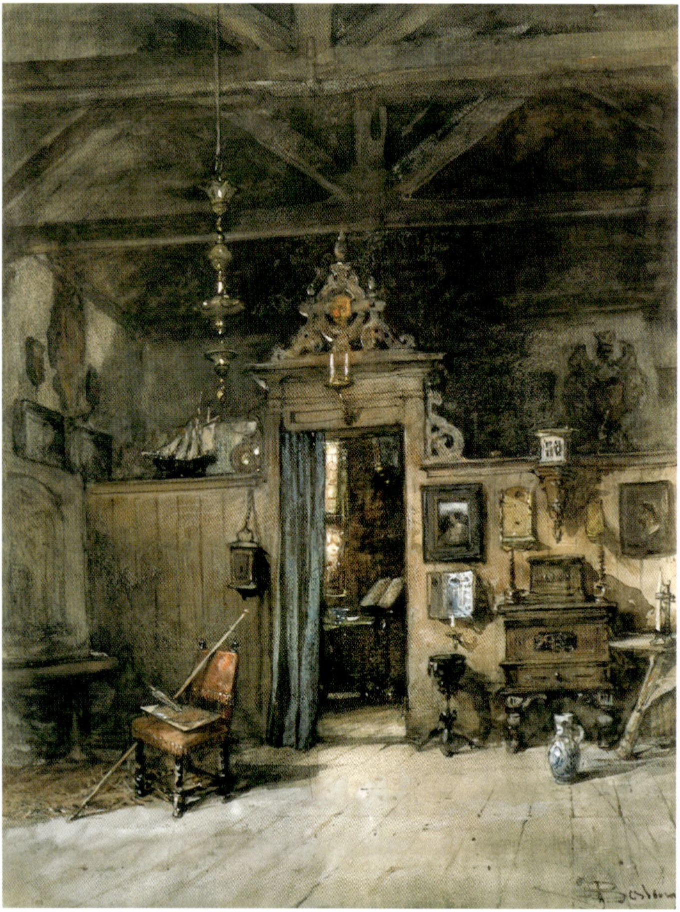

Johannes Bosboom, *The artist's studio on the Toussaintkade, The Hague,* n.d. (watercolour)

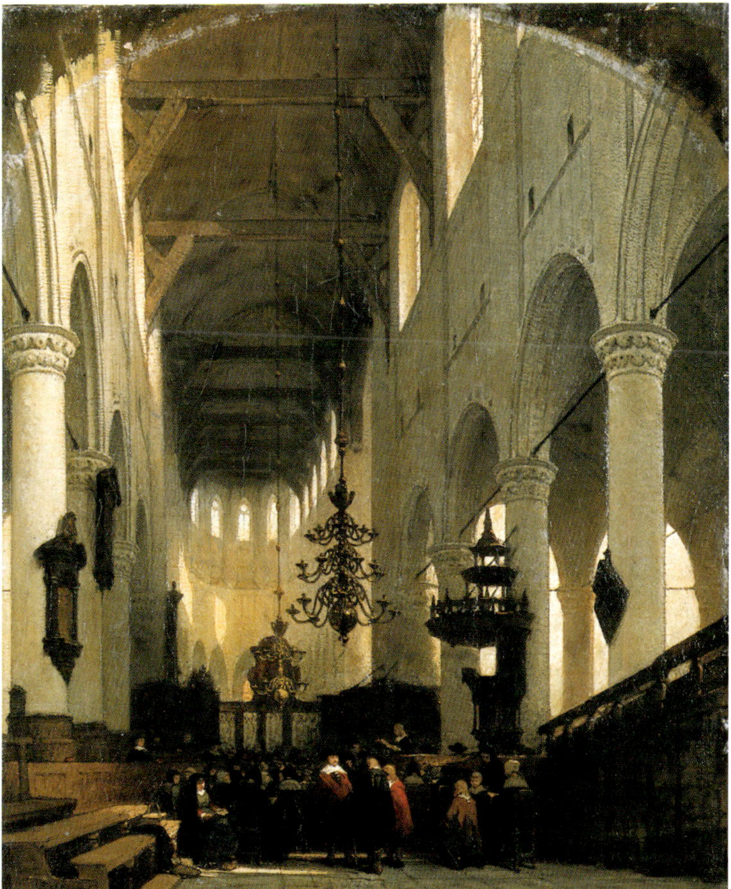

Johannes Bosboom, *The Pieterskerk in Leiden,* 1868

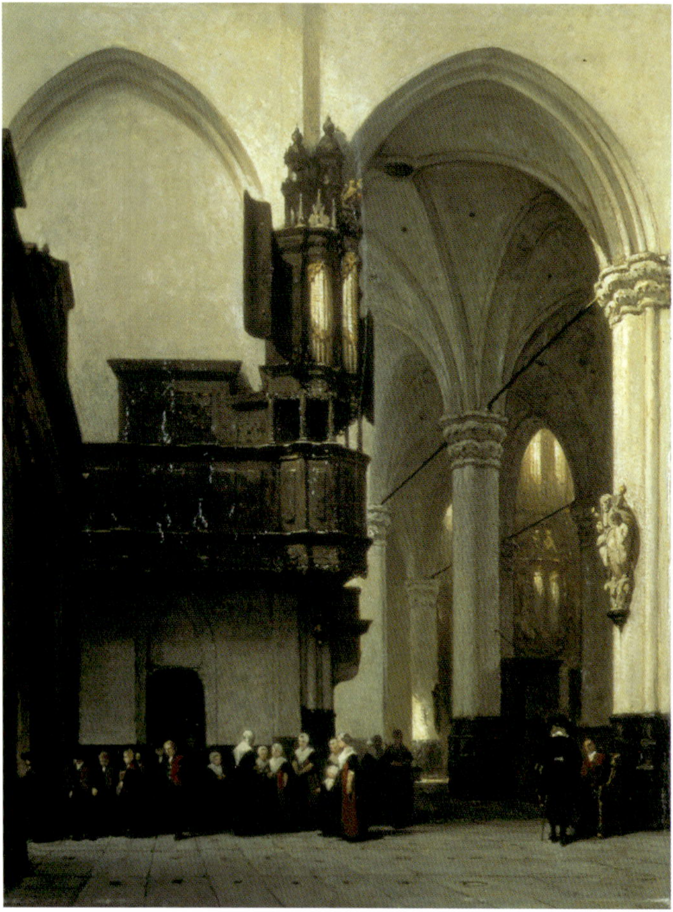

Johannes Bosboom, *The Nieuwe Kerk in Amsterdam,* ca. 1850-1855

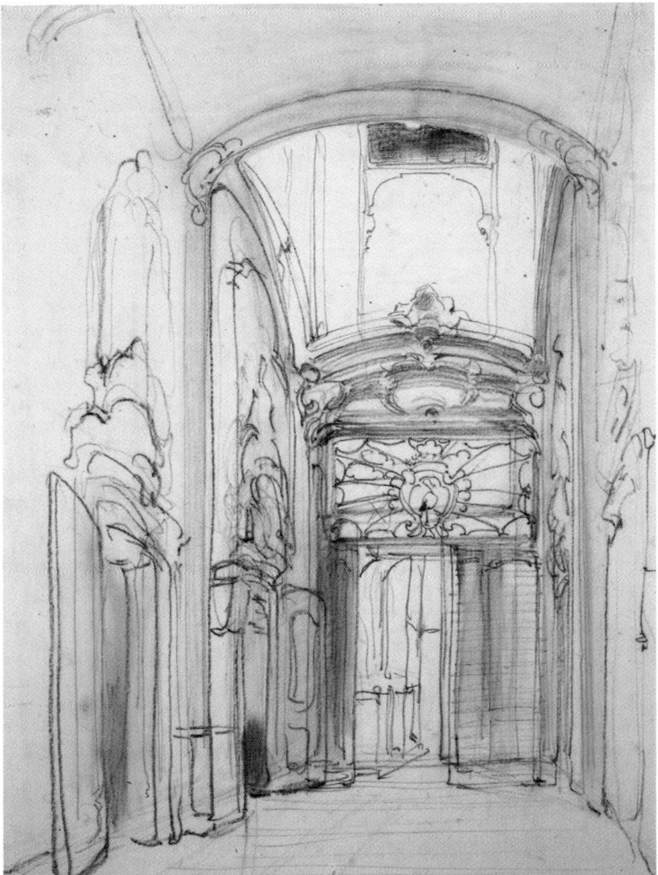

Johannes Bosboom, *Entry to the city hall on the Groenmarkt in The Hague,* n.d. (drawing)

Bosboom was not easily satisfied with his work, and often created several versions of an interior in these attempts, varying the staffage in each. From the many sketches of his churches, he not only created oil paintings but also studies in watercolours. He developed into an exceptionally capable watercolourist, and his watercolours gradually acquired a more individual character. In 1855, he became an honorary member of the Brussels Belgian Society of Watercolourists. From its very beginnings, he was a member of the Hollandsche Teekenmaatschappij (Dutch Drawing Society), which aimed at promoting the techniques of watercolour painting.

From 1862 to 1870, Bosboom became subject to varied and changeable moods. In 1862, his twin brother died, leaving a widow and seven young children. Bosboom was deeply affected by this and became depressed. Carel Ridder van Rappard, his friend from Utrecht, invited him to his summer house 'Heischoten' near Woudenberg. Van Rappard encouraged Bosboom to work outdoors in the surroundings of Woudenberg, Nieuw-Loosdrecht and Hilversum. Bosboom made drawings and watercolours of landscapes, farm yards, sheep barns, farm interiors and stables, expanding his subject matter from church interiors, the genre he had previously concentrated on. The following summer he and his wife were again guests of the Van Rappards. On this occasion they journeyed to Cleves. The cloister that Bosboom sketched there would often return in his work.

Shortly afterwards Geertruida Toussaint was taken ill with smallpox, which was then a deadly disease. As a result, Bosboom experienced such a severe crisis that he had to be treated by a neurologist. Against all expectations his wife survived, but it was only in 1865, after a trip together with his wife, that Bosboom was more or less back on his feet. They travelled to Huy (a small fortified town that Toussaint was using as a focus for a novel), Chaudfontaine (where Bosboom painted a watercolour of the chalk furnaces), and to Coblenz and Trier. From the sixties Bosboom's church compositions became more serious and oriented towards a specific element, such as a pulpit, choir screen, or organ. His use of paint became more direct and granular, with a lighter palette than before. He now chose as subjects cloisters and synagogues in Amsterdam and The Hague. Other themes that he often used were monks playing the organ and singing nuns.

Bosboom's choice of subject matter may seem to isolate him from the rest of the Hague School, but his search for ways to reproduce the spatial atmosphere through light, shadow and nuances of colour places him in the very mainstream of this group. In 1873, during his stay in Scheveningen, he painted many watercolours of town views, the dunes, the beach and the sea. It is possible that these watercolours encouraged Mesdag and Jacob Maris to concentrate further on the sea and the beach as subjects.

From 1877, when he moved into a new house and studio, he often painted himself as a scholar, sitting in his studio surrounded by historical relics. For many years Bosboom intensively collected antiques, which were a financial burden to him and his wife, much as the long time it sometimes took him to complete a painting and deliver it to the person who commissioned it.

In his sixties Bosboom travelled mainly within the Netherlands – to Groningen and Zuid-Laren (1876), Domburg (1878) and Hoorn (1880). We see these places in his later work as landscapes, city views, views of a town church and interiors. In 1886 his wife died, and shortly thereafter, his sister-in-law. The following year the seventy-year old painter was honoured with a one-man exhibition in Pulchri Studio. In 1890, he had a stroke and was confined to bed. After a long illness he died on 14 September 1891 in The Hague.

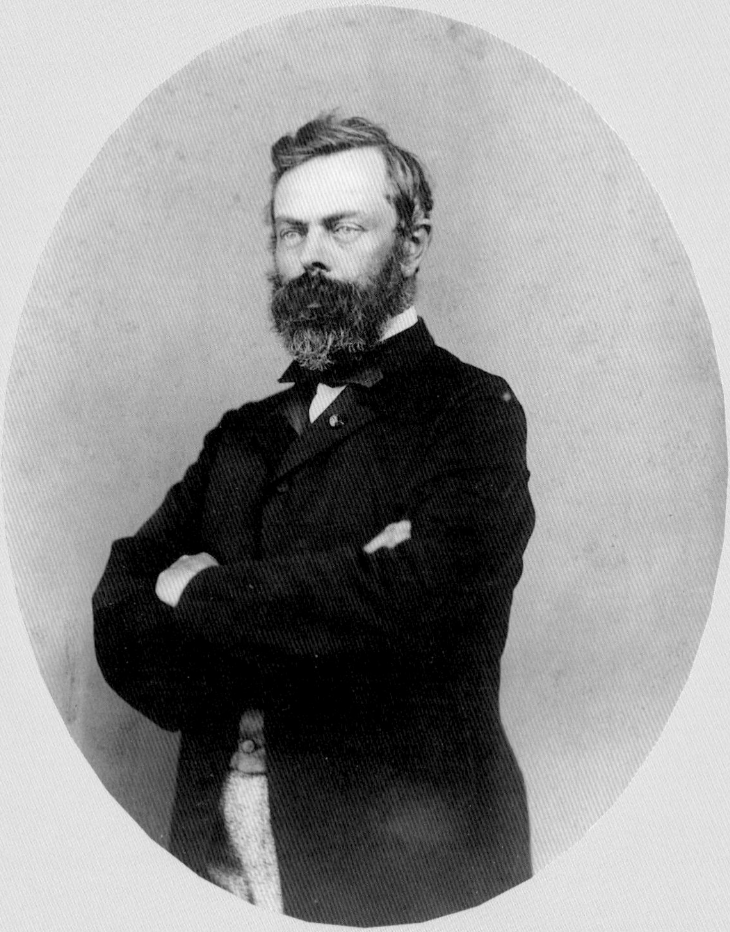

Photo-portrait
Willem Roelofs

Willem Roelofs

(1822-1897)

Willem Roelofs was born in Amsterdam on 10 March 1822. When he was about four years old, his family moved to Utrecht, where Roelofs' father had a tile factory. The family lived in a seventeenth-century country house called Rotsenburg. Even when he was very young Roelofs loved to draw; he also wrote poems and stories. He painted his first landscape at the age of fifteen, and took painting lessons from Abraham Hendrik de Winter, who, although he taught at a training course for cattle doctors, was also an amateur painter of landscapes, horses and cows. At about this time Roelofs exhibited his first paintings at the exhibition of Living Masters. It is likely that he visited The Hague in the summer of 1839, for it is from this period that his sketches of Scheveningen stem. In The Hague he was a student of Hendrikus van de Sande Bakhuyzen, a landscape and animal painter, and he was also registered at the Haagsche Teekenacademie (Hague Academy of Art). In the following year, Roelofs took a trip along the German Rhine together with his teacher, and returned to Utrecht afterwards. Although biographies often state that Roelofs only had lessons from Van de Sande Bakhuyzen for one year (from 1840 until 1841), it is possible that these lessons lasted longer, and Roelofs may have received advice and sketches to complete from Van de Sande Bakhuyzen while in Utrecht.

Roelofs worked in the surroundings of his parents' home. He took another trip to Germany in this period, this time including Gelderland as well. In 1846 he is back in The Hague, where he created studies of trees in the woods of Scheveningen. In the winter of 1847, he is one of the founders of the artists' society Pulchri Studio as were many of his

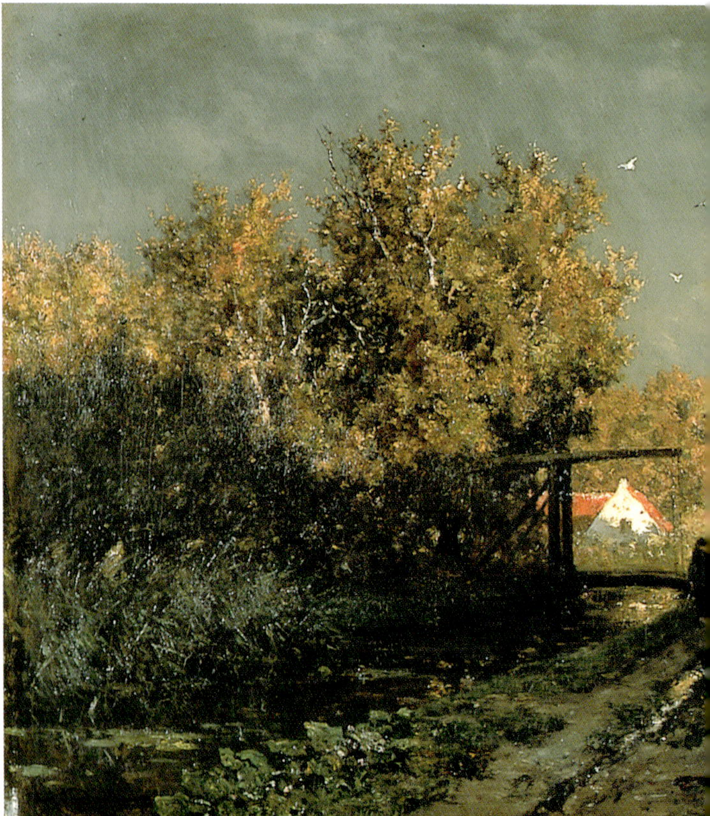

Willem Roelofs, *The rainbow (Evening after a rainy autumn day)*, 1875

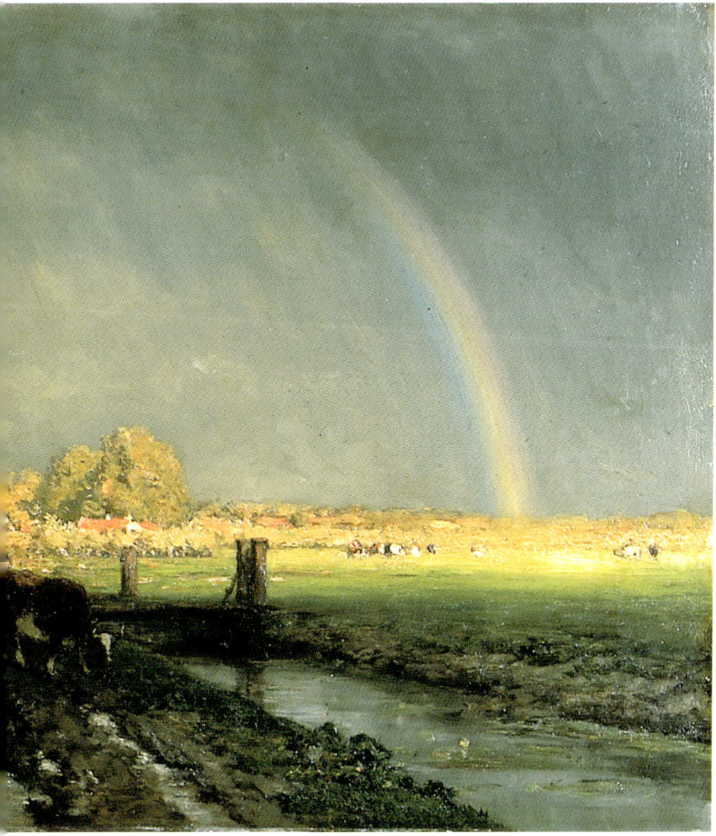

fellow students from the Hague Academy of Art. However, a few months later he moved to Brussels, where he was to remain for the next forty years. Nevertheless, he kept in touch with artistic life in The Hague, participating in Pulchri Studio's exhibitions and art reviews.

In those years Brussels was more favourable to artists than The Hague, Utrecht, or Amsterdam, for, as a result of the more thoroughgoing industrialisation there, the citizens of Brussels had more money to spend. In addition, Brussels had a well developed cultural infrastructure, with artists' societies, art dealers, its annual Salon, and the special support of Belgium's royal family. Moreover, Paris was geographically closer, and its cultural influence was more pronounced. Yet Roelofs' choice was unusual: most of the Dutch artists who worked abroad went to Düsseldorf, Munich, Rome, or Paris. Even Antwerp, with its strong, trend-setting reputation at the time in the area of historical painting, would have been a more likely choice. It is possible that Roelofs did not wish to remain in the Netherlands for reasons of the heart: he loved Johanna Adriana Verstraten, a miller's daughter. Because of her origins, his family probably did not view her as a desirable partner for Roelofs. Upon Roelofs' arrival in Brussels it was reported that Johanna was supported by him, 'whom she would soon marry'. Yet it would not be until 1852 that the marriage would take place.

Once having arrived in Brussels, Roelofs made friends with the Belgian animal painters, as well as with Jan de Haas (a Dutch painter and later Gerard Bilders' brother-in-law). Roelofs often worked in the area around Brussels, on the banks of the Senne, in Belgian Limburg, and in Kempen and Beaufort. He quickly became popular in Brussels. At the 1848 Salon he exhibited two landscapes, both very well received. He won a gold medal for his Gelderland landscape, and his Drente landscape was purchased by the Belgian king. Although the latter work is lost, it was probably very romantic, like the one of

Gelderland. In 1852, The Brussels Museum of Fine Arts purchased his 'Paysage avant l'orage', and in 1858 Roelofs was knighted as a member of the Order of Leopold. In Belgium he was valued as an innovator of the landscape genre. In his close studies from nature he expressed a very personal vision that the critics referred to as 'the poetry of the landscape'. His work was more gradually recognised in the Netherlands, however. Although the critics were more enthusiastic following a Dutch exhibition in 1851, it was not until 1870 that Roelofs' contribution to landscape art (and his ground-breaking role in this genre for other painters of the Hague School) was fully recognised.

Exhibitions of works from the Barbizon School were shown in Brussels relatively early, which enabled Roelofs to see paintings by Troyon, Rousseau and Millet. He also made friends with the French painter Francois-Auguste Ortmans, who had been a student of Rousseau's, and lived in Barbizon from 1854. In 1851, Roelofs visited the woods around Fontainebleau for the first time; he returned in 1852 and again in 1855. He was one of the first Dutch painters to visit this area, which confirmed his emphasis on studies directly from nature. The Barbizon painters believed, like the Dutch seventeenth-century masters, that nature should be the only teacher for a landscape painter. It was especially this aspect that caused Theophile Thoré, the most important spokesman of the Barbizon painters, to make an explicit connection between the works of Théodore Rousseau and Roelofs after 1860. The French influence can also be seen in Roelofs' use of colour.

It was not only his meticulous sketches of landscapes that embodied Roelofs' interest in nature: he was also completely taken up in a quite different type of observation of the natural world: entomology. He developed into a very valued scientist, especially in the area of weevils. Roelofs assembled an impressive collection of these small animals (in 1870 he had 5000 specimens); he also described other collections, published various articles, and discovered a new type of

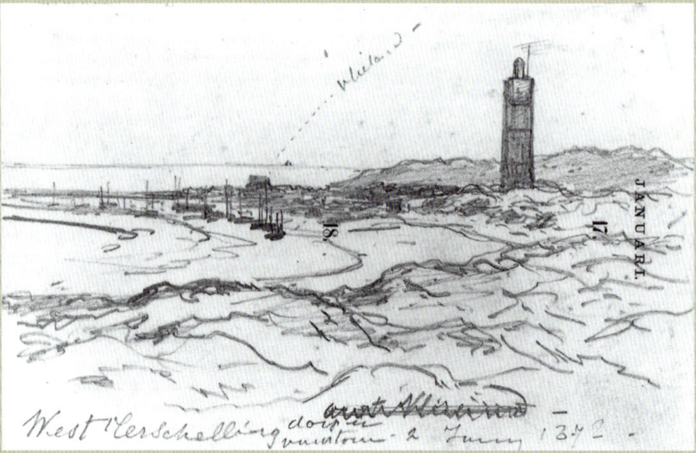

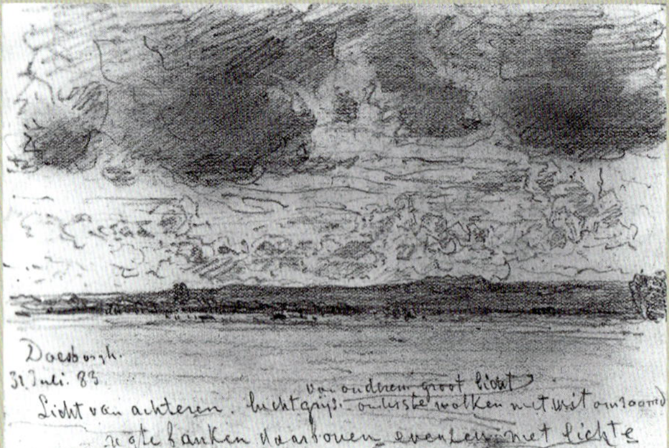

Willem Roelofs, *West-Terschelling, town and lighthouse,* 1872 (drawing)

Willem Roelofs, *The IJssel river near Doesburg,* 1883 (drawing)

weevil, which was named after him. For the most part the letters that have come down to us from him deal with this subject, and in 1855, the year he co-founded the Belgian Society of Watercolourists, he also founded the Belgian Entomological Society, whose chairman he would be from 1878 onwards. It is difficult to determine how these two almost equally important passions in Roelofs' life relate to each other. In all probability he received his main income from painting, while his collecting activities were simply an expense. In 1880, Roelofs felt forced to give up his entomological studies, selling his collection to the Museum of Natural History in Brussels.

From 1856, Roelofs regularly travelled throughout the Netherlands. One of his first trips was to Drente, which became the subject of his paintings; he also worked in the Gooi region and the area of the Vecht river, on the banks of the Gein river, the lakes at Nieuwkoop and Reeuwijk, and in the area of Loosdrecht. He was in part guided by where he could find interesting weevil environments. This took him to Ruurlo in the Achterhoek region, and prompted visits to the coast of the Zuiderzee and the island of Texel. Initially, the paintings he made were romantic: for example, his 'summers', with their ruins that catch the viewer's attention. But he gradually developed a more naturalistic view of the landscape, creating them in a very free style. His realism also entailed choosing landscapes that until then had been perceived as too ordinary for a painting. Open meadows with cows standing under an impressive array of clouds became characteristic of his style. In addition to paintings, Roelofs did many watercolour drawings, charcoal, chalk and pencil drawings, etches and lithographs.

His long stay in Brussels made Roelofs a beacon in this city for other Dutch artists. Among his students were Hendrik Willem Mesdag, Paul Gabriël and Alexander Mollinger. The directions Roelofs gave to his students have been written down and cited often. Although Gabriël was only six years younger than Roelofs, of all his

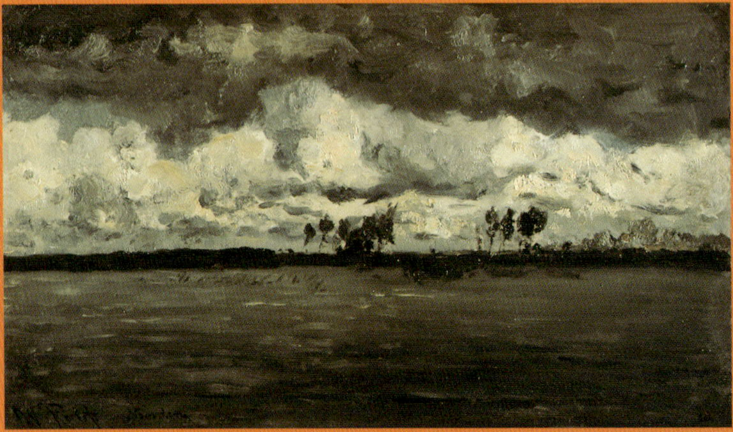

Willem Roelofs, *Lake at Noorden,* ca. 1882-1885

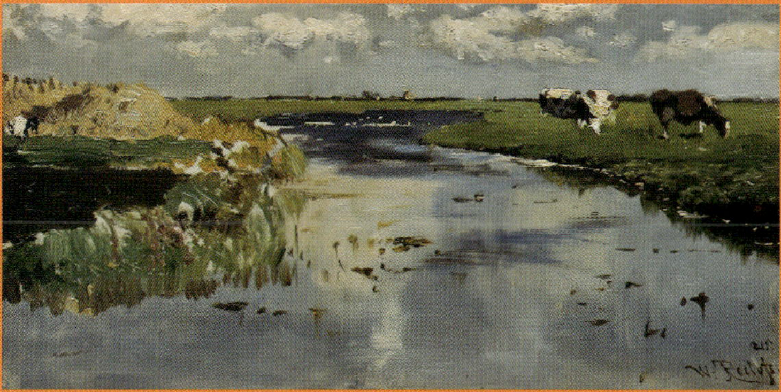

Willem Roelofs, *Study for the month of May in Noorden,* 1882

students he had the greatest influence on Gabriël, whose work critics would later associate often with that of Roelofs. In order to free himself from this dominating influence (but perhaps also because of temperamental differences) their relationship cooled somewhat later on. Roelofs worked together with Mollinger (a painter from Utrecht) in Drente. They sketched heath landscapes with *hunebedden* (a specific type of prehistoric stone graves) and shady village greens. In 1862, Mollinger introduced Roelofs to the Scottish collector John Forbes White. From that time onward Roelofs would sell many works to him and other Scottish collectors. When Mollinger died in 1867, Roelofs finished off his painting of a *hunebed*, so it would make a good impression on the very next exhibition.

For Roelofs the period from 1866 to 1870 was a time of reverses. His mother died in the spring of 1866, and thereafter his father and oldest sister moved in with him. Roelofs complains in his letters that all this was keeping him from working. In the winter of 1867, he was stricken with typhus and was ill for a long time. His wife had a breakdown in the spring of 1868 and suffered from hallucinations. She was unable to recover from this illness, and died in 1870. Thus, Roelofs was unable to concentrate on his work during this period. In 1871, he visited London, England and Scotland. On this trip he made many studies on the island of Skye. It is believed that the purpose of this trip was to help him forget the heartache of the previous years.

In 1873, he married Albertina Vertommen, who came from Flanders. She was already pregnant and was to bear him two sons: Willem Elisa and Otto Willem Albert, who would both become painters. Thus, Roelofs was later to be designated as 'senior'. In order to provide the boys with a proper education, Roelofs settled with his family in The Hague in 1887. In the meantime, the Hague School had established its reputation. Pulchri Studio and the Goupil art dealership ensured a flourishing cultural life. Moreover, Brussels increasingly became the showplace for a new generation that would give birth to symbolism, neo-impressionism, and other avant-garde movements. Roelofs no longer felt at home there.

His seventieth birthday was celebrated by Pulchri Studio with full honours. In the same year, however, his health deteriorated so much that his paintings no longer lived up to their promise, even though Roelofs continued to work on them. His friends Sadée and Julius van de Sande Bakhuyzen tried to encourage him and help him through. But after a stroke in 1894, his work became little more than painful, irregular scratches. Roelofs decided to spend his last years in Brussels, but on the way there he stopped at his brother-in-law's house in Berchem near Antwerp, where he died on 12 May, seventy-five years old.

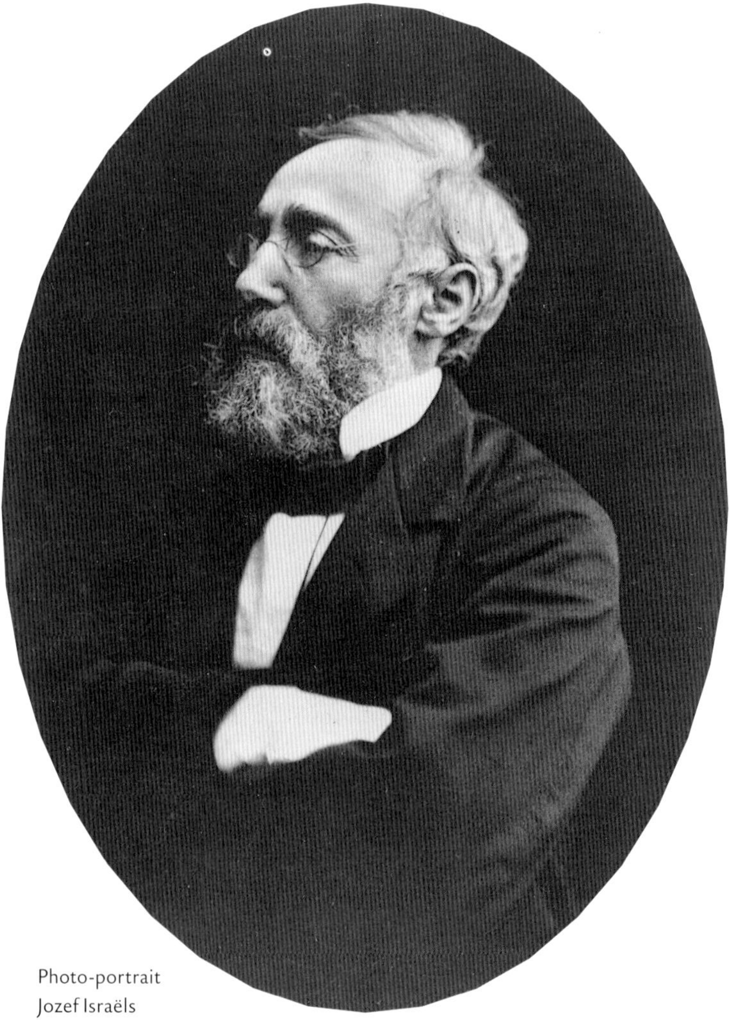

Photo-portrait
Jozef Israëls

Jozef Israëls

(1824-1911)

Jozef Israëls was born on 27 January 1824 in the Jewish quarter of Groningen. When he was young he was sent to the French School, as he was being considered for a rabbinical education. His parents belonged to the middle classes, and when still quite young Jozef began to work at his father's securities office. This work brought him to the home of the Mesdag family, where he got to know their son, Hendrik Willem, who would also become one of the most well-known painters in the Hague School. Jozef's father was a member of the Minerva Academy in Groningen, and was not against his son becoming a painter. Thus, from 1835, Jozef Israëls was permitted to take drawing and painting lessons at the academy in addition to his regular school work. He takes lessons from several local painters as well. Ferdinand de Witt, a Groningen dealer in paints, a member of the Pictura Painters' Society, and someone who knew many different painters, arranged for Israëls to get a place at the studio of J.A. Kruseman, a renowned portrait and historical painter. In 1842, the then fourteen-year old Israëls moved to Amsterdam, where he received lessons at the Rijksacademie from J.W. Pieneman in the evenings.

In 1845, he went to an exhibition where he saw the painting 'Gretchen at the spinning wheel' by Ary Scheffer, a Dutch artist who lived in Paris. Israëls was very impressed and decided to move to Paris, together with Jacobus van Koningsveld, a fellow student. He worked in Picot's studio in the morning, in the afternoon he and Van Koningsveld copied works by Rembrandt, Velázquez and Raphaël in the Louvre, and in the evening he took lessons at the École des

Beaux-Arts, where Pradier, Vernet and Delaroche were his teachers. In his training, Israëls chose to pursue the direction of historical painting, which was the most prominent one at the time. Together with Van Koningsveld he created his first paintings in that style.

Israëls returned to the Netherlands three years later and settled in Amsterdam. There he experienced his first success with 'Ophelia (daydreaming)', a representation inspired by Scheffer. The painting was purchased by Jeronimo de Vries, a renowned art critic. In 1850, Israëls painted several scenes that dealt with Dutch history, but these were not as successful, although costly to make because he had to hire models and historical costumes. From 1850 to 1853, he went to Düsseldorf, which was the centre of German Romanticism at the time, as well as to Oosterbeek, Paris and Barbizon. In Barbizon he bought farmers' costumes for his studies of farm interiors, which clearly heralded his change of subject around 1855.

The traditional explanation of this change is that Israëls began to suffer from rheumatism and wanted to be close to the sea. Thus, in the summer of 1855, he rented a place from the town carpenter in Zandvoort. Supposedly, he was so moved by the simple fishing life that he was inspired to make it the subject of his painting. Israëls himself cast some doubt on this myth when he wrote in 1900: 'One of my friends who lived in Amsterdam often spoke about a painter called Ritter who came from Düsseldorf. He had done such beautiful work portraying Dutch villages. When I realised that historical painting did not lead me to the true art of painting because it is not modelled from nature, I went to Zandvoort to look for my models and to study the interiors and the sea.' The fact that the Dutch market for historical painting was very limited and was even shrinking throughout Europe, combined with his introduction to the Barbizon School and the fishing genre from Germany and England, played at least as great a role as Israëls' stay on the coast.

When he changed his principal theme from history to everyday

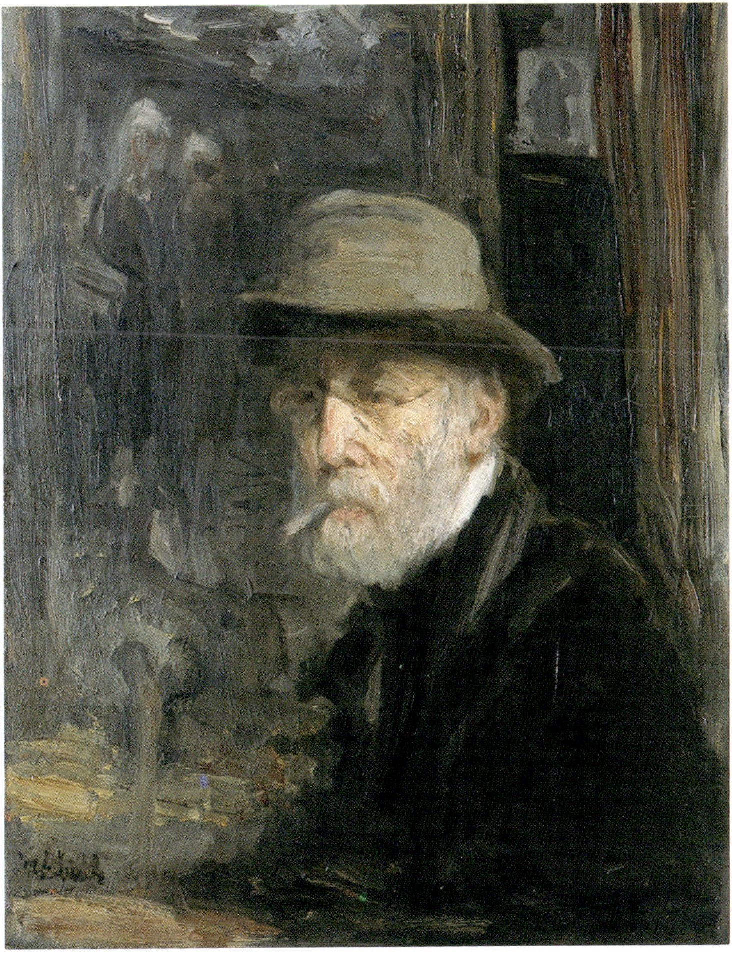

Jozef Israëls, *Self-portrait,* n.d.
Caldic Collection, Rotterdam

life, Israëls broke with academic tradition. In his paintings of interiors and fishermen in Katwijk, Zandvoort and Scheveningen, the poverty that these people often suffered from is very clearly present. This is especially true of the tragedy of deaths: the fisherman's widow or becoming older without being cared for. Israëls paints his Zandvoort landlord with his children in 'By mother's grave', for which he was acclaimed both within the Netherlands and abroad. The painting was purchased by the Rijksacademie in Amsterdam and received a silver medal. For his 'Unhappy woman' he won a gold medal at the Brussels Salon in 1860. When 'The drowned fisherman' was exhibited at the World Exhibition in London, Israëls travelled there. He sold the work at much too low a price because he did not know what the English pound was worth. This was an anecdote that he later delighted in repeating. His engravings for 'Children of the sea', a poetry anthology by Nicolaas Beets, were very successful in the Netherlands. After the first edition in 1861, the book would be reprinted many times. This book established Israëls' reputation as a painter of 'sensitive poetry'.

In 1863, he married Aleida Schaap. They had two children: Mathilde and Isaac, who would later also become a painter. The theme of death gradually disappeared from Israëls' work, as he more often began to paint scenes depicting household joy and mother love. Israëls' work is becoming increasingly recognised abroad, in part because he knew how to further his work in this market. In 1870, he travelled to Aberdeen in Scotland, where he visited John Forbes White, a well-known collector. Another famous Scottish collector, the railroad magnate James Staats Forbes, purchased his first painting from Israëls that year. He was later to acquire a prestigious collection of Dutch art, which would include about seventy works by Israëls. This awakened the interest of other British art lovers, and Israëls had to create small versions of his successful paintings in order to accommodate the demand.

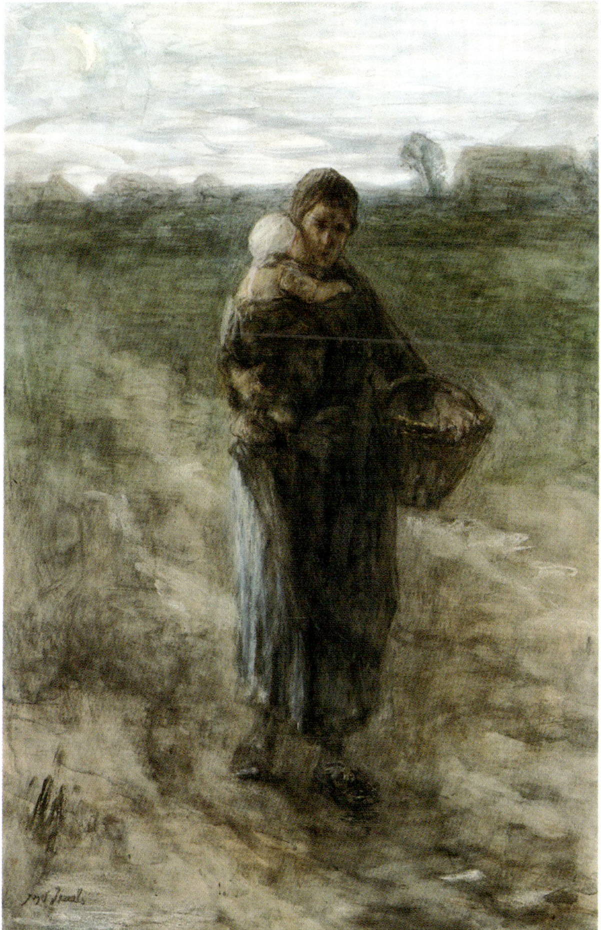

Jozef Israëls, *Mother and child,* ca. 1895-1903 (watercolour)

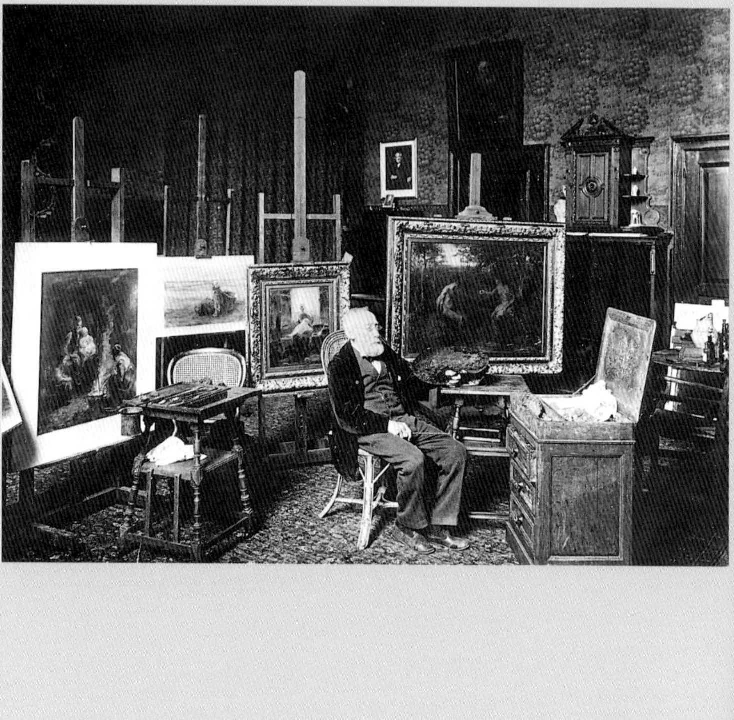

Jozef Israëls in his studio (photo)

Isaac Israëls, *Front of Israëls' house on the Koninginnegracht,* n.d. (drawing)

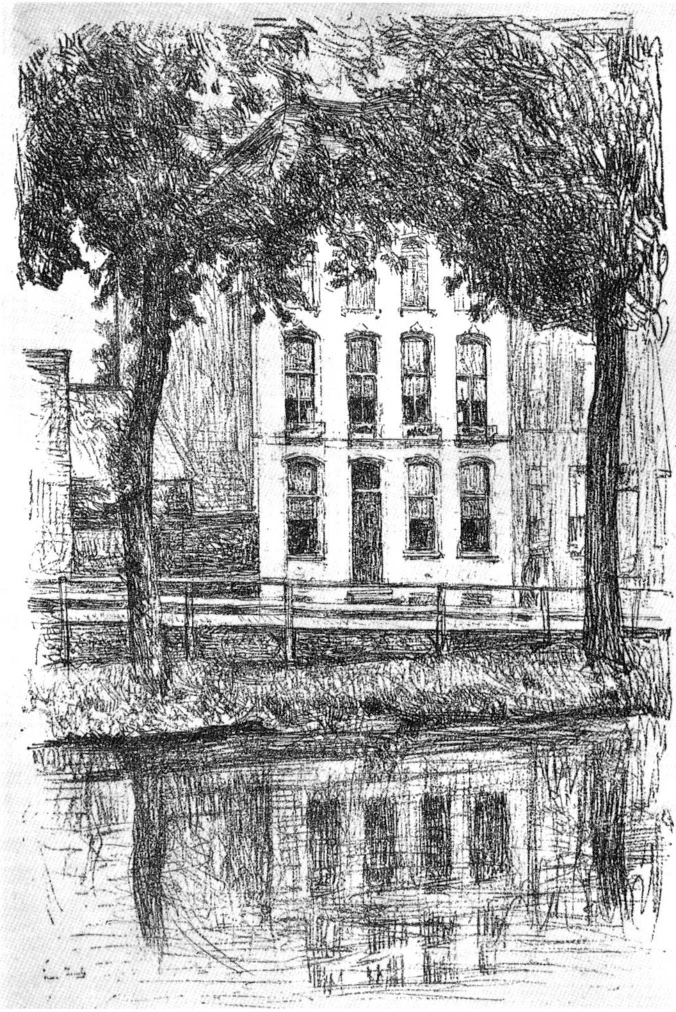

Around 1870, many prominent landscape painters settled in The Hague, including Israëls, who went to live on the Koninginnegracht in 1871. In the garden of his house he built a large studio, which contained his famous 'fisherman's corner', an imitation of a fisherman's house in which many of his models posed. Israëls became a member of both the Amsterdam artists' society Arti et Amicitiae and Pulchri Studio in The Hague. He was chairman of the latter from 1875 to 1878. He was also one of the founders of the Hollandsche Teekenmaatschappij (Dutch Drawing Society) in 1876. From 1885 until his death he remained chairman of this organisation, and it was there that he would exhibit and sell many of his watercolours. In 1877, he went on an extensive trip through Europe with his family. The trip was such a success that every year thereafter they all visited the Salon in Paris. Israëls was thus always very aware of developments in the international art world.

It was around this time that Israëls changed his work location from the fishing villages to the Gooi: he went to Laren for the first time in 1870. Later on he drew Mauve's and Neuhuys' attention to the town and the artistic farmer scenes that he encountered there. From 1875, ageing and human suffering again became important subjects in his work. His manner of painting changed: he used a broader stroke and stronger contrast between light and dark, but with transparent sections of shadow. He began to use a cooler palette: the shadows became more grey than brown. Israëls also began to omit some of the narrative details, and the figures acquire a spent appearance. In this way the mood of the work becomes the full focus.

The painting 'When one becomes old', is an example of this style: it portrays an old, bent-over woman warming her hands at a small fire. This painting was sent on an extensive tour of European exhibitions. But it was variously received: at the World Exhibition in Antwerp it received a first class medal, but in France and the Netherlands some critics believed his manner of painting was too coarse and the choice of subject too far-fetched and sentimental. In Scotland and America, however, his (financial) success was exceptional. That Israëls was praised far and wide is shown by the fact that a monograph about him had already appeared while he was still alive. In 1882, Ernest Chesnau published a book about Israëls and even published editions for the London and Paris markets.

In 1884, the Dutch literary critic Philip Zilcken wrote an article about Israëls for the series 'Grand Peintres Français et Etrangers'. Israëls' Jewish origins were mentioned for the first time in this article, which would have an important influence on subsequent international literature about Israëls. It was especially in the last phase of his life that Israëls himself began to highlight his Jewish identity. During his lifetime he always had several Jewish buyers who did not (or hardly ever) purchase the work of other Hague School painters. After 1890 Israëls painted several works with biblical themes, and after 1900 these became specifically Jewish, including: 'David and Saul' and 'A son of the Chosen People'. These themes, as well as the strong emphasis on the contrast between light and darkness, caused his work to be compared with Rembrandt's.

At the turn of the century, when symbolism and other modern art movements began to become popular among artists, criticism of Israëls' work increased: he was deemed too sentimental, insincere, and he had a poor command of contours (which his work had always suffered from). Vincent van Gogh is one of the few painters of the new generation who wrote with passion about Israëls' paintings.

When his wife died in 1894, Israëls' son Isaac and his friend Frans Erens took Israëls on a trip to Spain and North Africa. Israëls describes this trip in an amusing travel report, which was published in 1899, complete with his own illustrations. In 1895, his seventieth birthday was celebrated (which had been put off because of his wife's death) in which a tableau vivant that enacted 'A son of the Chosen People', one of his paintings, was set up in Pulchri Studio. There was

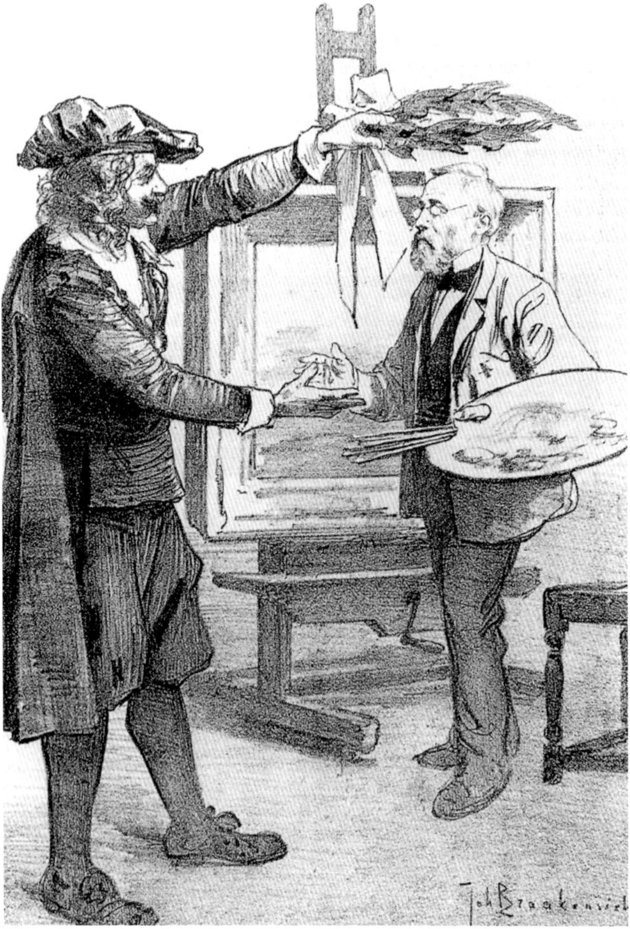
Joh Braakensiek

an even bigger celebration for his eightieth birthday: Pulchri Studio, Arti et Amicitiae and the Dutch Drawing Society together honoured the painter and he was accorded the Order of the Dutch Lion, which was an appropriate recognition for all the honours he had received, both in the Netherlands and abroad. In 1904, a major portion of the Dutch contribution to the Biennale in Venice consisted of his work, and in 1910 he was honoured there with an individual exhibit ('Mostra Individuale'). On 12 August 1911, Israëls died at his summer place in Hotel Oranje in Scheveningen. He was buried with great honours in the Jewish cemetery in The Hague.

Johan Braakensiek, *Rembrandt crowning Jozef Israëls*
(print from *De Amsterdammer*, 1895)

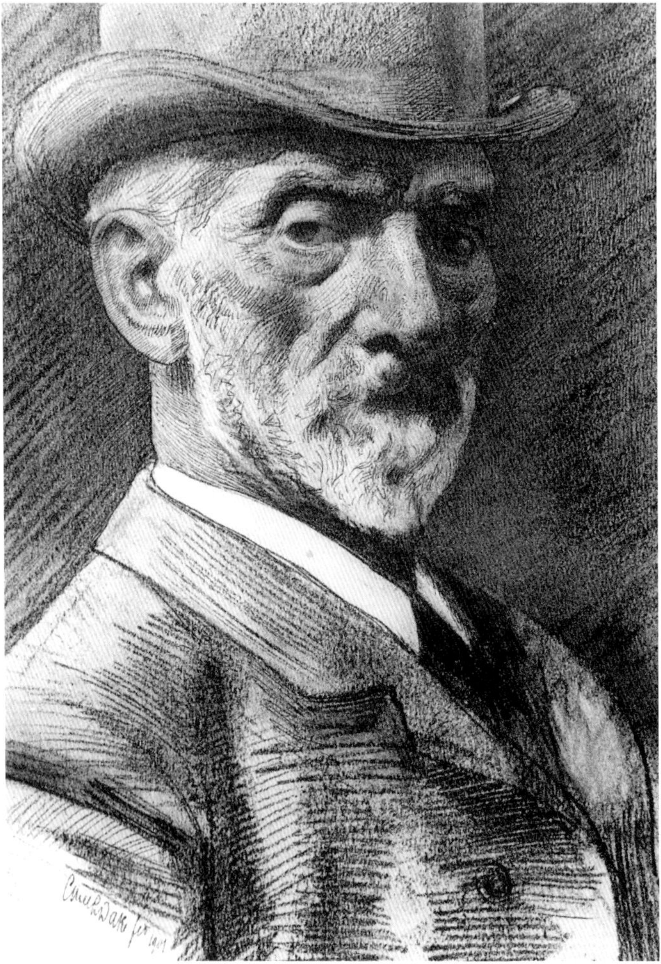

C.L. Dake, *J.H. Weissenbruch,* 1901 (drawing)

Jan Hendrik Weissenbruch

(1824-1903)

Hendrik Johannes Weissenbruch was born on 19 June 1824 on the Kazernestraat in The Hague. For the major portion of his life, Jan Hendrik, as he was called when he became an artist, would live in the house he was born in. He came from an artistic family; although his father was also a cook and owned a restaurant, he painted in his free time and collected art on a small scale. Among his collection were several works by Andreas Schelfhout and B.J. van Hove. Hendrik's cousin Jan was a well-known painter of romantic city views, and a brother, an uncle, and two cousins worked in the graphic arts. When Weissenbruch was sixteen years old he received drawing lessons from Johannes Löw. In 1843, he took evening classes at the Haagsche Teekenacademie (Hague Academy of Art); the classes were taught by B.J. van Hove. During the day Weissenbruch worked in Van Hove's studio, together with Johannes Bosboom and Samuel Verveer, helping to make pieces of scenery for the Royal Theatre. It is reported that they covered 'the canvases as if they were using brooms'.

Weissenbruch's early work showed the strong influence of the romantic painter Andreas Schelfhout. When he was invited to take lessons from this very celebrated artist, his older friend, Bosboom, advised him not to accept. 'I can't simply say "no, thank you" to Schelfhout!' sputtered Weissenbruch. Whereupon Bosboom said: 'But you should do that, Weiss! You have to learn to stand on your own and see through your own eyes.' In 1847, Weissenbruch first exhibited at the exhibition of Living Masters, and he became one of the founders of the artists' society Pulchri Studio. The following

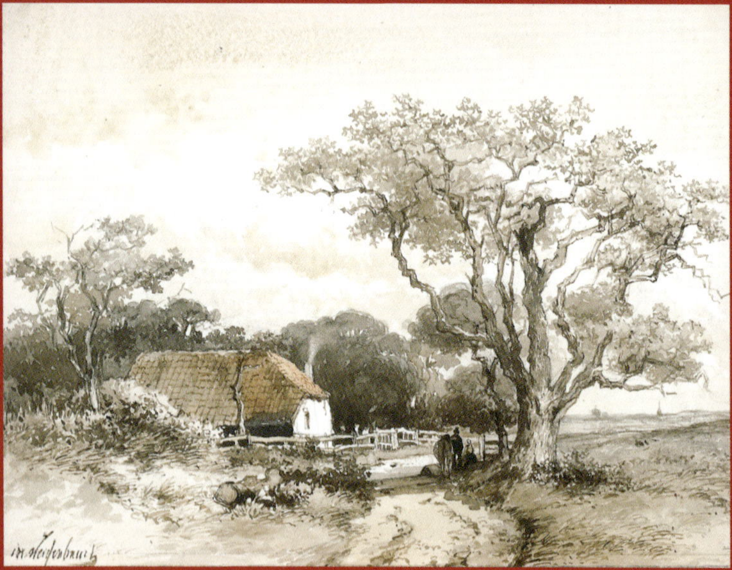

J.H. Weissenbruch, *Near Dekkersduin,* ca. 1850 (watercolour)

year the Teylers Museum in Haarlem purchased his major painting 'View of the Trekvliet' for what was then the very substantial sum of 250 guilders. The painting, which shows a canal with a towpath, mill and bleaching field alongside, is built up in a traditional way, using alternating light and dark planes, and is still somewhat clumsy in composition with sketchlike strokes.

For the panoramic 'View of Haarlem' Weissenbruch used the same wings to suggest depth. In its traditional subject matter, portrayal of depth and foreground dotted with colour, the style of the seventeenth-century Jacob van Ruisdael is clearly recognisable. The Mauritshuis was for Weissenbruch and other painters of his time one of the few places where they could see art. He spent time there copying works by Potter, Vermeer and Ruisdael. Later he would say about this: 'I remember that when I was still a boy I would visit the museums and stand absolutely dumbfounded, looking at the paintings of the old Dutch masters, especially how they were able to depict nature so that it really touched you. If I learned from anyone how to look at nature, then it was from our old masters.' But in his version of the panorama of Haarlem, Weissenbruch brings his own day to life on the canvas, with its smoking chimneys on the horizon and steam train riding through the landscape.

The commendable purchase of his painting by Teylers did not immediately result in a breakthrough for Weissenbruch. On the contrary: a couple of months later he was forced to sell one of his paintings for a meagre 52.50 guilders. Nor did the critics always regard his work favourably: they claimed that his work showed that he was not yet a finished artist, and when he painted landscapes he was accused of not taking sufficient care. This latter criticism probably related to the loose brushstrokes that Weissenbruch used to set up his landscapes. Nevertheless, he was not the type of person to allow such comments to guide his behaviour. He describes himself as: 'I was a healthy, strong, happy youth [...] and joyfully took long walks in and around

The Hague. When I saw beautiful corners, a lovely beach, picturesque canals, and lovely skies, or made my way through the dunes towards the sea, I was totally absorbed in the beauty and in nature. Sometimes it was even as if I received a blow from nature. And afterwards, when this happened, I was able to draw and paint whatever I had seen. I could capture it with a couple of strokes.'

Weissenbruch and his friend Johannes Destrée took trips through Haarlem and Arnhem. He also often made drawings around Dekkersduin, an extensive, wild area of dunes south of The Hague. Later on he worked near Delftse Vliet and in Schieland, to the west of Rotterdam. From 1860, Weissenbruch regularly visited the polder landscape near Schiedam, Delft, Gouda and Boskoop. It is possible that this was how he discovered the lakes around Nieuwkoop. It has often been written that Johannes Hendricus Sala, a frame maker from Leiden, owned a sailboat in which he took Weissenbruch, Gabriël and a few other painters to the lakes around Nieuwkoop in 1875. Although this is unlikely, Frans Sala, the frame maker's brother, did take Weissenbruch fishing that year. Fishing became one of Weissenbruch's favourite hobbies, which the artist later often combined with drawing and creating watercolours at the lakes near Nieuwkoop and Noorden. It is certain that, from 1882, he spent his summers in this area. Around the same period he could also often be found at the coastal side of The Hague, fixing his attention on the beach there.

Weissenbruch developed slowly, exchanging the panoramic landscape for a lower point of view. Thus, the sky above the polders began to play a more important role. His impressions of the landscape broke away from tradition and became less anecdotal and increasingly more personal. For Weissenbruch it was a matter of recreating his experience with nature. With his usual passion he said: 'when you just walk outside in nature and you see something beautiful, it gives you a real punch. When this happens you can't keep your hands still and you have to paint [...]. But the punch has an after

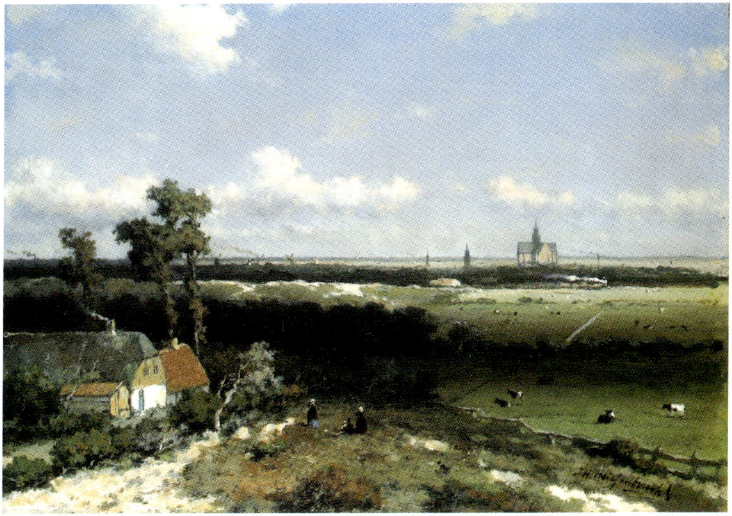

J.H. Weissenbruch, *View of Haarlem,* ca. 1845-1848

p. 235
detail of page 233

effect, and sometimes I think that I'm not going to get it and then I suddenly see it in the evening, and then I can give it a last kiss.'

His use of colour gradually became more restrained, his application of paint increasingly broader and looser. This made his landscapes more atmospheric, the bearers of light and clouds. Weissenbruch stressed the importance of both of these elements: 'The sky in a painting, that is what is important! The main thing! Sky and light are the great magicians. The sky determines what the painting is. Painters can never pay enough attention to the sky. We live from light and sunshine, and go with our palette through the dry periods.'

In 1863, he married Susanna Petronella Geertruida Schouw. Their son Willem Johannes, who was born in 1864, would also become a painter. Weissenbruch gave lessons to Willem Johannes as well as to Théophile de Bock and Victor Bauffe. And he was one of the few who perceived that the drawings by Vincent van Gogh showed great talent; he encouraged him by saying that he 'would easily be able to work after his studies'. Among his colleagues Weissenbruch took a special position, being known as the 'jolly Weiss'. At Pulchri Studio people said about him: 'He is like a storm wind [...] just listen to him effervesce and speak loudly and heatedly [...] he is always enthusiastic and happy; [he is] inventive and goes to the heart of the matter in the way he expresses himself ...].' His ability to express himself caused people to listen to and fear his judgements about art; he was called 'the sword without pity.'

His strong, broad watercolours were especially valued by his colleagues, and in 1866 he was invited to become a member of the Belgian Society of Watercolourists in Brussels. He had been a member of the Hollandsche Teekenmaatschappij (Dutch Drawing Society) from its very beginnings in 1876. However, he was more of a 'painter's painter', as it took a generation or more for the buying public to show interest in his work. Weissenbruch did not seem to have made much effort to change this state of affairs. In this light it

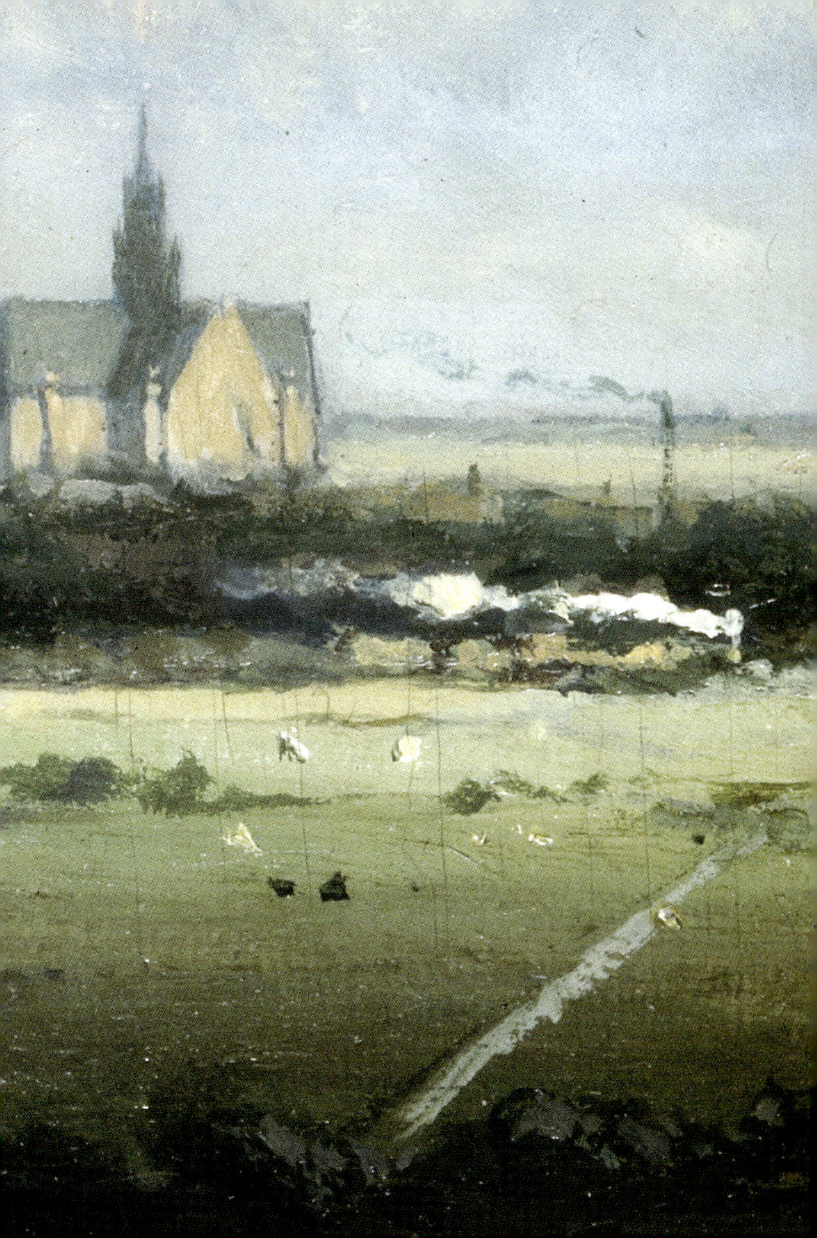

is not surprising that his works were mainly bought by museums: in 1871 the Gemeentemuseum in The Hague purchased 'View of the Trekvliet', and in 1873 the Rotterdam Museum Boijmans purchased 'Landscape with mill near Schiedam'. The Hague Museum Association purchased a beach view in 1887 in order to give it to the Gemeentemuseum. They only paid 800 guilders for this work, which was considerably lower than the prices that were paid for works by Mesdag or Israëls at that time. It was from this time that Weissenbruch's paintings and watercolours began to receive more attention at the exhibitions of Living Masters.

Nevertheless, the art dealer Theo van Gogh wrote to his brother Vincent in 1889 about the World Exhibition in Paris: 'The Dutch School is doing very well. There are two watercolours by J.H. Weissenbruch which I find especially beautiful [...] He is a world class artist, but Tersteeg says that he doesn't sell.' A couple of months later Theo wrote: 'I am happy that Tersteeg had the courage to buy from him [...]. Here where they can understand Jongkind, they'll also be able to understand him. In any case it's certainly worth trying.' Only after 1890 his paintings began to sell in America and Canada – much later than the works of other Hague School painters, most of whom became popular around 1870 on the English and Scottish markets, and somewhat later on the American continent.

The real breakthrough for Weissenbruch would come ten years later, at the retrospective in 1899 organised by the Amsterdam art dealer Frans Buffa to commemorate Weissenbruch's seventy-fifth birthday. Most of the work exhibited was sold. Articles written about Weissenbruch frequently quote from the introduction to the catalogue from this exhibition. And although the members of Pulchri Studio (especially Hendrik Willem Mesdag) would have preferred he had accepted their invitation, Weissenbruch did not want to accept a birthday dinner offered by the society. He was, however, obliged to receive the members in his studio where they honoured him with a wreath. The newspapers gave a complete account of this visit and Weissenbruch's remarks at the occasion were often and repeatedly quoted.

Around 1900, when Weissenbruch was already a dapper old man, he created bold, broad beach views, confirming his individuality by going off in a new direction. He had previously described his love of harsh weather conditions: 'When there are storms and rain, when there is thunder and lightning, I am in my element. You have to see nature at work. Then, outside, I put on my jacket, push my feet in wooden clogs, put on a type of hat, and go out walking. When the storms have passed, I take charcoal or black chalk and make a few sketches to hold on to what I see. As you work on it you will remember the tones and colours.' In these late beach views the sky, the light, the wind and the water – natural elements that he so gladly defied – are all present. The restrained use of colour is reminiscent of his watercolours, while at the same time Weissenbruch skilfully varies the extent of transparency of the paint in these large oil paintings: from very thinly layered grey paint to thick, creamy whites.

Weissenbruch submitted one of these beach views to the 1900 World Exhibition in Paris. This painting, 'Storm on the coast of Zeeland', was awarded a gold medal. Moreover, a substantial price was offered for this painting, although it is not entirely clear if the sale went through. This, together with the financial success of the Buffa exhibition, may have been the reason Weissenbruch decided to take a trip to Paris. With him on this trip went his student, Victor Bauffe, and the art dealer Jacobus Slagmulder and his wife. In addition to Paris, they also visited the very touristy Barbizon and Fontainebleau. Weissenbruch had never previously been abroad, and this trip was probably much like a pilgrimage to him, given the subjects that he chose to paint: Millet's house and the rocks of Gorges d'Aprémont, one of Théodore Rousseau's favourite places. These paintings occupy a special place in his œuvre with regard to the use of colour and brush strokes. Weissenbruch died on 24 March 1903 in The Hague.

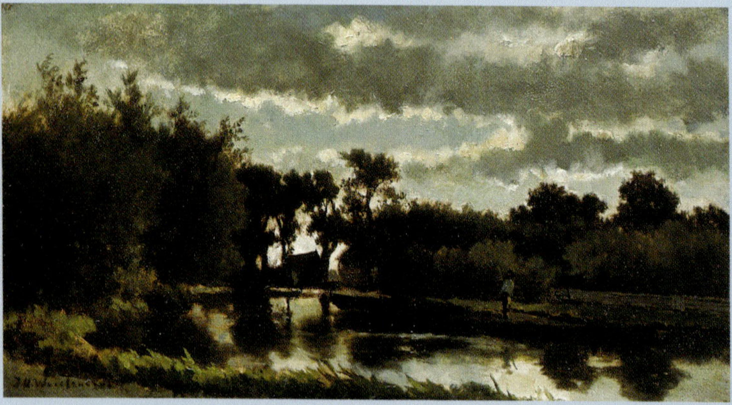

J.H. Weissenbruch, *Brook near Noorden (Stormy weather),* ca. 1890

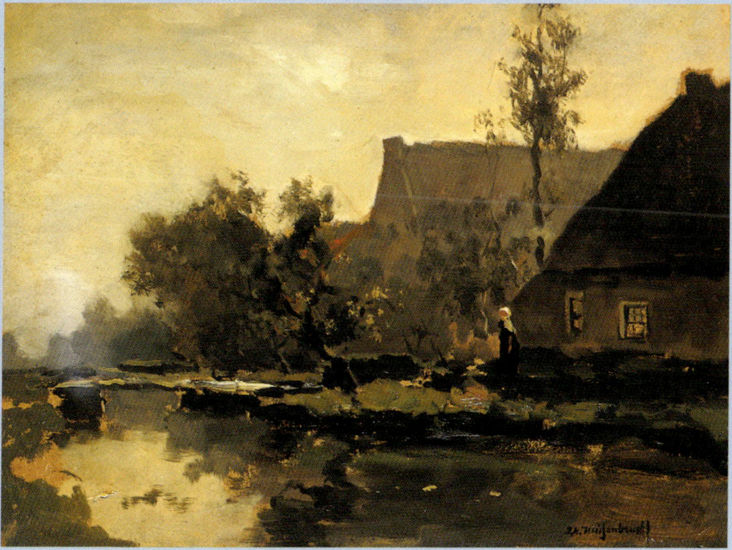

J.H. Weissenbruch, *Clogmaker's house in Noorden,* ca. 1900

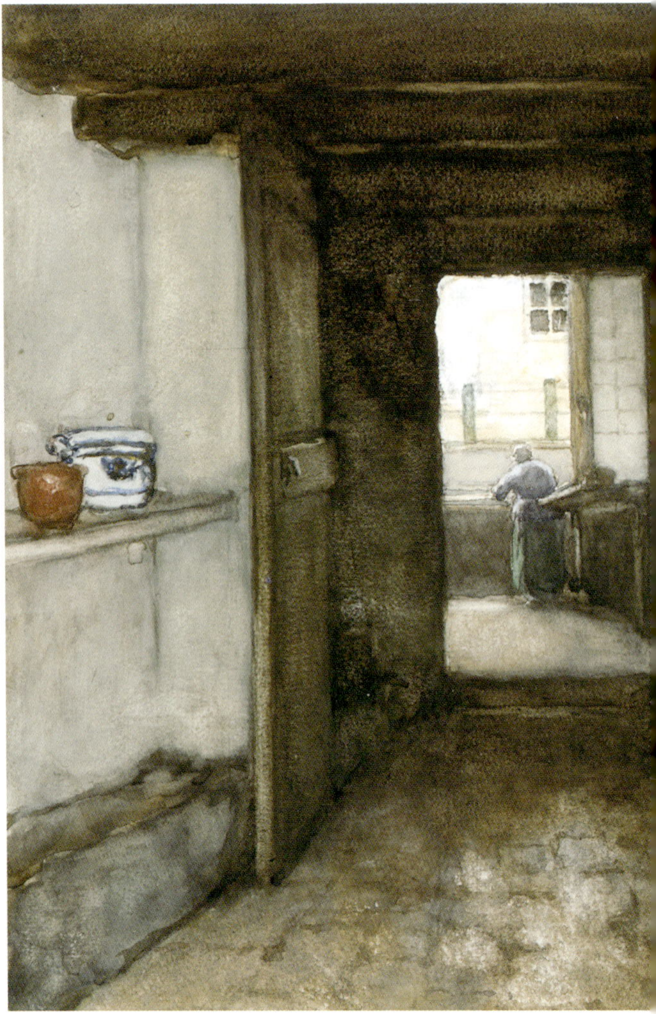

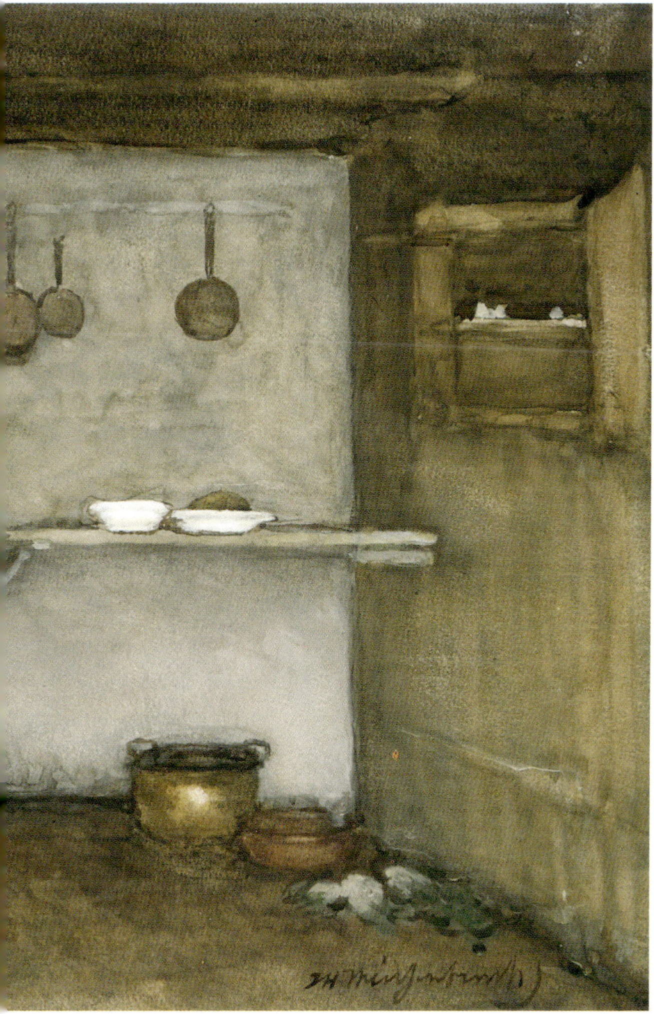

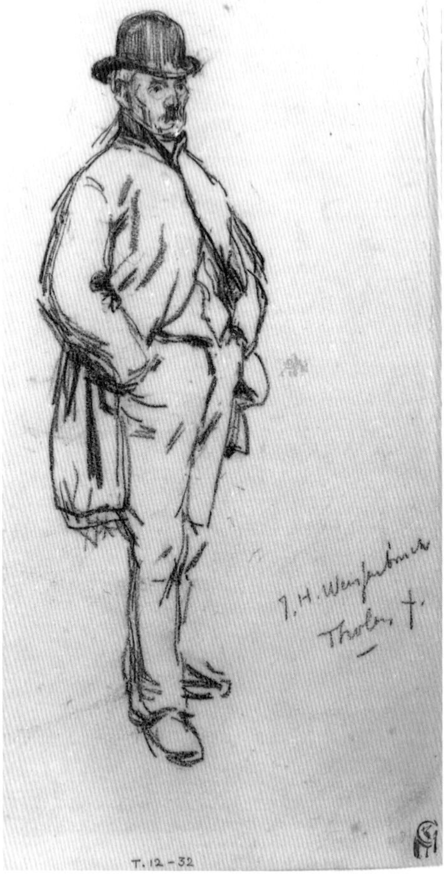

Willem Tholen, Sketch of J.H. Weissenbruch for 'Skating in the Hague Woods', ca. 1891

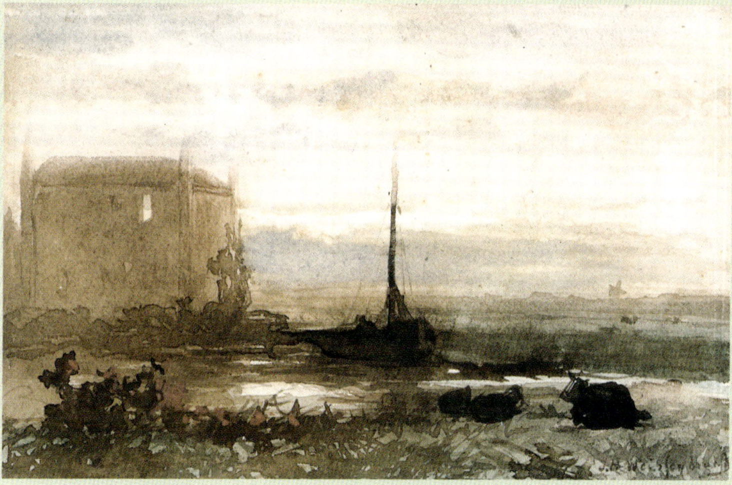

pp. 240-241:
J.H. Weissenbruch, *Kitchen interior (Kazernestraat)*, n.d. (watercolour)

J.H. Weissenbruch, *Canal near Rijswijk*, ca. 1870 (watercolour)

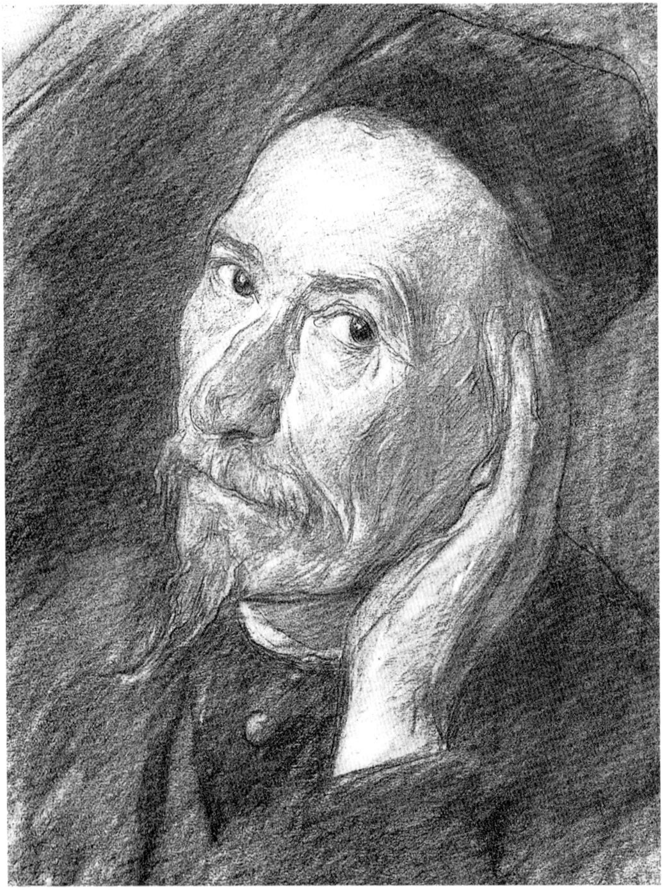

Jan Veth, *Portrait of Paul Gabriël,* n.d. (litho)
RKD collection

Paul Gabriël

(1828-1903)

Paul Joseph Constantin Gabriël was born on 5 July 1828 in Amsterdam. He was the son of the then celebrated sculptor Paul Joseph Gabriël, who died when the young Gabriël was only five years old. Gabriël Sr was director of the sculpture class at the Rijksacademie in Amsterdam, and his son was also destined to have an artistic career. He took evening classes in drawing at the Rijksacademie from the age of twelve. In 1843, he became Louis Zocher's student, who was an architect and amateur painter. The following year he went to the German town of Cleves, where Barend Cornelis Koekkoek, a landscape painter, had founded a drawing academy a few years earlier. Gabriël was set to copying studies by Koekkoek, which were regularly checked by his master. One year later Koekkoek did not yet believe Gabriël had learned enough to begin painting. Koekkoek is reported to have said that Gabriël didn't have it in him to become a painter.

Thus, Gabriël returned to the Netherlands, and after a while ended up in Haarlem, where he studied with the painter Cornelis Lieste. In this period Gabriël mostly did portraits and copied paintings in the Pavilion 'Welgelegen', at the time the place where the national collection of contemporary art was exhibited. Gabriël got acquainted with the animal painter Jan de Haas, as well as with the ten-year younger Anton Mauve, whom he was to work with often.

In 1853, Gabriël moved to Oosterbeek in Gelderland, also called the 'Dutch Barbizon', where landscape painter Johannes Warnardus Bilders had gathered around him many other young painters. The members of this group would later be central figures in the Hague School. Gabriël lived with a family called Wiesner, as did Jan de Haas

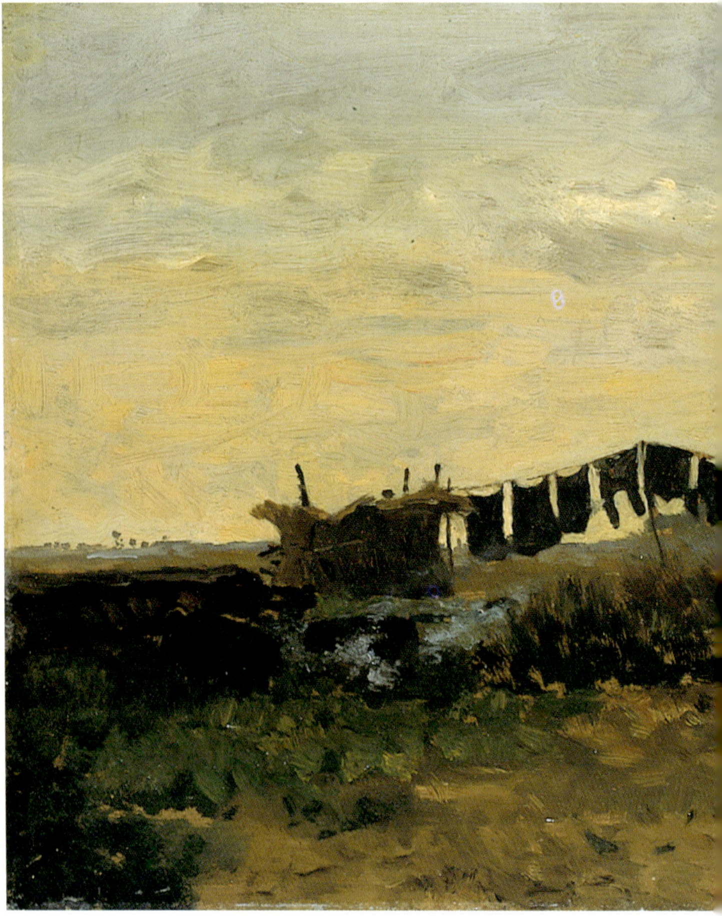

Paul Gabriël, *Cottage on the heath,* 1879

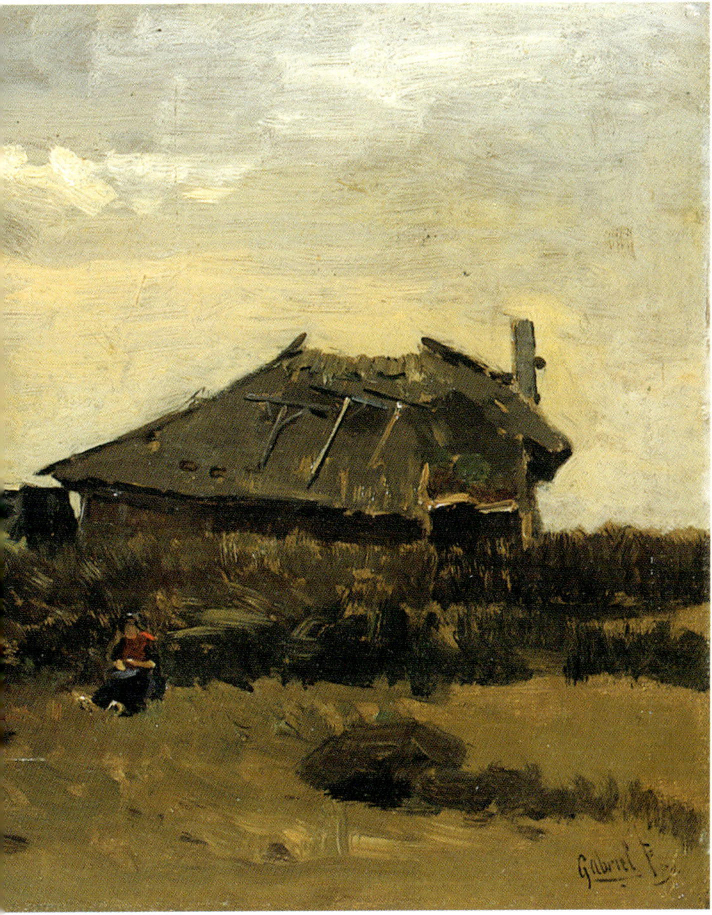

(who would later become old Bilders' son-in-law). Gabriël found nature studies very difficult but persisted. He would later write about this period: '[...] those days in Oosterbeek, what a crazy time, but we did work hard there!' In 1858, he introduced Anton Mauve to the area, who would return there ten years in a row and would become good friends with Gerard Bilders, Johannes Warnardus' son.

When Gabriël returned to Amsterdam to live he had a hard time. Hardly anyone wanted to buy his work, so he had financial difficulties. In 1860, Cremer, an art collector in Brussels, commissioned him to make a painting and asked him to come to Brussels to pick up the money. Gabriël packed his belongings and went to the Belgian capital, saying he 'preferred to have himself buried there than ever to return to Holland.' Although he had no immediate success in Brussels either, he did receive support from Willem Roelofs, who had been living and working there for some time. Despite the fact that he was only six years younger, Gabriël was enormously influenced by Roelofs. Gabriël benefited from Roelofs' social position in the art world of Brussels, and became a member of the same societies, the Belgian Society of Watercolourists and the Artistic and Literary Circle, where he filled various administrative positions. He made the acquaintance of H.W. Mesdag, also a student of Roelofs' and Mesdag's brother Taco. Jan de Haas, his friend from Haarlem, also settled in Brussels. Besides these, Gabriël befriended the Belgian sea painter Paul-Jan Clays.

In addition to still lifes with flowers, Gabriël painted landscapes in the area around Brussels: such places as Groenedael, La Hulpe and the edges of Zoniën forest. He is influenced by the painters of the Barbizon School, whose works were regularly exhibited in Brussels, as well as by the French painter Corot. Helped by Roelofs' suggestions, Gabriël developed into a good landscape painter, with a clear palette. Certainly in his later work he surpassed his master in the directness of his impressions. The Belgian press increasingly valued his work, and in 1875 he was made a Knight of the Order of Leopold. He had two

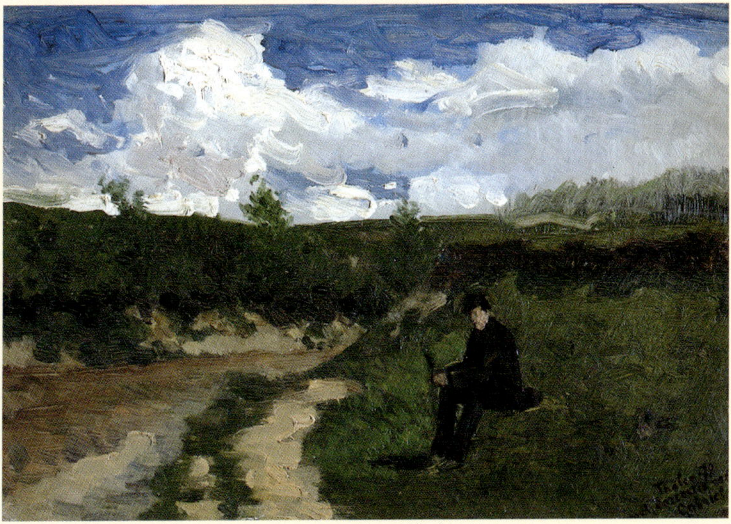

Willem Tholen, *The painter Gabriël working,* n.d.
(oil sketch with corrections by Gabriël) (private collection)

students: W.B. Tholen and Gesina Mesdag-van Calcar (Taco Mesdag's wife). Gabriëls' work was often compared with Roelofs', and in order to wrest himself from this influence, Gabriël increasingly distanced himself from him. The relationship between the two cooled significantly. Gabriëls' paintings stand out from the 'grey tones' for which the Hague School was so famous because of his clear use of colour. His work was less an impression of atmosphere than a consequence of the immediate registration of the sunny Dutch landscape. He consciously distanced himself from the 'grey school', which he characterised as 'an ensemble of cardboard paper with here and there a little colour'. (The somewhat grumpy tone he was known to use can be detected here.) The more he looked at the Dutch landscape, the more colour he perceived in it. He described the Dutch countryside as 'colourful, juicy, fat'. He said: 'Our land is not grey, even when the weather is grey.'

From 1862 onwards, Gabriël regularly embarked on study trips to the Netherlands: first to Arnhem and Oosterbeek, in 1866 to Veenendaal, in the seventies to Abcoude and Vreeland, and from 1875 to the lakes around Nieuwkoop near Noorden. Around 1880, he spent the summers in Kortenhoef, on Kampereiland and in Giethoorn. He visited the places in Overijssel with Tholen. But it was only in 1884 that Gabriël would permanently return to the Netherlands. At that time he moved to Scheveningen, where he bought a free-standing house next to his student Geesje Mesdag-van Calcar. Together they painted still lifes with flowers.

In this period he often painted the brook near Voorschoten, as well as in Broeksloot (1886), Oosterbeek (ca. 1887), Kinderdijk and Heeze. In 1886, he stayed with the Mesdags in their house in Vries in Drente, where he makes studies of the sands, barns and farms. In this period Gabriël also received recognition in the Netherlands: museums purchased some of his important pieces, including 'The peatery in Kampen', purchased by the Hague Gemeentemuseum in 1890. Gabriël died on 23 August 1903 in his home in Scheveningen.

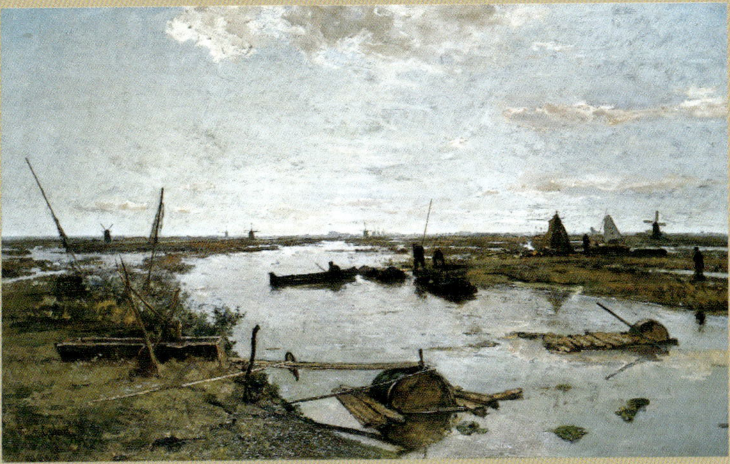

Paul Gabriël, *The peatery in Kampen (Zwijnsleger near Grafhorst)*, ca. 1889

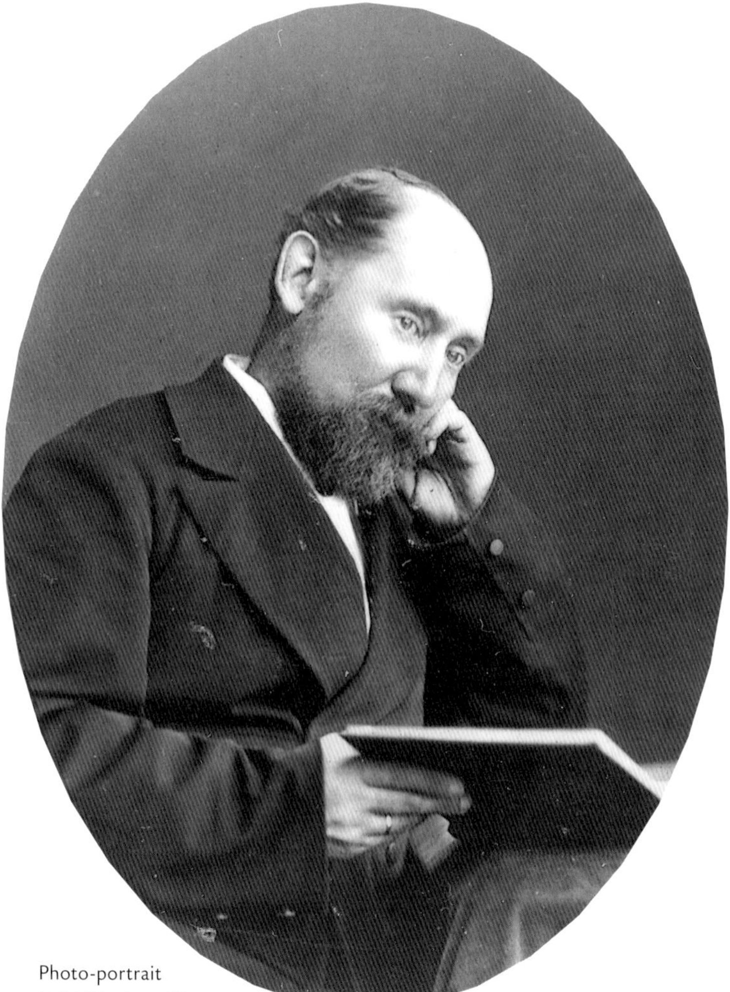

Photo-portrait
H.W. Mesdag, 1882

Hendrik Willem Mesdag

(1831-1915)

Hendrik Willem Mesdag was born on 23 February 1831 in Groningen. His family were fairly well-off Baptists. Mesdag's mother died when he was still a young boy. His father, who had first been a merchant and later a banker, was also an amateur painter who collected art. He saw to it that his sons Hendrik Willem and Taco took drawing lessons in addition to their regular schooling. When his schooling was finished, Mesdag went to work at Mesdag & Sons, where he was to remain for sixteen years. In his free time he continued to draw and paint.

In 1856, he married Sientje van Houten, who supported his painting aspirations. In 1861, Mesdag registered as a student at the Minerva Academy. He made accurate paintings of the Groningen landscape. When Sientje's father, a successful dealer in wood, died in 1864, he left her an inheritance of sixty thousand guilders. This enabled Mesdag to leave the family business and devote himself completely to painting. Although this has often been described in biographies as a sudden change, it actually took some time before Mesdag found his feet. In 1866, he wrote a letter to his cousin Lourens Alma Tadema, a painter of historical scenes who lived in Brussels. 'I am thirty-five. I have a wife and child. I have been trained to be a merchant, but I'm no good at this. I am a painter, help me.' Alma Tadema intervened and saw to it that Mesdag was able to take lessons from Willem Roelofs. The lessons would cost Mesdag 1200 francs a year.

Before Mesdag moved to Brussels, he spent the summer in Oosterbeek. There he visited Johannes Warnardus Bilders, who warned him not to become a 'little Roelofs'. The entire family – Hendrik Willem, Sientje and their son Klaas – moved to Brussels.

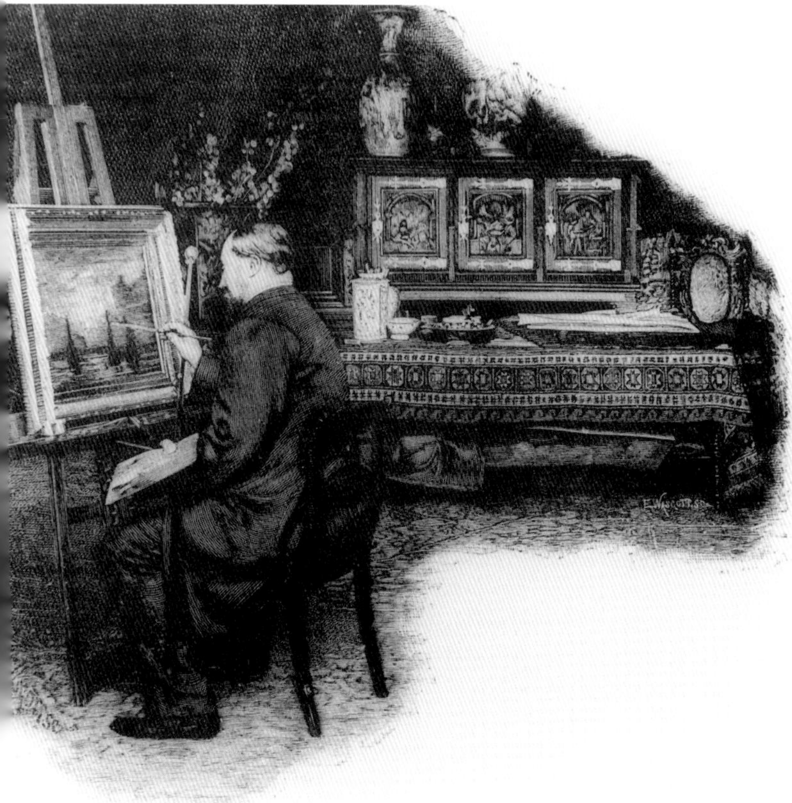

H.W. Mesdag in his studio (wood engraving)

Mesdag spent three years there as a student – years in which he industriously and doggedly tried to master the art of painting. As well as Roelofs' lessons, Alma Tadema's advice was very important to him. Mesdag's studies and paintings mainly included figures, sections of an interior, or views from a window: a staircase, walled-in back gardens, a cat on the threshold of a house, a pile of bricks on the street. All the details are rendered precisely and in a sketchlike way. Mesdag characterised himself as a 'realist'. He exhibited almost immediately upon arriving in Brussels, but the critics did not value his work: they called his choice of subject 'uneasy' and his style 'comical'.

In the summer of 1868, Mesdag visited Taco and his wife, who had a house in Vries, a village in Drente. Taco would later also become a painter. They went to the German island of Norderney together, where Mesdag became acquainted with the subject that would dominate the rest of his life: the sea. He made many drawings, which also show his obsession with details: he even took notes about the length of different types of gulls, both seated and flying. When he returned to Brussels his sketches were admired by his friends, and he tried to develop the studies into a painting. He could not quite manage this, and one of his friends would write: 'It was clear: if Mesdag wanted to paint the sea, then he had to be there where he could look at it daily – in all its broad lines and wonderful colours, its foam and waves, its forever-changing life.' In 1869, the Mesdag family settled in The Hague, where Mesdag went to Scheveningen every day to sketch. He even rented a room there to learn how to portray the sea and beach in all their varieties.

Mesdag had difficulty freeing himself from his image as an amateur painter. To his friends' surprise, he decided to submit two of his paintings to the Paris Salon in 1870 where a debate was going on about the uncompromising sea views that the painter Courbet, advocate of French realism, had submitted. The jury was more appreciative of Mesdag's 'Les Brisants de la Mer du Nord' – another painting without much narrative, consisting of little more than sky, sea water, the surge of the waves, and some wood flotsam on the beach. And although Mesdag was completely unknown, the jury awarded his painting the gold medal. Chaplin, one of the jury members, bought the painting, and another member, Millet, sent Mesdag a telegram congratulating him. For many years this telegram hung on the wall of Mesdag's studio. For long afterwards no one knew where the painting was, until Johan Poort in 1990 discovered that it had been cut in two and that both parts had had sailboats added to them. Now that it has been restored, it is donated to the Van Gogh Museum.

For Mesdag, winning the gold medal meant a real breakthrough: no longer would he be regarded as an amateur. Dutch recognition followed in 1872, when he again won a gold medal for 'The return of a fishing vessel to Scheveningen' at the exhibition of Living Masters. In 1878, King Leopold II of Belgium bought 'Scheveningen, ready to lift anchor' for a substantial amount. He appointed Mesdag Knight of the Order of Leopold. From this moment on he was valued for his realistic rendering of the sea. Van Santen Kolff, who gave the Hague School its name and was one of its champions, wrote: 'Whenever we ponder Mesdag's 'On the Dutch coast', we feel as if the salty sea air penetrates our nostrils and lungs, as if we can feel the fresh breeze of the beach playing with our hair, as if we hear the surf breaking [...] Here we have realism of the true, healthiest type. That is the way, I am convinced, that our landscape and sea painters sooner or later must go, if they want to create something lasting, according to the spirit of our time.' Joris-Karl Huysmans, an art critic at that time, wrote disappointingly about the Paris Salon of 1879 as well, but found that Mesdag's work stood out above the others and characterised him as a representative of modern art.

Contrary to what he wrote Alma Tadema, Mesdag had a good business sense and used this talent as artist as well. In his correspondence with art dealers he asked for the addresses of trustworthy

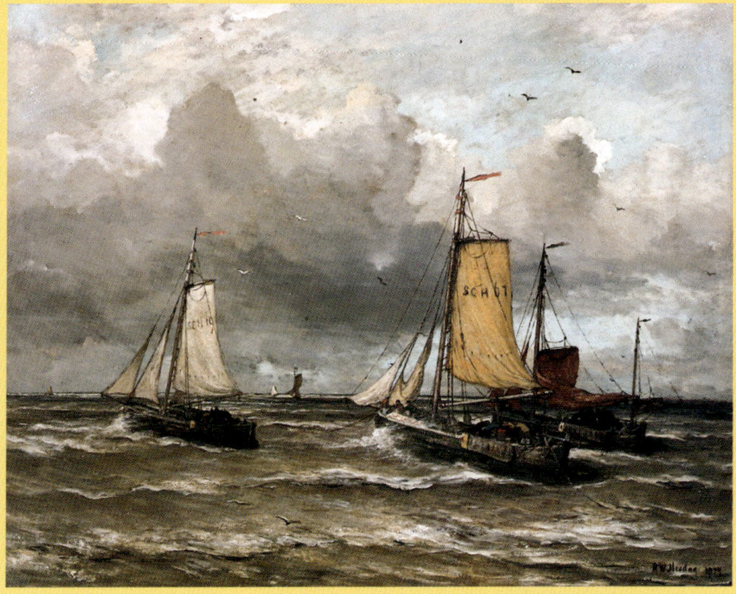

H.W. Mesdag, *Ships*, 1899
Panorama Mesdag collection, The Hague

dealers in other cities, and thus consciously extended his business network. When he would introduce himself to a new dealer in a letter, he did not only mention his French gold medal but also stated that his paintings were all of good quality, that they had to be exhibited in favourable places and that they were more than worth the high prices he asked for them. In business deals he held his ground, but if Mesdag noticed that the size of a painting or a subject did not please his public, he adjusted it to their wishes.

Now that he had mastered the technique of perspective and figure drawing, he concentrated on the composition and tonalities of his seascapes. He especially tried to catch the change of light during sunset in numerous sketches. His paintings increasingly consist of loose strokes. The notes he wrote with his sketches show a typically 'Hague-like' attempt towards rendering tonalities: he described the shades of the colours of the sea as 'a purplish grey', 'a greenish grey', and also having a 'warm light'. As subjects for his paintings he also chose life in the fishing community, ships, dragging the nets, the fish sellers, and the village of Scheveningen.

In 1871, when their son Klaas died just before his eighth birthday, Sientje also decided to devote herself to painting. In 1878, they decided to build a house on the Laan van Meerdervoort together with their brother-in-law Sam van Houten. Mesdag and Sientje each had a studio. To house their growing collection of contemporary French and Dutch art, they had a separate museum built in their garden. In 1903, Mesdag donated the major portion of his painting collection and the museum to the Dutch state, making it one of the few collections of contemporary art in the Netherlands that was open to the public. Although he always had a good financial base, also after 1866, Mesdag became a wealthy man when his father died in 1881. This enabled him to be a patron himself, and one of the recipients of his largesse was the young Italian painter Antonio Mancini. He bought several of his works as well as negotiating for him with other dealers.

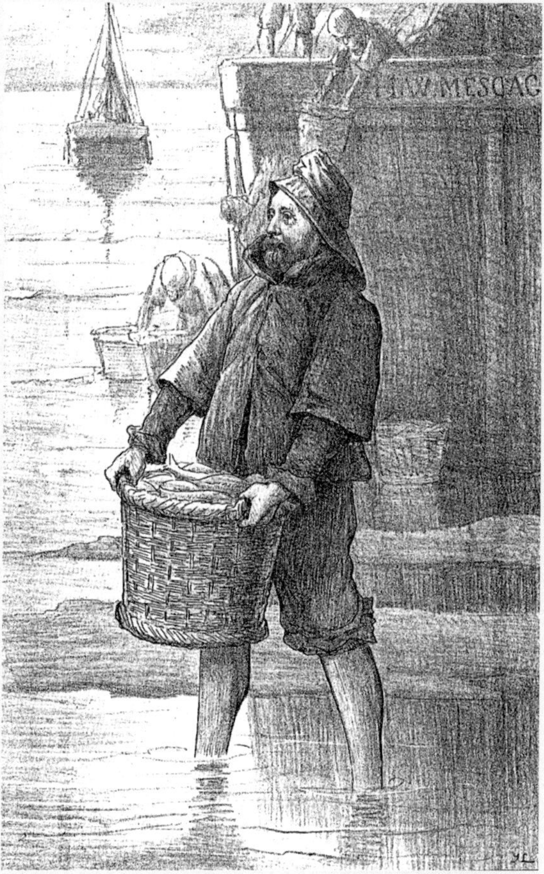

‘An ample ship master. Mesdag gathered the most beautiful that the close of the century has offered us. Because he preserve it for Holland, Holland thanks him’ (published in ‘De Nederlandsche Spectator’, 1903) (RKD collection)

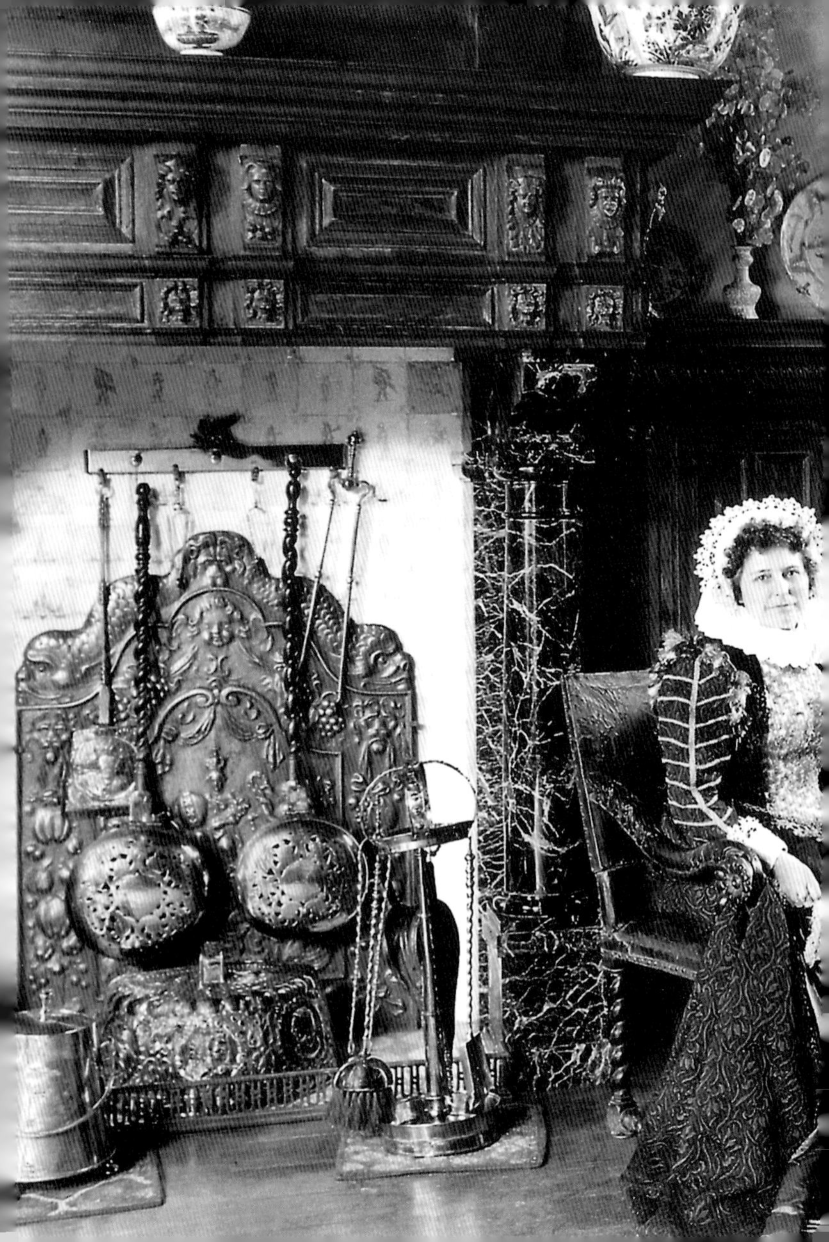

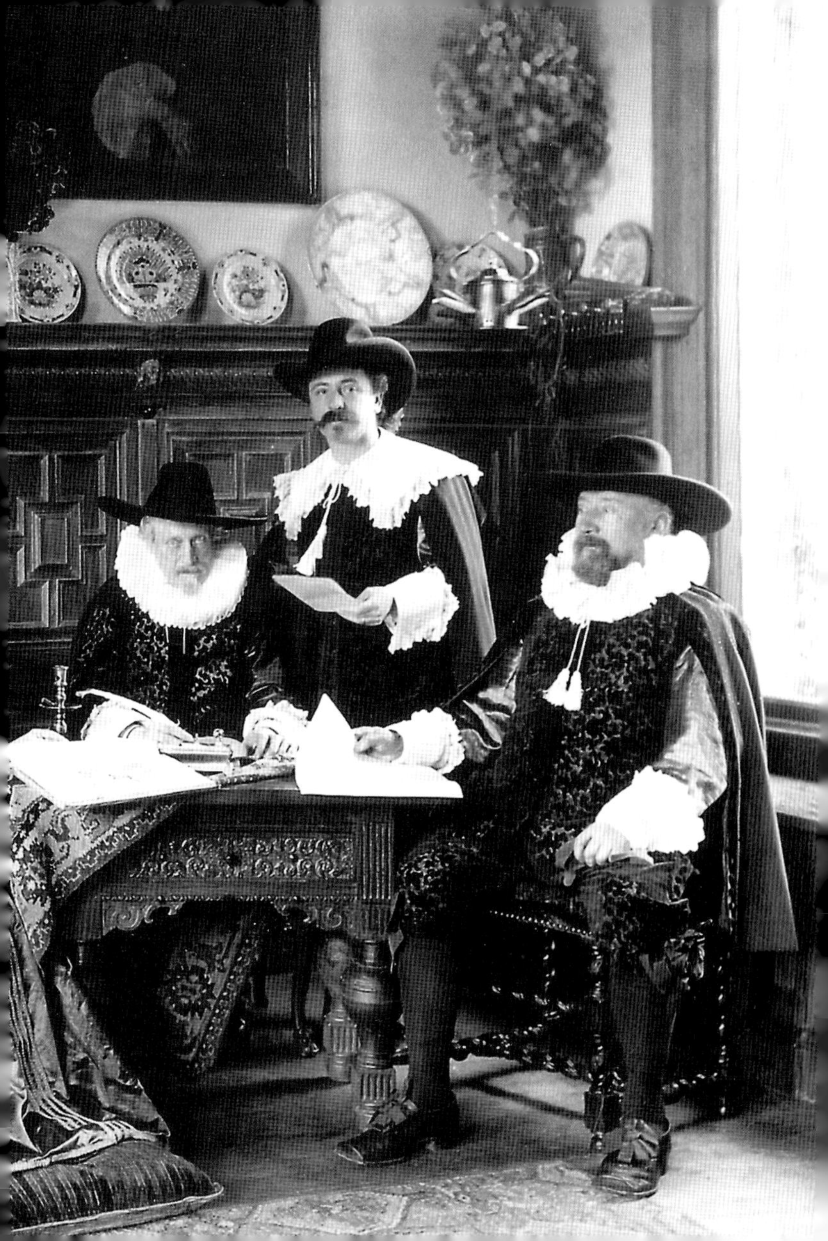

That same year he received a commission from a Belgian company to paint a panorama. The previous year the municipality of The Hague had announced that it would level the Seinpost Dune near Scheveningen, and Mesdag decided to make the view from this point the subject of his work. The enormous canvas measuring 1680 square meters was completed by Mesdag, his wife Sientje, Théophile de Bock, Bernard Blommers and George Hendrik Breitner in four months. It features a topographic compilation of many sketches of the sea, the dunes and the beach, the town of Scheveningen, fishing boats, bathing pavilions, Sientje painting on the beach and cavalry training. Various painters in the Hague spoke derogatorily about this undertaking. Van Gogh wrote to his friend Van Rappard that a pedantic painter had told De Bock that this type of thing was not at all artistic. De Bock's response was: 'What is more artistic – to do or not to do something?' When the Panorama was opened on 1 August, Mesdag's friends celebrated the occasion by going through the streets with music and torches. The painter viewed the Panorama as one of his most important works 'because it gave such a grand impression of nature', a characterisation that was true of all his work. Interest on the part of the public was somewhat disappointing, for the subject was much less spectacular than the battles shown in other panoramas in Rotterdam, Amsterdam and The Hague. After the Belgian company went bankrupt in 1886, the Mesdag family purchased the Panorama itself.

Mesdag was highly esteemed in the art life of The Hague: from 1869, he was a member of Pulchri Studio, and he was one of the founders of the Hollandsche Teekenmaatschappij (Dutch Drawing Society) in 1876. He was also chairman until 1885, and his work was always represented at the exhibitions and in the society's portfolio's containing works for sale. In 1889, he became chairman of Pulchri Studio, which he would remain until 1907, when he was made honorary chairman. The business sense that he used so advantageously for his own work, was also useful to the society: he devoted himself enthusiastically to the many foreign exhibitions of Dutch art and organised many highly publicised events for Pulchri Studio. Around 1900, he decided to move to a building on the Lange Voorhout. He and Sientje both invested money in renovating the building; the large hall with paintings, with its wonderful light from above, is still there.

At the end of his life Mesdag was greatly honoured. When he celebrated his seventieth birthday in 1901, he was made Commander of the Order of the Dutch Lion. In 1906, he and Sientje celebrated their fiftieth wedding anniversary, which led Pulchri Studio to host a party for them. All the city's art dealers exhibited his work. In 1909, Sientje died, and soon thereafter Mesdag's health began to fade. He died on 10 July 1915, after a long illness.

pp. 260-261:
Suze Robertson, Christoffel Bisschop, F.J. van Rossum du Chattel and H.W. Mesdag in historical costumes
(J. Poort photo collection, Wassenaar)

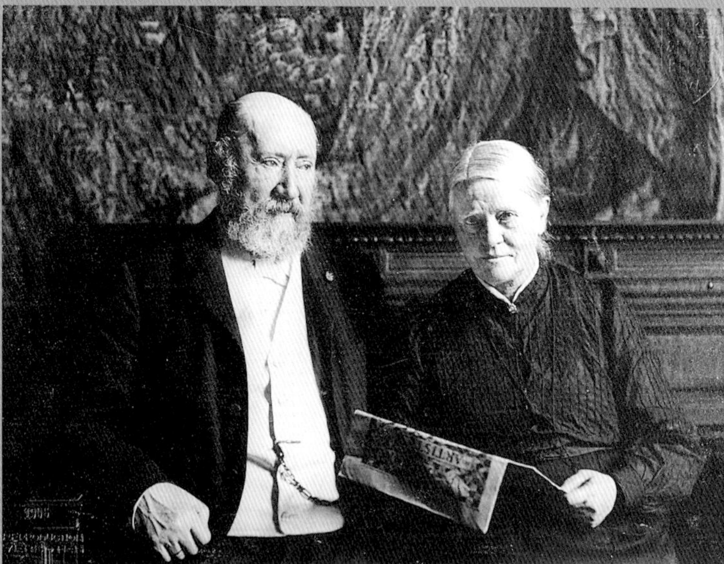

Photo of H.W. Mesdag and Sientje Mesdag-van Houten, 1906 (RKD collection)

Photo of H.W. Mesdag in his house on the Laan van Meerdervoort

p. 266:
Photo of Jacob Maris in his studio

pp. 268-269:
Photo of Mrs Maris and company wearing traditional costumes;
in the background is a self-portrait of Matthijs Maris

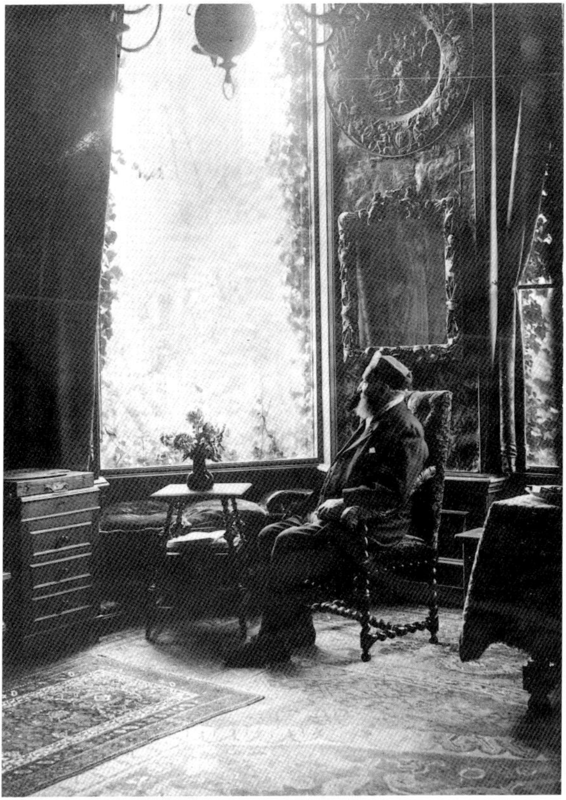

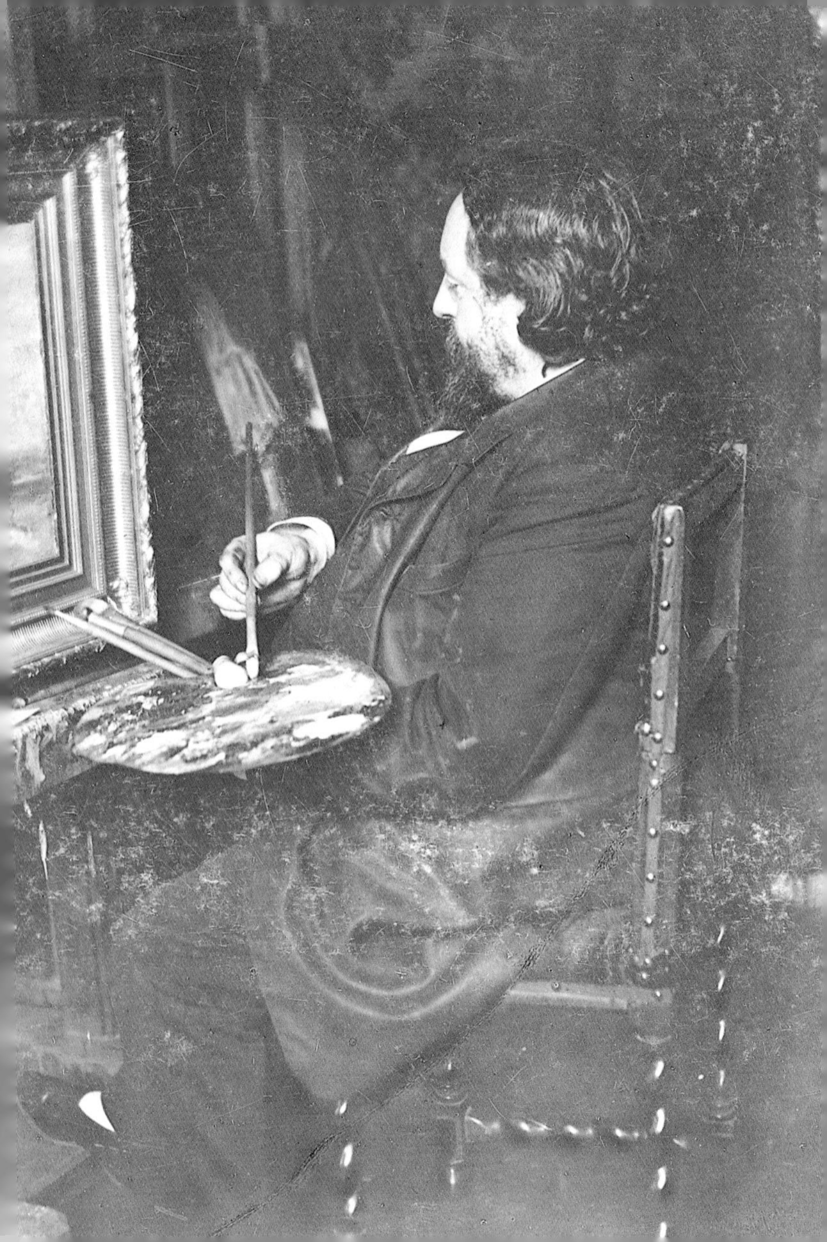

Jacob Maris

(1837-1899)

Jacob Maris was born in The Hague on 25 August 1837. He was the oldest in a family of five children. All three of the boys were later to become artists. Mattheus Maris, his father, was foreman at a printer's, and the children copied the prints and illustrations that he brought home. When he was twelve, Jacob Maris took lessons from J.A.B. Stroebel. Later, he enrolled in the Haagsche Teekenacademie (Hague Academy of Art). It is reported that A.A. Weimar, an art dealer in The Hague, saw Jacob and his brother Matthijs on the street drawing, and recognised their talent. He introduced Jacob to Louis Meijer, the sea painter, and saw to it that in 1854 Jacob was able to work in Huib Van Hove's studio. Van Hove also taught Stroebel. Both young artists painted interiors in the same fashion, after Pieter de Hoogh. Maris also practised interior, figurative and genre painting. Compared to his teachers, his interiors showed fewer anecdotal elements, concentrating more on the use of light. In 1854, Maris made his debut at the exhibition of Living Masters.

Van Hove moved to Antwerp because he had tax debts, and the nineteen year old Maris went with him. Although their relationship began to go downhill, Jacob remained at his teacher's studio because he depended on him financially. This was to change in 1855 when Matthijs Maris was granted a royal subsidy and joined his brother. Together they rented space which also had a room for their friend Lourens Alma Tadema. They took lessons at the Antwerp Academy. In order to make a living, both brothers made small paintings of interiors and biblical tableaux, which they sold for 5 to 10 guilders whenever they had a full chest, and these were then shipped off to America.

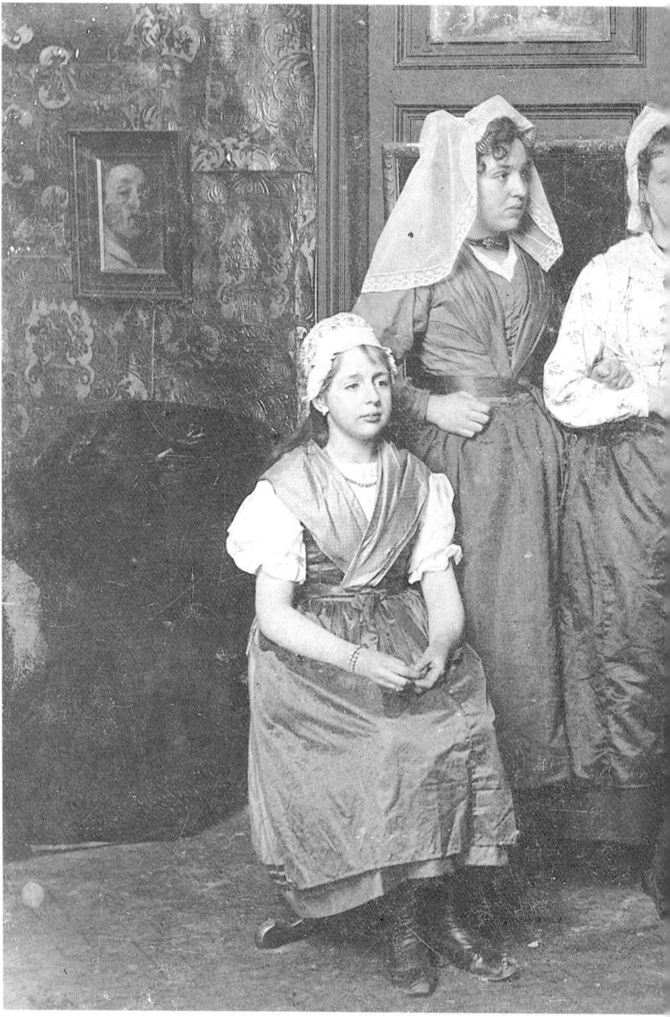

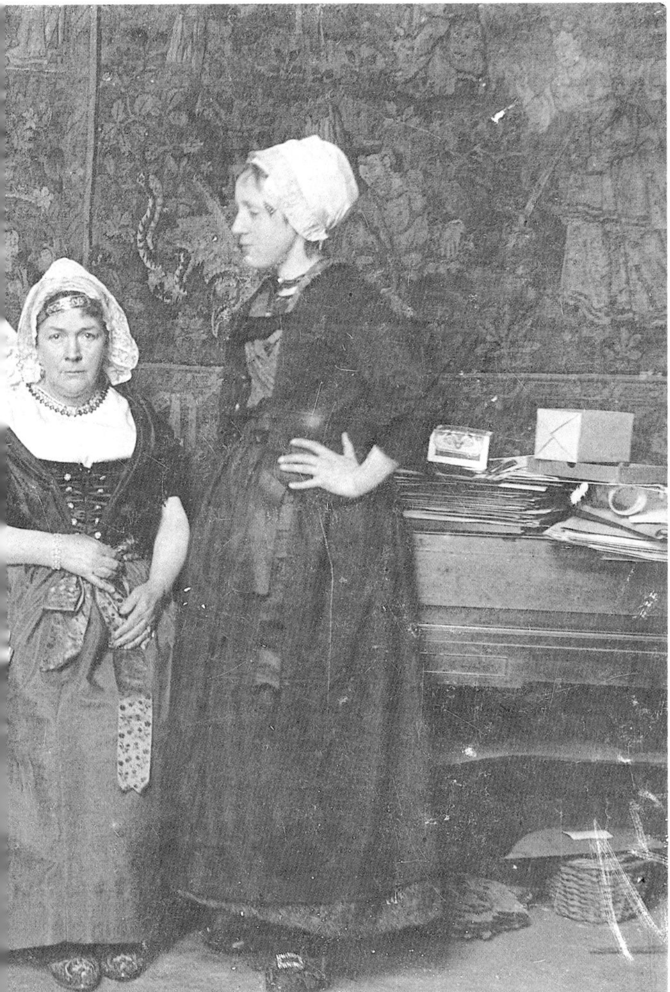

In 1857, Jacob Maris returned to The Hague, but Matthijs stayed another year in Antwerp before he again shared a studio with Jacob in The Hague. Around 1860, they were commissioned by Princess Marianne, the youngest daughter of King William I, to copy eight portraits of the House of Orange. The 700 guilders they earned from this allowed them to go to Oosterbeek and Wolfheze, where they met J.W. Bilders, his son Gerard, and other people who would later play important roles in the Hague School. The landscapes the brothers created showed much similarity. They went on a study trip together, which can be traced from their sketch book: they went from Cologne, Mannheim, Heidelberg and Karlsruhe to Switzerland (Basel, Lausanne, Neufchatel) and France (Dijon, Fontainebleau, Paris). When all their money was spent they again moved in with their parents. Jacob Maris again took lessons at the Hague Academy of Art and helped his rheumatic friend, the sea painter Louis Meijer, fill in his paintings.

In the summer of 1864, Jacob Maris again went to Oosterbeek, and possibly also to Fontainebleau and Barbizon. Following this trip he moved to Paris, which was probably made possible by his new financial security, owing to his good contacts since 1860 with Vincent van Gogh, a Hague art dealer and an uncle of the painter. Van Gogh was associated with Goupil, a Paris art dealer, and had been living in the French capital for several years. For a short time Maris worked in Ernest Hébert's studio (possibly arranged by Van Gogh). Hébert's paintings of Italian peasants were very well-known, as the 'Italian women' genre and its masculine equivalent, 'the Savoyards', were very popular at the time. Even at the Hague Academy and Pulchri Studio this theme was in fashion. Maris also worked in this genre, and in 1866 made his debut at the Paris Salon with 'Little Italian girl'. His painting technique is rich in colours, detailed and smooth. He also painted girls who were not in Italian dress, but would nevertheless be identified as part of this genre; for example, the 'Knitter on the balcony in Montmartre'. Goupil sold many of these paintings, for the most part to customers in America.

From this period on, Maris signed his paintings not as 'J.H. Maris' but as 'J. Maris'.

It had long been reported that Maris wanted to concentrate on landscape painting, but Goupil convinced him not to because the Italian girls were such a success. In 1868, with 'Shepherd boy by a river', Maris supposedly had completed his first landscape, and when he found that Goupil was not very enthusiastic about it, Maris submitted it to the Paris Salon on his own. Although it was hung in a place where it was difficult to see, the London art dealer Henry Wallis (who, as an experienced Salon visitor, was equipped with binoculars) did notice the painting and purchased it immediately. This event marked a turning point for Maris in his painting career: he had wrested himself from the grip of the demanding art dealer and in the future was to concentrate only on landscapes and city views. From the records of sale, however, it appears that Wallis really purchased this work from Goupil. Moreover, Maris had already been submitting landscapes to the Salon in Rotterdam in 1864, and had been making nature studies from his first visit to Oosterbeek in 1861. Even his visits to Fontainebleau, Barbizon, and later the villages of Marlotte and Montigny-sur-Loing show that he had been working on landscape paintings before. Despite Maris' change of subject matter, his contacts with Goupil in Paris and The Hague remained very close and lucrative for both parties. In this respect Wallis' valuation of Maris' landscapes may have been important as a final impetus in the new direction, possibly for both the painter and the art dealership.

At the outbreak of the Franco-Prussian War in 1870, which was succeeded by the French Commune, Maris, his wife Katrien and their young daughter Henriette moved back to the Netherlands. Initially, he had only planned for a brief stay, but he was to remain for the rest of his life. H.G. Tersteeg, manager of the Hague branch of Goupil, may have helped the family with moving expenses. They settled on the Noordwest Binnensingel.

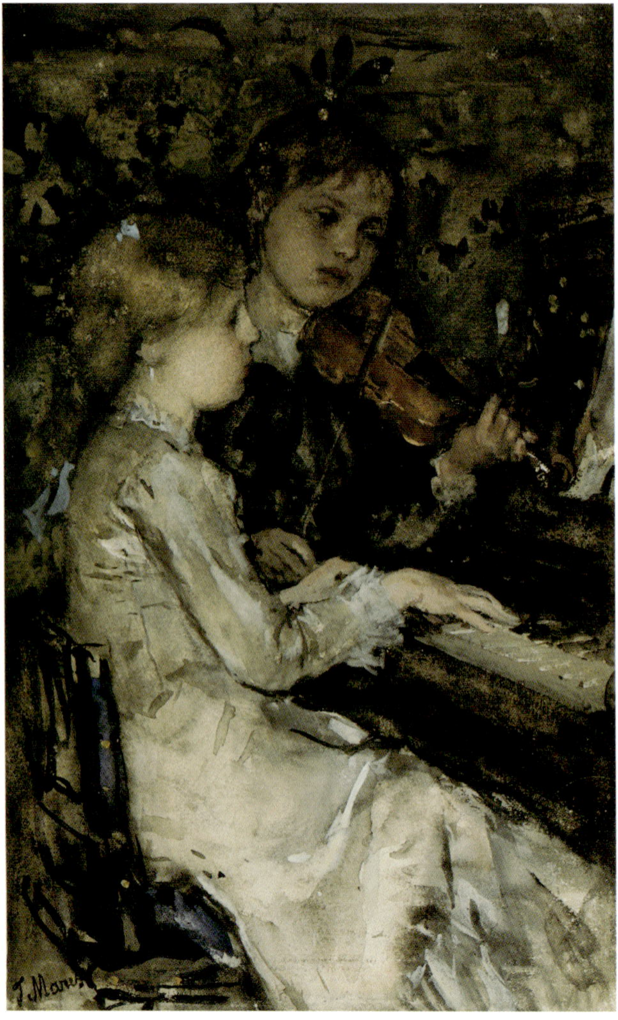

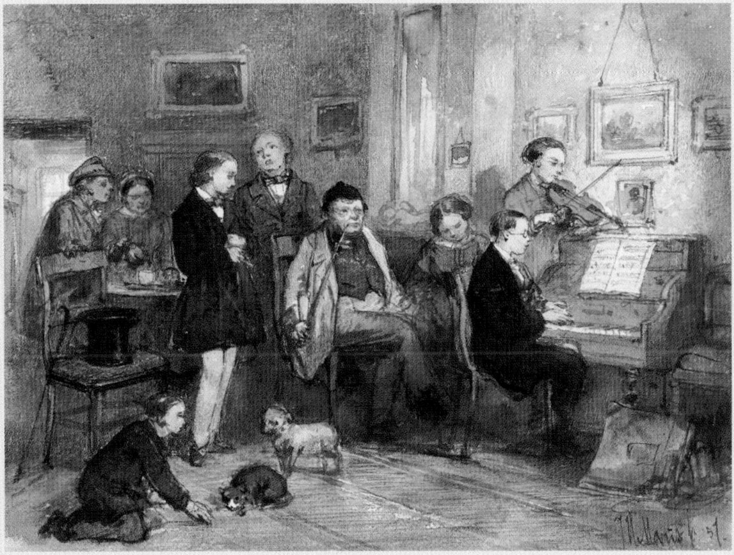

Jacob Maris, *The Maris brothers at a musical soirée at Mr Sierig's,* 1857 (watercolour)

Jacob Maris, *The duet* (watercolour)

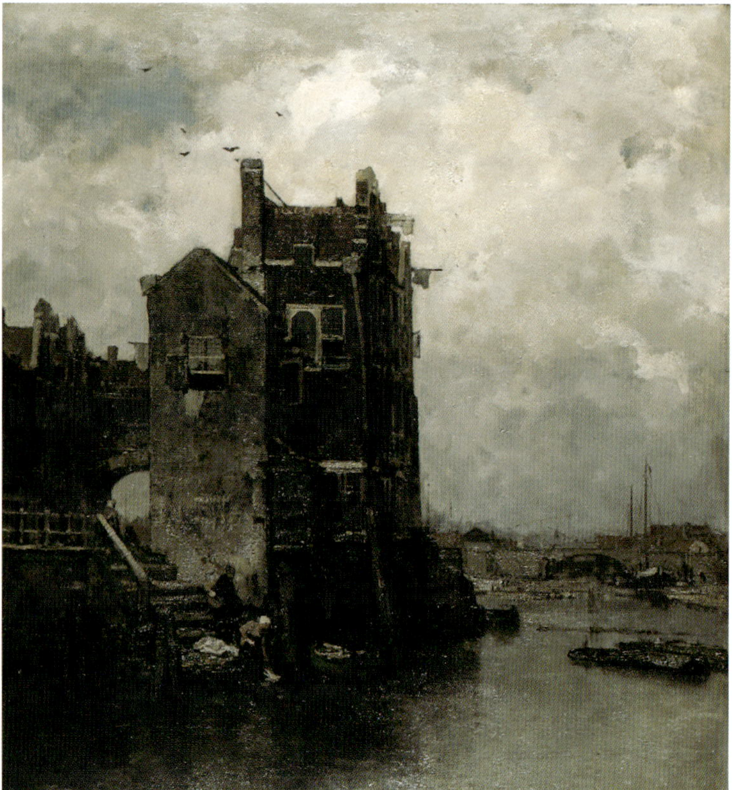

Jacob Maris, *Old Dordrecht (the old house),* 1876

In The Hague Maris mostly painted landscapes, many in the immediate area of his studio. Famous from this period is his 'Cut-off mill', a view that he was able to see and paint from his window. Even the small white bridge right near his house can be seen in many of his paintings. His style changed as well: from a sensitive figure painter, skilled at the accurate rendering of the texture of fabrics, he developed into a strong landscape painter. He painted rivers and canals, landscapes with mills and towpaths, and beach views with fishing boats. His stroke became broader and larger, combining this with impasto. His use of colour became more subdued and directed towards portraying the atmospheric depiction of clouds. This part of his work has been compared to the seventeenth-century painters Jan van Goyen, Jacob van Ruisdael and Johannes Vermeer. His way of working has been described in the following way: 'They say that he paints first and draws only afterwards. He applies the paint thickly, builds it up, fiddles around and messes with it – all gradually developing into a harmony of colours that establishes the major directions. Only then does he complete his figures with lively, thin brush strokes. But the final touch is done with a master stroke, and in the end the entire work is as solid as the tightest drawing.'

Maris was one of the few in the Netherlands who painted city views, often of Amsterdam but even more often combined locations and house facades from Amsterdam, Rotterdam, Delft and Dordrecht. These made up city views he perceived more as 'character images than portraits'. He said: 'Why isn't it possible for me to be able to build my own cities?', referring to the old painter Samuel Verveer, who had allowed himself the same freedom. The high skies with robust white clouds above these cities were his speciality. He went to great lengths to achieve this, and wrote: 'The most difficult thing about our art is to make the paint live: to make the clouds move in space, to make the light sing.' The commercial success of these works made Goupil continue to ask for similar works, and Maris must once have sighed: ‘Damn, again a city with white clouds!’ Nevertheless, he developed great virtuosity and self-confidence in the subject. The story goes that, when out on a stormy day, he bumped into an acquaintance who said, ‘What a beautiful sky, don’t you think?’ to which Maris supposedly replied: ‘Oh, never mind, I’ll paint it better’.

In 1871, Maris became a member of Pulchri Studio and would fill various administrative positions there. Socially he was completely accepted in The Hague. When the Hollandsche Teekenmaatschappij (Dutch Drawing Society) was founded in 1876, he became one of the first members of the board. Yet he sold more of his work through Goupil to America, Canada and England than in the Netherlands. It was only after 1876 that he experienced any renown in the Netherlands; his definitive breakthrough occurred in 1885. From that time on he was a very celebrated and much requested painter. As a leader of the Hague School his influence was enormous. Nevertheless, Willem de Zwart and possibly Bernard Blommers, had been his only students.

When he was in his sixties Maris began to suffer from asthma and corpulence. At the advice of his doctors he went to take the waters at Karlsbad, where he suddenly died on 7 August 1899. He was buried in The Hague.

Jacob Maris, *Mill in the snow,* n.d. (watercolour)

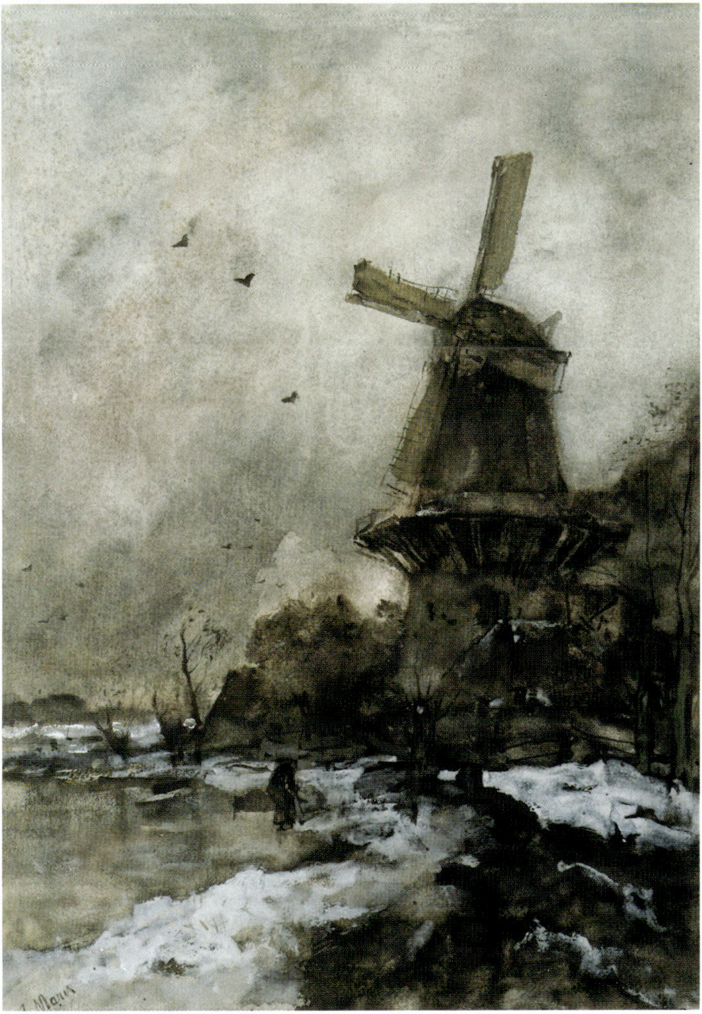

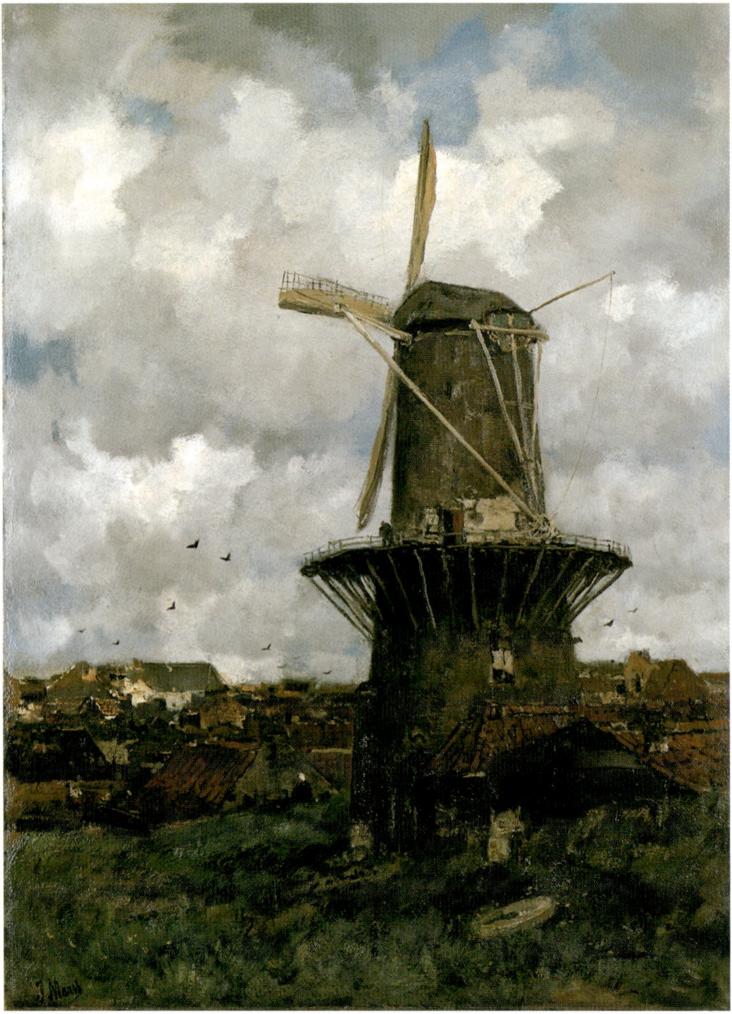

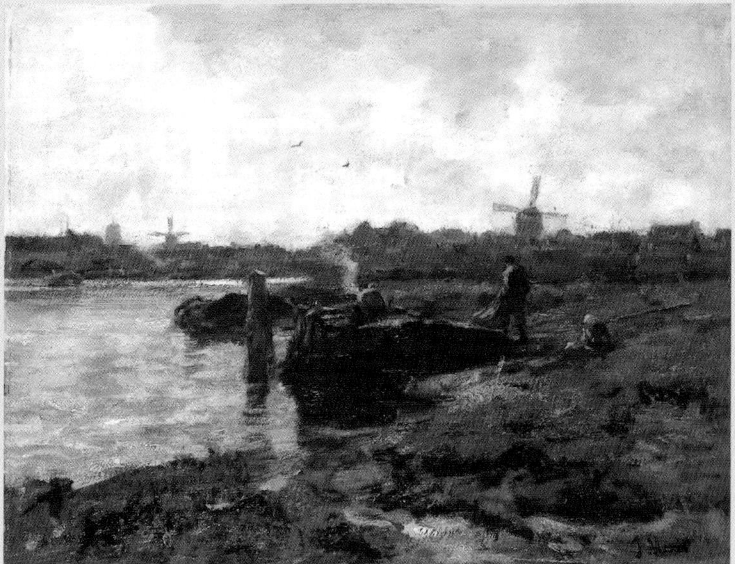

Jacob Maris, *Stone mill,* ca. 1890

Jacob Maris, *Near Dordrecht,* ca. 1890

p. 280:
Photo-portrait of Gerard Bilders
(Collection of the Gemeentearchief, The Hague)

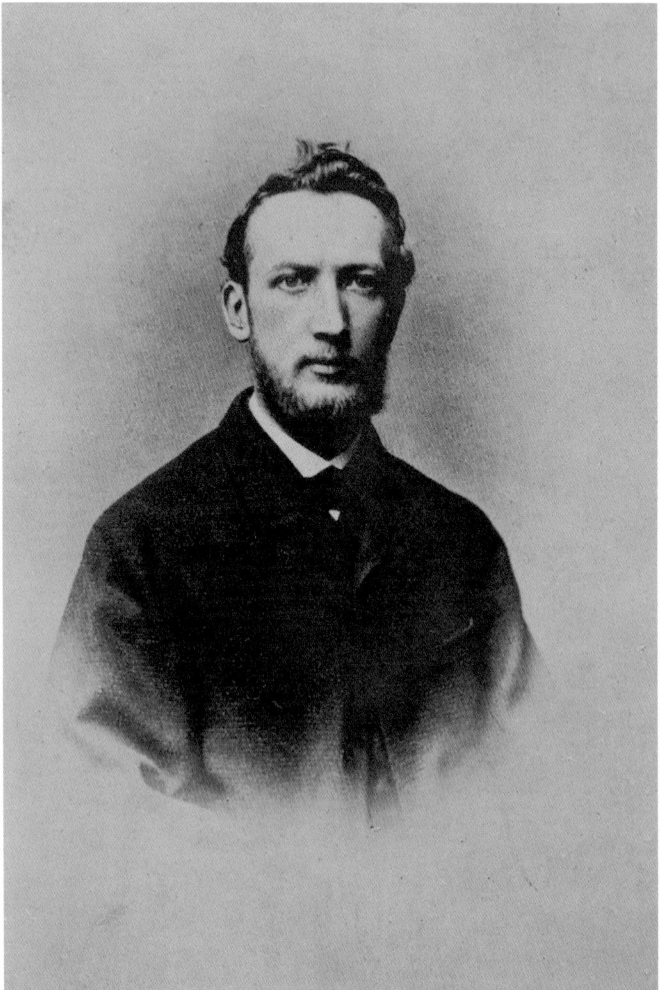

Gerard Bilders

(1838-1865)

Albertus Gerardus Bilders was born in Utrecht on 9 December 1838. His father was Johannes Warnardus Bilders, the well-known landscape painter and dean of the 'painters group' in Oosterbeek. Gerard grew up in Utrecht and in the Oosterbeek house called 'The Parre'. He received his first lessons in painting from his father.

After the Leiden literary critic Kneppelhout, well-known for his realistic but moralizing sketches of student life under the pseudonym Klikspaan, purchased the estate 'De Hemelsche Berg' as well as the surrounding areas that were part of it, he visited Bilders Sr's studio. There he met Gerard, whom he saw as an 'uncultivated, unspoiled child of nature', and decided to make something of him. Kneppelhout had an ideal in mind that he had articulated about ten years previously in his 'l'?ducation par l'amitié': tracing and developing, through friendship, the creative strength that was hidden in each person. With the approval of his parents Bilders became Kneppelhout's protégé. But the young painter was not his only protégé: the poet Petrus August de Génestet and the violinist Jan de Graan were also in Kneppelhout's custody. The same ideal prompted Kneppelhout to found schools, such as the Institute for Young Men in Oosterbeek.

Kneppelhout gave Bilders an allowance (albeit irregularly and not too generous) and arranged a place for him in the studio of Simon van den Berg, a painter of cattle who lived in the Hague. Bilders also visited the 'plaster classes' of the Haagsche Teekenacademie (Hague Academy of Art), although with little enthusiasm. He bought a sheep's head from a butcher, which he copied. And he also copied seventeenth-century masters in the Mauritshuis. Jacob van Ruisdael was his ideal 'who always painted and thought in the same poetic tone; what a genius he was!' He was impressed by Potter's portrayal of cattle in a powerful yet elusive, 'gentle' way. He made studies after the famous bull, although it was the sheep and the lamb in the background that captured Bilders' attention. The posture of the sheep, foreshortened and portrayed from the back, was to be a motive that would often be seen in his work.

Bilders' admiration for these renowned predecessors caused him to doubt his own future as an artist. Kneppelhout continuously sent letters with good advice to the young painter, providing him with recommendations, exhortations and warnings. From his written responses as well as his diaries, a picture emerges of Bilders as a worried young man, filled with enormous love for nature and the paintings of the seventeenth century, but always doubting his own work. Especially in the winter, when it was impossible to work directly from nature and he had to spend his time on working out sketches in the studio, he wrote about his fear that he would not be able to capture the living colours of the outdoors and would get stuck with the 'indoors tones'. Kneppelhout's influence on him was far-reaching, partly because of his insecurity, and Kneppelhout concerned himself with absolutely everything related to his protégé. For example, in March 1858 Bilders wrote: 'It is a pleasure for me that in your last letter you were so tough on me. I was especially surprised when you pointed out a flaw in my character, which I had already detected, that is, although I often talk about my many defects, I don't do anything to improve them.'

Bilders returned to Oosterbeek in the summer of 1857, where he preferred to study the anatomy of cows to plaster models. Just as his father had, he saw nature itself as the only true teacher, and said: 'I believe that once someone decides to become a landscape painter, it is important to live as much as possible among the bare skies, to eat, drink, read and sleep under the trees and in the grass.' In his admiration for the painters of the Golden Age he was also following in his father's footsteps. Yet his father's influence on Bilders' style can only be detected in his earliest works.

The following summer Kneppelhout gave him an opportunity to travel to Switzerland. For one month he received lessons in Geneva from Charles Humbert, a landscape and animal painter. Humbert was content with his student, and wrote that the young man had a lively feel for colour and that during his stay was able to get a better eye for the effects of light. Humbert advised him to visit the village of St. Ange. Bilders befriended the amateur painter Auguste, Count of Pourtalès, and they travelled together through Switzerland, making studies of groups of rocks. In September Bilders worked in the mountains near Chamonix, and subsequently returned to the Netherlands.

This trip enabled Bilders to free himself somewhat from Kneppelhout's restrained view. Thereupon Kneppelhout blamed Bilders for his lack of open-hearted friendship, but nevertheless continued to support Bilders and arranged rooms for him in Leiden. That way he could guide him better, as he himself lived on the Rapenburg in Leiden. Bilders worked in the area around Leiden, Leiderdorp and Zoeterwoude, mainly painting meadows with cattle. Cows, sheep and goats were always important in his work; people are present in his paintings, but always in subordinate roles. Yet he does not paint the 'cow for the cow' but rather as part of a 'great and beautiful' nature, which he approached with an almost religious worship. Bilders tried to reproduce the moods that the landscape evoked by using peculiar light effects as well as a 'coloured, fragrant, warm grey'. While he mixed all the colours of his palette with grey to get this effect, he was usually dissatisfied with the result. This attempt foreshadows the tonal painting style of the Hague School painters. However, at that age Bilders was better able to describe the effect he was striving for in his letters and diaries than he could achieve in his paintings.

In this regard, it is quite understandable why Kneppelhout stated that Bilders was a writer rather than a painter.

In November 1859, Bilders moved to a studio in Amsterdam, and the following spring he was made an honorary member of the Rijksacademie in Amsterdam. He reacted to this by saying: 'Certainly, this is an important honour, given my very limited talent: this makes me want more than ever to try to work my best in order to extend [my talent] to become more worthy [of the honour]'. Around 1860, Kneppelhout stated that Bilders must be able to stand on his own feet and ceased to support him financially. This led to Bilders often having money problems thereafter, which did not help his conviction and desire to work. His writings were punctuated with self-reproach, and he said that he used his knife and pumice stone at least as often to scrape paint from his canvases as he used his brush to apply paint. He believed his paintings suffered from a lack of seriousness, passion, mood and suffering: '[...] It simply comes down to the fact that in my paintings not only do I lack a compelling feeling, I do not know how to evoke any empathy. They look pedantic, lack youthfulness, and without that the whimsical fantasy is also lacking; they seem to have been created by an old man who was never very good.'

J.W. Bilders showed his work at an exhibition in Brussels, taking Gerard with him. There he became acquainted with the work of the Barbizon painters Troyon, Courbet, Diaz, Dupré and Robert Fleury. Bilders was deeply affected: he saw unity, rest, seriousness and intimacy in their paintings, and also recognised the inspiration of the Dutch seventeenth-century masters. At the same time he became so very disheartened (just as when he had been confronted with the painters of the Golden Age) that he got drunk. According to his own statements, in these circumstances he had 'often asked for directions, hoping [...] that he would go astray.'

When Bilders' mother died of tuberculosis in 1861, Kneppelhout feels sorry for the painter, and the relationship improves. They spent the summer in Oosterbeek: Kneppelhout on his estate and Bilders in a house in the water meadows. He spends a lot of time with Jan de Haas, an animal painter who would be marrying his sister Carolien the following year. It has often been said that he became friends with Anton Mauve and the Maris brothers, who at the time regularly worked in Oosterbeek and Wolfheze. In light of this it is remarkable that Bilders wrote to Kneppelhout in 1863 about a 'certain Marits'. His contacts were clearly not as close as would have been expected from a precursor. On the other hand, Willem Maris remembers his meeting with Mauve and Gerard Bilders as if both painters had worked and spent their free time together.

A number of studies have been preserved from this period, which through their fresh, spontaneous impression seem to have been accomplished with less difficulties. Bilders had some success, albeit on a modest scale. At times Kneppelhout purchased one of his works, even though he often asked Bilders to make some corrections. The same year, Bilders completed a painting that was unusually large for him: 'Landscape in the Betuwe with an impending storm'. After its exhibition in Utrecht he received favourable reviews; the work was sold for nine hundred guilders, which enabled him to keep four hundred fifty guilders after deducting his costs – at that time a very substantial sum.

In the autumn he went on a second trip to Switzerland, where he stayed with the De Pourtalès family in Geneva. Together with his friend Auguste he again visited the town of St. Ange. In 1862, Bilders sold several paintings: one to Arti et Amicitiae for two hundred and another in Stuttgart for nine hundred guilders. The criticism he received from purchasers of art was mostly directed at his sketchy way of working, while the reviews tended to concentrate on his sometimes excessive reproduction of light effects. That summer Kneppelhout proposed a trip abroad. While Bilders wanted to go to Paris where the 'torch of modern art' burnt and where he would be

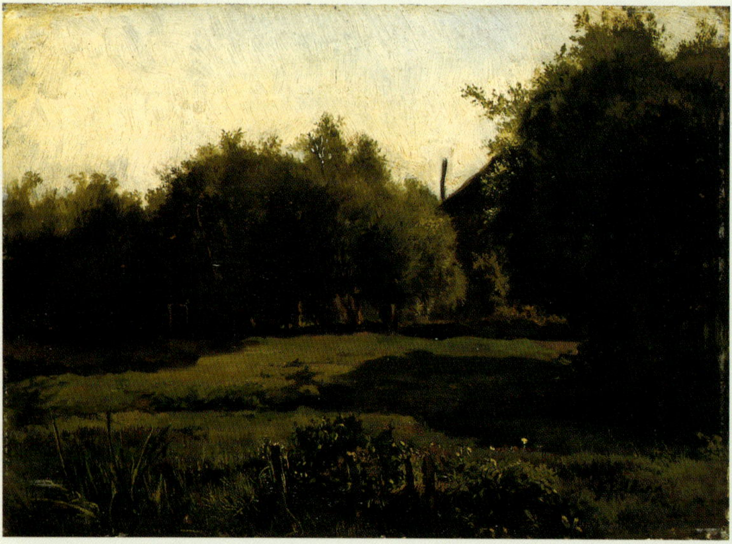

Gerard Bilders, *Haystack among trees (Farm near Wolfheze)*, ca. 1860-1863

able to see more of the Barbizon painters, Kneppelhout was thinking of Dresden, which was then still the centre of the German Romantic School. Bilders reacted by saying: 'I understand very well what you tell me about Paris. It is a dangerous flow, and most [of the painters] fail. But in Amsterdam it is the same. Those who were born to struggle have enough to fight about; the same bad angel lurks everywhere, but here people don't lose any sleep over it.' The two cannot agree, and instead decide to go to Lochem for a week. In Lochem Bilders became ill, spitting blood: the first clear sign of tuberculosis.

In 1864, Bilders went to Brussels in an attempt to find buyers for his work. He believed that in Amsterdam and Utrecht 'the customers had died out'. He only sold one painting. He spent the summer in Oosterbeek, but in November, when his health deteriorated, he moved in with his father in Amsterdam. When he was dying he asked Kneppelhout to visit him. He did not come, but wrote that a letter meant more to him than a visit, saying that Bilders should have become a writer rather than a painter. Bilders died on 8 March 1865, when he was only twenty-six. Kneppelhout did not go to his funeral, a few days afterwards. Bilders' pallbearers were his fellow painters Mauve, Allebé and Artz.

In his short life Bilders created some two hundred paintings. His work was characterised by an ambiguous view with respect to tradition and renewal. As a precursor of the Hague School, the meaning of his work was to be found not so much in his paintings as in the opinions he expressed about art. Kneppelhout posthumously published an extensive (but censored) selection from Bilders' letters and passages from his diaries. The first edition in 1868 was very limited: only twelve copies. The second edition in 1876 was possibly somewhat larger – one hundred copies. Yet Bilders' opinions about nature, mood, colour and art found their way among painters. They especially made a profound impression on Mauve, Gabriël and Willem Maris.

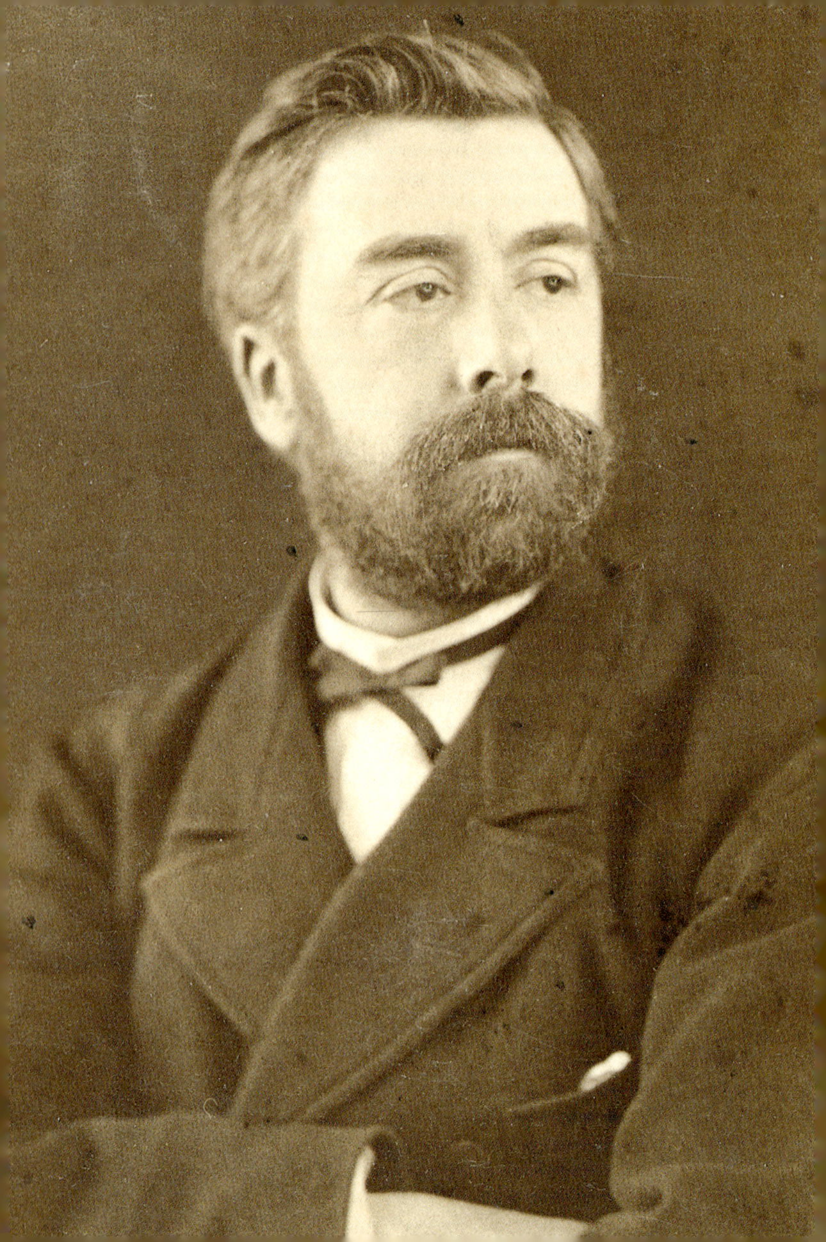

Anton Mauve

(1838-1888)

Anthonij Mauve was born on 18 September 1838 to a large family in Zaandam. His father was a Baptist preacher, who was called to Haarlem, where Mauve spent his youth. When he was sixteen Mauve went to study with the famous animal painter P.F. van Os. He worked there for about three years, and afterwards received lessons for a few months from Wouterus Verschuur Sr, who was known for his paintings of horses. Vincent van Gogh later sneeringly remarked: 'You can sometimes indirectly learn a great deal even from comparatively poor artists, as, for example, Mauve learned much from Verschuur with respect to bringing perspective to a stable, a cart and the anatomy of a horse, and yet, Mauve stands head and shoulders above Verschuur.' Whatever the case: Mauve's career started with the traditional genre of cattle painting.

Paul Gabriël, who was ten years older than Mauve, also lived and worked in Haarlem at that time. In the summer of 1857, he took Mauve to Oosterbeek. Mauve was introduced to the dean of the 'painters group', J.W. Bilders, his son Gerard Bilders and his son-in-law Jan de Haas. In the following years Mauve often went to Oosterbeek to work. The anecdote about how Mauve met Willem Maris became famous. Maris, who had come to Gelderland on his own, was a few years younger than Mauve and Bilders. When Mauve saw him working, he became very enthusiastic about Maris' drawing ability. In later years Maris loved to refer to this event, adding: 'The moment he met me resulted in a complete change in the way he painted. He came along to The Hague, even though he didn't know anyone there at all.'

Unlike other painters, Mauve not only stayed in Oosterbeek for the summer, but also during other seasons. Contemporaries characterised the area as an example of unspoiled nature, and compared it with Barbizon and Fontainebleau in France. Mauve particularly appreciated studies from nature, which in practice mainly involved the accurate drawing of landscapes and details. Thus Mauve developed a more realistic view of nature than he had learnt in the studios of Van Os and Verschuur. However, he was often hindered by his inability to reproduce everything that he saw and felt: 'whatever you saw was too much and too beautiful'. He later put these struggles into perspective when responding to the question what the secret of his art was: 'Well, you go outside, light your pipe, whistle a tune, and paint what crosses your path.'

Indeed, Mauve and Willem Maris became good friends, and Maris' broad manner of drawing surely served as an example for Mauve. They often worked together, even on the same painting, in order to improve and help one another. Mauve wrote letters to his friend in The Hague to convince him to come to Oosterbeek. These letters include lyrical descriptions like: 'Before sunset I went to the heath, you can understand what it looked like. Sweet, movingly sweet and very grand, the shepherd with his sheep came to the brook, and I can still hear their bells and clicking rustling in my ears, like the most beautiful music by Beethoven. Slowly I saw them cross the heath, and then they finally were lost to view.' But the arguments Maris had to succumb to were also more pragmatic: 'Come in the beginning of May, that month is excellently suited for studying the cattle, the cows are much quieter then because flies and other insects have not yet settled on them.'

From 1865 to 1871, Mauve lived in various places, including Amsterdam, Haarlem, Renkum, Wezep in Drente and Dordrecht; mainly in search of an inexpensive but light room where he could stay when he was not in Oosterbeek. In 1871, he lived in The Hague for a

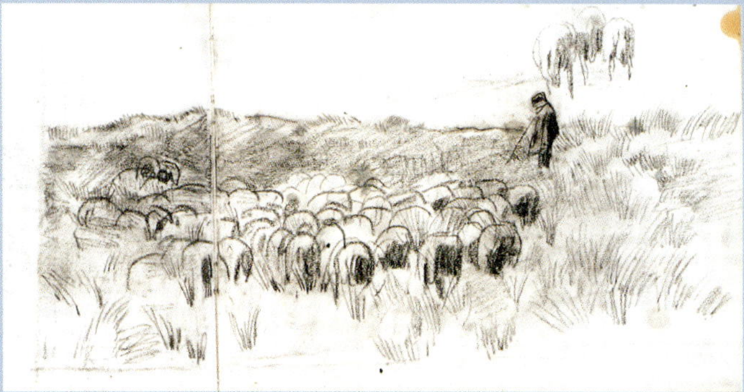

Anton Mauve, Page from a sketchbook, n.d.

p. 288:
Photo-portrait Anton Mauve

short while where he met Ariëtte Sophia Jeannette Carbentus. Mauve was often insecure about his work and increasingly suffered from depression. The doctor prescribed him a long vacation, and he lived for a while with his brother-in-law in Alkmaar. In 1873, he went to Bad Godesberg in Germany to take a rest cure. When he returned to The Hague, he married Jet Carbentus. Part of their honeymoon they stayed with Gabriël, who was living in Brussels at the time. The Mauves settled permanently in The Hague. Mauve was henceforth to remain in the Netherlands.

He worked in the area surrounding The Hague, especially around Dekkersduin, south of the city. The farm 'Kranenburg' was located on the Laan van Meerdervoort, then still in the middle of the dunes. Mauve had a studio there. He painted his first flocks of sheep and befriended the shepherds. This would later become one of his favourite subjects, also among his followers and art lovers. At the time however, this theme was still a self-willed choice, the more so because Mauve portrayed his subject in a realistic rather then a romantic manner. In addition, he developed into a very versatile painter, watercolourist and draughtsman. He painted meadows with cows, milking yards, sand paths, foresters in the woods, work horses and smart horsemen, interiors, portraits and the beach at Scheveningen, the fishing boats being drawn by draught horses as well as fashionable beach life. He was increasingly valued for his easy brushstrokes, informal compositions, and his portrayal of the silver light that was often associated with the Hague sea air. His drawings earned a great deal of admiration as well: 'In leaving out and sacrificing what was unnecessary, he was classical par excellence. There are scratches among these sketches, which completely express a landscape in five or six lines.'

In The Hague Mauve actively participated in the social aspects of the artist's life. In 1876, Mauve, Mesdag and Willem Maris together founded the Hollandsche Teekenmaatschappij (Dutch Drawing Society). Mauve was a very talented watercolourist, and submitted

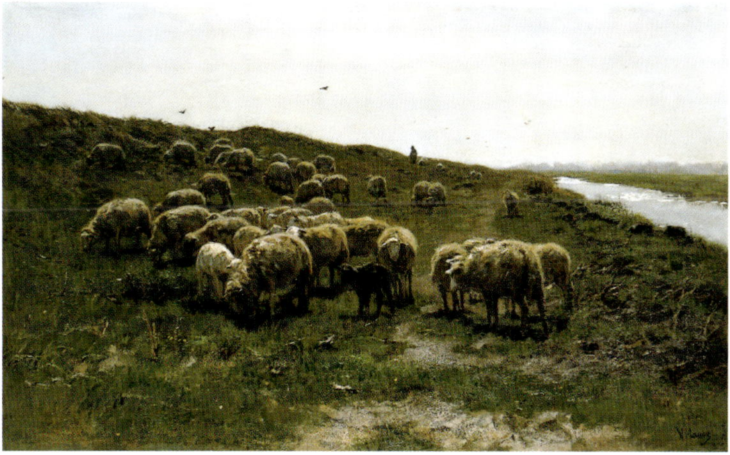

Anton Mauve, *Sheep on a dike,* ca. 1870

many canvases for the organisation's sales folders. High-flown descriptions of these paintings have been preserved: 'When Mauve paints a watercolour, poetry gently strikes [...] its wings on the paper and blows life into it. His sheep bleat on the damp heath, nudge each other, and a breeze carries the penetrating and wonderful fragrance of the trampled grasses to us.' From 1878 to 1883, he was a member of the board of Pulchri Studio, first as 'Governor of Art Reviews' and later as treasurer. Things also went well financially, even though Mauve had to work hard to achieve this: the books of art dealer Goupil show that between 1880 and 1889 some 160 paintings by Mauve were sold.

His wife was a cousin of Vincent van Gogh, and in 1881, the young Van Gogh asked Mauve for advice. When Van Gogh worked in Mauve's studio for a few weeks, Mauve suggested he try watercolours: the smaller format made it easier to sell watercolours than paintings. They also discussed Millet's work, who Van Gogh greatly admired. He wrote enthusiastically to his brother Theo about a series of paintings showing draught horses in Scheveningen. According to him, the way in which Mauve had portrayed the slender, tired horses, expressed an almost religious sympathy. He added that if Millet would have been able to see these paintings, he would have mumbled: 'Il a du coeur, ce peintre-là'. Some time later Van Gogh and Mauve quarrelled, which caused a break in their relationship.

At this time the area around The Hague became increasingly urban. Around 1880, Dekkersduin, an area loved by Mauve and J.H. Weissenbruch, was levelled in order to create the Duinoord district. This caused many painters in The Hague to look elsewhere for subjects. Jozef Israëls drew Mauve's attention to the beauty of the weavers' town of Laren in the Gooi. Mauve first went there in the summer of 1882, returned many times, and moved into Villa Ariëtte in 1885 with his wife and four children. Neuhuys, who had known about the town somewhat earlier, introduced Mauve to various farm

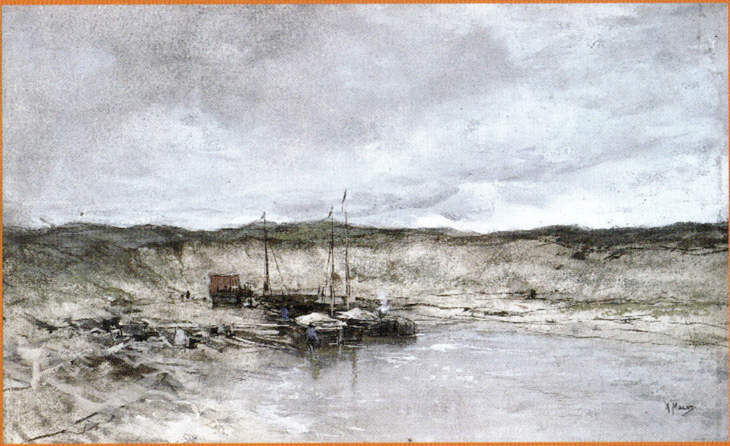

Anton Mauve, *Sand excavation near Scheveningen,* n.d. (watercolour)

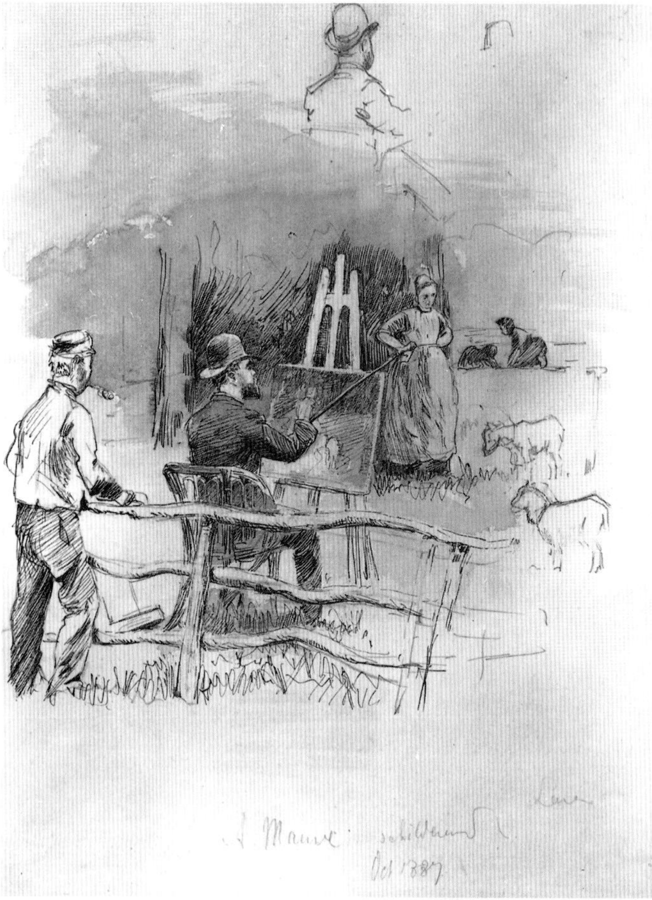

Jan Hoynck van Papendrecht, *The painter Anton Mauve outdoors,* 1887 (drawing)

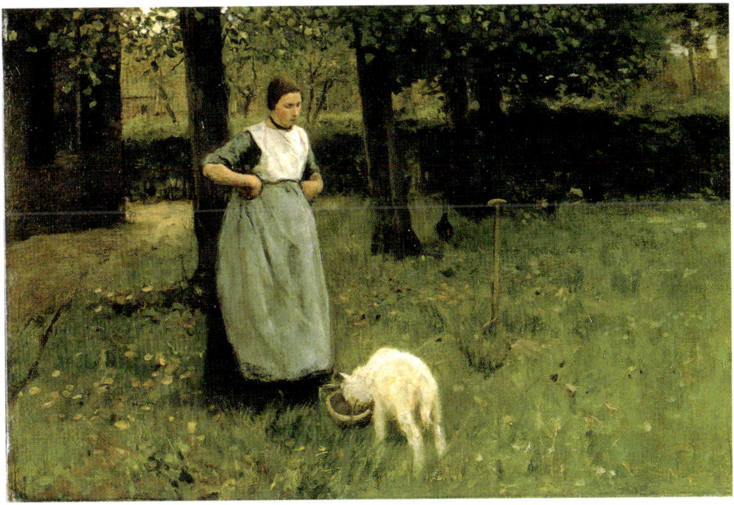

Anton Mauve, *Woman with lamb in Laren,* 1885

families. Mauve painted many heath landscapes with sheep; these paintings were especially in demand in England, Scotland and America. The art dealer Tersteeg (who worked at Goupil in The Hague) was reputed to take half painted canvases with him in order to accommodate his clients' wishes. E.B. Greenshields, a Canadian, wrote in his 1906 book, 'Landscape Painting and Modern Dutch Artists': 'It is a rare thing to find anyone who does not like the paintings of Anton Mauve.' Mauve has many followers in Laren, although he actually gave lessons to very few painters. Even the German impressionist Max Liebermann admired his paintings, and came to Laren to work. This led to Mauve becoming known as the 'initiator of the Laren School' and the area around Laren being called 'Mauve country'. However, Israëls and Neuhuys were equally important in making Laren famous.

From 1884, Mauve was often invited to Ewijckshoeve near Baarn, the country home of the painter Willem Witsen and his family. Mauve also made the acquaintance of other young artists such as Willem Bastiaan Tholen and Piet Meinders. Their admiration for Millet caused Mauve to show more interest in peasants working. He painted housewives doing the laundry, the corn harvest, sheepshearers, and people working in a vegetable garden. His use of colour changed as well: his former silver tone became clearer and more distinct. The younger painters and their contemporaries in particular esteemed these changes in Mauve's work.

As Mauve approached fifty he became overstressed. He suffered from melancholia, for which he was prescribed complete rest. When he went for a short stay with his brother in Arnhem, he had a stroke, dying unexpectedly on 5 February 1888. News of his death was a great shock, for not only Mauve but the entire Hague School was at the pinnacle of fame. That was why Mauve was not given the type of elaborate commemoration that some other painters received at the end of their lives. Yet the burial was almost as big and perhaps as promoted an event; it was extensively reported in the newspapers and magazines. A Laren birch was planted by Mauve's grave, and Jozef Israëls' words at the burial have often been cited: 'O, where can we find another Mauve! Where can we find another Mauve!'

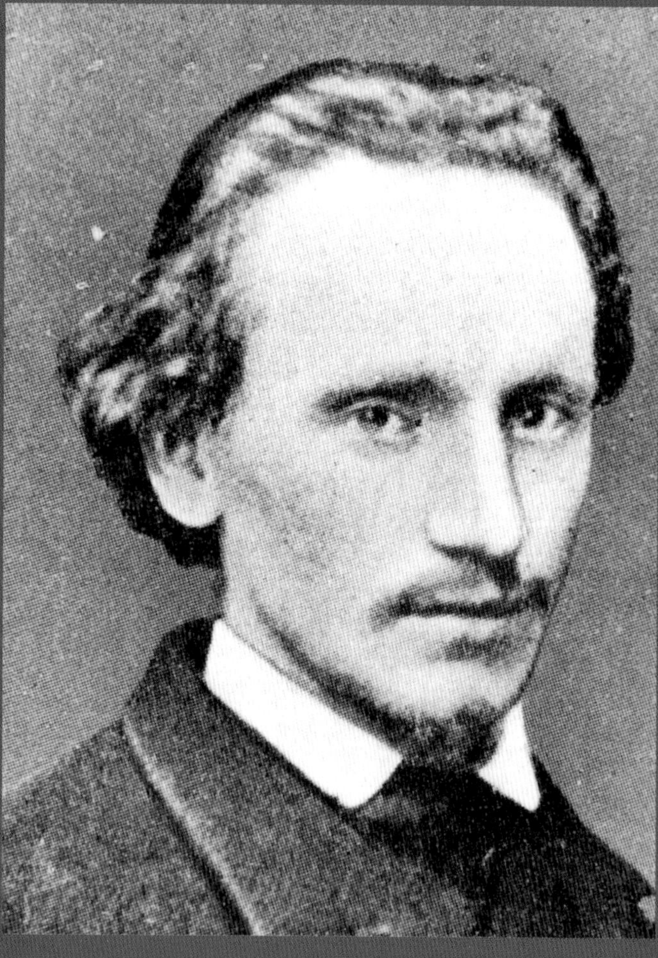

Photo of Matthijs Maris, ca. 1870 (RKD collection)

Matthijs Maris

(1839-1917)

Matthijs Maris was born on 17 August 1839. He was the second son in a family of five children. The Maris children copied prints that their father brought home from the printing house he worked at. Matthijs' brothers, Jacob and Willem, also became artists. When Matthijs was twelve he registered at the Haagsche Teekenacademie (Hague Academy of Art), but did not pass the entrance examination. Therefore, he took lessons from Isaac Cornelis Elink Sterk, secretary of the academy. One year later he was admitted. He took lessons from the academy until 1855, and in the meantime served his apprenticeship with the sea painter Louis Meijer.

Meijer had good contacts with the court and arranged for a monthly allowance for Matthijs from Queen Sophie. These 40 guilders a month allowed Matthijs to follow his brother Jacob to Antwerp in 1855 to study at the academy there. They rented rooms together, to be joined later by their friend Lourens Alma Tadema. In order to add to their monthly stipend, the Maris brothers painted small works for the American market. At the academy, the German painter George Laves introduced Maris to the work of the German romanticists Von Schwind, Rethel, Kaulbach and Richter, masters who would have an important influence on Maris. He developed into a good draughtsman, and Jacob would later say that 'Matthijs can do everything'. In this period he created many genre pieces and everyday scenes of urban life: the market, the pawnshop, and workers eating on the street.

In 1858, Matthijs Maris returned to The Hague, where Jacob already had a studio that they would again share. Around 1860, the

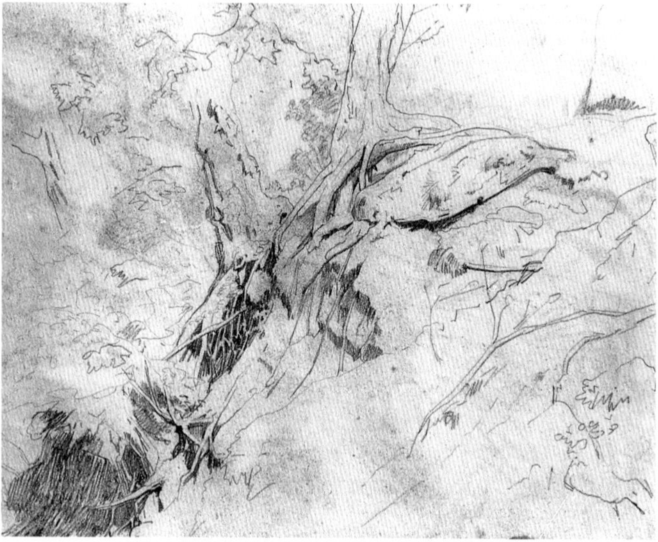

Matthijs Maris, *Study of tree roots,* n.d. (drawing)

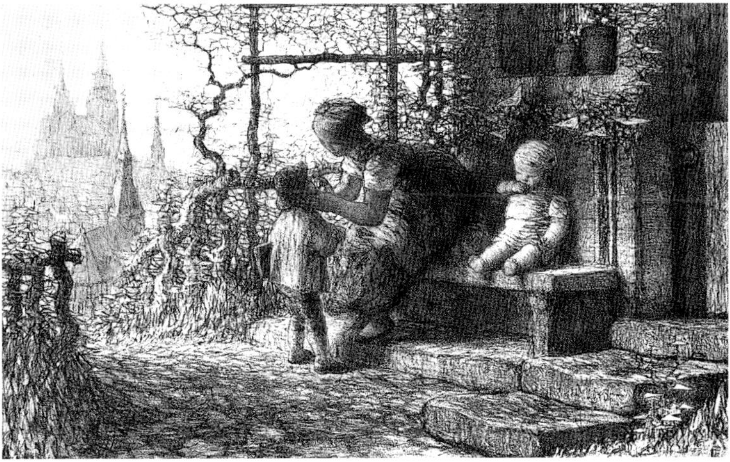

Matthijs Maris, *Before going to school,* n.d. (etching)

brothers copied eight portraits of royal persons for Princess Marianne's estate Rustenhof. This commission earned them enough to spend some time in Oosterbeek and Wolfheze, making studies from nature. The brothers strongly influenced one another, and sometimes it is not even clear who painted which painting. Matthijs painted sheep barns, tree stumps and brooks in warm brown and green tints, with subtle shades from dark to light. It is these works that link him to other painters of the Hague School such as Mauve and Gerard Bilders. Nonetheless, even at this time, to him painting from nature was not the main thing, but rather a means to 'express his own mind', causing him to be characterised as a romantic-symbolic painter rather than as a Hague realist.

The trip the brothers took in 1861 along the Rhine to Switzerland and France was very important to Matthijs Maris. In Cologne the brothers saw an exhibition that presented an overview of German art since 1800, which intensified the influence of German Romanticism on Matthijs. The mountains, wooden houses and the castle and cathedral of Lausanne became returning motifs in his paintings. The watercolour 'Baptismal procession in Lausanne' earned him an honorary membership of the Belgian Society of Watercolourists in 1863.

Upon his return to the Netherlands Matthijs Maris exhibited his landscapes, genre paintings and portraits in The Hague and Amsterdam. The press and public repeatedly reacted unfavourably, which led Maris to become bitter and withdrawn, especially now that he no longer had any direct support from his brother Jacob who had gone to Paris. He decided not to participate in any more exhibitions, and became depressed. His mother and younger brother Willem tried to convince him to move to Paris as well, and Jacob wrote him inviting letters. So, in 1869, Matthijs again moved in with Jacob, who had meanwhile gotten married, had become a father of a daughter, and lived in an apartment in Montmartre.

Following the Franco-Prussian War of 1870-1871, many painters

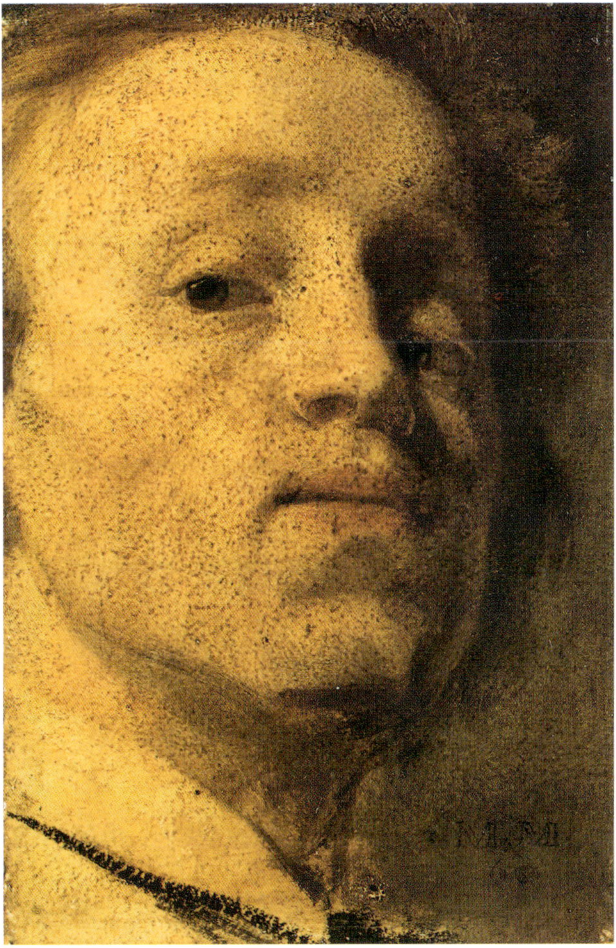

Matthijs Maris, *Self-portrait,* n.d. (collection of the Rijksmuseum, Amsterdam)

left the chaos of Paris, including Jacob, who took his family back to The Hague. Matthijs supposedly joined the National Guard and later fought with the Communards. Although he put this rumour to rest as a story made up by a journalist, he did remain in Paris. During these years he suffered from poverty and loneliness. He was partly cheered up when his sister Henriette, who had married a Frenchman, came to take care of him. Maris' productivity in this period was relatively large: he painted a few of his most famous works, including 'Butterflies', 'Souvenir of Amsterdam', 'The spinner', 'Girl at the pump' and 'The sisters'. In these paintings his main theme had already become clear: the loss of innocence through the search for knowledge.

Many of these works were bought by the art dealer Goupil. Maris hated working for the commercial market, but felt constrained to conform to it. He wrote: 'I was hungry, my hunger was real and made me totally subordinate'. Later Maris would distance himself from these works, dismissing them as 'potboilers', only painted in order to put bread on the table. He would also regret it that both his brothers had become 'bread painters' because they'd had families to support. He differentiated himself from them when he said: 'I am not a painter. Jaap and Willem were painters. I'm a dreamer.'

Through Goupil Maris came into contact with Elbert Jan van Wisselingh, assistant at the art dealership. Van Wisselingh introduced Maris' work to Daniel Cottier, a London art dealer, who, perceiving that Maris had great talent and was likely to become a commercial success, convinced Van Wisselingh and Maris to come to London. Maris wanted to 'work from his imagination' and hoped that Cottier would give him the freedom to do this. In 1877, he moved in with Cottier, and together they took trips to Norway, Ireland, Brittany and Paris. The contrary expectations of both men caused the relationship to worsen, which eventually led to a break after ten years.

Van Wisselingh continued to give Maris financial support, and arranged rooms for him in the London working-class district of

Hampstead. Maris was to live there for nineteen years. Finally he was able to transform his internal images into paint. Sometimes he would spend years on end working on the same paintings. He wrote: 'I am not a painter. I do not paint pictures. I try to produce work. It may take me two years or it may take me fifty. But it is the same at the end as it was in the beginning. It is finished in my mind before I touch the canvas. But I have to do it again and again before I get it right.' With his fairy-tale princes and princesses, goatherds, spinners and enchanted castles, he retreated into a fantasy world. These dream-like scenes, executed in very muted colours and with granular, runny transitions, do not really belong to the Hague School. In the distinction Maris made between 'matter' and 'spirit' he anticipated the emerging symbolist movement – despite his romantic, nostalgic choice of subjects.

In the hundreds of often bitter letters Maris wrote from London to his family and a few friends – in a wonderful mixture of English and Dutch – he repeatedly airs his abiding hatred for art dealers, collectors, critics, and all the other people who were driven by money. He also repeatedly refers to academic education that robs artists of their innocence and 'imagination'. He paints a picture of himself as a reluctant recluse, someone who has been exploited and excluded from a society that cares only for money.

In part because of this, Maris became a legend in the Netherlands. He got few visitors, and the visits by Jan Veth and later Lodewijk van Deyssel and Jan Toorop were always depicted as a type of pilgrimage. Van Deyssel in particular regarded Maris (lovingly called 'Thijs') as an honest artist but also a strange fellow, an unworldly person near the breadline, living in a tiny, dirty room. But there must have been a different Maris as well. Isabella Angus, E.J. van Wisselingh's wife, described him as: 'Thijs was always ten years old and full of wit and sun, so gay at times, singing and working, sometimes singing whole operas, always a magic person, a sage and profound.'

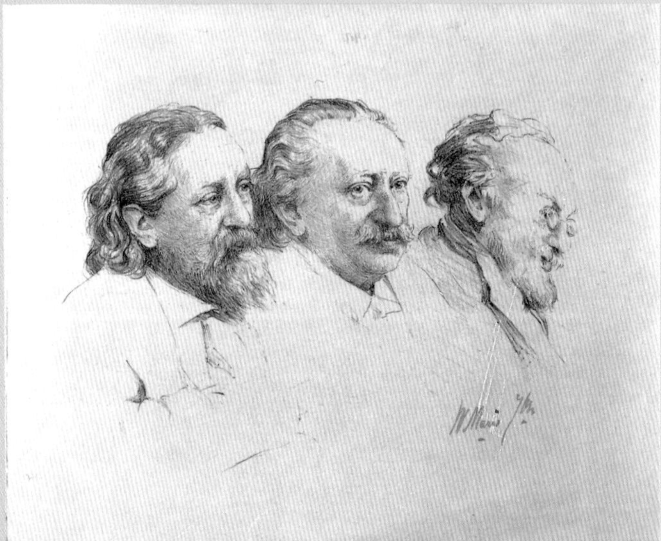

Willem Maris Jr, *The Maris brothers,* n.d. (drawing)

In 1908, Maris moved for the last time, to a comfortable two-room apartment on Westbourne Square. When Van Wisselingh died in 1912, his widow and the Rotterdam ship owner P.F. Thomsen took over financial responsibility for Maris. He worked for ten years on end (with some interruptions) on a chalk drawing, commissioned by the Museum Boijmans. Because of his immense self-criticism he was no longer able to complete a single painting. He died on 22 August 1917, when he was seventy-eight, following a short illness, and was buried in London.

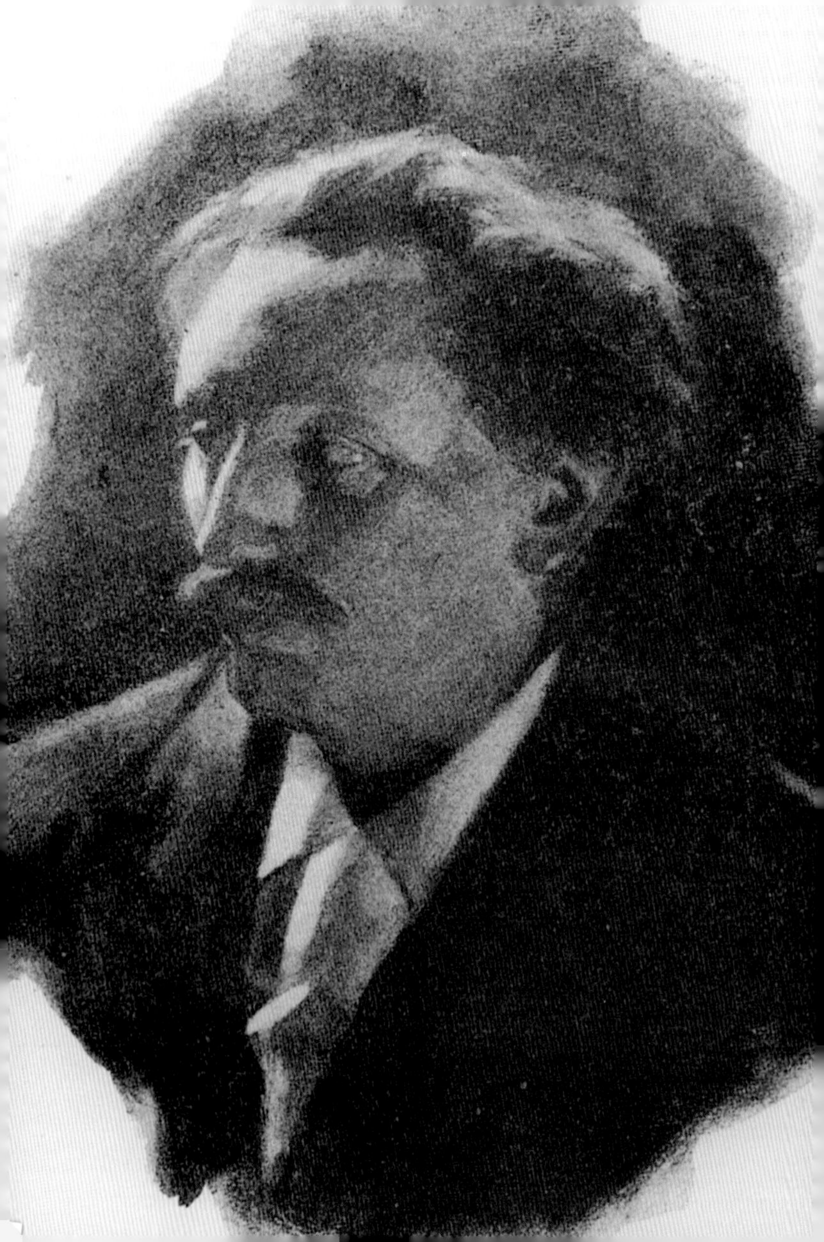

Willem Maris

(1844-1910)

Willem Maris was born on 18 February 1844. He was baptised 'Wenzel', after his Prague grandfather Wenzel Maresch, whose family name had been turned into Dutch. Willem was the third in a family of five children. His two brothers preceded him in the painting profession. In literature he is often characterised as a self-taught man, and Maris describes his study years as follows: 'From the time I was young I worked outdoors. Even before I was twelve I would sit in the meadow and watch the cows before and after school. As my brothers were older than me, naturally I got part of my training from them, and in the winters I went to the Teekenacademie [Academy of Art], where I often drew from plaster [plaster models] and also often practised drawing in perspective. In the summer I always studied outdoors, and in the winter in the stable.' Maris also received advice from the cattle painter Pieter Stortenbeker, who gave him work to copy.

In 1862, Maris made his debut with 'Cows on the heath', submitted to the exhibition of Living Masters in Rotterdam. This work may have been painted in Oosterbeek, which he visited for the first time that year. It was in Oosterbeek that he met Gerard Bilders and Anton Mauve. Maris would write about his legendary meeting with Mauve: 'a couple of days afterwards I was sitting somewhere and painting – when one of these braggarts came up behind me. Well, hey, when you're young, you don't think that's very nice. And suddenly the guy throws his arms around me and roars: 'I sit here all day long plodding away with a pencil – scratching and scratching – and you get it right away!' It was … Mauve.' They would remain good friends for the rest of their lives.

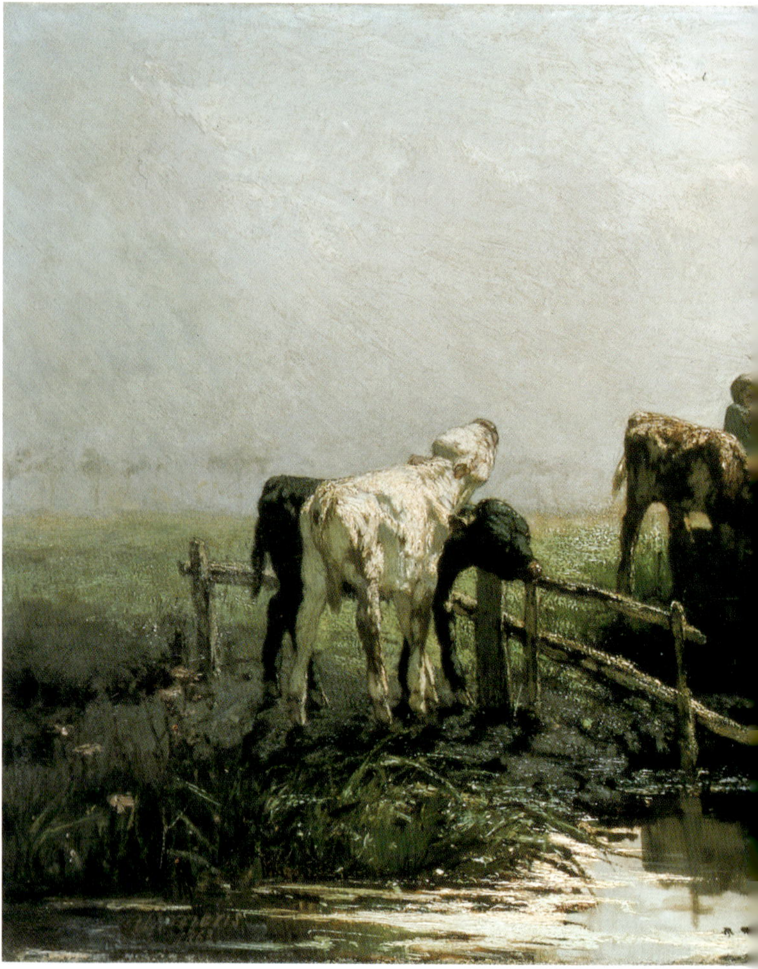

Willem Maris, *Calves near a trough,* 1863

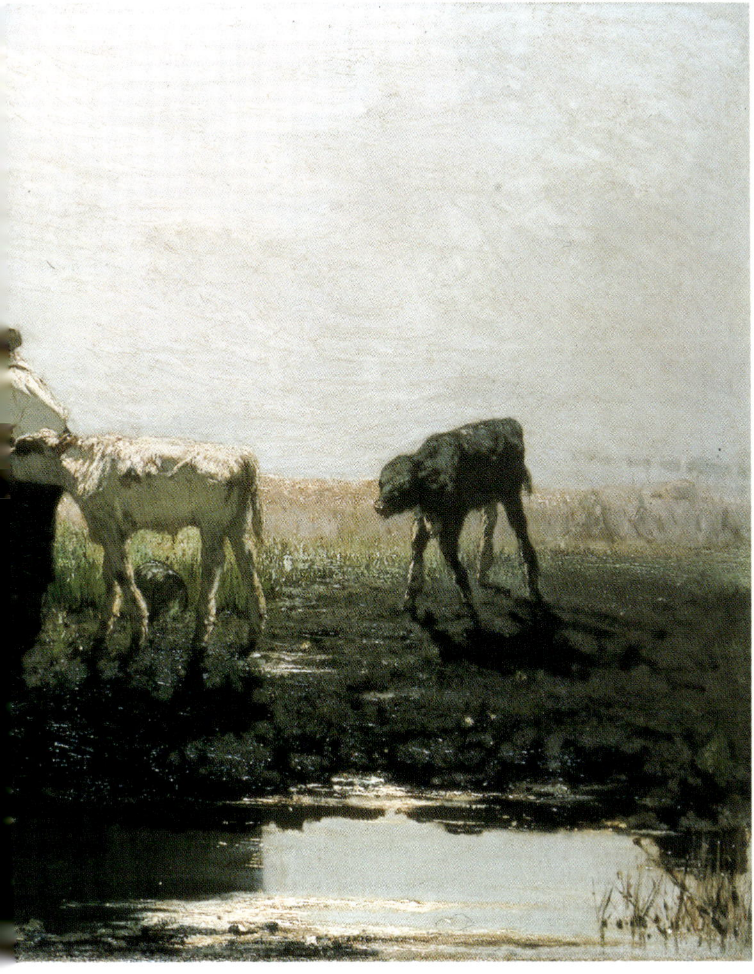

In 1863, the Maris family moved house and set up a studio. The house had three front windows; behind each window was a painting easel, one for each brother. As Jacob and Matthijs had done before him, Willem, too, took a trip along the German Rhine. His travel companion, Bernard Blommers, would later recount anecdotes about the adventure. It has often been written that Maris spent a few weeks in Paris in 1867, on the occasion of Jacob's marriage. At that time he supposedly became acquainted with the Barbizon School, but the correspondence among the brothers themselves and with Mauve contradicts that. At the time he shared a studio with Blommers on the Juffrouw Idastraat in The Hague, where Matthijs Maris and Mauve could also be found often. In the Mauritshuis Maris copied Potter's work, a seventeenth-century cattle painter who had also inspired Gerard Bilders, Jan Hendrik Weissenbruch and the Barbizon painters. Studies from this period show that each tree leaf was very carefully drawn, as was each small hair of a cow's hide.

Maris' last long trip abroad was in 1871. He travelled for three months along the Norwegian fjords with F. van Seggeren and Alexander Wüst. Although he made many drawings on this trip, by his own account he never turned them into a painting. Yet two paintings of Norwegian landscapes do exist: 'Study in Norway' and 'Mountain landscape in Norway'. He also added cows and eagles to Wüst's paintings, as well as cows to Théophile de Bock's paintings.

Apart from a few short trips to Kalmthout in Belgium, Maris mostly worked in his own country, painting in the area of The Hague, Gouda, Reeuwijk and Sluipwijk. He also often returned to Oosterbeek. Mauve often stayed for longer periods in Gelderland, and wrote letters trying to convince his friend to visit him there: 'how beautiful it starts to be here, one more impetus for you quickly to change your domicile and come to Oosterbeek [...] Come, come, I call to you. You won't regret it.' But Maris did not want to settle in the countryside because he believed it was not fruitful for a painter to live outdoors:

'Do you know where always being outdoors will get you? You'll end up [...] copying. [...] And that's why we made so many beautiful things in our studio on the Juffrouw Idastraat; the studio was not so special. It was noisy. But going outside all of a sudden, moves you all the more...'

Maris married Maria Jacoba Visser in 1872. They had two sons. The eldest, Simon Willem, would also become a painter. In the meantime, Maris had been a member of the board of Pulchri Studio for several years, and in 1876, together with Mauve and Mesdag, he founded the Hollandsche Teekenmaatschappij (Dutch Drawing Society) modelled after the Belgian Society of Watercolourists. This society was very important for the flourishing of the Hague School in general, and of watercolour art in particular.

Willem Maris was the only one among his brothers who was and remained successful since his debut. His painting career progressed regularly and harmoniously, and he maintained a steady production. For his entire life he remained true to the subject he had chosen in his youth: meadow landscapes with willows and ditches, cows or calves in a meadow, by a river or pond, and later ducks and chickens. His paintings and watercolours are best known for his emphasis on light. Maris' often cited motto was: 'I don't paint cows, but rather effects of light'. His early work in particular often contains a cool, cloudy atmosphere. Someone wrote: 'In those days, the young painter had a pronounced preference for shrouds of mist, which is quite peculiar. On several occasions he angrily broke off his study trips as soon as the sun and wind had chased away the early-morning mist.'

As Maris often repeated the motifs he used, and because he no longer dated his works since the seventies, it is difficult to assign a chronological order to his work. Still, three major phases can be distinguished in his work. The first works are characterised by an exact reproduction of the surroundings. Maris was still finding his way in the anatomical portrayal of cattle. In the second phase he had

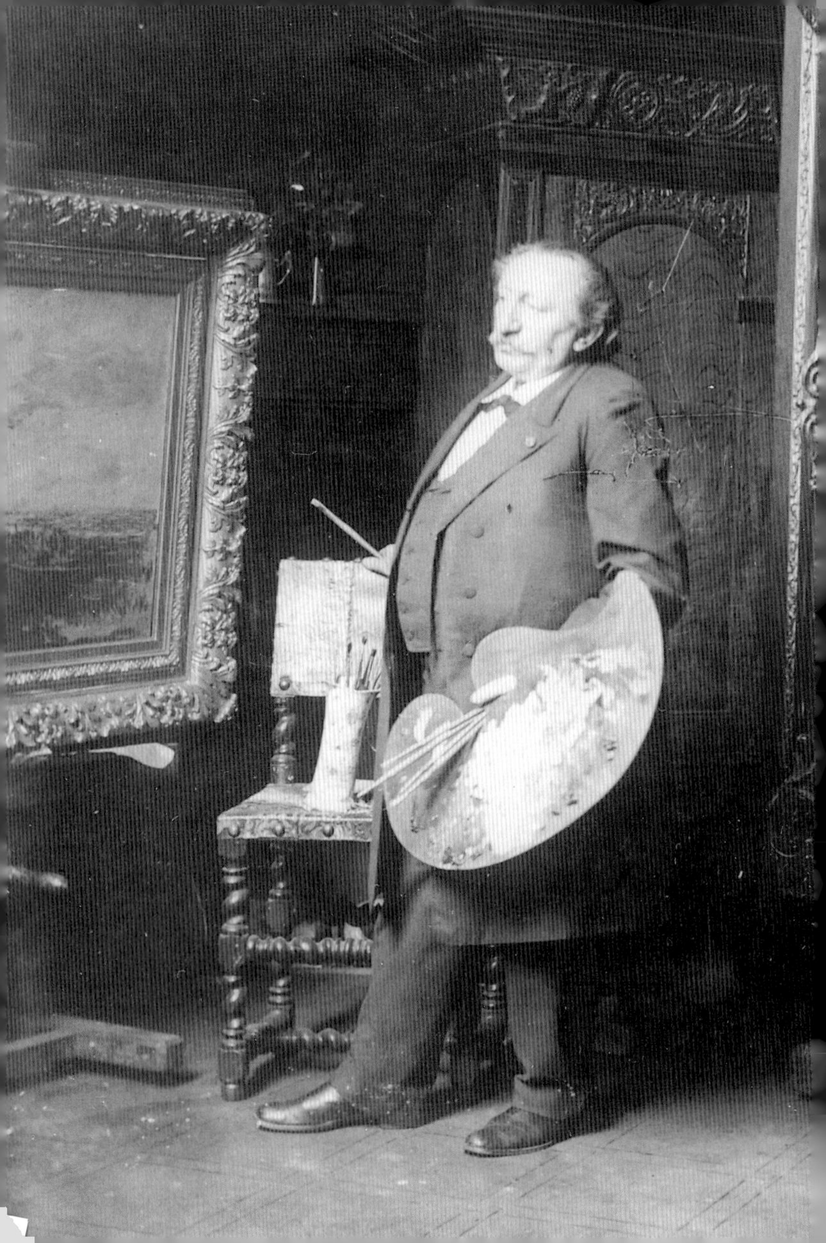

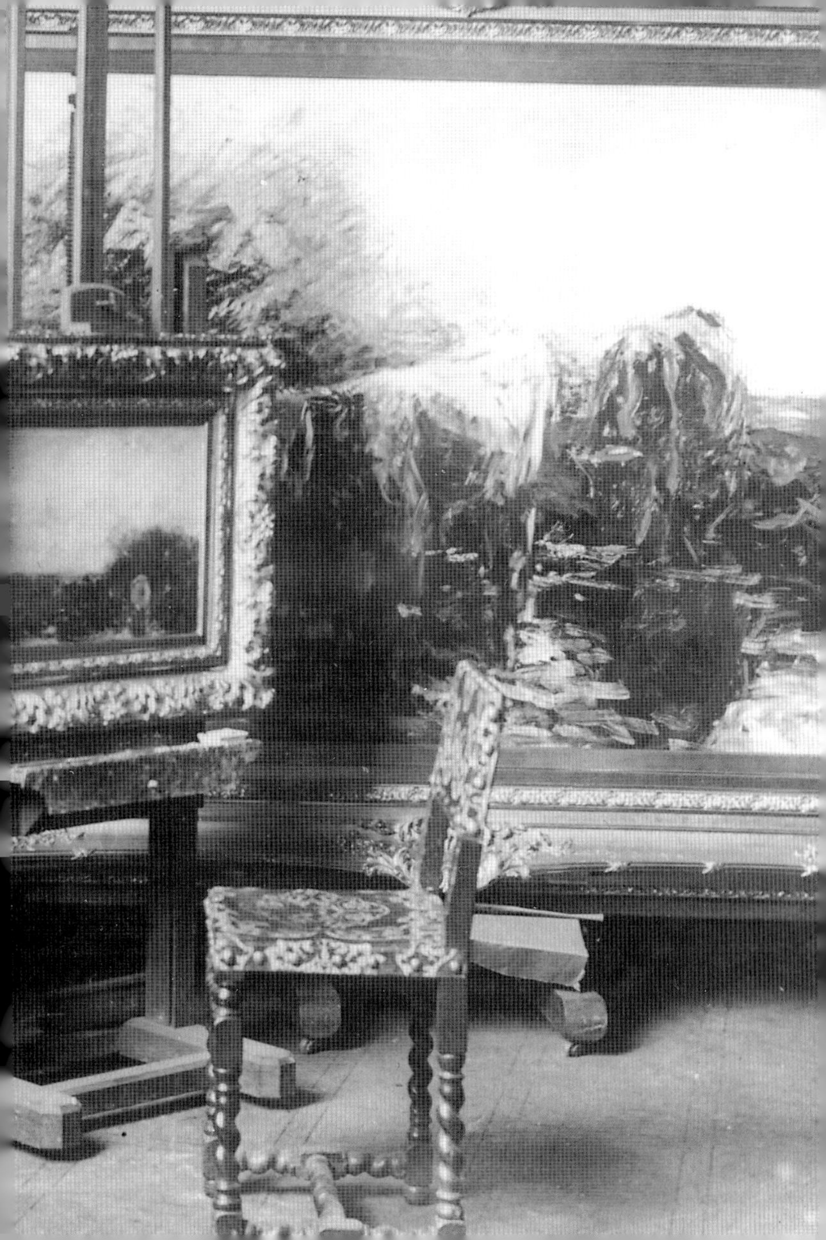

complete mastered this, and his use of colour became more definite. The meadows and trees are painted in gradations of saturated shades of green. Around 1880, he began using broader strokes, combining this with impasto. Yet these works have an intimate atmosphere. His lively use of colour distinguished Maris from the 'grey mood' of his contemporaries, and he was often called the 'impressionist' of the Hague School.

Maris received many honours during his life, including a gold medal in 1886 at an exhibition in Amsterdam as well as a gold medal at the World Exhibition in Brussels a few months before he died. In 1905, a critic praised him as follows: 'The abundance of sun that Willem Maris applies to his "ponds" with such strength of colour and tone, enraptures the viewer. It is a rare gift to reproduce light and sun the way he does, the vastness of the waters, the wonder of such a beautiful day, the tenderness of the meadow.' Nevertheless, his work also received criticism. Initially people had to get used to his portrayal of light, in which the cows' backs were touched by sunbeams in the backlighting. The style was characterised as 'theatrical rather than natural light'. His continuous repetitious choice of subject matter also gave rise to comments: 'No matter how much one admires Willem's sunny, radiant meadows full of living nature with their shining cattle and juicy greens, each piece is too much like the others.'

When he was about thirty-five, Maris lived in a villa called 'Oud-Rozenburg' in Rijswijk. (Later on the Rozenburg delftware works were established on this spot.) Maris created a duck pond in his garden so he could paint intimate scenes of ducks with their offspring near his home. Maris wrote that he never had any students, although 'Several young people did let me see their work and judge it.' Yet, around 1880, George Hendrik Breitner must have studied with him for a year. He also taught his son Simon Willem. And Maris' influence on the work of Geo Poggenbeek, Constant Artz and Fedor van Kregten is unmistakeable.

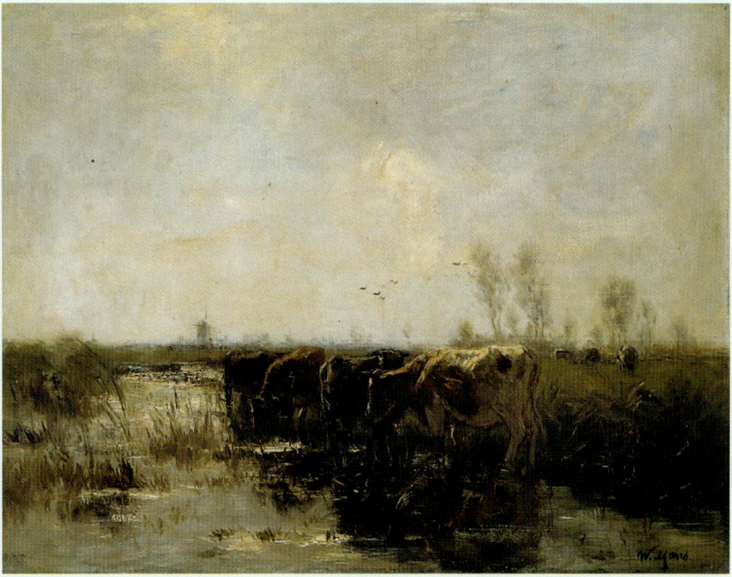

Willem Maris, *Cows in a ditch,* n.d.

pp. 316-317:
Willem Maris in his studio

In 1889, his wife died. The following year Maris married the twenty-two year younger pianist, Johanna Antonia Gijsberta Bijleveld. Two daughters were born from this marriage. When Maris was in his sixties he often seemed tired of life. He went to Karlsbad a couple of times to take the waters, as his brother Jacob had previously done. On 10 October 1910 he died in The Hague.

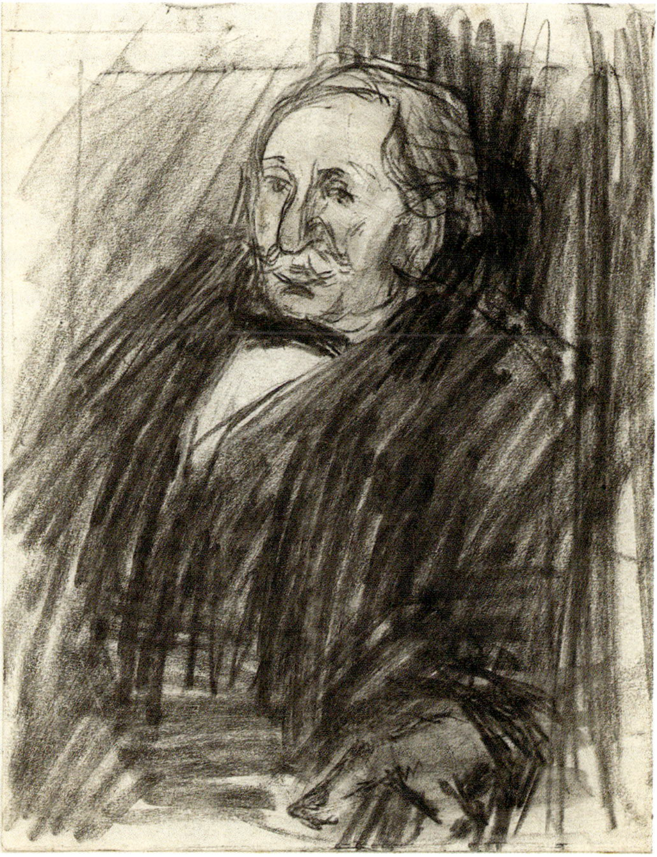

Floris Arntzenius, *Portrait of Willem Maris,* n.d.
(private collection, drawing)

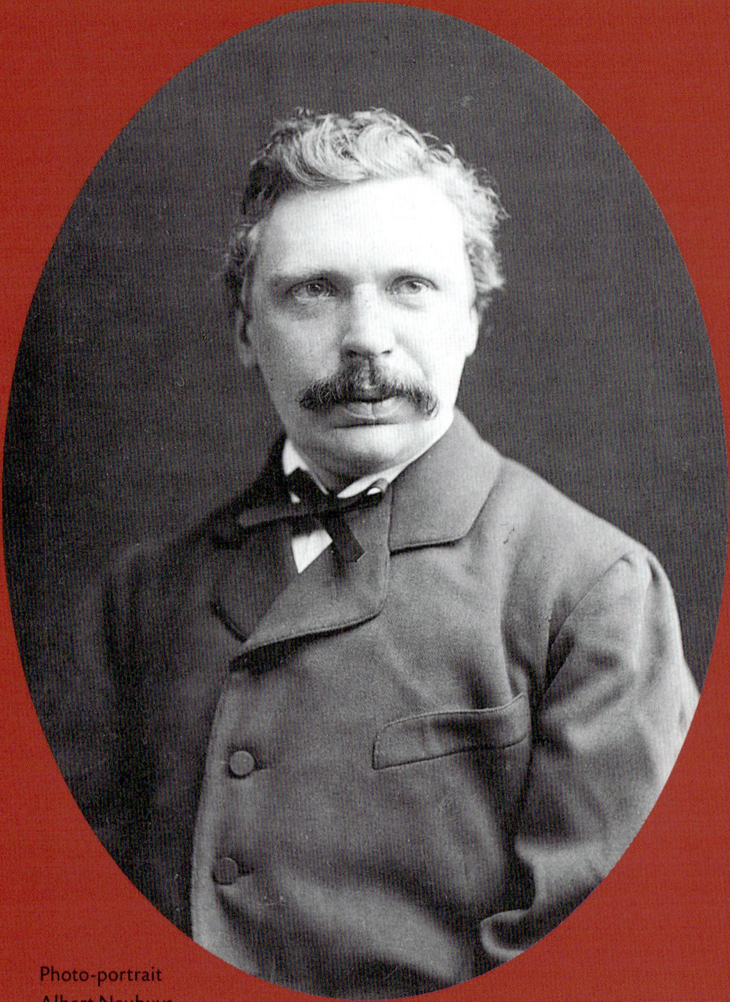

Photo-portrait
Albert Neuhuys

Albert Neuhuys

(1844-1914)

Johannes Albert Neuhuys was born in Utrecht on 10 June 1844, the youngest in a family of eight children. His oldest brother, Jan Antoon, went to the Antwerp Academy where he made friends with Lourens Alma Tadema, who was to become famous as a painter of figures and historical scenes. Albert was also interested in painting, but his musical talent caused him to think about becoming a pianist rather than an artist. Neuhuys Sr was not enamoured of having two sons become painters, so he prevailed upon Albert to choose the more financially secure profession of lithographer. Thus, Neuhuys went to the Municipal Drawing School in Utrecht from 1858 to 1860; he won silver medals for his studies in 1859 and in 1861. He then went to work for the lithographer Van de Weyer in Utrecht, who unfortunately went bankrupt two years later. From that time on, Neuhuys completely devoted himself to drawing and painting. His younger brother, Jozef Hendrikus, would also become an artist.

His tutor was Gijsbert Craeyvanger, a talented lithographer, whom Neuhuys probably met at Van de Weyer's. He received lessons in genre painting, historical pieces and portrait painting. In that style he made his debut in 1863 at the artists' association Kunstliefde in Utrecht with 'The weathercock' (based on a poem by Génestet). When an art dealer commissioned him to create anonymous portraits from photographs he was able to live off his earnings for two years. Neuhuys also painted interiors of the well-to-do – often taking his parents' house as a model – in a detailed style with a great deal of attention to texture.

From 1868 to 1872, he took lessons at the Antwerp Academy,

where he was awarded prizes twice. From 1871, he was supported by a royal stipend. The interiors he painted at that time were filled with ladies, noblemen and knights, in line with contemporary Belgian fashion. He was especially skilled at expressing the texture of fabrics, particularly at reproducing the shine of satin clothes. These 'satin pieces' (after the example of seventeenth-century artist Pieter de Hooch) were very popular. From 1867, Neuhuys became more interested in painting poor farmers' houses, and in 1868 he exhibited 'Farmer's home in Nunspeet' in Utrecht. In addition to farm interiors, he worked on fishing scenes and mothers with children. His work during this period can be compared to that of Christoffel Bisschop, who is known for his Hindelopen interiors.

After he moved to Amsterdam, Neuhuys lived with his parents for several years. In Amsterdam he met Jozef Israëls, Anton Mauve, and the Maris brothers. When Neuhuys married Neeltje Broeder in 1876, they decided to settle on the Noordwest Binnensingel in The Hague. They were to have three children: Christina (1878), Johannes Albertus (1883), and Pieter Etienne (1892). Neuhuys' neighbours were Jacob Maris and the animal painter Simon van den Berg, and he shared his studio with his older brother Jozef. It was especially Maris' painting style that fascinated Neuhuys. Much like the other Hague School painters, his detailed manner of painting changed to a much looser stroke, following Maris' example. His use of colour, too, was inspired by Jacob Maris: his watercolours became famous for their sparkling transparency and the use of light was always very important in his compositions. In his choice of subject matter Neuhuys was closer to Jozef Israëls, even though his models are always well-fed and the tableaux are always sunny.

Living and working in The Hague, among so many fellow artists, benefited Neuhuys' work a great deal. As someone wrote: 'It is wonderful to note how Albert Neuhuys' work is becoming more and more mature, increasingly more solid and poetic. In the last three or four years his progress may be called truly colossal. I recently saw a painting of his from '75 or '76; it was nothing like it. He's worked his way up to be one of our four best figure painters (Israëls, Blommers and Jacob Maris are the other three) and particularly one of our finest colourists.' From 1880, Neuhuys added a new theme to his repertoire: loving couples. His 'Fisherman's Courtship' was purchased by the Amsterdam Rijksmuseum, which marked a major recognition.

The increasing urbanisation of the area around The Hague forced the painters of the Hague School to look further afield for their subjects. Israëls pointed out to Neuhuys how picturesque Laren was, and from 1872 on he regularly worked there. In 1883, he purchased a house in Laren, which was easy to reach from Amsterdam since the train had begun to stop there two years earlier. Two years later Mauve also moved to that town in the Gooi region and became his neighbour. Together with Mauve, Neuhuys was regarded as the founder of the 'Laren School'. He painted the farmers and weavers in their homes, and he rented a flax barn where he drew and painted spinners. The German painter, Max Liebermann, also took advantage of this opportunity. Neuhuys built an interior in his studio for posing his models, just as Israëls did with his fishermen in his 'fishermen's corner'. This allowed him to avoid the often bad hygienic conditions of the actual farmhouses. Neuhuys also worked in Schellinkhout in the North of Holland, in the Kempen region, in the Belgian province of Limburg, and in Markelo in the eastern Dutch region of Twente. He travelled around Brabant with Bernard Blommers, painting in the villages of Heeze, Bladel and Dongen.

In his time Neuhuys was an especially celebrated artist in his own country as well as abroad. His paintings sold well, according to some reports even without a frame. Because his work was so commercially successful, he copied many of his paintings as watercolours, which he sold through the Hollandsche Teekenmaatschappij (Dutch Drawing Society), among others. He had been a member of this society since

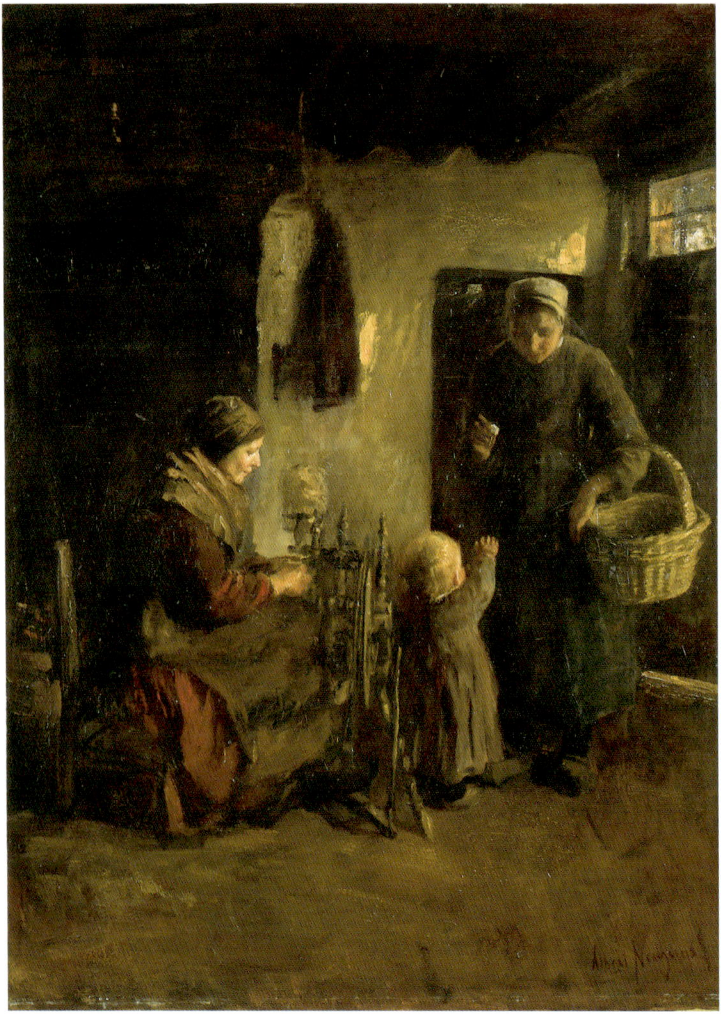

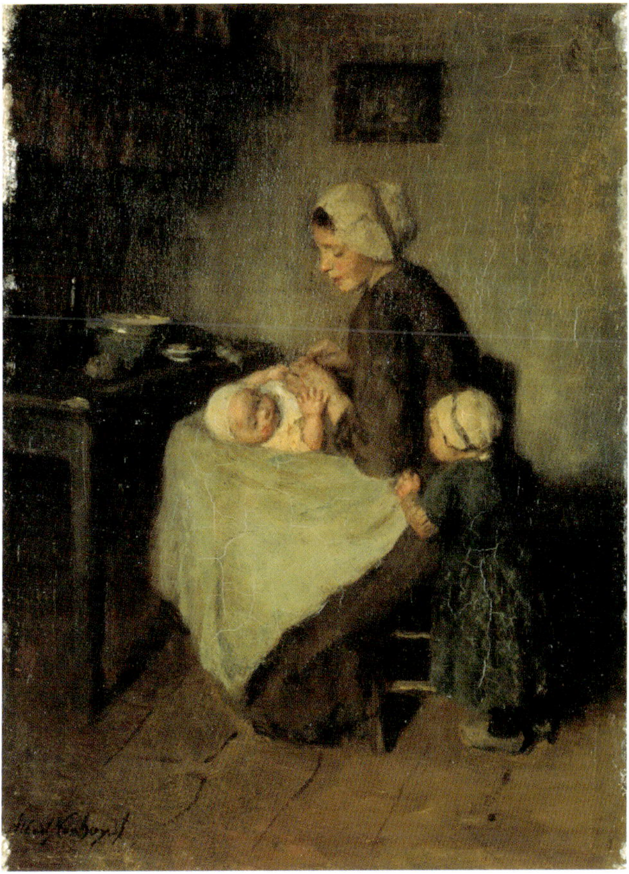

p. 326:
Albert Neuhuys, *Mother's darling,* n.d.

Albert Neuhuys, *Mother with children,* n.d.

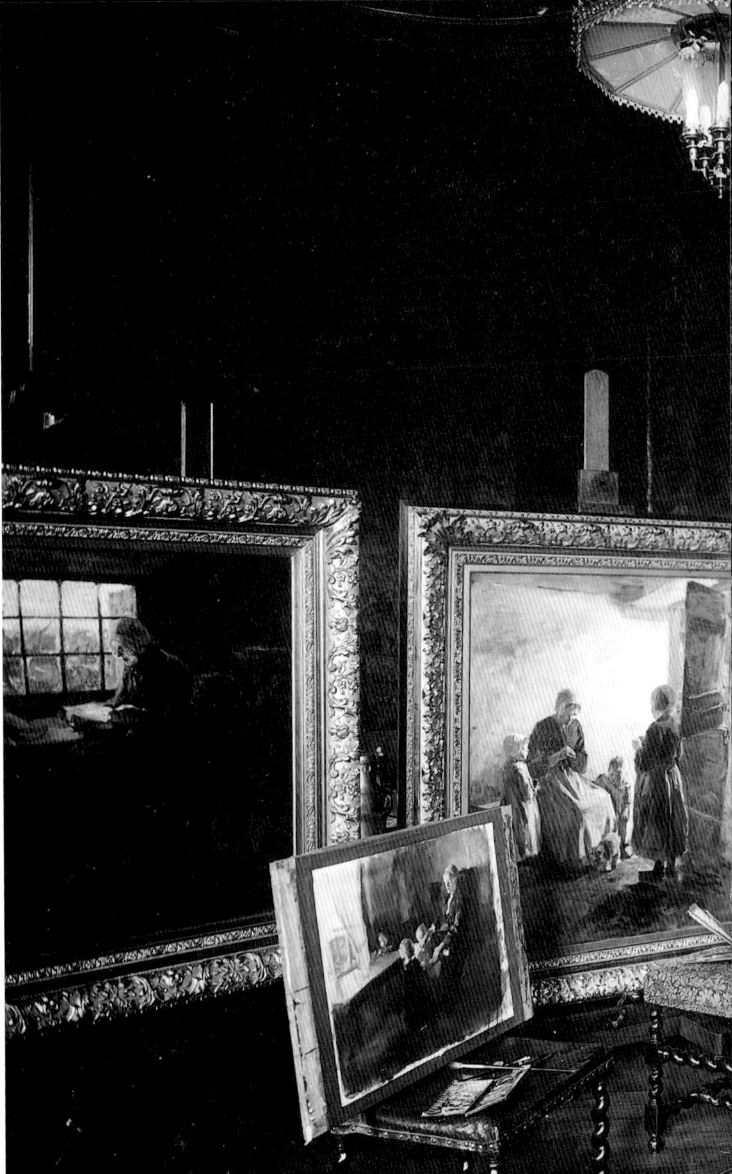

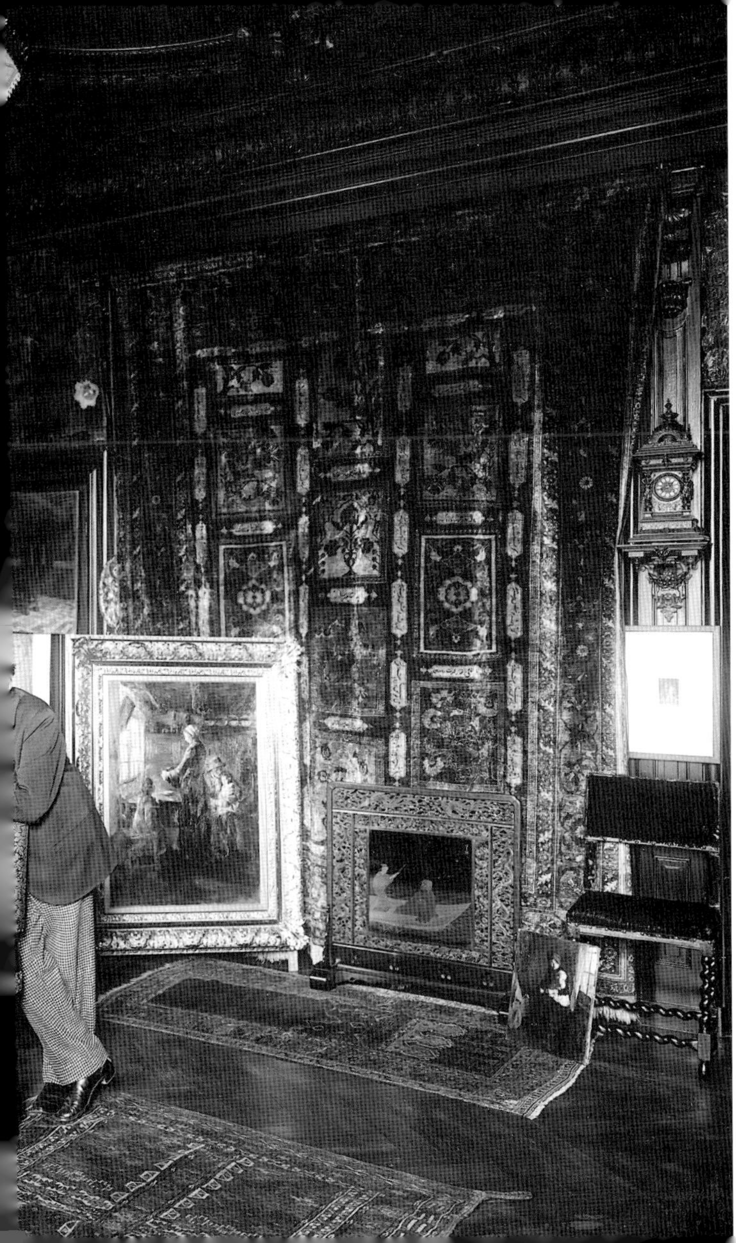

1876 and joined its board in 1884. Neuhuys earned Dutch as well as international honours throughout his entire career, for example in Amsterdam (1883 and 1889), Munich (1888), Vienna, Chicago and Budapest. But there was also criticism of his work. When, in 1890, his manner of painting became even looser, one reviewer thought it was degenerating into coarseness: 'The good public, even when it remains at the required large distance, is uncertain about several things and has the right to complain.' In 1904, on the occasion of his sixtieth birthday, Neuhuys was honoured with a retrospective exhibition at the Rotterdam Art Circle; he was also made a Knight of the Order of the Dutch Lion. Four years later he was celebrated by Arti et Amicitiae, who added his name, with those of Matthijs and Willem Maris, to the plaque commemorating 'the great Visual Artists of The Netherlands' in the society's staircase on the Amsterdam Rokin.

Until the end of his life Neuhuys loved to travel. He travelled to France, Germany, Austria, Scandinavia, Italy and Spain, but also visited more exotic destinations like Yugoslavia, Montenegro and Albania, Algiers and Corfu, Poland and Russia. These trips did not noticeably influence his work, however. In 1904, 1908 and 1910 he travelled to the United States. His first time there was at the invitation of the art dealers Arthur Tooth and Knoedler in New York. He made both the other journeys as a member of the jury for the International Exhibition at the prestigious Carnegie Institute in Pittsburgh.

From 1900 to 1910, Neuhuys lived on the Sarphatikade in Amsterdam. He retained his great interest in music, often going to the Concertgebouw as well as playing the piano for his friends at musical soirees. In 1910, Neuhuys moved to Zurich, but continued to visit Laren in the spring and autumn. He generally spent his summers at Castle 'De Erp' in Baarlo, Limburg. He died on 6 February 1914 in Orselina near Locarno, and was buried at 'Oud Eik en Duinen' cemetery in The Hague.

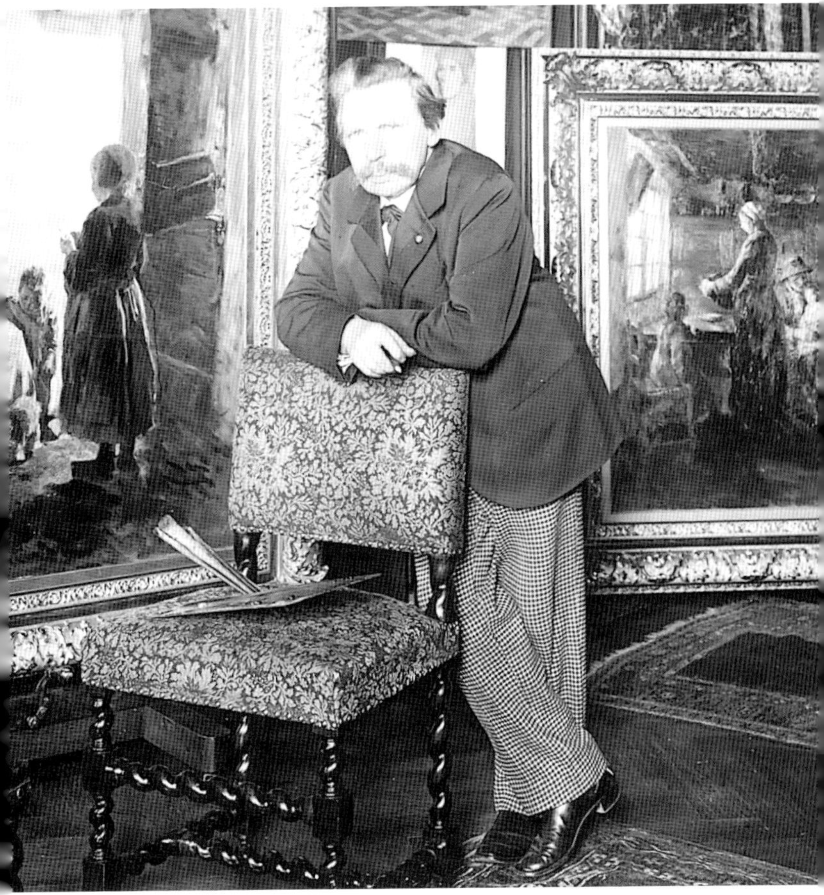

Detail from pp. 328-329

pp. 328-329:
Photograph of Albert Neuhuys in his studio (RKD collection)

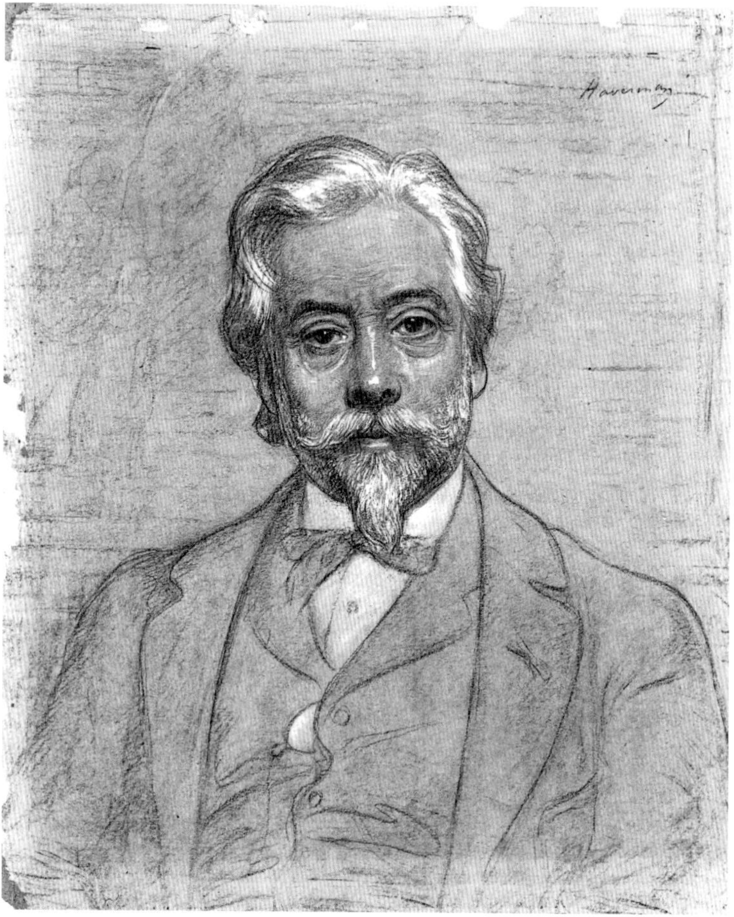

H.J. Havermans, *Portrait of Bernard Blommers,* n.d. (drawing)

Bernard Blommers

(1845-1914)

Bernard Blommers, the only son of Anna Maria van Balen and Pieter Blommers, was born on 30 January 1845. His father owned a lithographer's shop on the Spui in The Hague and he was initially trained to be a lithographer. But Bernard's heart was set on painting, and from 1863, he worked in his father's shop during the days, while taking lessons at the Haagsche Teekenacademie (Hague Academy of Art) in the evenings. It is reported that he also painted in Christoffel Bisschop's studio, who was known for his Hindelopen interiors.

At the academy Blommers became friends with Willem Maris. They took a walking and boat trip in 1865 along the German Rhine, which was then a favourite with young painters because of its picturesque landscapes and towns. The trip was not without incident, however. Many German cities had invoked martial law because of the Schleswig-Holstein issue (a border dispute between Germany and Denmark). In such a situation artists who sketched outdoors were automatically suspect, and the young men were arrested twice. Blommers would later repeat the story of his adventures to anyone who would listen.

He made his debut that same year with the painting 'Scheveningen interior with net-menders' at the exhibition of Living Masters in Amsterdam. The painting was given a place of honour, next to a large beach view by Jozef Israëls. It was reported that about this time Blommers met Israëls on the beach at Scheveningen, and when they started talking about the beautiful sea-view Israëls discovered that Blommers was also a painter. It is entirely likely that Blommers had consciously searched out the renowned painter, who was twenty

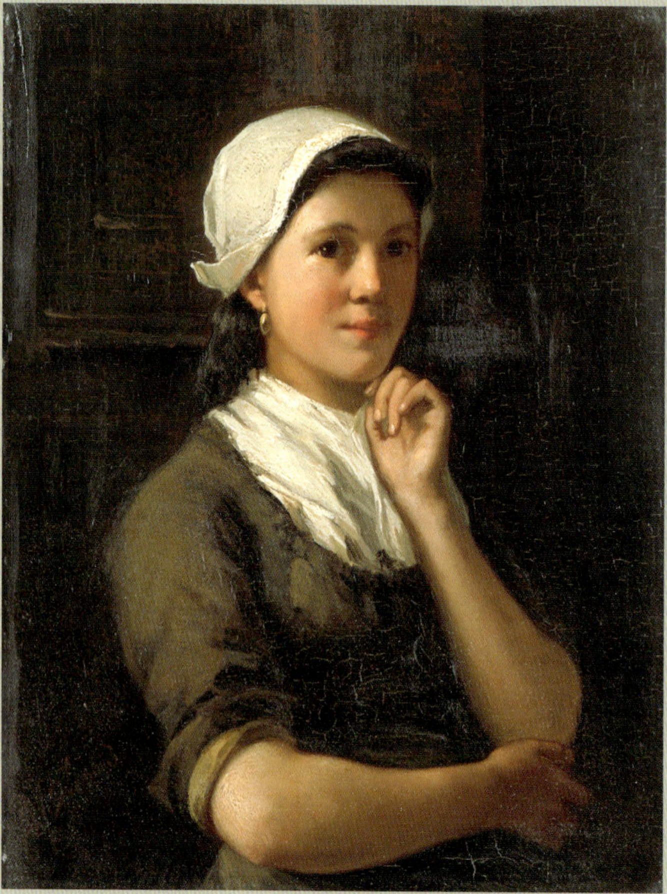

Bernard Blommers, *Young Scheveningen woman (Portrait of Anna van Toorn)*, 1869

years his senior. The fact is that from that time Israëls became a friend and adviser to the young painter. Israëls greatly influenced Blommers' choice of subjects: he, too, decided to paint fishermen's and farmers' interiors, as well as seascapes and dune landscapes in which figures played prominent roles. Israëls similarly influenced D.A.C. Artz, Albert Neuhuys and Philip Sadée.

Blommers finished his studies at the academy in 1868 and then shared a studio with Willem Maris on the Juffrouw Idastraat. Matthijs Maris worked there as well before moving to Paris in 1869. Anton Mauve visited the studio, as did Philip Sadée, Theo Mesker, Elchanon Verveer, George Hendrik Breitner and Louis Apol at that time. It was there that Blommers painted one of his first children's portraits: the little daughter of Siebenhaar, the landlord. Again Blommers' painting was successful: he won a gold medal for his 'Fisherman's Children' at an exhibition in The Hague. When Blommers was fairly young he became a member of Pulchri Studio and was active on the board right from the beginning. In 1870, he went to Paris to visit Jacob Maris, thinking he might want to settle there, but was forced to return to The Netherlands because of the Franco-Prussian War. The conflict also made him abandon his intended trip to Barbizon.

The young girl in the 'Fisherman's Children' was probably the Scheveningen fish seller Anna van Toorn. She was often Blommers' model; sometimes he even 'lent' her to his painter friends. The couple married in 1871, with Anton Mauve and H.W. Mesdag as their witnesses. The Blommers moved into a house on the Jacob Catshofje. It was at this time that Blommers taught Tony Offermans (1854-1911), who would later become famous for his intimate interiors showing tradespeople at work.

Blommers was an optimistic type and liked to paint the sunny side of fishing life. Unlike Israëls, his portrayal of Scheveningen life was not so much dramatic as domestic. Moreover, he did not explicitly paint the poverty around him, as Philip Sadée did. Instead, his scenes

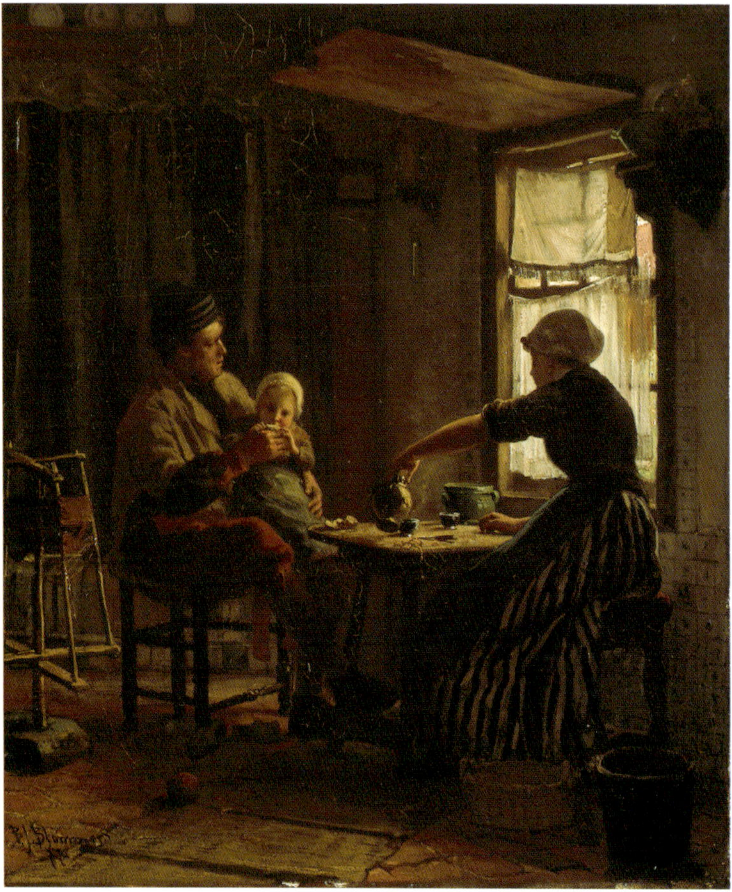

Bernard Blommers, *Fisherman's family,* 1877

are often unpretentious and anecdotal, in an easy style and painted in warm colours. Later, some critics of the Hague School would denigrate his bourgeois mentality (Knuttel and De Gruyter) and lack of depth (H.P. Bremmer). Yet Bremmer was charmed by his technique and the liveliness of his work. Blommers' marriage was a happy one and blessed with many children, and, from the birth of his oldest daughter Johanna in 1874, motherly love became a familiar theme in his work. And although critics had initially thought that children playing on the beach were too close to Israëls' 'Children of the Sea', this theme was later to become a trademark of Blommers.

His work was very popular, and during his lifetime he received many honours. Collectors such as H.W. Mesdag and J.H. van Eeghen owned some of Blommers' work, as did the Scots magnates James Staats Forbes and John Reid, who purchased his paintings and watercolours. His success enabled him to build a house in 1882, which he named after his daughter Johanna. His new home was very near Théophile de Bock, who became his friend. For a short time Blommers worked on the Panorama Mesdag, as did De Bock.

The urbanisation of The Hague drove the Hague painters to other areas in the countryside. Blommers chose Heeze in North Brabant, and also worked with Albert Neuhuys in Bladel, which was nearby. After 1906, Blommers found that Heeze was becoming too crowded and claimed: 'Last year there was an entire international group on the hunt for things – even in America Heeze near Eindhoven is not unknown!'

Following the 1894 storm it was decided to construct a sea harbour in Scheveningen, which led to the area developing into a modern seaside resort very quickly. It became too fashionable for Blommers, and he turned to Katwijk. Initially he stayed with Hidde Nijland, but in 1899, he built a house that he called 'Thérèse' (after his youngest daughter), next to the church. He found a new subject in Katwijk: the shellfisher. Together with several other painters, including his son-in-law Zoetelief Tromp, he hired a fisherman as a model. Katwijk was a very popular spot in those years: between 1899 and 1904, as many as 170 names of Dutch and foreign painters were recorded in the local hotel registers. Blommers got so involved with the town that he was named honorary chairman of the Katwijk Artists' Association.

The growing fame of the Hague School quickly drove up prices in the United States and Canada. Blommers' paintings and watercolours, too, were very popular there. In the long run his work was thought to be too anecdotal at home, but across the ocean his children washing their feet were avidly purchased. In 1904, Blommers, his wife and his oldest daughter travelled to the United States. It was a glorious tour: they visited Joseph Jefferson, a famous author of the day who boasted some of Blommers' paintings in his collection. In Philadelphia Blommers was made an honorary member of the Art Club, and Thomas Eakins painted his portrait. To cap it all off, they were received by President Theodore Roosevelt.

Blommers remained active in the Dutch art world well into his sixties. When he returned to The Hague he often hosted American painters, and in 1911, following Israëls' death, he became chairman of the Hollandsche Teekenmaatschappij (Dutch Drawing Society), which he had co-founded in 1876. In 1912, he again travelled to America. Two of his sons, Bart and Pierre, decided to stay in America to build their own careers there. Blommers was also chairman of the committee that championed the interests of Dutch artists at the Venice Biennale. This would lead to the establishment of the Dutch Pavilion. In 1897, 1899 and 1907, Blommers himself exhibited at the Biennale. He died on 15 December 1914 in The Hague.

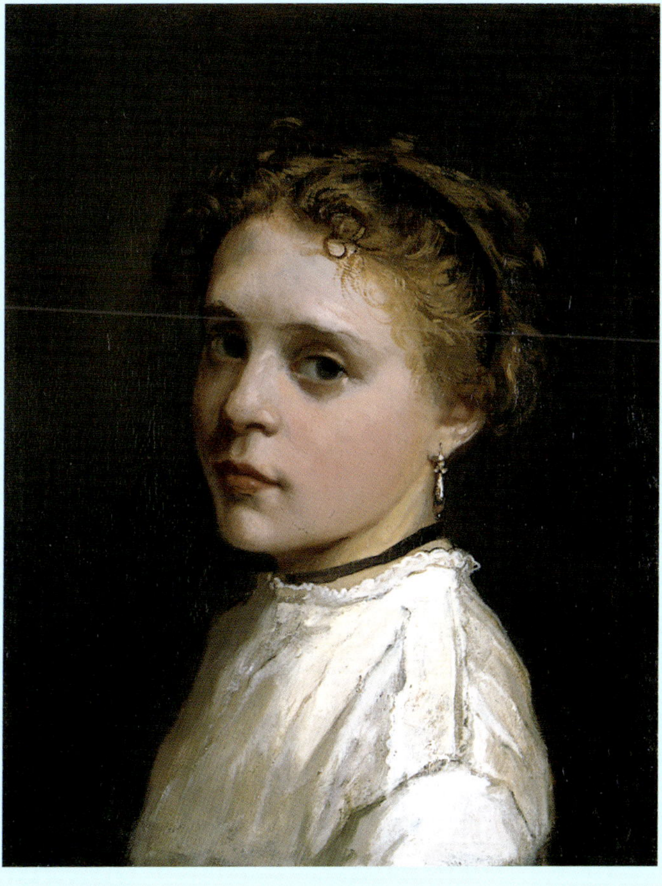

Bernard Blommers, *Head of a girl (the daughter of Mr Siebenhaar)*, 1868

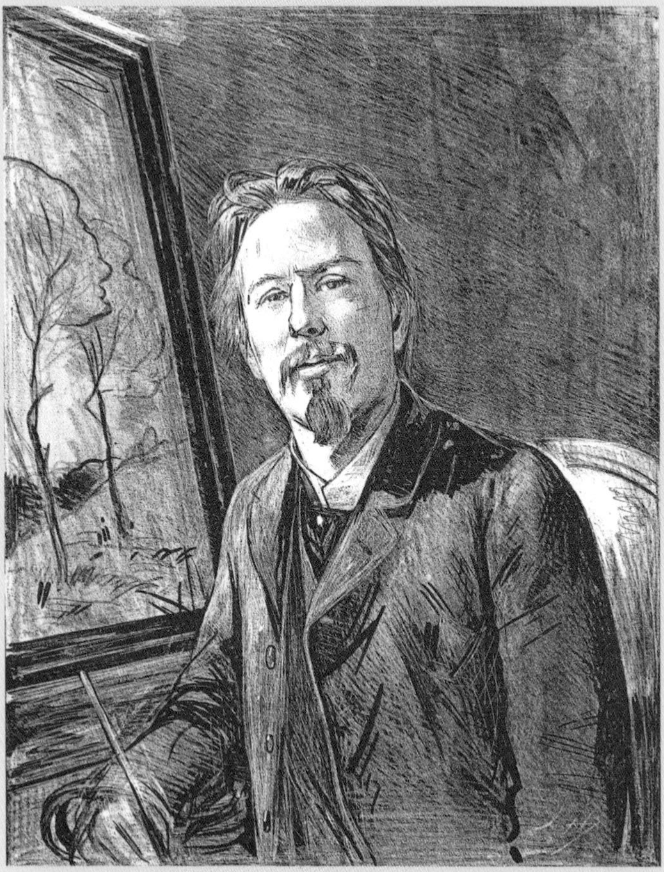

Portrait of Théophile de Bock
(print from 'Elseviers Geïllustreerd Maandschrift', RKD collection)

Théophile de Bock

(1851-1904)

Théophile de Bock was born on 14 January 1851. His parents, Heinrich de Bock and Willemien Thomassen, did not marry until three years afterwards, after they had had two children. They were to have five more children after they were married. De Bock Sr also had four children from a previous marriage and later was to have five more children from his third marriage. His unconventional behaviour forced him to leave the military, and the family moved to Delft, where Heinrich became a civil servant.

When he was eighteen Théophile de Bock went to work for the HIJSM railway company in The Hague. He was soon fired, however, because he took his drawing tools to work with him – and did not leave them idle. It was reported that after he had been fired he asked if he could have a three-month free pass for the company's railroads, so he would be able to continue drawing in the area around The Hague. This was refused. From that time on, he was to devote himself completely to drawing and painting. Moreover, De Bock received a royal subsidy that enabled him to be financially independent for a time.

Johannes Kneppelhout, a literary critic, acted as a patron for the young artist, and proposed that Simon van den Berg become his teacher, just as he had done for Gerard Bilders. Although De Bock did receive support for a while from Kneppelhout, he cut his ties early, freeing himself from Kneppelhout's influence. He worked in the studio of the landscape painters J.W. van Borsselen and J.H. Weissenbruch. In 1872, he made his debut with the painting 'Around Nootdorp' at the exhibition of Living Masters in The Hague. Jacob Maris returned from Paris in the same year, and settled in The

Hague. Maris became the primary example for De Bock, and when the latter exhibited 'Landscape full of trees' in 1875, although he received much criticism about this 'grey painting', Jacob Maris valued it and bought it.

De Bock also saw a great deal of the younger Willem Maris. From 1875 to 1877, they lived together at Engelenburg House on the Loosduinseweg. Later, he was thought to have been Willem Maris' student. It is true that Maris did sometimes provide cows and other figures for De Bock's landscapes. De Bock later moved to the Rozenburg House, where Tony Offermans, a painter of interiors and one of Blommers' students, and Jan Antoon Neuhuys, a historical painter and Albert's older brother, also lived. The following year, in 1878, Willem Maris joined them. By hanging the motto 'Praise to the Knights of the Grey Fog' in the entrance, De Bock presented himself as a painter of the new direction.

Around 1880, De Bock travelled to Paris and Barbizon, where he would often return, perhaps because of his appreciation for Millet's and Corot's work. It was especially Corot who would influence De Bock greatly. In all likelihood, however, Jacob Maris probably had a greater impact on him than is generally believed. Whatever the case, at the Living Masters exhibition of 1881, the results of his influence are very clear in 'On the Marne' and 'Evening at Fontainebleau'.

When Mesdag, his wife, and Breitner worked on the Panorama in 1881, De Bock was responsible for the air and dunes. He enticed Van Gogh to come and see the final work, and Van Gogh wrote enthusiastically about it in his letters to his brother Theo. Although many denigrate De Bock's work as too grey and too sketchy, Hague School champions love his work. Even Van Gogh was convinced of De Bock's 'artistic temperament', although he eventually found his choice of subject too limited, and tried to get De Bock to paint figure studies. But De Bock stuck to the subject he was good at: the Dutch landscape. He characterised his own choice of subject when he wrote lyrically: 'Let the spider spin its web, the bird fly, the fish swim, the worm creep, the frog jump, but let me paint in my own way: the wonderful light of a strong sun, the muted moonlight, the twinkling of the stars in the deep blue air; the velvety green woods, the rattling water, everything, everything, everything that appears beautiful to me, for I believe that everything belongs to and is meant for me.'

Around 1880, he worked a great deal in Scheveningen and in the area of Loosduinen, and from 1884, he also visited other areas. In the autumn of 1885, he went to Drente for the first time, and when he returned there the following summer, he took Isaac Israëls with him. His landscapes seemed to exude sombreness and blackness, and his oil sketches of the megaliths were often monumental. Although he hardly ever drew figures, his interest in the farmers was apparent from the number of short stories he wrote about farm life in Drente.

In September 1887, De Bock again settled in The Hague and married Catharina Petronella Bloklander, mother of his then ten-year old daughter Neeltje and the six children that followed. His work sold well, and De Bock passionately started collecting stoneware and porcelain from Japan, China and Delft, a collection that was to become one of the most important in the Netherlands.

Along with other painters of the Hague School, De Bock's reputation was becoming increasingly established. In 1883, he received a silver medal in Amsterdam; in 1889, he won a gold medal in Paris, the first of five international honours. Above all his paintings and chalk drawings of Gelderland were popular in Great Britain, the United States and Canada, without having been shown in his own country. Yet there was always a great deal of criticism about the work of 'the birch painter', as De Bock was often unjustly called. The various camps in the art world – conservative or radical – were responsible for this, but so was the uneven quality of his work.

In 1889, he had his first one-man exhibition, first at Arti et Amicitiae and then at Pulchri Studio. It offered an overview of his work up to that time: drawings and paintings of dunes, woods, rivers and seascapes done around The Hague, Fontainebleau, Diepenveen and Oosterbeek. The many shipyards that he did in this period, in the areas around Deventer and Zwartsluis, were also included. The most famous work in this group, 'The Zwartewater', was described as follows: 'This capital painting ... is so powerful, but at the same time so broad in its conception, so impressive in its reality; it is, moreover, so soundly and finely painted, that I do not hesitate to include it as one of the great masterpieces of our newer painting school.'

In 1891, at De Bock's initiative, the Hague Art Circle was founded in the spirit of the emerging Wagnerian ideal of 'the Gesamt Kunst'. The association's goal was to promote the various artistic expressions such as the visual arts, crafts, architecture, music, musical arts and writing. De Bock became chairman of the department of Visual Art and of the board. Although many painters were members of both associations, the Art Circle offered the generation after 1850 an alternative to Pulchri Studio, in which the renowned Hague School painters such as Mesdag, Israëls and Jacob Maris retained close control of the administration of exhibitions and admission of new members. The exhibition that was organised in 1892 by Jan Toorop, which included works by Vincent van Gogh, was a major success, and the avant-garde reputation of the Hague Art Circle was established. Other expositions followed, which included works by the Brussels artists' association Les Vingt (1892), Renoir, Monet, Sisley, Pissarro (1893) and Redon (1894). De Bock tried to keep in step with this new generation, and briefly flirted with the pointillist use of colour, but the critics did not take to this at all.

When he became seriously ill in 1894, he resigned the chairmanship of the Hague Art Circle. Following his recovery he and his family moved to Renkum, where he again threw himself into the town's social life. He was co-founder of the VVV (tourist organisation) in Renkum, and became honorary chairman of the artists' association

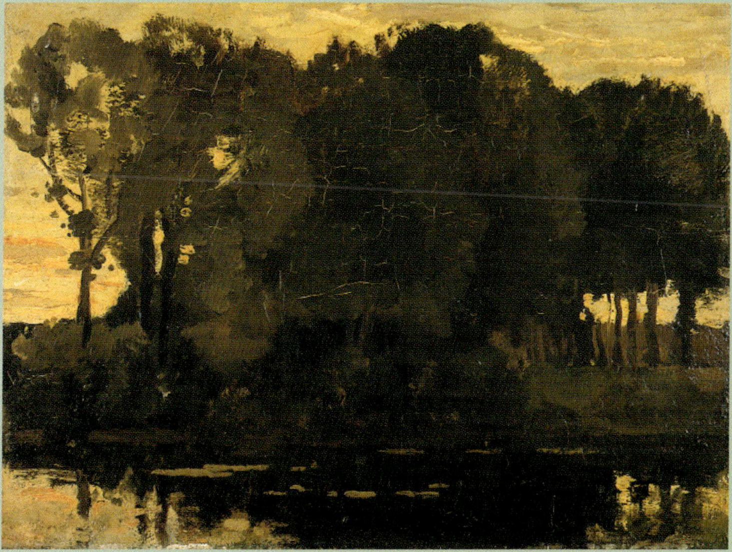

Théophile de Bock, *Landscape with trees,* n.d.

Pictura Veluvensis. Yet De Bock maintained his contacts with artistic life in The Hague, and in 1896, the Hague Art Circle celebrated its fifth anniversary with an exhibition of his work.

He lived in Renkum until 1902, when he moved to Haarlem because he wanted to be closer to cultural life again. 'Besides, now I want to search for a different kind of nature. In the long term, Gelderland has something heavy about it.' De Bock was very productive in his Haarlem period, and his success continued. For two winters he was also writing a book about Jacob Maris, which was published in 1903. When he became ill with severe bronchitis in the spring of 1904, he travelled to France, including Arcachon on the Atlantic coast and Barbizon. When he returned to The Netherlands he again fell ill; he died in Haarlem on 22 November.

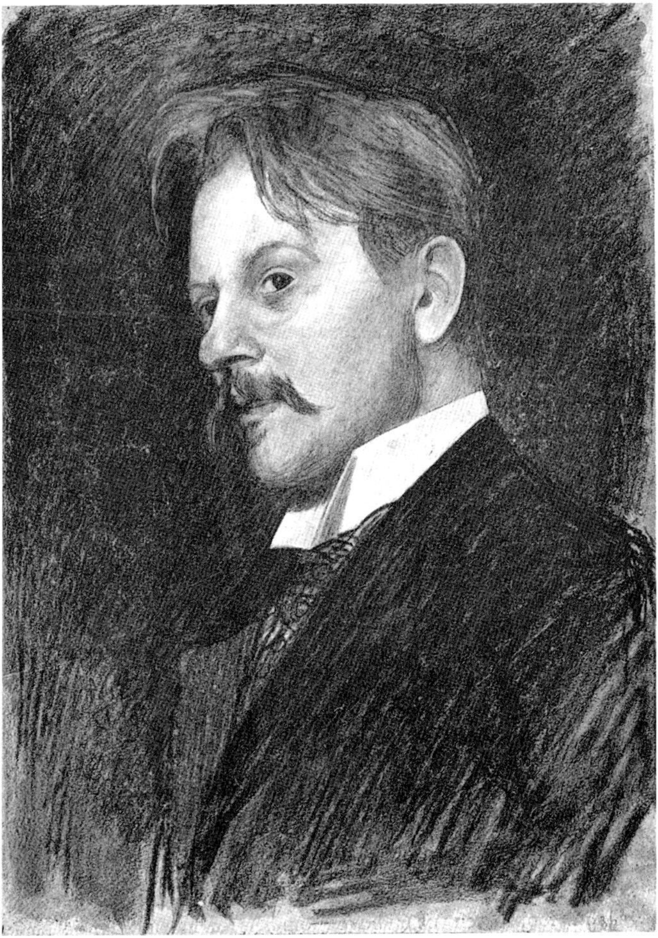

Portrait of Théophile de Bock
(print from 'De Lantaarn', 1889, RKD collection)

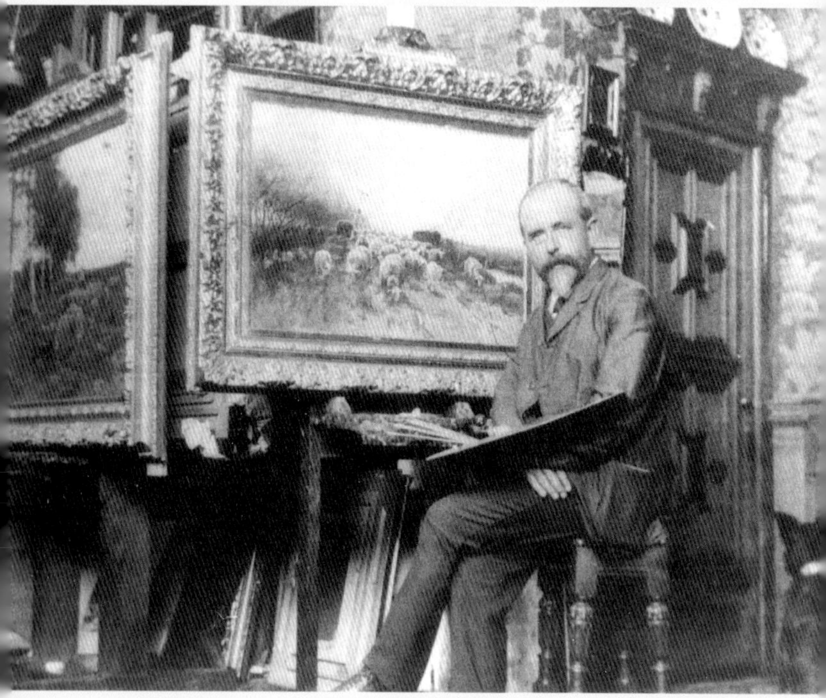

H.J. van der Weele in his studio on the Statenlaan
(RKD collection)

Herman Johannes van der Weele

(1852-1930)

Herman Johannes van der Weele was born on 13 January 1852 in Middelburg. He was the second youngest child in a family of nine. Herman was allowed to go to school until he was eleven, but then he had to look for a job. He found one as a clerk in a tax office, and with the money he earned he paid for private lessons, and later for drawing lessons from Van der Meer Mohr. The earliest example of his painting dates from the time when he was fifteen. It is a naive view of the village of Koudekerke in Zeeland. Van der Weele worked his way up to become special inspector of sea and harbour works for the province of Zeeland. When he was twenty he went to The Hague, with financial support from a few Middelburgers. He registered at the academy there, where he received lessons from J.W.F. Kachel. A year later he received his teaching certificate.

Van der Weele gave drawing lessons at a secondary school from 1873 onwards, which he continued to do even after he was able to earn a good income from selling his work. The writer Haaxman praised his pedagogic talent: 'Seldom have I seen someone speak so easily about art as Van der Weele did ... A discourse with him about theories and principles of art, about the great men of the past and the present, is a true pleasure. If all teachers had so much enthusiasm and conviction, then young people would find studying much more to their taste.' When he was young Van der Weele himself received advice from Mauve and Bosboom. Bosboom saw one of his paintings (a landscape showing the effect of sunlight) at an exhibition. Van der Weele had made the contrast so sharp that it seemed to give the impression of moonlight. Bosboom looked up Van der Weele in his studio and said to him: 'That certainly is an ugly painting there, but it is very studied! Just continue working hard and you'll get there.'

In addition to paintings, watercolours and drawings, after 1880, Van der Weele made etchings that were greatly appreciated: 'For example, if you take his etchings from that period, such as 'The pig pen' or 'The dead lamb', the powerful treatment is surprising, the polishing and re-polishing that was applied to such an animal hide, until the full strength of the light and its reflections is portrayed. In such an etching it is possible to see tones without colour even stronger than in many another very clever painting.' His chalk drawings of a shepherd with a flock of sheep or a sheep barn under tall trees are also characterised by strong lines, a subtle use of grey tones, and skilful light effects. The etchings that Van der Weele did from Anton Mauve's watercolours and paintings were published by Goupil, the art dealer. At the 1889 World Exhibition in Paris he won a medal for one of these etchings, and at the Chicago World's Fair, the etching 'A sandy road' was similarly honoured.

Mauve's influence can also be detected in Van der Weele's paintings. His compositions have the same simplicity, and Van der Weele's choices of subjects are very like those of Mauve. He painted flocks of sheep, sheep barns, stable interiors, meadows with cows, sand drifts, foresters with horses, farmers ploughing with an ox team, milkmaids tending cows, street scenes with coaches, and sand quarries. Van der Weele occasionally worked in Limburg and Drente, but he usually spent his summers in the area around Nunspeet in the Veluwe. In 1892, he remodelled a farmer's barn in Elspeet into a studio which he called 'Bosschenbroek'; he kept this studio until 1912. His work quickly became very popular, even in England, America and Canada.

In 1878, he married Johanna ('Jans') Stam. Her father had been a respected wood engraver. Following her husband's death in 1874, her mother had opened a shop under her maiden name, Liernur, which sold drawing supplies. Van der Weele's mother-in-law's shop was located on the Papestraat and became a meeting point for many artists. The young couple was to have three children: Herman (1879), Mary (1881) and Gonnie (1885). Only Mary would survive her parents. Van der Weele and his wife often supported other artists. In addition to works by Jacob and Matthijs Maris, Bosboom and Israëls, the Van der Weele collection mainly included work by contemporaries: Floris Arntzenius (who had painted a portrait of Van der Weele), Tholen, Breitner, Termeulen, Van Essen, Martens, Akkeringa, Steelink and De Zwart.

Van der Weele had a prominent place in the art life of The Hague. In 1876, he became a working member of Pulchri Studio, where he was also responsable for the exhibition halls for a while. His art judgement was also highly respected: 'Van der Weele was especially good at making the appropriate comment about his art colleagues' work. He was very welcome at studios where works were in progress. About the manner and the reason for things, about the beauty of the lines of the composition, the appropriateness of a figure in the landscape, the opposition of tones and their relative values, he knows how to speak with such taste and such fine, discerning judgement that even highly sophisticated artists welcome him to their studios and value his advice.'

Although he did not win especially great praise for his own work, it did receive appreciation: the compassionately painted thin, worn-out draughthorses that he exhibited in 1883, for example, were greatly praised by Isaac Israëls and Vincent van Gogh. Van Gogh's admiration was not returned, although Van der Weele did see Van Gogh, who was almost the same age, fairly often. Van Gogh encouraged Van der Weele to make lithographs and gave him double copies from his own collection of wood engravings in order to start Van der Weele off with his own collection. They also went to the sand quarries in The Hague

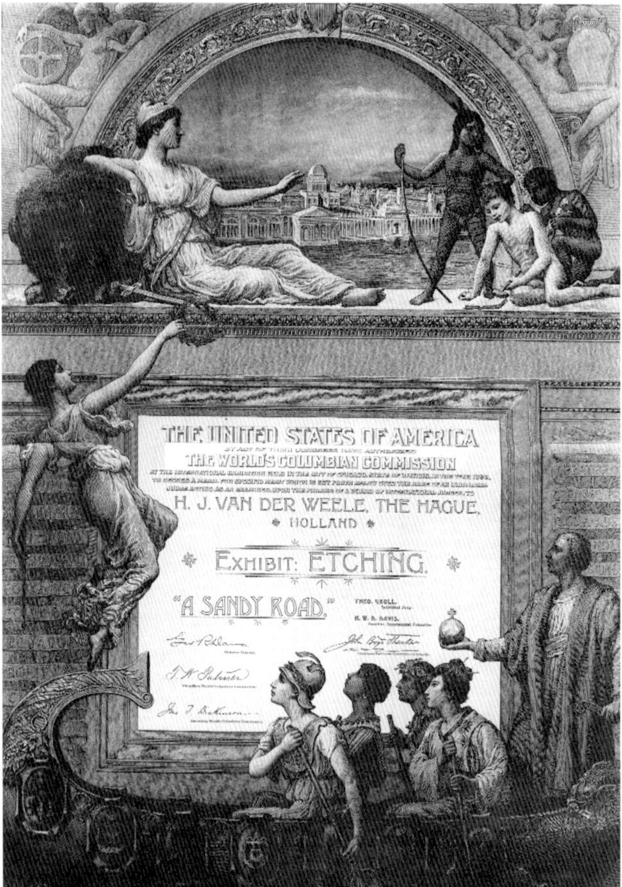

Honour awarded for the etching 'A sandy road'
at the Chicago World's Fair, 1893 (RKD collection)

to draw together. Van Gogh also wrote extensively about the works of Breitner hanging on the walls at Van der Weele's home.

Van der Weele was very close with George Hendrik Breitner. Described as an 'open, calm, harmonious man, an ardent atheist, without any eccentricity' he was very much the opposite of the five-year younger and volatile Breitner. He introduced Breitner to the English dealer, Peacock, and to the American Richardson. He also urged Breitner to accept an American commission to copy Rembrandt's 'The anatomy lesson'. Breitner dedicated his well-known 'Self-portrait with lorgnette' to Van der Weele, who was to bequeath the painting to the Gemeentemuseum of The Hague.

After Breitner had moved to Amsterdam in 1886, he and Van der Weele exchanged many letters, which survive as visible traces of their friendship. They exchanged news about the art world kept each other informed about their health, their commissions, and the progress of their various paintings. They also wrote about which exhibitions they submitted work to, and encouraged the other to submit to that exhibit as well. Thus Van der Weele submitted his work to the Munich International Exhibition in 1897, where he won a gold medal, second class. A catalogue for an exhibition in Chicago in the same year showed work by both of them, and they expressed their satisfaction in writing. Both of them also submitted works to the Saint Petersburg exhibition in 1896.

In their letters they exchanged information about etching techniques, paper qualities, inexpensive paints and photography. Van der Weele had probably become interested in photography somewhat earlier than Breitner, and also used photographs as studies for his paintings. Breitner wrote to him in 1888 or 1889: 'Please be so good as to let me know by return mail, through a drawing and an explanation, how I can build a camera like the one I saw at your place.' They exchanged their results, which is attested to in a letter from 1896: 'If you don't need my camera any more, send it back to me as soon as possible. I am curious to see the photos that you took with it.' Around 1898, Breitner finally wrote: 'Please do me the pleasure in your return letter of letting me know if perhaps you have my photographic device, 9 x 12, which you have already borrowed from me a couple of times. I can't find it anywhere.'

In 1892, when Breitner had to rest again because his eyes had deteriorated, he stayed at Bosschenbroek in Elspeet for a while, and wrote to Van der Weele and his family that they should send him cans of sardines. Breitner nevertheless had to go to hospital. When he was better and had returned to his Amsterdam studio, he found that his turtle had died. He regretted this and asked Van der Weele the best way to stuff it: 'Now it is full of worms.' Apparently Van der Weele was an expert in that area, for he also taught Breitner how to stuff the birds that they had shot in the Hague Woods.

From April 1885, the Van der Weele's rented part of a country estate, 'Het Kleine Loo', near the Hague Woods. The estate was owned by Zilcken, and had once belonged to King Willem III. At the time Willem de Zwart had rented the coach house on the estate. The stylish residence became a favourite place to stay for Breitner and other artists. In 1889, Van der Weele moved to the Koningin Emmakade, and in 1902, he bought a house on the Statenlaan, at that time one of the newest districts of the city. He had the place completely rebuilt to allow for a large studio. He furnished the reception area for clients with antiques from Zeeland. The artists F.P. van der Meulen, Willy Martens, Jan van Essen and Willem Steelink lived on the same road. They were all followers of the Hague School who often painted sheep. For that reason the road also came to be known as Sheep Lane. It had another playful name: since many of the above painters sold a great deal of their work on the American market, the road was sometimes referred to as United States Lane.

Van der Weele remained alone in the big house after his wife had died at the age fifty-six. Two of his children also died young: Gonnie in

1905 and Herman in 1909. In the final years of his life Van der Weele engaged in various honorary functions in the art world. Thus he had a seat on the board of the commission that granted subsidies to young visual artists, and he was a board member of the Royal Academy for Visual Arts in The Hague. After he retired, he was appointed an honorary member. He also worked for the widows and orphans fund. He died on 2 December 1930 at the age of seventy-eight.

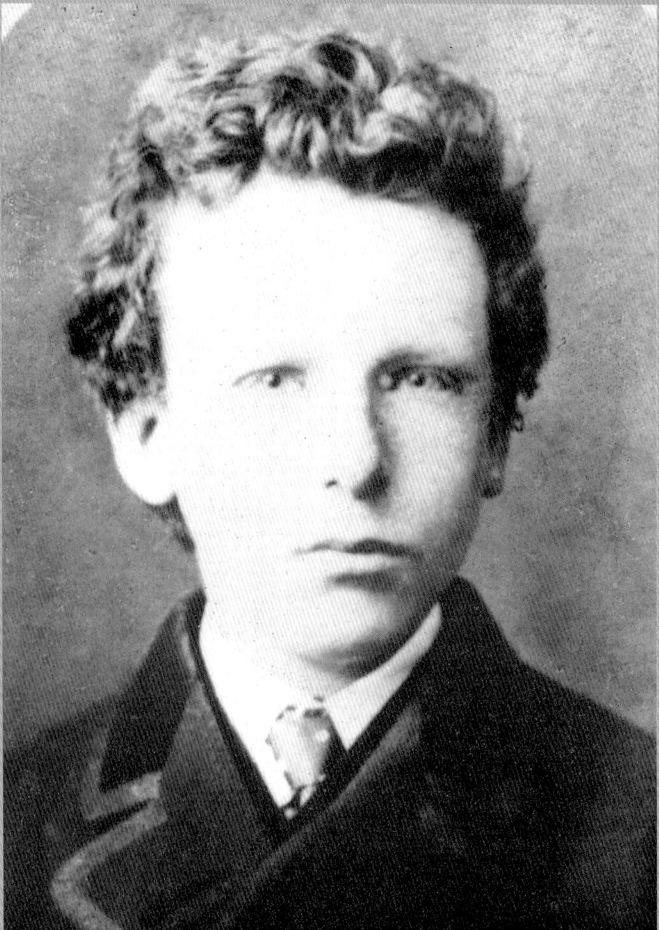

Portrait of Vincent van Gogh, ca. 1866 (RKD collection)

Vincent van Gogh

(1853-1890)

Vincent van Gogh was born on 30 March 1853 in Zundert, the son of the town's pastor, Theodorus (Dorus) van Gogh. The eldest of six children, Vincent spent his youth in Zundert. In addition to producing a number of pastors, the Van Gogh family was also quite rich in art dealers: Uncle Hein had an art business in Rotterdam which would later become well-known under the name Oldenzeel, C.M. van Gogh (uncle Cor) traded in art on Amsterdam's Leidsestraat and in The Hague, Vincent van Gogh ('Uncle Cent') ran an artists' supply shop located on Spuistraat, with Johannes Bosboom and J.H. Weissenbruch among his customers. Uncle Cent, too, decided to become an art dealer, affiliating himself with the renowned Goupil art dealers in Paris, where he successfully exploited the then still wide-open market for art reproductions. In 1858, Uncle Cent accepted Goupil's offer of a partnership in the firm, which in turn took over his Hague business and moved it to a new address at the Plaats.

Through Uncle Cent's intervention, the 16-year-old Vincent Van Gogh entered Goupil's employ in 1869, working at the Hague branch, which was run by H.G. Tersteeg. In the initial years of his employ, Van Gogh had to work hard for little pay as a shop assistant. But his efforts were rewarded in 1872 with a sizeable pay rise. The works and reproductions which passed through Van Gogh's hands through his work at Goupil constituted his first extensive confrontation with modern art, and it was in this manner that he became familiar with the School of Barbizon. And because Goupil had exclusive reproduction rights for the works of Jozef Israëls, these too became etched in his memory.
In the spring of 1873, Van Gogh was transferred to the company's

London branch, and two years later, against his will, to the Paris branch. Despite his growing fascination for the art around him, the career of art dealer interested him less and less, and when he failed to turn up for work during the busy Christmas period, he was sacked because of his indifferent attitude.

From 1872, Van Gogh wrote his four-years-younger brother Theo hundreds of letters, which provide us with much valuable information concerning his life and work. Theo, too, was in the employ of Goupil. Working at the Hague branch from 1873 to 1878, he developed into an esteemed art dealer, and ultimately became director of a branch of Goupil's at the Boulevard Montmartre.

Following his sacking in 1876, Van Gogh worked as a religion instructor at a boarding school in Ramsgate, England, and subsequently in Isleworth. He then worked for a short time as assistant in a bookstore in Dordrecht. In 1877, he resolved to become a pastor, preparing for the university entrance examination in Amsterdam. However, his impatience put pay to his plan to study theology, and he decided to try his luck as a lay preacher in de Belgian mining area of Borinage. There, he began drawing on a regular basis. In his letters to Theo, he compared his impressions of the region with Bosboom's watercolours of the lime furnaces of Chaudfontaine and other industrial installations, works with which he had become acquainted through his job at Goupil in The Hague.

After drawing had gradually become his main activity, Van Gogh, now 27, decided to become an artist. The artist who most inspired him was Jean-François Millet, who had gone to live among the peasants in the French countryside to depict their way of life. In 1880, Van Gogh tried to become a part of the cultural scene in Brussels. He enrolled at the Academy of Fine Arts, where he made the acquaintance of Theo van Rijsselberghe, Anthon van Rappard and Willem Roelofs. However, living in Brussels proved too costly for him, forcing him to return to his parents, who now lived in Etten, but he was neither able to work there nor to readjust to life with his parents. Following Christmas, 1881, he left to settle for the second time in The Hague.

Here, for a period of a few weeks, he received instruction from his fifteen-years-older cousin through marriage, Anton Mauve. Through Mauve, Van Gogh was able to become an associate member of the artists' society, Pulchri Studio, which made it possible for him to take life classes twice per week. Mauve also advised him to paint small watercolours, as there was a market for these. Van Gogh aspired to have his pen-and-ink drawings of different folk types reproduced in the same illustrated magazines whose wood engravings in this genre he collected. These engravings, especially those he found in French and British magazines, were a great source of inspiration to him. Van Rappard was one of the few who shared Van Gogh's interest in them. Bernard Blommers, who was also positively disposed to the project, submitted to Pulchri Studio's executive committee the idea of holding talks inspired by these illustrations, but the proposal only elicited sneers: after all, such material could be found in every coffee house.

1881 saw the unveiling of Mesdag's Panorama. Although panoramas were considered nothing more than popular entertainment, Van Gogh was extremely enthusiastic about this 'boundless' painting. The exhibition held in 1882 commemorating the 200th anniversary of the founding of the Haagse Teekenacademie (Hague Academy of Art) was also important for him, as it enabled him to see works by, among others, the Barbizon painters Troyon, Rousseau, Corot, Daubigny, Dupré, Diaz de la Peña, Jacque and Courbet. In his Hague period, Van Gogh made a number of views of the centre of The Hague and of Scheveningen. He made the acquaintance of the young George Hendrik Breitner, and together they went to The Hague's slums, soup kitchens and potato market to draw people. The relationship which developed between Van Gogh and the prostitute, Sien Hoornik, led to quarrels with Mauve.

The works from this period bespeak much admiration for the painters of the Barbizon and Hague Schools. Van Gogh, who had by now become personally acquainted with many of the Hague School painters, became a fervent admirer of the work of Jozef Israëls, putting him on almost as high a pedestal as Millet, the former's influence being particularly evident in 'The potato eaters.' In letters to his friend Anthon van Rappard, Van Gogh mentions Mauve, Israëls and Jacob Maris in a single breath in the context of innovation: 'a painting by Mauve or Maris or Israëls tells us more than Nature herself.'

Van Rappard wrote to Van Gogh enthusiastically about the province of Drente, at that time popular among painters, and in the autumn of 1883 Van Gogh journeyed to the heaths and peateries around Hoogeveen and Nieuw Amsterdam. He found it quite desolate here, and the desperate poverty of the peasants saddened him. When the winter set in, he once again went to live with his parents, this time in Nuenen. Here, he painted, in addition to peasant types, still lifes and landscapes in the sombre colours which characterise his early works. Van Rappard had much criticism for the technique employed in the most important of the works painted here, 'The potato eaters.' Van Gogh took the criticism very hard, causing a permanent cooling of their friendship.

In 1886, Van Gogh studied for a short period at the academy in Antwerp, where he learned to appreciate the art of Japanese prints. He then went to live with his brother Theo in Paris, taking classes at the studio of Fernand Cormon, a professor at the École des Beaux-Arts, and drawing from plaster and live models. In this period, he made the acquaintance of such impressionist and post-impressionist painters as Gauguin, Degas, Toulouse-Lautrec, Seurat, Pissarro and Signac, and saw the work of many others, as well. However, the hecticness of the city had a negative psychological effect on him, and he moved, in the early spring of 1888, to the southern town of Arles.

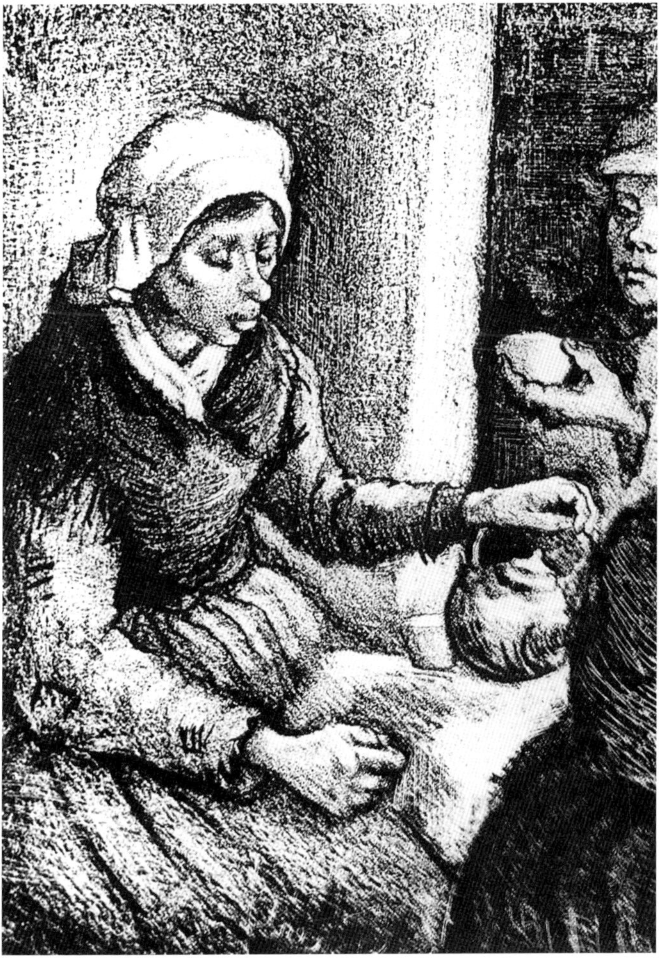

Vincent van Gogh, *The potato eaters* (detail of p. 145)

In the period which followed, Van Gogh made the post-impressionist palette entirely his own. It was a productive time, in which he painted the corn harvest, sunflowers and nocturnal landscapes. From time to time, he sold his work, and took part in exhibitions, but the great success for which he hoped never materialised. In September, Gauguin joined him, but left again in December, following a great row in which Van Gogh injured his own ear.

This attack of mental illness was the first of many. Van Gogh had himself hospitalised in the mental asylum Saint-Paul-de-Mausole in Saint-Rémy, where he painted productively between his episodes of illness. In mid-May 1890 he was released from the asylum. Following a visit to Paris he went to settle in Auvers-sur-Oise, where he was looked after by the physician, Paul Gachet. On 27 July, Van Gogh shot himself in the chest, and he died from his injuries two days later, in the company of his brother Theo.

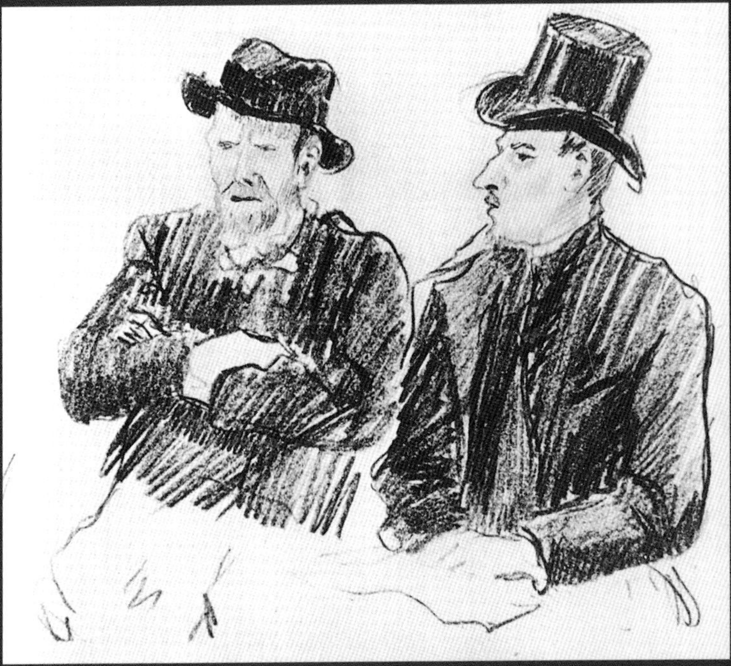

Lucien Pissarro, *Vincent van Gogh and Félix Fénéon,* n.d. (collection of the Ashmolean Museum, Oxford) (drawing)

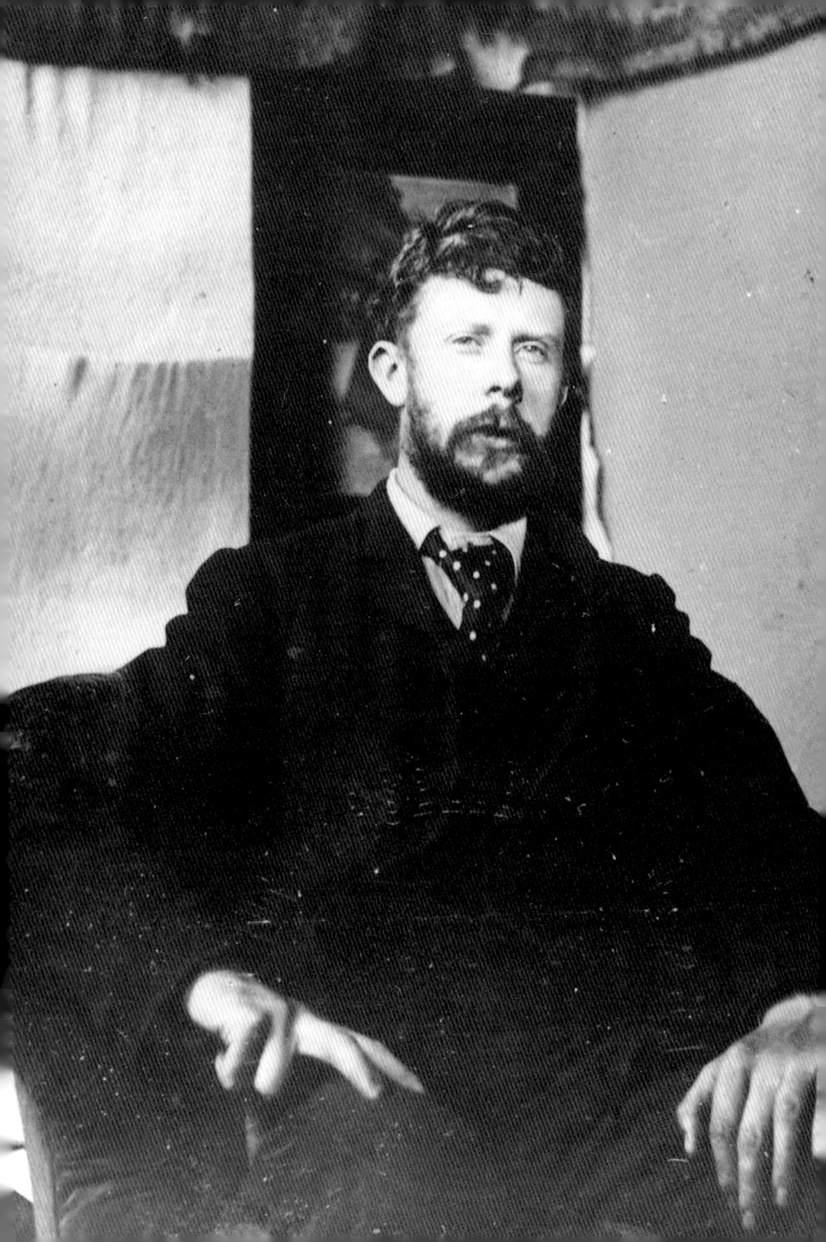

George Hendrik Breitner

(1857-1923)

George Hendrik Breitner was born in Rotterdam on 12 September 1857, the son of a trader in grain shares. Among Breitner's father's business contacts were the grain merchants A.P. and C.E. van Stolk. As a child, Breitner liked to draw, often basing his drawings on war reportage illustrations in magazines. A school friend would later recount: 'A few bent lines with a couple of dots for heads represented the backs of hundreds of soldiers, who, in long rows, came rushing on at top speed; a single curved sabre, carefully added, marked the excitement of the struggle.' Breitner was often caught drawing at school, as he had a tendency to inflate his cheeks when he really got wrapped up in a drawing: 'the greater the challenge, the more his cheeks would expand.'

Breitner attended school until he was fourteen, when he went to work as an assistant in his father's company and in other firms. He took drawing lessons from Christoffel Neurenburg, who introduced him to the painter of historical tableaux, Charles Rochussen. Rochussen was, above all, a source of moral support and inspiration to the young Breitner, who aspired to painting scenes from military history with the same technical mastery as his mentor. Both Rochussen and A.P. van Stolk gave their approval to his wish to enrol in an art academy. From 1877 to 1883, Van Stolk would help Breitner financially, take an active interest in his development and try to mediate in the sale of his work. Eventually though, Breitner's style and choice of theme would diverge to such an extent from historical themes, or in any case, sellable art, that Van Stolk would ultimately withdraw his support.

Breitner moved to The Hague in January 1876, where he would live for the next ten years. He enrolled in the Haagsche Teekenacademie (Hague Academy of Art), and was, initially, a very diligent student. He won a number of awards and took classes in the drawing of ornaments

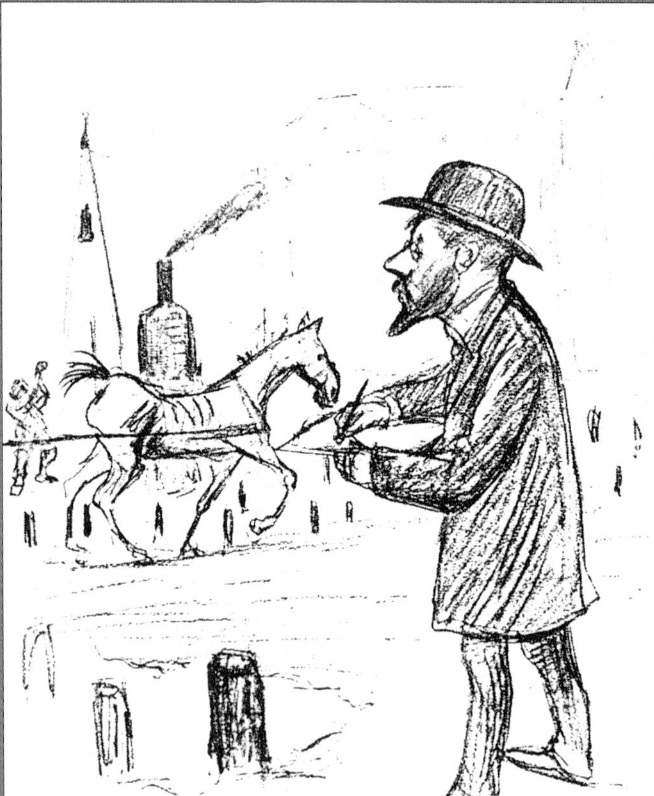

Breitner at work (caricature, n.d., RKD collection)

at the Polytechnic School in Delft. He went to a riding school to make studies of horses. Within a year, he had received his secondary school teaching certificate, and in 1878, received diplomas for various courses at the academy. Breitner became an instructor at the Leiden art academy, Ars Aemula Naturae. During the same period, he tried to gain admission to the studios of Rochussen, Philip Sadée and Blommers, but was unsuccessful in this. Breitner's attendance of classes at the Hague academy became less and less frequent. The academy's director, J.D. Koelman, believed in a strict and traditional method of instruction and was completely opposed to any form of modernism, referring to the work of the Hague School as 'realistic filth.' Breitner later wrote: 'Koelman indicated to me then that it would be my undoing if I went to listen to those younger painters [such as] W. Maris.' Breitner, however, retained his great admiration for the work of the Maris brothers, Mauve, Mesdag and Israëls. In 1880, when, in a quarrel with the school's janitor, Breitner destroyed the board with the academy's rules, he would ultimately be expelled from the school.

At the exhibition of Living Masters of 1879, Breitner exhibited a painting of his own for the first time: a still life with vegetables. In the autumn of the same year he worked in Delft, Schiedam, Rotterdam and Dordrecht, painting city views characterised by light colours, free strokes and a hint of the romantic genre piece. Following the example of his favourite Hague painters, he began to draw landscapes in the environs of The Hague. His friend from the academy, H.J. van der Weele, was instrumental in his becoming an associate member of Pulchri Studio. From 1880, Breitner came into contact with the Hague painters not only at the society, but in 'Oud-Rozenburg,' as well, the country house of Willem Maris in Loosduinen, where he had his own room. Both Willem Maris and his older brother, Jacob, exerted much influence on Breitner. By the time Breitner moved into his own studio on Juffrouw Idastraat a year later, he had accumulated a number of themes in his repertoire: city views, still lifes with flowers, landscapes, mounted soldiers and urban construction sites. He tried to obtain portrait commissions through Van Stolk, painting self-portraits in order to prove his skills in this genre.

In 1880, Mesdag invited Breitner to work on his Panorama. His official task was to paint the group of exercising hussars, but other figures on the beach and many of the almost sketchy housefronts of the village of Scheveningen are also probably from his hand. His contacts with the painters of the Hague School were intensified as a result of this commission; his strokes now became wider and more daring, reflecting the influence of Jacob Maris. Matthijs Maris is said to have exclaimed upon seeing Breitner's work during this period: 'Yes, Jacob is the great influence these days.' A note of Breitner's in one of his sketchbooks demonstrates clearly that he also had an eye for light effects: 'Corner of Paleisstraat. The sun hits the houses from above. The ones furthest back shine – the shapes as well! –, the red transparent. Toward the sky, toward the houses – marvellous.' During the same period, though, Breitner also often painted in the more refined style in which he had painted prior to this time, and he was not unreceptive to Van Stolk's desire for him to involve himself more with the painting of historical pieces. He tried to find suitable themes and scenes, but was unable to, attributing this to the fact that, as he saw it, many legends and histories were only available in Latin.

In the autumn of 1881, large-scale military exercises were held in the province of Brabant, and Breitner travelled there to make sketches of on-rushing cavalry, riders resting and the blacksmith, but also of the peasants as they picked potatoes. While working out these studies, he again discovered affinities to Rochussen, still an important influence, and to the historical genre in general. In regard to style, however, Breitner was embarking on a completely new path: his manner of painting no longer gave a precise representation of the manoeuvres or the uniforms, which had now been reduced to an impression. When, some years later, the national government had purchased a large canvas from Breitner, a critic would write: '... And Breitner's much-discussed mounted artillery? In a gallop, the team of horses flies from the dunes. It shall not be easy to attain unanimity about such work. Nothing is drawn with care, and one must not gloss over the sharp white streaks this colourist and impressionist gives to a stirrup or a sabre sheath. But what speed and storminess of movement, what a feeling for poetry in this glistening, dusty, turbulent ensemble!'

After returning to The Hague, Breitner spent much time with Vincent van Gogh, who wrote: 'These days, I often go drawing with Breitner, a young painter [...]. He draws with skill and very differently from me, and we frequently sketch in the soup kitchens or the station waiting room.' Breitner's city views became increasingly populated by urban types: ladies and chamber maids, drunks and coachmen. After the symptoms of gonorrhoea had made it necessary for Breitner to be hospitalised, Van Gogh and Breitner lost contact for a time, despite the fact that, a few months later, Van Gogh himself entered the same hospital with the same complaints. A curious aspect of their collaboration is that the two painters appear not to have liked one another's work. Concerning a few of Breitner's starts at paintings, Van Gogh wrote: 'From a distance they are nothing but haphazard fields of colour, such as on bleached and decayed and mouldy wallpaper, and in this respect, they exhibit qualities which I ultimately find totally unpalatable.' Alluding to the side-effects of the illness which both of them had recently experienced, he added: 'It is impossible for me to comprehend how a person can arrive at something like this. It reminds me of what one sees when one has a fever, and is as impossible or meaningless as something from a dream devoid of rhyme or reason.' Later, after visiting the Van Gogh exhibition of 1892, Breitner wrote for his part: 'I cannot help but find it to be art for Eskimos: I derive no enjoyment from it. I find it truly coarse and rude, bereft of any distinctiveness and, besides, it is all stuff he stole from Millet and others.' The two quotes underscore precisely how the painters differ from one another: Van Gogh criticised Breitner's work for lacking meaning, while he himself always tried to impart a deeper worth to his peasant and folk types – his realism was humanitarian in nature. What

Breitner, on the other hand, criticised about Van Gogh was his lack of 'distinctiveness,' the very quality he aimed for when using his powers of observation to depict reality.

From his hospital bed, Breitner had often written to Van Stolk, who tried to help him by improving his contacts to Rotterdam art lovers. These attempts met, however, with only moderate success. Nevertheless, Breitner did succeed in selling work during this period, writing: 'That happens quite often. I recently sold the same painting to two different people, so I'll have to make two, which is quite annoying, as both are familiar with the original. I'll wager that they don't notice anything!' However, because of his debts to Van Stolk, he now found it necessary to teach again, this time at the academy in Rotterdam. After his stay in Brabant and his hospital stay, Breitner's style became more expansive and daring, featuring larger forms and greater colour contrasts. Unable to give his approval to such changes in Breitner's way of painting, Van Stolk cancelled most of his support. In the autumn of 1883, Breitner journeyed through Drente. Few studies from this trip have been preserved. The following spring, he travelled to Paris, presumably again with financial help from Van Stolk, and worked for a period of a month at the studio of Fernand Cormon, to whom he had been introduced by either Theo van Gogh or art dealer E.J. van Wisselingh. Here, Breitner produced a number of somewhat academic studies of armour, heads and architecture, but devoted himself increasingly to painting tableaux of the great city. In Montmartre, he made various studies of horses with wagons and coaches.

A year later, in The Hague, the choice of theme with which he would make his reputation in Amsterdam already predominated in his work. He wrote during this period: 'As for me, I shall paint human beings on the street and in their houses, the streets and houses they have built, and above all, life itself. I shall endeavour to become 'le peintre du peuple,' or, to put it more correctly, I have already become that – because it is what I want to be.' In September, he moved from

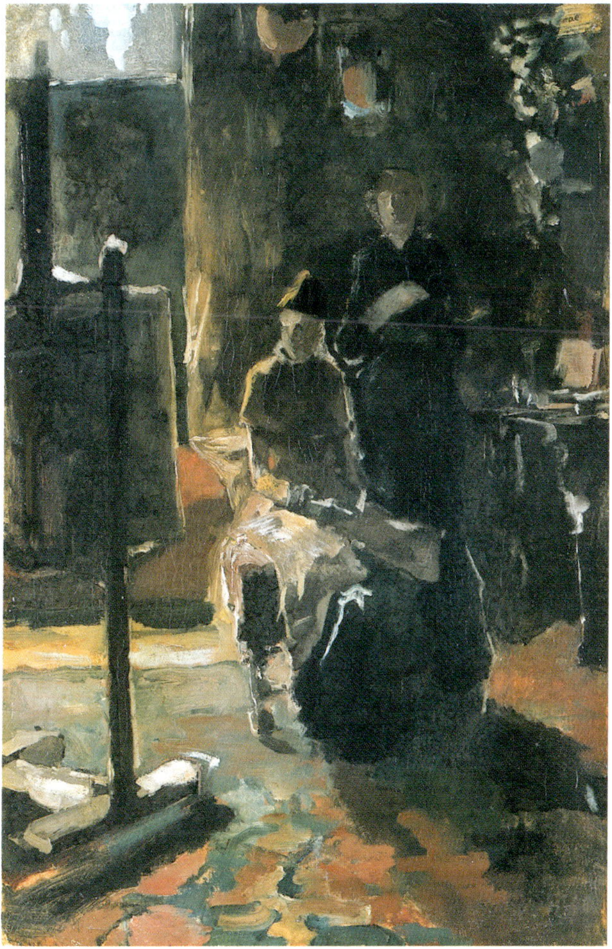

G.H. Breitner, *In the studio,* n.d.

the dignified and peaceful The Hague to bustling Amsterdam, where, together with Isaac Israëls and Willem Witsen, he formed the core of the group which would be known as the 'Amsterdam impressionists.' The misty, muddy and 'foul smelling' views of Amsterdam which Breitner was painting were now worlds removed from the pleasantly shining streets with down-pouring rain and elegant ladies which Floris Arntzenius was producing back in The Hague.

Although already thirty years of age, Breitner enrolled in Amsterdam's Rijksacademie, where he hoped to improve his drawing. He was given his own studio and received coaching from director August Allebé, but Allebé found him, as he put it, 'out of place,' and the other students reacted with amazement, one later recounting: 'Imagine, him, already a renowned artist, at our academy, supposedly to learn how to draw!' Allebé helped him become a member of the artists' society, Arti et Amicitiae, and, with the various administrative functions he gradually accumulated, Breitner would play an increasingly important role in the Amsterdam art world.

In 1901, Breitner married his model, Maria Catharina Josephina Jordan, and in the winter of 1901/1902 had his own retrospective at the artists' society, Arti et Amicitiae. Now, critics no longer breathed a word about 'sloppiness' in his work, or excessive sketchiness, but rather, praised Breitner's manner of direct registration, one remarking: 'I have never known anyone who could become so ecstatic about visible reality. [...] The freedom and accuracy with which he expressed the essential, and ignored the rest, without any apparent strain, were of the most pleasing mastery.' This marked the beginning of wide recognition for his work. In 1903, he moved into a villa in Aerdenhout, and from that moment, missed increasingly the contact he had had with the new generation of avant-garde artists, his move back to Amsterdam in 1906 notwithstanding. From 1914 until his death, Breitner hardly painted any longer, instead involving himself more and more with worthy projects of a cultural nature. He died as a result of a heart attack on 5 June 1923.

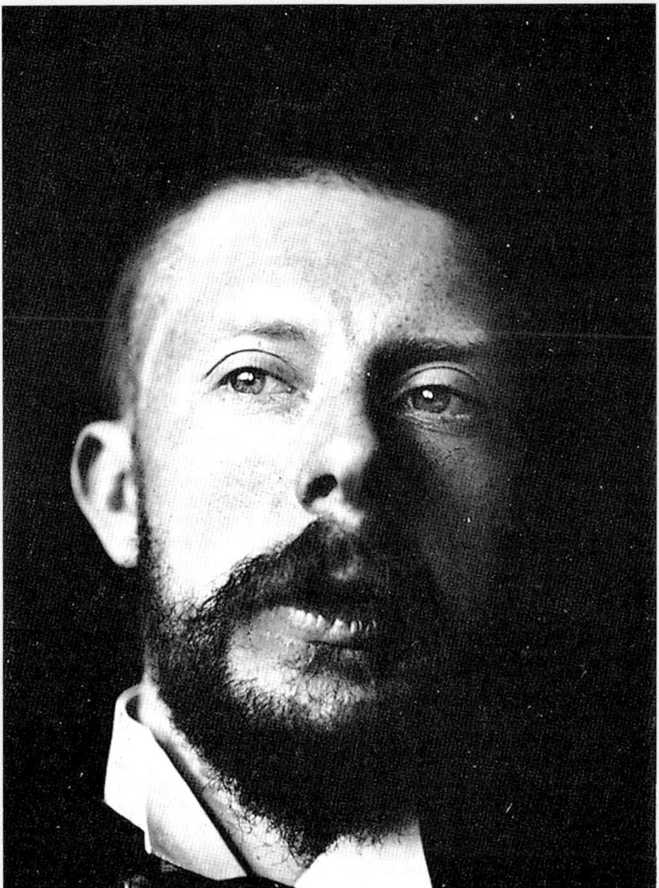

Portrait of G.H. Breitner, photographed by Willem Witsen
(collection of the Van Gogh Museum, Amsterdam)

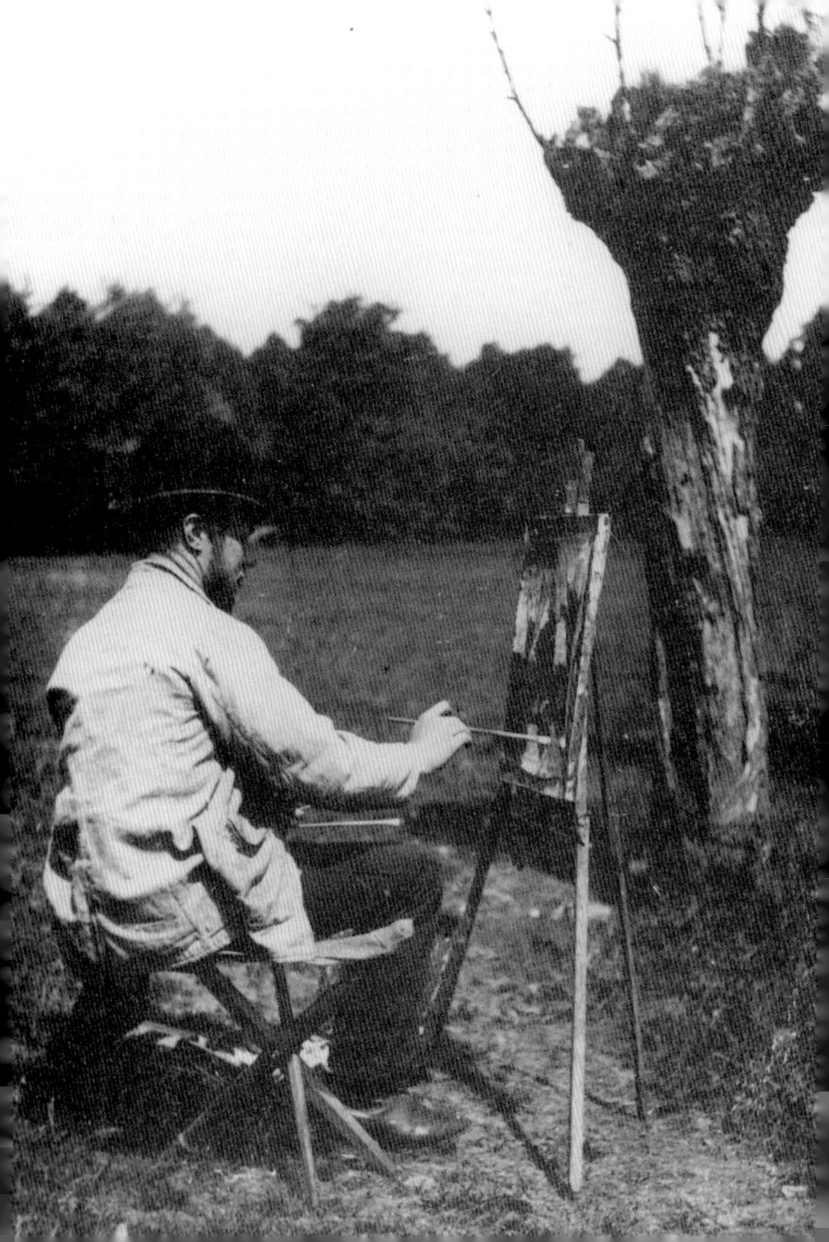

Anthon van Rappard

(1858-1892)

Anthon Gerard Alexander Ridder van Rappard was born in Zeist, in the Dutch province of Utrecht, on 14 May 1858. He grew up in an art-loving milieu, and when he decided, at the age of eighteen, not to join the navy, but rather, to become an artist, his parents reacted positively. Van Rappard moved to Amsterdam and was admitted to the Rijksacademie, where he studied until 1879. In the autumn of the same year, he left for Paris, becoming a pupil in the studio of J.L. Gérome, famous for his historical and exotic tableaux. It was probably during a visit to the art dealers, Goupil & Co., that he made the acquaintance of Theo van Gogh.

Having returned to Utrecht, Van Rappard became, in 1880, member of the artists' society, Kunstliefde, in the city of Utrecht. From the start, he was one of the society's more prominent members, and two years later, his father would be chosen as its chairman. At the evening drawing sessions, the new member set the poses taken by the models, and was subsequently successful in his initiative to have nude male models to draw from. When, however, in 1886, he tried to introduce female nudes, this met with the opposition of the society's executive board, prompting him, together with his friend, Willem Wenckebach, to leave the society. In the summer of the same year, he went sailing and drawing with Siebe ten Cate on the Loosdrecht Lakes. Presumably spurred on by Ten Cate, who was a student at the Royal Academy in Brussels, Van Rappard decided to enrol there as well, and moved to the Belgian capital in the autumn.

In the same year, Vincent van Gogh, too, enrolled at the Brussels academy, having decided to become an artist after a disappointing period as lay preacher in the mining district of Borinage. Van Gogh was eager to strike up friendships with fellow students, and on the advice of his brother Theo, paid a visit to Van Rappard's studio. The two became friends, and in the spring, Van Gogh often came to work at Van Rappard's studio. Together, they went walking and drawing in the environs of Brussels. The two artists had strongly contrasting characters. Van Rappard was known for his social talents, and Van Gogh characterised him as a 'gentleman.' He was a nobleman, enjoyed the backing of his parents in his choice of profession, was skilled at drawing and already had a great deal of academic training under his belt. In contrast, Van Gogh had grown up in austere circumstances, was headstrong, impulsive and short-tempered and lamented his parents' negative attitude to his decision to become an artist.

Van Rappard is often characterised as merely 'a friend of Van Gogh's,' with his significance being confined primarily to the documentary value of the letters which Van Gogh sent him. Their friendship however had greater depth than this would indicate. Van Gogh and Van Rappard were convinced of the quality of each other's work. They stimulated one another in their choices of theme and in regard to technique. Van Gogh, who found it difficult to maintain friendships, received from Van Rappard the kind of moral support which he otherwise only got from his brother Theo: Van Rappard did not reproach him because of his friendship with the prostitute, Sien Hoornik, as Anton Mauve would. He lent Van Gogh money when it was necessary. Van Rappard's influence did not, however, go beyond the encouragement Van Gogh needed to pursue his own development.

Conversely, Van Gogh's friendship did have a direct effect on Van Rappard's work. Van Gogh's enthusiasm for wood engravings in French and British illustrated magazines rubbed off on Van Rappard, who also started collecting them. Such magazines often published articles about the life of urban labourers as well as about houses for the poor and orphanages. The accompanying engravings after works by such internationally known masters as Millet and Breton exerted a direct influence on Van Rappard's choice of theme, his composition and the position of his figures. The uncompromisingness of presentation and contrast-rich 'black-and-white technique' of these wood engravings confirmed the conviction of both artists that one's choice of motif was a work's single most important aspect.

In 1881, Van Rappard returned to Utrecht, and Van Gogh went to live with his parents in Etten. Van Rappard went to visit him twice that year. When he told Van Gogh of his plan to return to the academy in order to draw from models, Van Gogh tried his best to talk him out of the idea, even formulating his criticisms of academic methods systematically on paper. Here he asserted that, for his friend, the academy functioned like a 'mistress who will prevent a genuine, warm and fertile love for art from awakening in you.' Although Van Rappard, too, considered devotion as the first criterion of art, he stressed the importance of having a good technique: 'Otherwise, the public will stumble over poorly drawn motifs before they can discover the character of one's work.' The two were unable to agree. That autumn, Van Rappard took life classes at the academy of St.-Joost-ten-Noode and exhibited for the first time at Arti et Amicitiae in Amsterdam. This was followed by regular exhibitions in Utrecht and elsewhere. A period of estrangement between the two set in.

Van Rappard made his first journey to Drente in the summer of 1882, together with Willem Wenckebach; the four succeeding summers would also bring him here. In Drente, he made sketches of people and landscapes, which he would transform into paintings in his Utrecht studio, viz., the studies he made in 1882 and 1883 in the house for the poor in Rolde, and the paintings featuring women at the spinning wheel which resulted from them. One of these canvases was rejected for the exhibition held the following autumn at Arti et Amicitiae, but in 1884, a comparable work was awarded with a silver medal at the International and Universal Exhibition in London's

Crystal Palace. Van Rappard's enthusiastic letters about Drente prompted Van Gogh to go to Hoogeveen and Nieuw Amsterdam in the autumn of 1883. In the same period, Van Rappard made his first studies in Utrecht's home for the blind. He would be ill the entire winter long.

By the spring of 1883, Van Rappard had recovered, and began writing his 'Kunstbeschouwingen in Kunstliefde' (artistic reflections of an art lover), published in the daily newspaper, the Utrechts Provinciaal en Stedelijk Dagblad, continuing to do so, anonymously, for three years. In these articles, he presented a notion of art in which, to be sure, skill and trueness to nature play an important role, but in which sentiment and character take pride of place: '[...] sentiment: it is there that not only the craftsman's hand was at work, but where it was guided by the heart; sentiment: it is the language of the artist's emotional world.'

The following year, Van Rappard's friendship with Van Gogh seemed to have recovered, and the two met three times. In the summer, Van Rappard stayed, for health reasons, at a health resort in Bad Soden, Germany. He then went to Drente and the Frisian Islands. In the autumn, he painted one of his best-known canvases: 'The home for elderly women on West Terschelling.' Van Rappard concentrated increasingly on working people, painting homes for the poor, tile painters, blind brush and mat makers and the labourers in a silver and a cotton-dying factory. His scenes are not anecdotal or filled with labourers' heroism, nor does he thematicise explicitly the poverty or working conditions of the labourers: he focused on the structure which the worktables, windows and people form in space, allowing the contrasts between light and shadow, the spatial effect of planes and the alternation of horizontal and vertical elements to dictate the composition.

When Van Rappard visited Van Gogh in Nuenen in May 1884, the two went drawing in the town's vicinity, producing, almost synchronously, works with the same motifs. They made studies of weavers, spinners, ox carts and portraits of the people. Van Gogh criticised Van Rappard's dark colours, but during his friend's second visit, in October, he himself employed a comparable palette, the colours for which his Nuenen period are now known. Nonetheless, the standpoints of the two concerning the importance of technique were no closer than they had been in their old disagreement. This became clear when, in 1885, Van Gogh sent a study after his 'Potato eaters' to Van Rappard, who reacted negatively because of its caricatural nature and virtual absence of technique. Van Gogh returned Van Rappard's letter unanswered. The friendship was now definitively over, and Van Rappard's subsequent attempt at a reconciliation was fruitless.

Van Rappard decided to make a large canvas which he planned to send on tour in both Holland and abroad. The resulting work was, however, somewhat stiff, and failed to depict the labourers of the stone works, 'Ruimzicht' in Jutphaas, in a convincing manner. Van Rappard enrolled once again in the Rijksacademie in Amsterdam. He lived and worked in that city, while still maintaining his contacts in the Utrecht art world.

In 1889, Van Rappard married his cousin, Henriette Elisabeth Camp del Campo, and the couple settled in the village of Santpoort, near Haarlem. A peaceful and productive period ensued. Van Rappard became more retiring and did not actively venture forward with his work. He painted dune landscapes, portraits of his wife, still lifes with flowers and, occasionally, seascapes. The portraits from this period reflect the influence of the Amsterdam impressionists; the landscapes still exhibit the influence of the Hague painters. Van Rappard died of pneumonia on 21 March 1892, aged only 33. He left behind a relatively modest œuvre.

p. 374:
Photo-portrait of Anthon van Rappard (RKD collection)

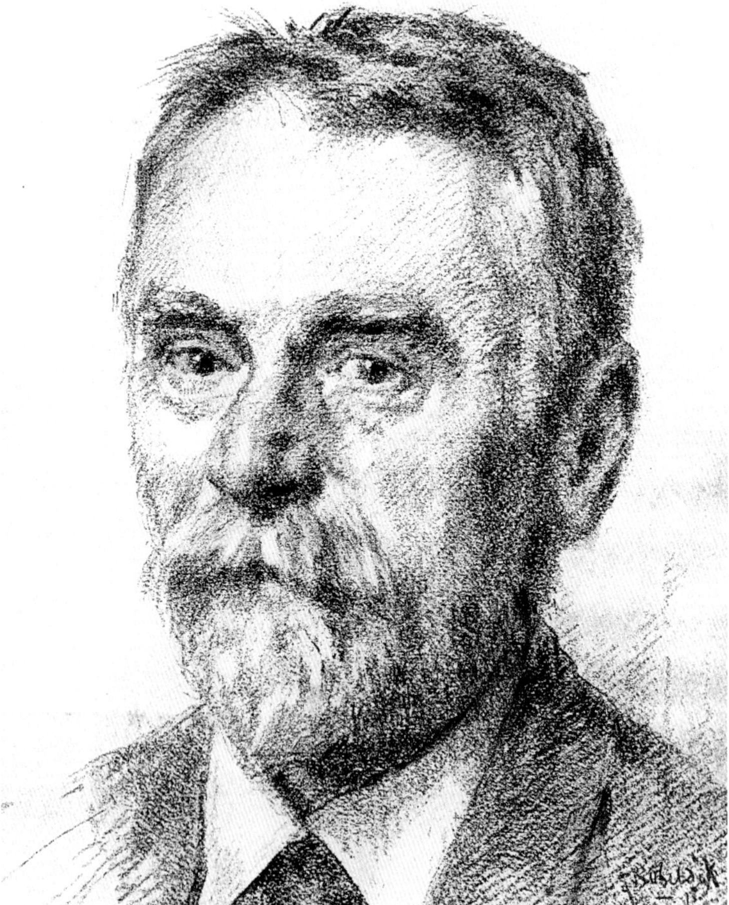

F. Bobeldijk, *Portrait of Willem Bastiaan Tholen,* 1913 (lithograph)

Willem Bastiaan Tholen

(1860-1931)

Willem Bastiaan Tholen was born in Amsterdam on 13 February 1860, the only boy among five siblings, to a well-to-do middle-class family. Although a merchant, his father had also taken drawing classes, and the family counted artists among its friends, one of whom was Paul Gabriël. Margo, Tholen's youngest sister, would also become an artist.

When Tholen was only five years old, the family moved to the town of Kampen. Tholen made friends with the three-years-older Jan Voerman, who shared his love for drawing, and together, they attended the Evening Drawing School where they received – apparently not very inspiring – instruction from C.H. Hein. The two boys, however, did have a high opinion of the old drawing instructor of Willem's father, J.D. Belmer, about whom Tholen later wrote: 'Belmer must certainly not be forgotten! It was through his efforts that Voerman and I [...] became what we became. Without Belmer, Voerman probably would have remained a farmer, and I would have become a street sweeper, which my father was always predicting I would become because I found it so difficult to sit still at school.' Tholen attended the first three forms of secondary school, and had to repeat the third. Belmer convinced both boys' parents of their talent, and prepared them for the entrance examination at the Rijksacademie in Amsterdam. When, at the age of sixteen, Tholen first enrolled at the academy, his fellow students included, aside from Voerman, Anthon van Rappard and Willem Witsen, and he would become good friends with the latter. Tholen earned his certificate of proficiency within a year, in turn enrolling in the Polytechnic School in Delft, where he attended drawing classes for two years. Having concluded his studies there in November 1878 with a secondary school teaching certificate, he went to work as a drawing instructor at the evening secondary school in Gouda.

The following year, he went to Brussels for approximately three months, where he was coached by Paul Gabriël. In subsequent letters, Gabriël expressed concern regarding Tholen's further development, and recommended his working outdoors a great deal, as he considered nature to be 'the only bible of God's greatness.' He also encouraged Tholen to pursue his own path: 'Found whatever school you wish: just make sure it comes from you. But you, yourself, must not belong to a school.' Tholen returned to Kampen and taught drawing there, as well. This proved a strain, and when his old teacher, Belmer, offered to take over some of his lessons, he gladly accepted the offer. In the same period, he went travelling together with Gabriël through the countryside around Kampen. They painted the peat cutters in the peateries and the villages of the, at that time still isolated, Giethoorn district. Gabriël's influence on him would gradually diminish, but the latter's economical use of paint would also continue to be a feature of Tholen's work throughout his career. A journey about which little is known is that which Tholen made together with his school friend, G.P. Rouffaer, to Rome, Capri and Naples.

In 1885, Willem Witsen invited Tholen to visit his family's country house, the 'Ewijckshoeve,' in the environs of Baarn, where their contemporaries, George Hendrik Breitner, Jan Veth and Jacobus van Looij were also frequent guests, as was the better-known Anton Mauve. Willem and Coba Witsen were close friends of Coba Muller, a slightly older, intelligent and well-read woman, who was very popular among the menfolk. She no longer had any close family of her own, and lived with the Witsen family. Bram Arntzenius was also a frequent guest. He was a widower and father of six, all nephews and nieces of the Hague painter, Floris Arntzenius. Quite unexpectedly, Coba Witsen and Arntzenius married, and went to settle, with the family, in The

Hague. A short time later, Tholen and the seventeen-years-older Coba Muller also married, a move which came as a great surprise within the Ewijckshoeve circle. It was, as well, a substantial blow to the friendship between Witsen and Tholen. Nevertheless, although the two would never return to being as close as they had been, they would never lose touch and continued to write and visit one another.

Tholen, too, settled with his wife in The Hague, with the proximity of the Arntzenius family probably being one important reason, although the extremely art-friendly climate developing at the time in the city may also have played a role in their decision. The two Coba's' need to be near each other can be seen from the fact that the family quickly went to live with the Tholens. As the Tholens themselves remained childless, they came to regard the six children, particularly the three youngest – the triplets Péronne, Constance and Paul – as their stepchildren.

From the start of his marriage in 1886, Tholen devoted himself entirely to his artistic career. The several portraits he made of the Arntzenius children are characterised by a mood of intimacy. Paul, who received his first lessons in painting from Tholen, developed into a fully fledged artist. Tholen established his reputation in The Hague with his landscapes of the countryside around Kampen and views of the woods near Baarn. He also frequently painted views of The Hague, the woods of Scheveningen and a series of interiors in which a window typically provides a view outside: a garden, a street illumined by sunlight or the rhythmically grouped roofs of a city. He painted the fishing boats on the beach in Scheveningen, but in contrast to Jacob Maris (whom he greatly admired), Tholen did not employ the desolate sea as a backdrop, but rather, the bustling village. He used the hustle-bustle of the city more often as a theme than was generally the case in the Hague School, depicting such subjects as construction sites, slaughterhouses, stonecutters and the sand excavations and sand barge captains on the canal between The Hague and Scheveningen.

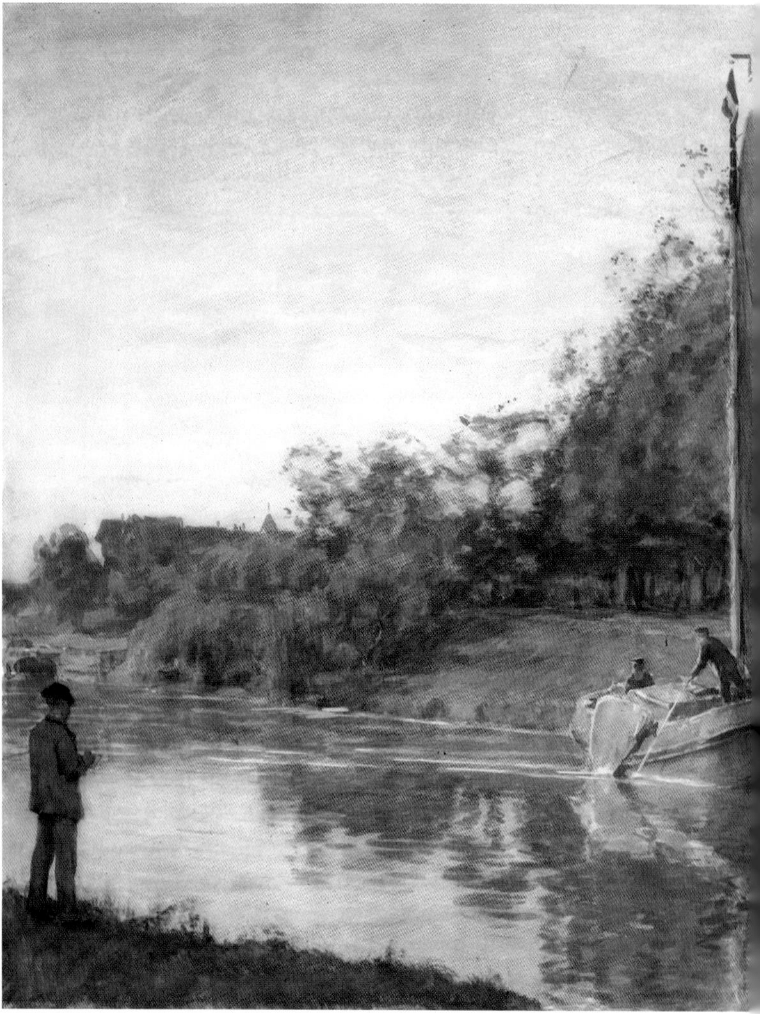

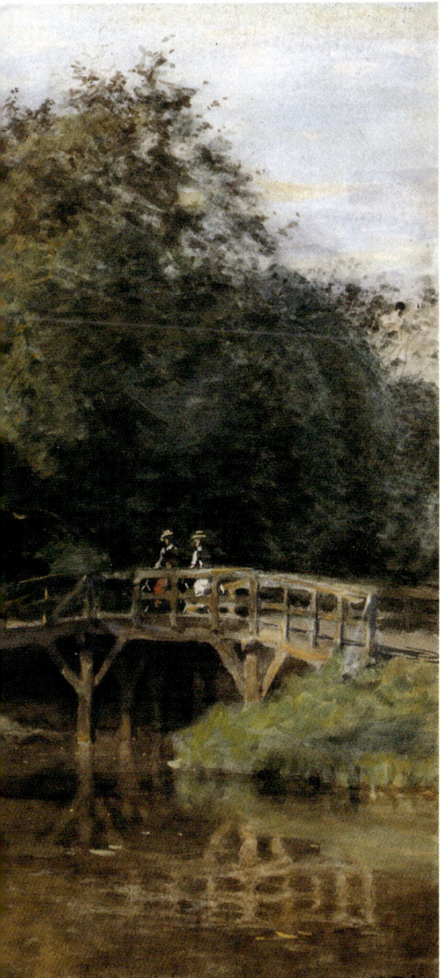

Willem Tholen,
The Koninginnegracht (with the sailing yacht Eudia and, in the background, Tholen's house), n.d.

A winter landscape, 'Skating in the Hague Woods' teems with people, with many of the established painters of the Hague School recognisable among them.

Nevertheless, much of Tholen's work from this period is subdued in character. From 1895, he worked with increasing frequency on the coast of the Zuiderzee, painting, in subtle colours and translucent paint, the sailboats, harbours and façades of the towns Enkhuizen, Monnikendam, Volendam, Nijkerk, Harderwijk, Vollenhoven, Blokzijl and Lemmer. His evening landscapes of this period, which often feature the silhouette of Enkhuizen's 'Dromedaris' lighthouse, have a subdued tenderness. The many details and relatively bright palette of his earlier work gradually disappeared and his strokes became freer, while browns and greys began to dominate, and a critic summed up Tholen at this time as a 'calm, sensitive observer of nature.' However, as these changes had taken place very gradually, they cannot be directly associated with innovations in painting then current. They have their origin in the personal development of a steadily persevering painter, and his striving for perfection. The most uncompromising painting from this group of works, but one nonetheless characterised by great sensitivity, is 'The Zuiderzee,' in which no boat, bird or cloud, and no tower on the horizon can be seen. Here, Tholen only painted transparent waves and a silver-coloured light. The studies he painted outdoors – he called them his 'little boards' – however retain the fresh and thicker paint application which was a feature of his earlier work.

Tholen's work was selling well. He, too, profited not only from the fame which the Hague School had now attained in its own country, but, as well, from the network of trade contacts it now had in England and the United States, making it possible for much of Tholen's work directly to be bought overseas. At thirty, Tholen could afford a villa on the canal between Scheveningen and The Hague, and in 1901, he had a fishing boat converted into the sailing yacht he named the

Eudia, in which he sailed on the Zuiderzee and the waters of Zeeland.

That the preponderance of the reviews Tholen now received was positive had something to do with his friendship with Albert Plasschaert, a critic normally known for his acerbity, but who, when characterising Tholen's work, used such terms as 'intimacy,' 'simplicity' and 'sincerity.' Nonetheless, his work was always – throughout his career – the subject of criticism, with, interestingly enough, the same features often being cited, regardless whether these were adjudged positively or negatively. For example, some considered him – in a negative sense – old-fashioned, because of his eschewing of innovation, while others admired the timelessness in his work and his quest for internal perfection. Another critic asserted: 'He is more original in his conventionality than the ostentatious modernity of many a "genius."' While one writer found him deficient in depth and passion, another found in his work honest and pure depictions, free of cheap effects. What one could criticise as excessive care was characterised by many as 'tenderness' and 'understatement.' However, virtually every critic praised Tholen's great thematic range and his mastery of technique, viz.: 'One seldom encounters a painter so at home in such a variety of registers and who nevertheless always remains himself, always authentic. [...] his confident stroke, his perseverant development of a theme, and adherence to it: in this all his works are alike.'

Coba's death in 1918 created a caesura in Tholen's artistic career. However, already in the following year, he married, at the age of 59, the 43 year old Lita de Ranitz, whom he probably had known for some time, as a result of a portrait commission from her father dating from 1916. Lita had been a childhood friend of Queen Wilhelmina, and through his wife's contacts, Tholen was able to obtain numerous portrait commissions, including from court circles. His painting portraying Princess Juliana sitting informally in a garden and his state portrait of Queen Wilhelmina were the result of such commissions. The majority of these portraits, however, do not go beyond being technically correct, dutiful renderings, and lack the directness of, the portraits of the Arntzenius children.

Tholen was a member of both Pulchri Studio and the Hollandsche Teekenmaatschappij (Dutch Drawing Society), whose minutes he himself published in 1914. Already in 1885, he had, together with Witsen, Jan Veth and Antoon Derkinderen, founded the Netherlands Etching Society. However, he would in fact produce no more than three etchings for sale in a portfolio, and left the society after only four years' membership. The almost customary honours are also not absent from Tholen's biography: at an exhibition in Lyon he was awarded a bronze medal, in Nice, and then Nîmes, one in silver and, at the World Exhibition in Antwerp, a honourable mention. Tholen was an honorary member of the Belgian Society of Watercolourists. In 1904, Tholen's first one-man exhibition was held in the rooms of Amsterdam's Preyer art dealers. Two years later, a more comprehensive retrospective took place at the Rotterdamsche Kunstkring artists' society. At the occasion of Tholen's 70th birthday in 1930, a monograph from the pen of his friend Reinier Bakels was published, and the painter was made a Knight of the Order of the Lion of the Netherlands. Willem Tholen died in The Hague on 5 December 1931. It is said that on that day, the flag of Enkhuizen's Dromedaris lighthouse flew at half-mast.

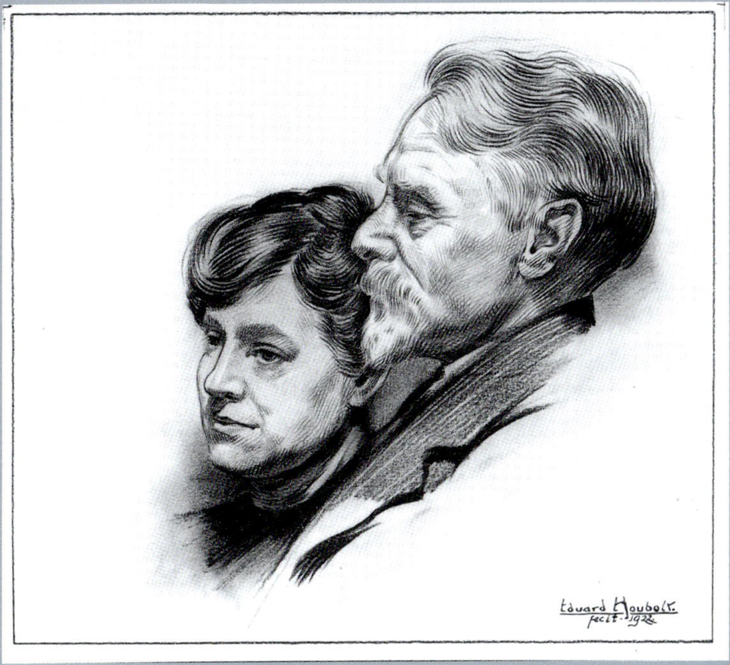

Eduard Houbolt, *Willem Bastiaan Tholen and his wife*, 1922 (drawing)

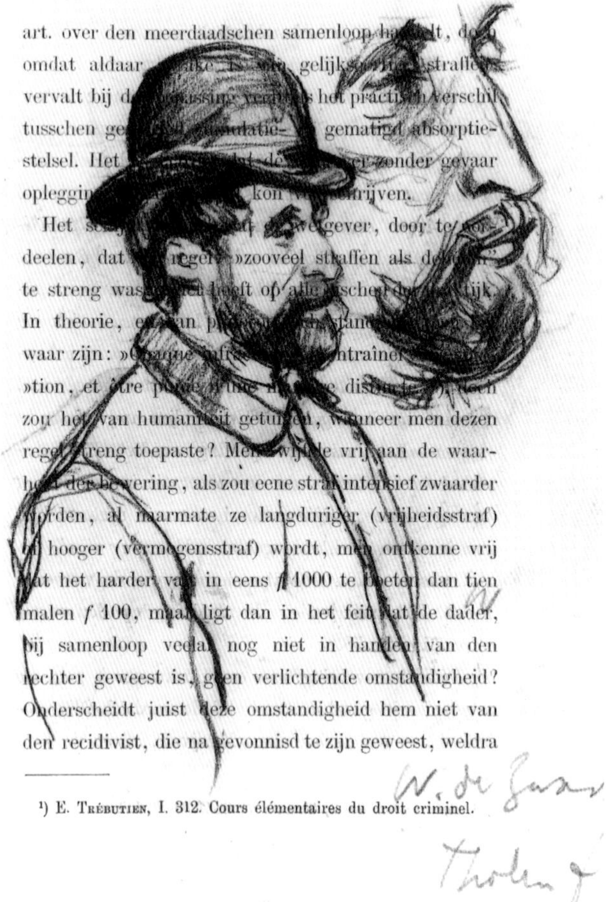

Willem Tholen, *Small sketch of Willem de Zwart for 'Skating in the Hague Woods,'* ca. 1891

Willem de Zwart

(1862-1931)

Wilhelmus Henricus Petrus Johannes de Zwart was born in The Hague on 16 May 1862, the eldest of eight children. His youngest brother, Pieter, would also become a painter. His father painted carriages for a living, and in 1875 the fourteen-year-old Willem was apprenticed to a carriage maker to learn the same trade. In his spare time, he copied prints he found in magazines, and a year later he enrolled in the evening class at the Royal Academy of Visual Art in The Hague. The following year, he was admitted at the studio of Jacob Maris. In the three years that he remained here, it is probable that he got to know many of the leading lights of the Hague School. Maris had him paint still lifes, and in one of the surviving studies a self-portrait of Matthijs Maris can be clearly recognised. Maris also sent De Zwart on a journey to the coast, without drawing materials, and had him work out his impressions directly on canvas when he returned to the studio.

De Zwart made several copies of works by 16th and 17th century masters in the Mauritshuis. He was most interested in the works of Vermeer, Paulus Potter's 'Bull,' and Rembrandt's 'Self-portrait as an officer,' but studied paintings by German and Italian masters, as well. Sometimes he produced copies on commission. In this period, he also made detailed studies of animals, concentrating particularly on their legs, heads and snouts. De Zwart developed a fastidious painting style with a sober, predominantly brown palette. When, in 1880, he was called up for military service, friends purchased his exemption, thus enabling him to continue painting without interruption.

In 1881, De Zwart began working in his own studio. He exhibited his work for the first time at an exhibition of Living Masters. A royal grant made it possible for him to immerse himself further in the old masters, and from 1883 he earned part of his living by painting tile tableaux for the Hague delftware works, Rozenburg. He had already become a member of both Pulchri Studio and the Netherlands Etching Society. Most of his contact at this time was with his contemporaries, Breitner, Zilcken and Van der Maarel. Throughout his life, though, De Zwart tended to keep to himself, never choosing to take an active role in the societies to which he belonged and only taking part sporadically in their exhibitions. He was characterised by those who knew him as 'retiring' and 'serious.'

De Zwart's landscapes continued to reflect the influence of his mentor, Jacob Maris. He sought his subjects in the polders of South Holland, both on the beach and at sand excavations, which at the time were considered picturesque by many artists. An important feature of De Zwart's painting at this time is his backlighting, which he employed to portray persons, trees or boats as silhouettes. In October 1885, De Zwart and Breitner journeyed together to Drente, where they worked in the vicinity of Hooghalen. Although none of the studies De Zwart made here have survived, it is probable that they had the same subjects as those employed by Breitner: peasants, carts and the occasional *hunebed* (a specific type of prehistoric stone grave). In general, when it came to his choice of theme, De Zwart tended, in this period, to emulate Breitner, viz., his use of such folk types as a blacksmith, and melancholic still lifes with flowers. In contrast to Breitner, though, he painted not just bouquets but, in addition, flowers lying individually or arranged in wreaths, with their petals illuminated before a dark background.

From 1886, De Zwart rented the coach house of 'Het Kleine Loo,' a vacation house on The Hague's Bezuidenhoutseweg. Part of the house was rented by the Van der Weele family, who often had other artists lodging as guests. Breitner, who on the urging of Van der Weele had accepted a commission to copy Rembrandt's 'Anatomy lesson,' sold his sketches to De Zwart, who in turn finished the commission. The house was the property of Philip Zilcken, a prominent member of the Nederlandsche Etsclub. Zilcken, who had his own press, encouraged other artists to become proficient in the technique of etching. De Zwart, too, began etching and would develop into a highly esteemed and productive etcher. In addition to the fanciful trees in barren dune landscapes which occupy a prominent place in his etchings, he also produced portraits, city views and studies of animals and labourers in the medium. Although De Zwart also made several etchings after his own paintings, he regarded the technique as a fully fledged artistic medium, a view which corresponded to the philosophy and objectives of the Etsclub. De Zwart devoted much attention to tonality, sometimes even scratching away paper from an already printed work to create the effect of white highlights.

In 1889, De Zwart moved to Loosduinen, together with his wife, Maria Helena Reevers, and on 5 August of that year, their daughter, Maria Hendrika was born. His wife was likely the model for a group of paintings of which those of girls in kimonos, the 'Girl in white' and the 'Girl with a Japanese parasol' are the best known works. The deep, luminous colours of these paintings definitively mark the end of the influence of Maris and other Hague tonalists on his work. De Zwart's choices of theme were now closer to the urban impressionism of the Amsterdam painters, Breitner, Witsen and Isaac Israëls. His paintings in oils or watercolours now featured carriages being stationed, still lifes, children playing, beach landscapes and fishermen. The Loosduinen countryside also continued to be an important source of inspiration to him.

In 1889, De Zwart was awarded honourable mention at the Paris World Exhibition, and in 1891, he stayed in that city for a short time. The conspicuously bright and clear atmosphere of the painting, 'Porte de St. Denis,' made after the visit, is remarkable and has led some to hypothesising that De Zwart had lightened his palette under the influence of the pointillist works he had seen there. The change is, however, more likely attributable to that of the Belgian and Dutch neo-impressionists, whose works were at that time frequently on view at exhibitions of the Haagsche Kunstkring artists' society. In 1892, De Zwart became a father for the second time, with the birth of Willem Paul Valentinus, and earned extra income by producing illustrations for a book and the monthly magazine of publisher Elsevier.

A year later, he concluded a long-term contract with the Amsterdam art dealers, Van Wisselingh & Co. De Zwart was given a current account, from which he could withdraw 200 guilders per month. In return, he sent in work, sometimes only in preliminary form. For the work it approved, Van Wisselingh & Co. would make a proposal for the purchase price of the corresponding completed work. These proposals were often accompanied by criticisms or suggestions for improving the paintings. A condition was that De Zwart himself could not sell any of the works. Because, as far as is known, De Zwart did not maintain intensive contact with his colleagues, his correspondence with the art trade is one of the few sources of information we have concerning his life and work. As a result of this contract, much of De Zwart's work was acquired directly by private collectors, and to this day, relatively few of his works can be found in public collections.

In 1894, the De Zwart family went to live on the outskirts of Soest, and would remain in the Gooi district for six years, moving, in 1897, to Hilversum, and in 1898, to Laren. As Jozef Israëls, Mauve and Neuhuys before him, De Zwart now began painting themes typical of the Gooi district: peasant women, stable interiors, landscapes with cattle, dunes eroded by wind with pines, and wagons with piles of brushwood. One theme with which De Zwart truly excelled during this period was the Hilversum cow market. In these works, he let the backs of the cattle reflect bright sunlight. The red and blue clothing of the peasants and tradesmen contribute additional colour intensity, while their faces are hardly worked out. These paintings derive their vibrancy from the true-to-life manner in which the postures and motions of the figures are portrayed as they talk and deal. In this period, De Zwart also drew and etched a great deal. The etchings are less sombre and more compact than those from the preceding years, this owing to the lattice patterns he employed in rendering such volumes as walls and groups of trees. Particularly successful motifs recur repeatedly in both oils and watercolours. This appears in part to have resulted from market demand, and in part through the artist's own need for stability.

In the same year, Jacobus van Looij settled in Soest; the Amsterdam artists Willem Witsen, Jan Veth and Wally Moes also worked nearby. Nevertheless, it is probable that De Zwart had close contact with none of them. Only Dijsselhof and Isaac Israëls are mentioned in passing in letters. The latter probably helped De Zwart in finding a place to live in Amsterdam, where he moved to in 1900. It is from this period that an anecdote comes which casts a different light on the seemingly ever-sombre De Zwart: 'One evening, Willem de Zwart, Breitner and Isaac Israëls went celebrating at the dancing house on Zeedijk. When they left the place hours later, they stood outside in a state which would hardly have permitted their returning to the studio. They went to the grounds of the IJ station which later burnt down, where they found large empty glass crates filled with straw, and all three painters piled into one of them to sleep off their intoxication.'

In the period from 1903 to 1910 there was much interest in De Zwart's work. In 1903, Van Wisselingh & Co. organised an exhibition devoted to his work; in 1906, Arti et Amicitiae and Amsterdam's Van Gogh art dealers held retrospectives and in 1908, a comprehensive retrospective took place at the Rotterdamsche Kunstkring artists' society. In 1910, the Hague art dealers, Krüger's exhibited work of his. These exhibitions in turn led to a great deal of attention being paid to De Zwart in the press. In general, it was his work from before 1894 which received the most praise. His 'wild' use of colour, characterised as 'aglow with inner fire' and 'powerful and full of passion,' was the subject of much interest. One critic also wrote that: '[...] his etchings contain the finest states of inspiration and the subtlest turns of his rational faculty.' Nonetheless, there were also critical words: 'The artist is now revealed in full portrait, with all his virtues, but all his deficiencies, as well; we admire his beautiful bronze tonality, but, at the same time, it becomes apparent how, under less favourable conditions, this can easily turn into something unpleasantly iron-like; we admire the mastery with which he fills the canvas, but cannot escape noticing that he loses this ability as soon as he takes on canvases of larger dimensions. Then, his organisation becomes poor, his colours coarse and out of balance.'

In 1905, De Zwart moved to Bloemendaal. In the same year, he began to have problems with his mental health. Even after Van Wisselingh's had helped him to purchase a house in Scheveningen, his condition did not improve. In fact, he experienced both this financial support and an increase of his monthly remit to 300 guilders not as a help, but as additional pressure upon him. Several times, he requested his paintings back so that he could make improvements to them, and diminishing self-confidence is reflected in what he wrote about his work. Ultimately, he was hospitalised in the mental asylum, Oud-Rozenburg, in Loosduinen in August 1906. The diagnosis: paranoia. He remained here until the spring of 1907, when he rejoined his family, who now lived in Veur, near Leidschendam. In the winter of 1909/1910, De Zwart concluded that he could neither tolerate his workload nor Van Wisselingh's comments about his work any longer, and he terminated his contract with the art dealers. In 1911, he was divorced from his wife and remained by himself in Veur. From this time on, he earned a living presumably by painting portraits, and a few female portraits have been preserved from this period.

In the last phase of his life, De Zwart lived in The Hague, and created here some of his most profoundly personal works. Around 1916, he painted a triptych with biblical scenes, with, as unifying theme, human sin and godly punishment, viz., the expulsion from Paradise, the Flood and the Fall. The latter theme was employed in 'The fallen angel,' a work which can be regarded as symbolic for De Zwart's entire life. He was now increasingly besieged by 'daemons,' whom he visualised as the mask-like heads in the triptych by the same name dating from 1924. De Zwart could often be found in the billiard room of Pulchri Studio, and in the Gemeentemuseum. He derived the greatest consolation from the paintings of Tholen, Breitner, Van Gogh, Robertson and Verster, works which also made him feel that he was among friends. He donated the few works he had produced in these years to the Gemeentemuseum, and curator Gerard Knuttel described him as he '[...] shuffled in his curious clothing, with small and trembling steps, standing still often and for long periods, always with his folding stool and paint box under his arm and with a kind of powerless fanaticism in his eyes.' De Zwart's last known works were drawings of exotic birds which he had studied in The Hague zoo, and a screen. Willem de Zwart died in a Hague hospital on 11 September 1931.

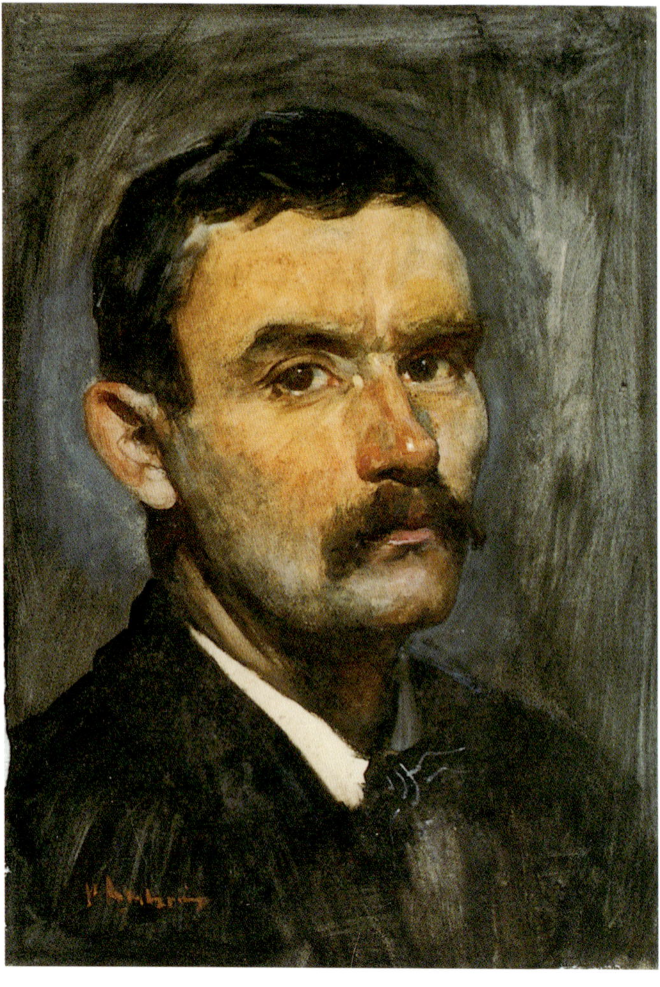

Floris Arntzenius, *Self-portrait,* n.d. (private collection)

Floris Arntzenius

(1864-1925)

Pieter Florentius Nicolaas Jacobus Arntzenius was born on 9 June 1864 in Soerabaya on the island Java, the son of an officer with the Royal Netherlands- Indies Army (KNIL). When he was approximately eleven years of age, Floris and his older sister, Charlotte, were sent home to the Netherlands to attend school. Charlotte went to a boarding school in The Hague, Floris stayed with an aunt and uncle in Amsterdam, where he attended secondary school.

At this time, Arntzenius, who already knew that he wanted to become an artist, began preparing for the entrance examination for the academy, receiving help from Frederik Nachtweh, a painter who specialised in traditional portraits and landscapes. Arntzenius was admitted to Amsterdam's Rijksacademie in 1881, and continued to study there, with interruptions, until 1888. His debut probably took place in 1886. Subsequently, a satisfied purchaser wrote Arntzenius' mother a letter full of praise for his work. His canvas, 'For submission,' was painted in 1888 when friends came to help him select works to contribute to an exhibition at the artists' society, Arti et Amicitiae. In the same year, he left for Antwerp, to continue his studies for two more years at the academy there. He opted for this school, despite its reputation for being traditionally oriented, as instruction was carried out there in Dutch, which was not the case at the more progressive Brussels academy.

From a presumed stay in New York City, not much more has been preserved than a small drawing and a list of items for the journey. When he returned to Amsterdam, Arntzenius became a member of Arti et Amicitiae and exhibited there, among other works, an interior reminiscent of 17th century paintings, 'Corner of a studio.' From the start, Arntzenius' work had always been quite well-received, and he regularly found buyers. He nevertheless found it necessary, in this period, to supplement his income by painting low-priced portraits. The following year, Arntzenius also became a member of St. Lucas, an artists' society with a more innovative orientation than Arti et Amicitiae. In the same period, he entered the competition for the Willink van Collem Prize, submitting his 'Monday drunkards,' whose subject consisted of three drunken men, making their way across the Amsterdamse Sluis. Some twenty years later, it was recounted that, for this work, Arntzenius had taken genuine drunkards off the street and brought them to his studio. In order to keep them upright, he had given them a ladder to lean against, thus giving literal meaning to the Dutch expression *ladderzat,* meaning completely smashed. (According to the story, the men were sober when they left the studio again.)

In 1892, following the death of his father, Arntzenius' mother moved to The Hague, at the time home to a large community of *Indië-gangers* (people with connections to Indonesia, a former Dutch colony). Arntzenius moved in with her, even though this meant leaving the cultural focal point of the Netherlands – after all, Breitner and Isaac Israëls had recently moved to Amsterdam, and in The Hague, the older generation of Hague School painters, now a bastion of the establishment, were setting the tone in artistic matters. From 1893 to 1895, Arntzenius shared a studio with C.A. van Waning on the Spui. Together, Arntzenius and Van Waning journeyed to Paris and Bordeaux. In 1900, Arntzenius married Lide Doorman, herself a talented painter of floral still lifes who had lived across the street from his mother. From the couple's honeymoon in Bruges, Lide wrote of her plan to return there to sketch the town's façades, but this was not to be: she would eventually give birth to four daughters, and her painting activities would recede into the background.

Arntzenius rapidly made a name for himself in The Hague art world. He produced illustrations for the illustrated monthly, Elseviers Geïllustreerd Maandschrift, and besides his landscapes, interiors and still lifes, he became well-known for his views of The Hague.

While the older generation had turned away from the city as theme, Arntzenius' made his immediate living environment his primary source of material. Despite the many changes in the city's appearance since then, the streets and squares he repeatedly portrayed are still recognisable in his oil paintings and watercolours, this despite the fact that it was not so much his aim accurately to depict streets and squares, as it was to give his impressions of modern urban life. Weather conditions often played an important role in these renderings, and Arntzenius was a master in the depiction of busy shopping streets in rain or mist. Façades, signs and people are reflected in the wet asphalt, which may explain his preference for Spuistraat, Venestraat and Vlamingstraat, as around 1900, only these three were asphalted. Employing an extremely spontaneous style, he captured the representatives of various walks of life: ladies taking a stroll, the butcher's assistant, a chambermaid, a fisherman's wife, the handicapped woman selling matches near the Passage and occasionally, the painter himself, walking down the street, in a bowler hat, carrying a walking stick. Cyclists and automobiles were also not absent from his scenes, and often he let a yellow streetcar contrast with the weather's grey tonality.

However, Arntzenius also often journeyed elsewhere in order to work. He travelled to all parts of the Netherlands in search of suitable subjects, e.g., the picturesque streets and quays with historic façades he found in Overschie, Schiedam, Vlaardingen, Gorinchem, Dordrecht, Rotterdam, Haarlem, Leiden, Sluis, Hoorn, Enkhuizen, Deventer, Arnhem and Utrecht. Industrial Zaandam failed to inspire him, however: 'Everywhere windmills with ugly little houses (all painted green); and besides these, the great factories.' Sneek, as well, was too modern for his tastes; on the other hand, he admired Bolsward's quaint canals. He would return a number of times to Hoorn, Enkhuizen and Amsterdam. Here, too, weather conditions played an important role. Arntzenius wrote from Overschie to his wife: 'Pity that it's not grey this morning – with these clear skies, almost nothing

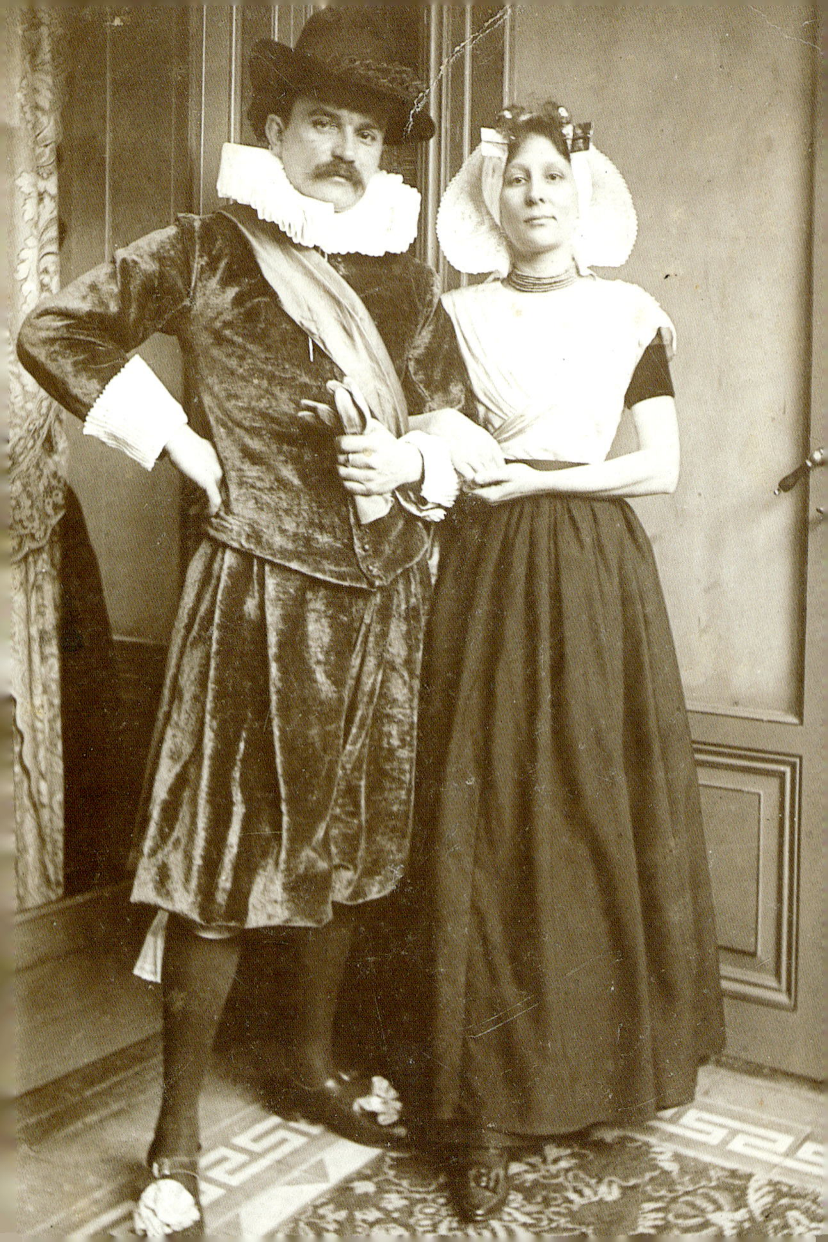

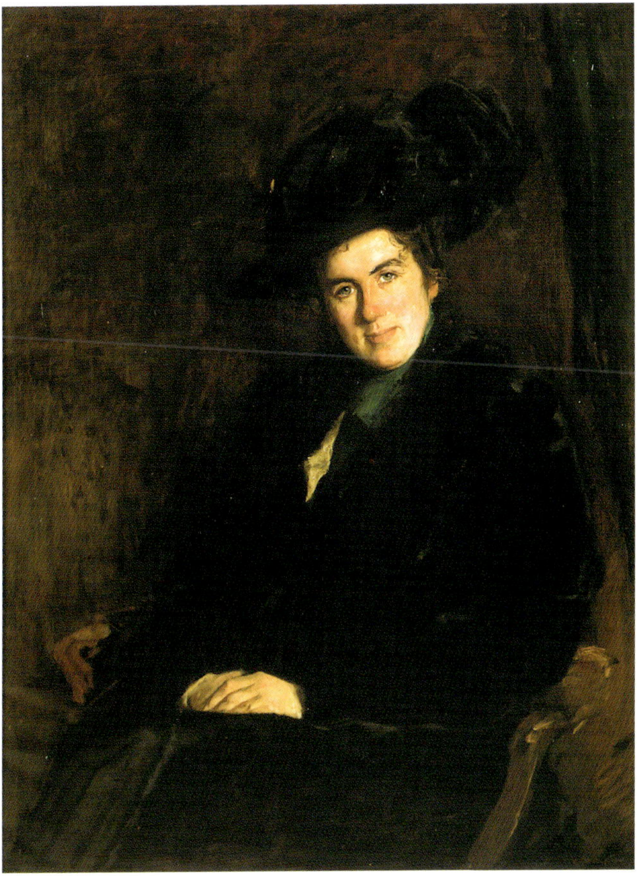

Floris Arntzenius with his daughter Charlotte in fancy dress
(photograph, private collection)

Floris Arntzenius, *Portrait of Lide Arntzenius-Doorman,* painted before 1913

looks right.' One could almost assume that Arntzenius painted more often under an umbrella than under a parasol, as the older generation of Hague School painters had done. If the weather changed, he could become quite cross: 'Yesterday I started doing the quay in grey weather, but today there was more sun: I had to change the whole thing; otherwise I would have had to stop.' In order to work out his ideas without distraction, Arntzenius often rented a 'window': 'When I've found a good street or canal, I go looking to see if I can't rent a window somewhere. Sitting on the canal itself with all my paraphernalia is not really practical: too many people looking over your shoulder. Behind a window you can work in peace.'

Arntzenius was more versatile than one would gather from the above. In addition to the street scenes with which he became famous, he cultivated a number of other genres. His floral still lifes in watercolours are extremely intimate in character, as are his portrayals of subjects drawn from his own household, such as the activities of his four daughters. In his interior views of Café Riche and Pulchri Studio, he recorded his impressions of the social life around him. One will not find fishermen as subjects in his Scheveningen scenes: Since the storm of 1894, fishing boats were no longer to be found on the beach, and since the time of Israëls, Maris, Mesdag and Mauve, the fishing village had turned into a fashionable seaside resort. The beach was now populated by ladies on rattan beach chairs under parasols and children playing in the sand. And yet, these beach scenes are never truly sunny ones: Here, too, Arntzenius demonstrates his preference for grey days. Arntzenius also reflected a modern outlook in the way he chose to spend his leisure time: he was a cricket and tennis enthusiast. However, he does not appear to have regarded these activities as suitable themes for a painting: only photographs of him and his fellow players have survived.

Employing free strokes, Arntzenius depicts himself in his self-portraits as a bon vivant in shoddy clothes, with a cigarette hanging diagonally from the corner of his mouth. Yet such portraits have more to do with the at that time prevailing conception of an artist than with a reflection of his actual lifestyle. Arntzenius did not lead the life of a bohemian, nor was his work primarily innovative – already during his lifetime, his paintings and watercolours were characterised as a 'competent continuation of what greater predecessors have already shown to be beautiful.' Arntzenius was well aware of this and consciously opted for this role. When the Laren art dealers, Van Harpen's, sent him a form with the question 'How would you sum up your style of painting?', he answered, somewhat ironically: 'If judged by present standards, it is the wrong style.' In the Netherlands, his accurate and technically strong works had many admirers. His works sold well throughout his career, through, among others, the Hague art dealers, Biesing and Goupil, and he was the recipient of honours at exhibitions in Munich, Venice, Pittsburgh and Brussels. It was only the influential critic, Albert Plasschaert, whose view of Arntzenius was almost always negative, due to his insufficient interest in innovation.

Although the ballot at the Hollandsche Teekenmaatschappij (Dutch Drawing Society) had become very strict, Arntzenius was accepted as a member in 1896, because of his exceptionally good watercolours. He was also a prominent member of Pulchri Studio, and in 1897, became its secretary. Highly valued for his eye for quality, he was always happy to give advice to the art lovers among the members, viz., bankers, lawyers and Indië-gangers. Among his friends were the painters, Willem Maris, Tholen, Blommers and Van der Weele. In 1910, Arntzenius founded a studio for art students. In this period he painted several portraits, primarily stemming from commissions from the great and the good. This continued until his relatively early death from tuberculosis on 16 February 1925, at the age of 58.

pp. 406-407:
Floris Arntzenius, *Artistic reflections ('For submission')*, 1888

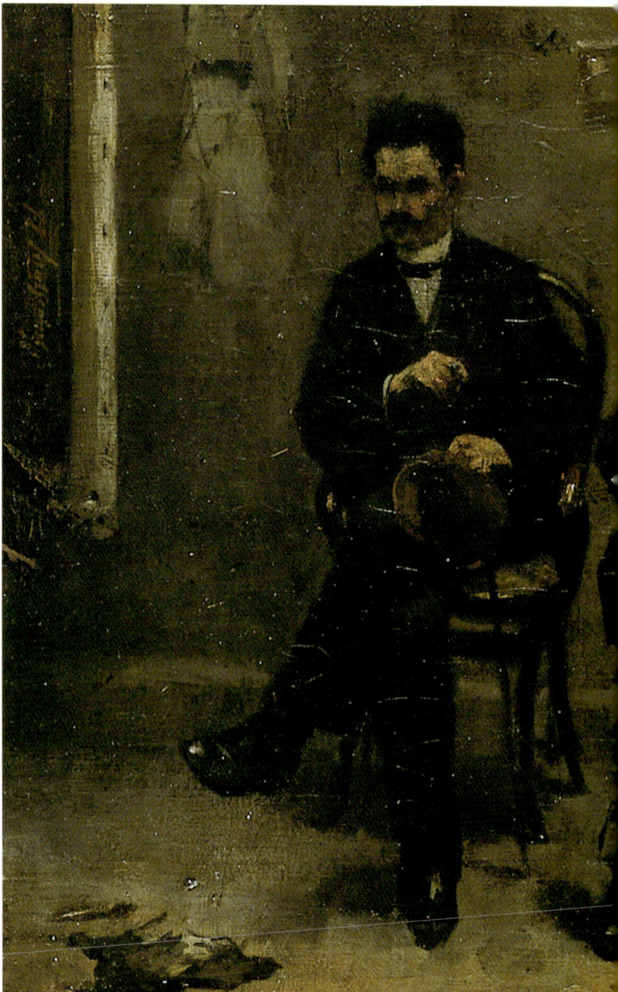

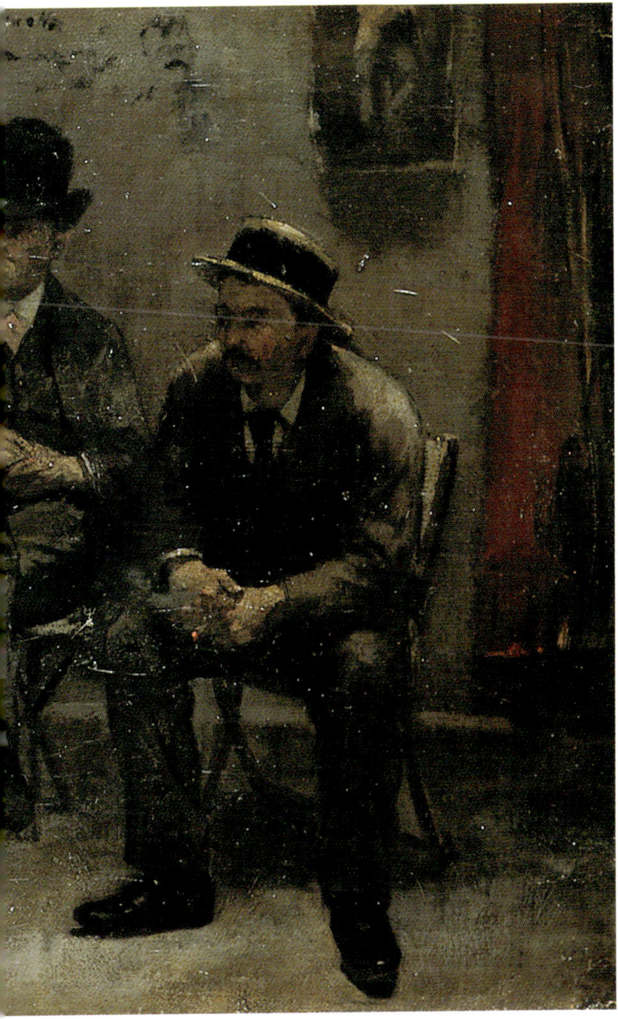

Index

Gabriël, Paul
biography: pp. 245-251; illustrations on pp. 129, 246-247, 251
bibliography: H.F.W. Jeltes, 'Brieven van Gabriël', *Oud Holland,* Vol. 43 (1926), pp. 117-127; *Land van Gabriël,* Kortenhoef 1991

Gogh, Vincent van
biography: pp. 357-363; illustrations on pp. 103, 123, 124, 125, 126, 127, 136, 138, 139, 140-141, 143, 145, 361
bibliography: *Brieven van Vincent van Gogh aan Anthon G.A. Ridder van Rappard,* Amsterdam 1937; R. Groot and S. de Vries, *Vincent van Gogh in Amsterdam,* Amsterdam 1990; M. van der Mast and C. Dumas, *Van Gogh en Den Haag,* Zwolle 1990

Israëls, Jozef
biography: pp. 217-227; illustrations on pp. 14-15, 70, 86, 87, 88, 90, 91, 92, 122, 144, 146, 147, 148-149, 219, 221
bibliography: D. Dekkers, *Een Visserstragedie groot geschilderd. Jozef Israëls' 'Langs moeders graf',* Zwolle [sa]; D. Dekkers, *Jozef Israëls. Een succesvol schilder van het vissersgenre,* Leiden 1994; D. Dekkers, *Jozef Israëls. 1825-1911,* Zwolle 2000

Maris, Jacob
biography: pp. 267-279; illustrations on pp. 5, 51, 68, 69, 75, 76, 77, 79, 83, 100, 272, 273, 274, 277, 278, 279
bibliography: T. de Bock, *Jacob Maris,* Amsterdam 1903; J. de Raad, T. van Zadelhoff and J. Bethe-van der Pol, *Maris. Een kunstenaarsfamilie,* Zwolle 1991

Maris, Matthijs
biography: pp. 301-309; illustrations on pp. 43, 44, 45, 56, 62, 72, 80, 81, 82, 84, 85, 94-95, 302, 303, 305
bibliography: M. Haveman (ed.), 'Matthijs Maris. Een vreemd bestaan', *Kunstschrift,* 1990 (special); J. de Raad, T. van Zadelhoff and J. Bethe-van der Pol, *Maris. Een kunstenaarsfamilie,* Zwolle 1991

Maris, Willem
biography: pp. 311-321; illustrations on pp. 6, 110, 111, 128, 312-313, 319
bibliography: M.H.W.E. Maris, *De geschiedenis van een schildersgeslacht,* Amsterdam [1943]; A.B. de Vries, 'Willem Maris. Winter in het dorp', *Openbaar Kunstbezit,* (1961), no. 37; J. de Raad, T. van Zadelhoff and J. Bethe-van der Pol, *Maris. Een kunstenaarsfamilie,* Zwolle 1991

Mauve, Anton
biography: pp. 289-299; illustrations on pp. 47, 93, 102, 112-113, 130-131, 172-173, 291, 293, 295, 297
bibliography: E.P. Egel, *Anton Mauve (1838-1888). Bronnenverkenning en analyse van zijn oeuvre,* Utrecht 1967; F. Leeman, 'Mauve's aquarellen', *Bulletin Rijksmuseum Vincent van Gogh,* Vol. 2 (1988), n.p.; S. de Bodt and M. Haveman, *Anton Mauve en de Haagse School. 'De meester van het zilveren licht',* The Hague 1997
Mesdag, Hendrik Willem
biography: pp. 253-265; illustrations on pp. 150, 151, 152, 154-155, 158-161, 162-163, 164, 165, 166, 167, 257
bibliography: S. de Bodt, 'Schetsboeken van H.W. Mesdag', *Jong Holland,* Vol. 1, no. 1 (1985), pp. 36-45; J. Poort, *Hendrik Willem Mesdag. Leven en werk,* Wassenaar [1991]; H. Pennock, 'De levens van twee neven. Hendrik Willem Mesdag en Lourens Alma Tadema', *Jong Holland,* Vol. 9 (1993), no. 1, pp. 8-19; *Hendrik Willem Mesdag en Pulchri Studio,* Wassenaar [1995]; J. Poort, *H.W. Mesdag. De copieboeken of de wording van de Haagse School,* Wassenaar 1996; John Sillevis, *Mesdag en de zee,* Zwolle 1999; P. Thoben, *Hendrik Willem Mesdag. 1831-1915. Zeeschilder van de Haagse School,* Eindhoven 1999
Neuhuys, Albert
biography: pp. 323-331; illustrations on pp. 326, 327
bibliography: J.C. Ebbinge Wubben, *Albert Neuhuys,* Rotterdam [sa]; J. van Rijn, *Rijkdom der eenvoud. Albert Neuhuys 1844-1914. Schilderijen, aquarellen, tekeningen uit privéverzamelingen,* Maastricht 1987; M. van Seumeren-Haerkens, *Albert Neuhuys (1844-1914). Schilderijen, aquarellen, tekeningen,* Laren / Eindhoven 1987
Rappard, Anthon van
biography: pp. 375-379; illustration on p. 120
bibliography: *Brieven van Vincent van Gogh aan Anthon G.A. Ridder van Rappard,* Amsterdam, 1937; J.W. Brouwer, J.L. Siesling and J. Vis, *Anthon van Rappard. Companion en correspondent of Vincent van Gogh. His life and all his works,* Amsterdam 1974; H. Schopping and L. Smit, *Een schilderij centraal. Arbeiders op steenfabriek Ruimzicht van Anthon G.A. van Rappard,* Utrecht 1980
Roelofs, Willem
biography: pp. 205-215; illustrations on pp. 40, 48, 49, 67, 206-207, 210, 212, 213
bibliography: H.F.W. Jeltes, *Willem Roelofs. Bizonderheden betreffende zijn leven en werk,* Amsterdam 1911; H.F.W. Jeltes, 'Brieven van Willem Roelofs aan

Mr. P. Verloren van Themaat', *Oud Holland*, Vol. 42 (1925), pp. 86-96 and 131-140; W.F. van Rappard, 'Enige onuitgegeven brieven van Willem Roelofs aan Carel Vosmaer', *Oud Holland*, Vol. 104 (1990), pp. 293-305; S. de Bodt, *Halverwege Paris. Willem Roelofs en de Nederlandse schilderskolonie te Brussel 1840-1890*, Ghent / Amsterdam 1995

Tholen, Willem Bastiaan

biography: pp. 381-389; illustrations on pp. 192-193, 242, 249, 384-385, 390

bibliography: A. de Jong, *Willem Bastiaan Tholen (1860-1931)*, Gouda / Assen 1993

Weele, Herman Johannes van der

biography: pp. 349-355; illustrations on pp. 109, 119

bibliography: P.A. Haaxman Jr., 'Herman Johannes van der Weele', *Elseviers Geïllustreerd Maandschrift*, Vol. 14 (1898); P.A. Haaxman Jr., H.J. van der Weele, *Het Vaderland*, 3 December 1930; P.H. Hefting, 'Brieven van G.H. Breitner aan H.J. van der Weele', *Nederlands Kunsthistorisch Jaarboek*, part 27 (1976), pp. 112-172

Weissenbruch, Jan Hendrik

biography: pp. 229-243; illustrations on pp. 1, 2-3, 20, 21-22, 52, 58, 59, 98, 178-179, 180-181, 190-191, 230, 233, 235, 238, 239, 240-241, 243

bibliography: W. Laanstra and H. Ooms, *J.H. Weissenbruch 1824-1903*, Amsterdam 1992; E. Jacobs, H. Janssen and M. van Heteren (eds.), *J.H. Weissenbruch*, Zwolle 1999

Zwart, Willem de

biography: pp. 391-397; illustration on p. 134

bibliography: H.E. van Gelder, *Suze Robertson. Willem de Zwart*, The Hague 1942; R. Bionda, *Willem de Zwart. 1862-1931*, The Hague / Alkmaar / Laren 1984

Books and other publications for further reading

Apects of Dutch culture. From the collection of the Haags Gemeentemuseum, Nagasaki 1985

De Haagse School met Schevenings werk, Scheveningen 1989

Koninklijke Academie 300 jaar. Haagse School in Pulchri, The Hague 1982

Landschaft im Licht. Impressionistische Malerei in Europa und Nordamerika 1860-1910, Cologne 1990

Nieuwkoop en Noorden in de schilderkunst. 1875-1940, Nieuwkoop 1982

Oost-Nederland model. Landschappen, stads- en dorpsgezichten. 17de-19de eeuw, Enschede 1980

Van Veluwezoom naar Haagse School. Schilderijen van de 19de eeuwse landschapschilders, De Steeg 1983

D. Bieber, *Katwijk in de schilderkunst*, Katwijk 1995

R. Bionda and C. Blotkamp (eds.), *De schilders van Tachtig. Nederlandse schilderkunst 1880-1885*, Amsterdam / Glasgow 1991

S. de Bodt, 'Pulchri Studio. Het imago van een kunstenaarsvereniging in de negentiende eeuw', *De Negentiende Eeuw*, Vol. 14, no. 1 (1990), pp. 25-43

S. de Bodt, *De Haagse School in Drenthe*, Assen 1997

S. de Bodt, S. Gubbels and W. Pijbes, *Mesdag en zijn vrienden*, Rotterdam 1997

J. Boschma and J.M. de Groot (eds.), *Meesterlijk vee. Nederlandse veeschilders 1600-1900*, The Hague 1988

W. Brakman and J. Prince, *De Haagse School*, The Hague 1994

S. de Clercq, *Schilderku(n)st Scheveningen. Van Haagse School tot heden*, Scheveningen 2000

D. Dekkers, 'Goupil en de internationale verspreiding van Nederlandse eigentijdse kunst', *Jong Holland*, Vol. 11, no. 4 (1995), pp. 22-36

D. Dekkers, '"Where are the Dutchmen?" Promoting the Hague School in America. 1875-1900', *Simiolus*, Vol. 24 (1996), pp. 54-73

R. Dorn, K. Albrecht and J. Sillevis (eds.), *El joven Van Gogh y la Escuela de La Haya*, Madrid 1996

R. Dorn, K. Albrecht and J. Sillevis (eds.), *Van Gogh e la Scuola dell'Aia*, Milan 1996

R. Dorn, K. Albrecht and J. Sillevis (eds.), *Van Gogh und die Haager Schule*, Vienna 1996

D. Duijzer and G. Jansen, *Het Haagse Platteland. LTO-Nederland, de Haagse School en de nieuwe tijd*, The Hague 1999

M.A. Goley, *The Hague School and its American Legacy*, Washington 1982

F. de Graaf, 'Eenvoudig en oprecht. Nederlanders op de Salon', *Kunstschrift*, Vol. 39, no. 3 (1995), pp. 29-33
M. Haveman, *Het feest achter de gordijnen. Schilders van de negentiende eeuw 1850-1900*, Amsterdam 1996
M. Haveman (ed.), Aan zee, *Kunstschrift*, Vol. 40, no. 4 (1996) special
J.J. Heij (ed.), *Een Vereeniging van ernstige kunstenaars. 150 jaar Maatschappij Arti et Amicitiae 1839-1989*, Amsterdam 1989
J.F. Heijbroek and E.L. Wouthuysen, *Kunst, kennis en commercie. De kunsthandelaar J.H. de Bois (1876-1946)*, Amsterdam / Antwerp 1993
M. van Heteren, G. Jansen and R. de Leeuw, *Poëzie der werkelijkheid. Nederlandse schilders van de negentiende eeuw*, Zwolle 2000
L. Heyting, *De wereld in een dorp. Schilders, schrijvers en wereldverbeteraars in Laren en Blaricum 1880-1920*, Amsterdam 1994
A. Hoogeboom, *De stand des kunstschilders. De positie van de kunstschilders in Nederland in de eerste helft van de negentiende eeuw*, Utrecht 1991
M.H. Hurdalek, *The Hague School. Collecting in Canada at the turn of the century*, Toronto 1983
H. Janssen, W. van Sinderen and J. Kapelle, *De Haagse School*, Zwolle 1997
T. van Kalmthout, 'Tempels aan de muzen gewijd. Multidisciplinaire kunstringen in Nederland tussen 1880 en 1914', *De Negentiende Eeuw*, Vol. 14, no. 1 (1990), pp. 95-110
R. de Leeuw, J. Sillevis and C. Dumas, *De Haagse School. Hollandse meesters van de 19de eeuw*, Paris / The Hague / London 1983
T. de Liefde-van Brakel, 'Kunstvereeniging "Katwijk"', *Pulchri*, Vol. 23, no. 3 (1995), pp. 2-4
J. van Lindert, 'De natuur zelf op het doek. Schilders van de Haagse School', *Ons Erfdeel*, Vol. 40, no. 5 (1997), pp. 695-702
W. Loos, R.J. te Rijdt and M. van Heteren, *Langs velden en wegen. De verbeelding van het landschap in de 18de en 19de eeuw*, Amsterdam 1997
E. Maas, *Kneppelhout en de Veluwse Schildersbent. Van Oosterbeek naar Haagse School*, Heelsum 1983
B. Meijs-de Werd and J. Aerts, '*... toch wilde ik in Heeze werken*'. *70 jaar schilderkunst in en rond een Brabants dorp*, Helmond 1985
K. Roodenburg, *Kunstenaars op de Noordwest Veluwe 1880-1930. Een speurtocht*, Harderwijk / Nunspeet 1991

J. Sillevis [et al.], *Een feest van kleur. Postimpressionisme uit particulier bezit*, Zwolle 1990
J. Sillevis, *Mesdag en de zee*, Zwolle 1999
J. Sillevis and R. Dorn, *Die Haager Schule. Meisterwerke der holländische Malerei des 19. Jahrhunderts aus Haags Gemeentemuseum*, Mannheim 1987
J. Sillevis, R. Dorn, and H. Kraan (eds.), *De Haagse School. De collectie van het Haags Gemeentemuseum*, The Hague 1992
J. Sillevis and C. Heilmann, *Die Haager Schule in München. Meisterwerke der holländische Malerei des 19. Jahrhunderts aus dem Haager Gemeentemuseum und den Bayerischen Staatsgemäldesammlungen*, Munich 1989
J. Sillevis and H. Kraan (eds.), *De school van Barbizon. Franse meesters van de 19de eeuw*, Ghent / The Hague / Paris 1985
J. Sillevis and H. Kraan, *The Barbizon School. Dutch collections*, Osaka 1987
J. Sillevis, S. van Smoorenburg, T. van Kalmthout, M. Trappeniers and A. van der Woud, *Licht, lucht en water. De verloren idylle van het riviergezicht*, Zwolle 1993
J. Sillevis and A. Szinyei Merse, *A Hagai Iskola*, Budapest 1995
C. Stolwijk, 'De Tentoonstellingen van Levende Meesters in Amsterdam en Den Haag 1858-1896', *De Negentiende Eeuw*, Vol. 19 (1995), pp. 193-221
C. Stolwijk, *Uit de schilderswereld. Nederlandse kunstschilders in de tweede helft van de negentiende eeuw*, Leiden 1998
T. Streng, *Realisme in de kunst- en literatuurbeschouwing in Nederland tot 1875*, Amsterdam 1995
P. Thoben, *De Haagse School. Thema van een collectioneur*, Eindhoven 1992
L. van Tilborgh and G. Jansen, *Op zoek naar de Gouden Eeuw. Nederlandse schilderkunst 1800-1850*, Haarlem 1986
E. van Uitert, 'Het oog wil ook wat. Over het beeld van de negentiende-eeuwse schilderkunst', *De Negentiende Eeuw*, Vol. 16 (1992), pp. 41-54
C. Vergeer, *Toen werd schoot en boezem lekkernij. Erotiek van de Tachtigers*, Amsterdam 1990
G. Willems, H. Vuijsje and K. van Zomeren, *Gras en wolken. Een beeld van het groene hart*, Woerden 1996

Photographic credits

Ashmolean Museum, Oxford: p. 363
Haags Gemeentearchief: pp. 194, 280
National Gallery, London: pp. 14-15
Panorama Mesdag, The Hague: pp. 150, 151, 153-161, 257
Netherlands Institute for Art History (RKD), The Hague: pp. 197, 244, 259, 264, 300, 328-329, 340, 347, 348, 352, 356, 366, 374
Rijksmuseum, Amsterdam: p. 305
Stedelijk Museum, Amsterdam: p. 70
Van Goghmuseum, Amsterdam: p. 373
private collections: pp. 47, 109, 144, 146, 147, 152, 162-167, 219, 249, 263, 321, 398, 402

front cover: J.H. Weissenbruch, see pp. 190-191; W. Maris, see p. 6; back cover: J. Maris, see p. 79; J.H. Weissenbruch, see p. 20; back cover: A. Mauve, see p. 297; J.H. Weissenbruch, see p. 230; J. Maris, see p. 75; A. Mauve, see p. 130; A. Neuhuys, see p. 326; A. Mauve, see p. 93; title page: J.H. Weissenbruch, View of Haarlem, ca. 1845 (detail)

List of abbreviations

ca. = circa
n.d. = no date of publication given
n.p. = no place of publication given
RKD = Netherlands Institute for Art History, The Hague

The medium is oil on canvas, except where otherwise specified.

The works reproduced are from the collection of the Gemeentemuseum Den Haag, except where otherwise specified. The author and the publisher wish to express their gratitude to the owners of the works reproduced in this book for making available the images used, especially to:

The heirs of Floris Arntzenius	Caldic Collection, Rotterdam
Panorama Mesdag, The Hague	J. Poort, Wassenaar
L. van Sinderen, The Hague	RKD, The Hague

We would also like to thank:
Hans Janssen, Marjan Pols, Marcella Sleeuwenhoek and Claudette Warning.

Colophon

Publication
Waanders Publishers, Zwolle
Gemeentemuseum Den Haag, The Hague

Authors
John Sillevis, Anne Tabak

Design/layout
Gijs Dragt bNO/Annelies Mikmak

Printers
Waanders Printers, Zwolle

First published in Dutch in 2001 by Waanders Uitgevers, Zwolle

ISBN 90 400 9037 8

NUR 646, 640

Additional information about Waanders Publishers
can be found at www.waanders.nl
Additional information about the Gemeentemuseum Den Haag
can be found at www.gemeentemuseum.nl